Standing Naked in the Shower

NATHAN K. BRYCE is the author of an extensive collection of books, training presentations, course materials, lesson plans, news articles, and multimedia publications which teach a variety of cognitive, social, personal, family, and employment skills that help people succeed in life. In 1994, he invented and patented the *Insight Personality Instrument™*, the first product of his company, Insight Learning Solutions, LLC.

Standing Naked in the Shower

Life-Enriching Insights That Expose Human Nature

Nathan K. Bryce

Published by Insight Learning Foundation, 1439 East 880 North, Orem, Utah 84097-5414. Item #N202A. (800) 320-4788.

First printed: August 2002
Latest revision: April 2007

10 9 8 7 6 5 4 3 2 1

Printed in the United States of America

ISBN 1-932044-01-9

Acknowledgements

Throughout history, countless philosophers, psychologists, scientists, and researchers have attempted to describe, predict, and understand human behavior. Many of these experts have developed effective systems to examine conduct by categorizing people who share certain attitudinal and behavioral characteristics. They often refer to these characteristics as personality temperaments or types.

There are several excellent personality-typing instruments currently on the market, most of which are based on extensive research and experimentation. For many years, I have systematically reviewed these tools as well as their successful and unsuccessful predecessors. This examination revealed that the "perfect" instrument—one that combined accuracy, simplicity, and affordability—was not yet available.

The Insight Personality Instrument™ is an attempt to be this device. It's my hope that this tool, and the information in this book, will be used to solve the communication and relationship problems that occur from time to time in most of our lives.

There are many authors, scholars, educators, psychologists, and other professionals who have provided insight, and countless others who have validated this work based on their own experiences. I truly appreciate the direct and indirect contributions of these people.

I owe special recognition and thanks to those colleagues, friends, and family who reviewed and encouraged my efforts. There's Russ Kesterson, Judy Edward, and George Nelson, my hardworking partners at the Insight Learning Foundation. And Lisa Hawkins, Jen Drake, and John Middleton, my brilliant editors and collaborators. And Rick Lehtinen, a gifted wordsmith who toiled with me for hundreds of hours to complete the manuscript. But above all, I pay tribute to my wife Kristin, the lovely mother of our four sons, who has patiently endured and sacrificed in order to see my dreams come true.

— Nathan K. Bryce

Contents

INTRODUCTION

Laying the Foundation

Discovering the components of your unique, individual personality spectrum is the first step in exploring the world of temperament. This introductory chapter will expose some important foundational principles and concepts that will guide the rest of your journey.

First Things First

Minds far greater than mine have established that by identifying and understanding personality style—also known as temperament, disposition, character, nature, spirit, psyche, makeup, persona, and perspective—you can learn a great deal about yourself and those around you.

You can determine how people prefer to think and feel, work and play, learn and teach, speak and write, lead and follow. You can identify the attributes they admire, the values they cherish, and the activities that bring them joy. You can detect the kinds of jobs they prefer to do in the workplace and at home, how they respond to stress and conflict, and how they prefer to relax and enjoy themselves. You can determine what they want from their relationships, how they show affection, and what strengths and liabilities they bring to the home. You can even get some pretty significant clues into what they like to read, what television programs they enjoy, what clothes they choose to wear, how they decorate their homes and offices, what kinds of toys they play with, what kinds of cars they drive, even what they'll do at a backyard pool party. The amount of information you can gather is really quite impressive.

Therefore, the first objective of this book is to teach you how to identify your own style and the styles of others. Then it will show you how to use this knowledge to benefit your life in many new and exciting ways. Among other things, you will gain insight into why people think, feel, and act the way they do—perhaps one of the most important and practical pieces of information a person can learn. This understanding will influence the way you see yourself and others from now on.

As a result, your life may never be the same. Your relationships can't help but improve and be lifted to greater heights. New windows of opportunity will open to you, and your understanding of people will reach new levels you never thought possible. When you finish this book, you will see through an entirely new set of eyes. Because it has the ability to increase your tolerance, respect, and sensitivity to the needs, values, and attitudes of others, you will have an empowering perspective and advantage few people ever obtain.

Well, enough of objectives and highfalutin' promises. It's time to begin your journey and discover how to understand people better than they understand themselves.

Discovering Your Colors

The information in this book is based on the Insight Personality Instrument™, a tool that accurately identifies an individual's personality profile. The tool describes four archetypal temperaments from which all personality styles are derived. To help people learn and remember these temperaments, each one has been named after a color: *Blue, Gold, Green,* and *Orange*.

For the most part, each person is born with one color that fits his or her personality more than any other. This is the person's primary color. Over the past several decades, several million people throughout the world have used the Insight Personality Instrument or related tests to determine their primary color. Approximately 44 percent of the general population has a clear preference for the Gold temperament, 40 percent prefer Orange, 10 percent prefer Blue, and 6 percent prefer Green. Women and girls account for half of all Golds and Oranges, three out of five Blues, and two out of five Greens.

In addition to a person's primary color, a combination of the other three colors affects his or her personality to a lesser degree, forming a color spectrum. An individual's color spectrum is unique. There aren't many people who share exactly the same blend of personality types. However, by simply understanding someone's primary color, you can find out a lot of information about that person and understand why the individual does the things he or she does.

The next section of this chapter contains the full text of the Insight Personality Instrument™. If you haven't yet used this device to identify your primary color and your personal color spectrum, please take the time to do so. However, before you proceed, there's one extremely important concept to discuss.

Standing Naked in the Shower

Before you can accurately identify your temperament, you need to stand completely naked in the shower. Of course, you're probably asking yourself, "How does standing naked in the shower help me understand my personality?" Good question. Let's discover the answer by examining an analogy.

Most of us have a rather large wardrobe of clothing. Some clothes we wear to the office, others we wear as we putter around the garden or change the oil in our cars. We wear one type of clothing when we go swimming and something completely different to a wedding. Regardless of what we choose to put on, the clothes are fulfilling a function—a role, if you will. Their role is to help us fit in with others, work more efficiently, or simply clothe our nakedness. However, they often hide our true selves, our real natures. Only when we take these clothes off, as happens when we take a shower, do we catch a glimpse of our true identities, undressed, unfettered, unobstructed, unadorned.

So it is with our inner selves. Some call these our spirits, characters, personalities, temperaments, or dispositions. Whatever you decide to call them, they're the combination of attributes, characteristics, and preferences you were born with and taught, all of which make you unique. Unfortunately, we don't get to see this inner self very often.

As you and I go throughout life, we are like actors, performing a variety of roles that cause us to act in ways we don't normally prefer. For example, in the "parent" role you may act as an unsympathetic disciplinarian who metes out justice to misbehaving children, when in fact you'd much rather let them off the hook and take them to the amusement park. Or you may be in the "dedicated worker" role and act like an organized employee who loves to file folders in their proper places, even though deep down inside you'd rather be flinging the files off a cliff. But you know you'll eventually be well paid for your performance, so you keep your mask and costume on and keep your dreams to yourself, until the play is finally over.

Sometimes, especially if you've played the role long enough, you not only fool the audience, but you begin to fool yourself. You believe you're one particular way when you're really another. It's that true self, your native self, that we're trying to reveal. And to do that, you must strip yourself of your roles and your responsibilities. You need to get rid of all the things that you, or others, think you should be. You need to stand naked in the proverbial shower.

This may be hard to do. It's a significant struggle for most people to take an objective, impersonal look at themselves. But that's exactly what you need to do as you read through this material; otherwise, you might misinterpret the information and get all skewed up. To help you do this, pretend you're a solitary castaway on a deserted island. You have all the food, water, and shelter you need, but no one is around to tell you what you must do, ought to do, or could do. You're free to do whatever you feel like doing. What would you do? How would you spend your time? More likely than not, your true preferences—the things you value above other things—will come out of hiding and make themselves known loud and clear.

So, before you continue reading, strip off your roles and responsibilities and jump into the shower. Take a close look at what you see. When you're ready, start plowing through this information with an open mind. Before long, you'll be able to clearly see your true nature and understand your values, needs, and strengths. Then, once you understand yourself, you can turn your focus outward and begin to understand others—even better than they understand themselves!

The Insight Personality Instrument™

This test will identify your complete color spectrum—your unique blend of all four colors. It presents each color in ten different categories: Values, Motivation, Communication, Work, Supervision, Recreation, Childhood, Youth, Education, and Love. Each page features a different category.

Starting with the first category—Values—carefully read all four paragraphs. If you want, compare each paragraph to the other three. Then determine how much each paragraph describes you. Use the following scale to assign a point to each paragraph and fill in the appropriate box:

Always like me (100% of the time)	4 points
Usually like me (75% of the time)	3 points
Sometimes like me (50% of the time)	2 points
Seldom like me (25% of the time)	1 point
Never like me (0% of the time)	0 points

For example, if you feel that one or two paragraphs from a category are like you 75 percent of the time, give each paragraph three points. If another paragraph isn't like you at all, give it zero points. Repeat this step until all ten categories have been scored.

You must be honest to make sure your results will be as accurate as possible. Don't respond the way you think you should or how other people think you should. Don't respond the way you wish you were or would like to be—answer the way you truly feel, deep down inside.

Don't consider your current roles, responsibilities, and duties. Avoid making a choice based on particular words or phrases—consider the entire paragraph. Take your time, but don't over-analyze the words. When you're done, go to the end of the test to calculate your spectrum.

Category 1: Values

The following statements describe the general attitudes, values, dreams, hopes, and ambitions of each personality type.

A
☐ 4
☐ 3
☐ 2
☐ 1
☐ 0

I dream of assets, wealth, influence, status, and security. I place high value on dependability, accountability, and responsibility. I respect authority, loyalty, and obligation, and highly regard service and dedication. I promote structure, associations, and organizations, and work to maintain the order, stability, and traditions that keep our society together.

B
☐ 4
☐ 3
☐ 2
☐ 1
☐ 0

I dream of peace, love, affection, and authenticity. I place high value on compassion, sympathy, and rapport. I respect nurturing, empathy, and the sharing of feelings, and highly regard meaning, significance, and identity. I promote growth and development in others and can be relied on to take care of people's physical, spiritual, and emotional needs.

C
☐ 4
☐ 3
☐ 2
☐ 1
☐ 0

I dream of perfection, accuracy, and truth. I place high value on answers, resolutions, and intelligence. I respect innovation, knowledge, and capability, and highly regard progress, efficiency, and increased output. I promote effectiveness, competence, and expertise, and like to explore new ideas and add to humanity's understanding of the universe.

D
☐ 4
☐ 3
☐ 2
☐ 1
☐ 0

I dream of being free, spontaneous, and impetuous. I place high value on finesse, grace, and charisma. I respect skill and artistic expression and highly regard opportunities, options, and competition. I promote stimulation, challenge, and courage, and bring fun, excitement, and adventure to society. I am willing to take risks when others won't.

Category 2: Motivation

The following statements describe the fundamental characteristics that motivate and drive each personality type.

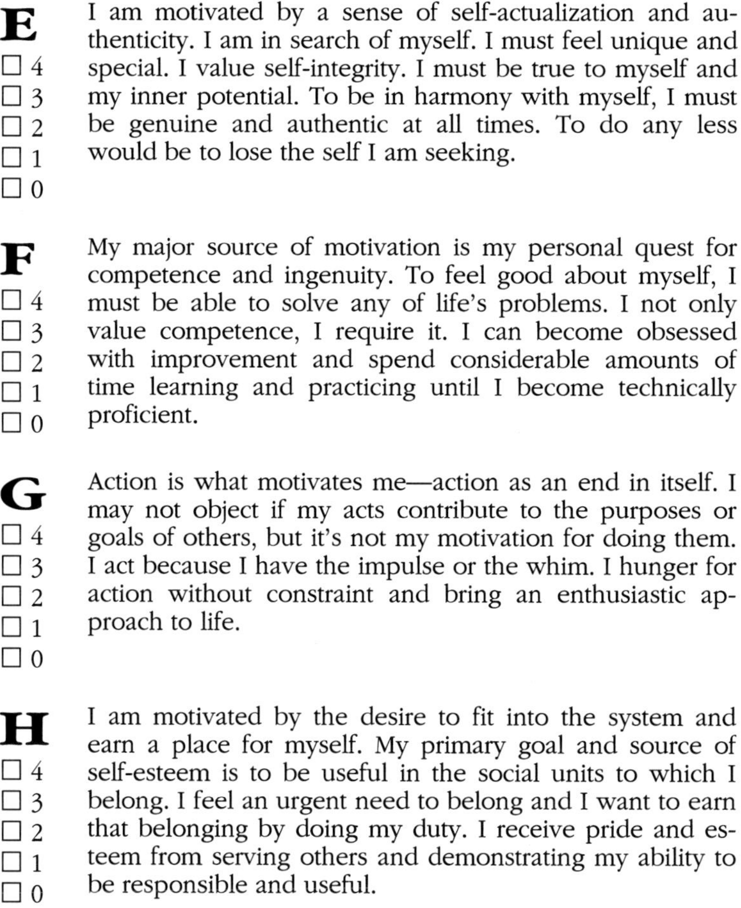

E

☐ 4
☐ 3
☐ 2
☐ 1
☐ 0

I am motivated by a sense of self-actualization and authenticity. I am in search of myself. I must feel unique and special. I value self-integrity. I must be true to myself and my inner potential. To be in harmony with myself, I must be genuine and authentic at all times. To do any less would be to lose the self I am seeking.

F

☐ 4
☐ 3
☐ 2
☐ 1
☐ 0

My major source of motivation is my personal quest for competence and ingenuity. To feel good about myself, I must be able to solve any of life's problems. I not only value competence, I require it. I can become obsessed with improvement and spend considerable amounts of time learning and practicing until I become technically proficient.

G

☐ 4
☐ 3
☐ 2
☐ 1
☐ 0

Action is what motivates me—action as an end in itself. I may not object if my acts contribute to the purposes or goals of others, but it's not my motivation for doing them. I act because I have the impulse or the whim. I hunger for action without constraint and bring an enthusiastic approach to life.

H

☐ 4
☐ 3
☐ 2
☐ 1
☐ 0

I am motivated by the desire to fit into the system and earn a place for myself. My primary goal and source of self-esteem is to be useful in the social units to which I belong. I feel an urgent need to belong and I want to earn that belonging by doing my duty. I receive pride and esteem from serving others and demonstrating my ability to be responsible and useful.

Category 3: Communication

The following statements list the characteristics you possess as a communicator. Consider both verbal and written communication.

A

☐ 4
☐ 3
☐ 2
☐ 1
☐ 0

I use proper language and etiquette while communicating. I am thorough and detailed, especially when giving directions. I can reach conclusions and make up my mind quickly. I prefer orderly and controlled conversations and don't like to become side-tracked. I focus on what needs to be done, who is going to do it, and when they will report on what they have done.

B

☐ 4
☐ 3
☐ 2
☐ 1
☐ 0

I love to communicate about anything and everything. I am sensitive to non-verbal communication and am concerned with how what I say might affect others. I am a good listener and people often come to me for sympathetic reassurance. While I can be articulate and persuasive, I prefer to avoid issues that might end in conflict or debate.

C

☐ 4
☐ 3
☐ 2
☐ 1
☐ 0

I dislike redundancy and small talk and want my communications to be succinct, factual, and logical. Because I am naturally skeptical, I will ask many questions and take plenty of time to make up my mind. Since I am frequently oblivious to non-verbal messages and the emotional overtones in the communication of others, some may find me to be cold, distant, and enigmatic.

D

☐ 4
☐ 3
☐ 2
☐ 1
☐ 0

I am a dynamic communicator who likes to keep the conversation lively and interactive. I am bold and aggressive and apt to say what is on my mind. I don't hesitate to embellish a story or situation with exaggeration or jokes, and might even argue just for the sake of arguing. I focus on action, results, and cutting right to the heart of a problem.

Category 4: Work

The following statements list the occupations that appeal to specific personality types, as well as the characteristics you possess as a worker, both at home and on the job. Don't consider your current vocation unless it really appeals to you.

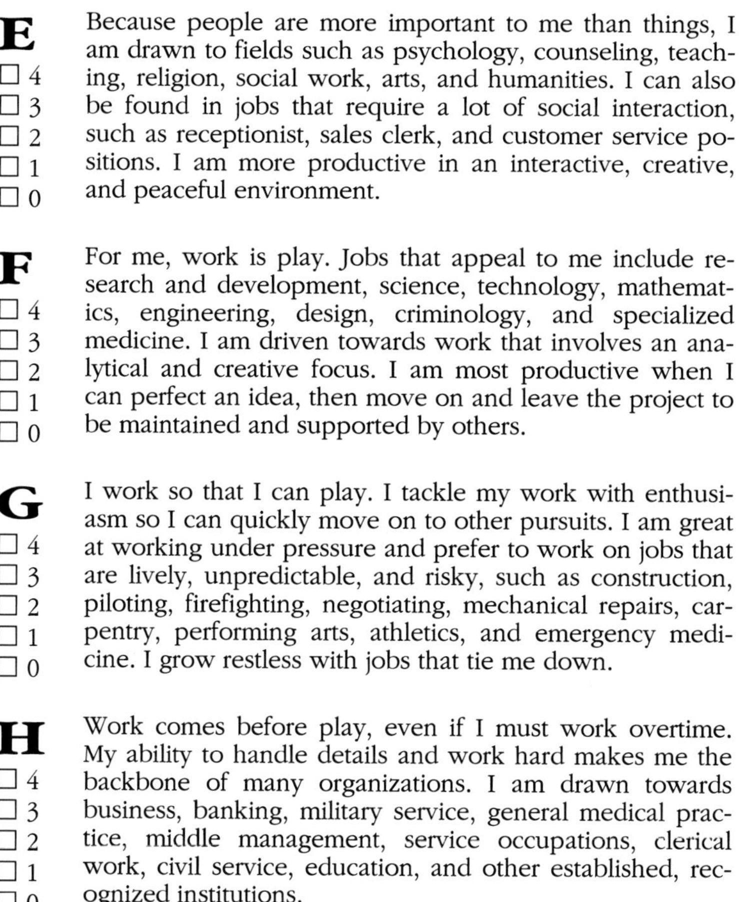

E

☐ 4 ☐ 3 ☐ 2 ☐ 1 ☐ 0

Because people are more important to me than things, I am drawn to fields such as psychology, counseling, teaching, religion, social work, arts, and humanities. I can also be found in jobs that require a lot of social interaction, such as receptionist, sales clerk, and customer service positions. I am more productive in an interactive, creative, and peaceful environment.

F

☐ 4 ☐ 3 ☐ 2 ☐ 1 ☐ 0

For me, work is play. Jobs that appeal to me include research and development, science, technology, mathematics, engineering, design, criminology, and specialized medicine. I am driven towards work that involves an analytical and creative focus. I am most productive when I can perfect an idea, then move on and leave the project to be maintained and supported by others.

G

☐ 4 ☐ 3 ☐ 2 ☐ 1 ☐ 0

I work so that I can play. I tackle my work with enthusiasm so I can quickly move on to other pursuits. I am great at working under pressure and prefer to work on jobs that are lively, unpredictable, and risky, such as construction, piloting, firefighting, negotiating, mechanical repairs, carpentry, performing arts, athletics, and emergency medicine. I grow restless with jobs that tie me down.

H

☐ 4 ☐ 3 ☐ 2 ☐ 1 ☐ 0

Work comes before play, even if I must work overtime. My ability to handle details and work hard makes me the backbone of many organizations. I am drawn towards business, banking, military service, general medical practice, middle management, service occupations, clerical work, civil service, education, and other established, recognized institutions.

Category 5: Supervision

The following statements list the leadership characteristics you possess, both at home and on the job.

A

☐ 4
☐ 3
☐ 2
☐ 1
☐ 0

I am a stabilizer and an organization-oriented leader. I am highly accountable, thorough, and dedicate a great deal of time and energy to maintain my administration. I am good at establishing policies, procedures, and rules. I encourage team efforts and support traditional values. I am comfortable with established routines and well-ordered meetings.

B

☐ 4
☐ 3
☐ 2
☐ 1
☐ 0

I am a people-oriented leader who is committed to the personal and professional well-being of my staff. I am an enthusiastic spokesperson for my organization and demonstrate a gift for language. I am comfortable in unstructured, democratic settings and listen attentively to the contributions of each person present. I promote flexibility, harmony, and cooperation.

C

☐ 4
☐ 3
☐ 2
☐ 1
☐ 0

I am a visionary leader. I am system-oriented and a keen analyst of the dynamics of my organization. I attempt to address problems with a logical and almost scientific perspective. I constantly re-evaluate policies and procedures and am often the pioneer of innovative change. I am confident of my abilities and surround myself with competent individuals.

D

☐ 4
☐ 3
☐ 2
☐ 1
☐ 0

I am an action-oriented leader who makes things happen when other leaders just sit and wonder what happened. I am excellent at solving problems and emergencies in a quick and efficient manner; in fact, I tend to elevate problems to a crisis level in order to solve them. I welcome change and take risks.

Category 6: Recreation

The following statements list the ways different personalities like to spend their leisure time. Remember, these are preferences, and may or may not reflect what you ultimately do with your time.

E
☐ 4
☐ 3
☐ 2
☐ 1
☐ 0

My leisure activities usually involve my close circle of friends or family. It doesn't matter what we do, just as long as we do it together and take advantage of the time to strengthen our relationships. When I want to be by myself I read novels, listen to music, garden, or watch dramatic television or movies. Sometimes I spend my spare time with societal movements or special causes.

F
☐ 4
☐ 3
☐ 2
☐ 1
☐ 0

I am likely to continue the pursuit of perfection even at play or on vacation. In strategic or athletic games, I am constantly thinking about how to improve previously noted errors. I hate to be mentally idle and feel that I need to be reading, watching educational television, working with a computer, or adding to my knowledge in some other way.

G
☐ 4
☐ 3
☐ 2
☐ 1
☐ 0

I love to play and do all I can to maximize my leisure time. I'm usually involved in activities, particularly sporting ones, either as a player or an active spectator. I live for physically challenging and daring adventures. I prefer to associate with others who are fun or exciting to be with, but don't mind solitary activities that deal with tools, toys, or other tangible objects.

H
☐ 4
☐ 3
☐ 2
☐ 1
☐ 0

I do not allow myself to indulge in recreational activities until I have fulfilled all my other responsibilities. My play activities are usually well thought out, organized, and oriented towards some goal, such as improving family relationships, maintaining health, or entertaining others. I appear to be strait-laced but can be fun-loving when appropriate.

Category 7: Childhood

The following statements list the general characteristics of children.

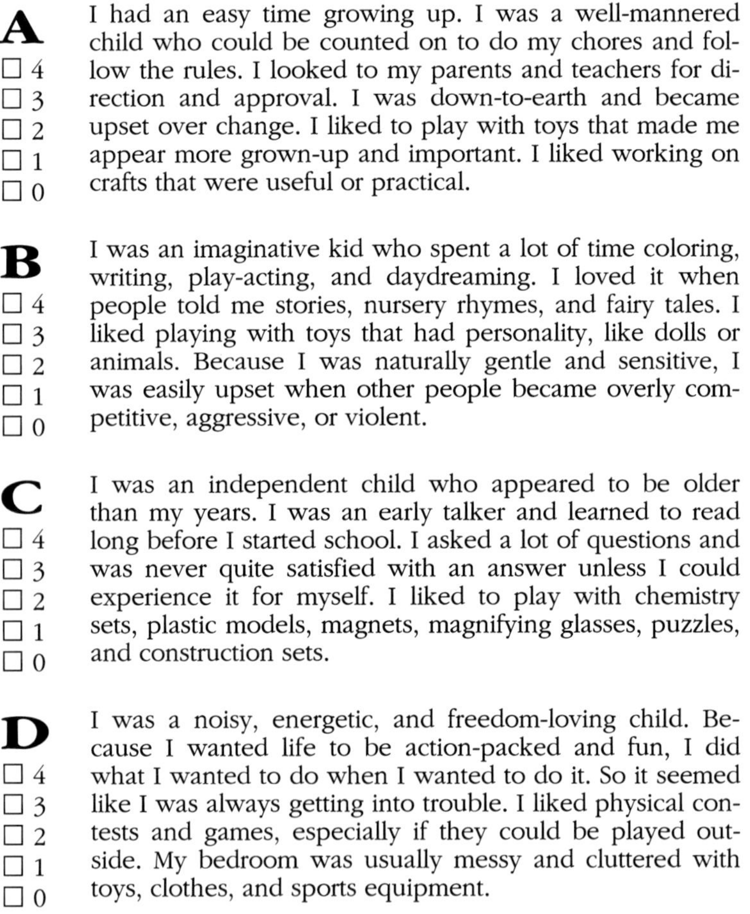

A

☐ 4
☐ 3
☐ 2
☐ 1
☐ 0

I had an easy time growing up. I was a well-mannered child who could be counted on to do my chores and follow the rules. I looked to my parents and teachers for direction and approval. I was down-to-earth and became upset over change. I liked to play with toys that made me appear more grown-up and important. I liked working on crafts that were useful or practical.

B

☐ 4
☐ 3
☐ 2
☐ 1
☐ 0

I was an imaginative kid who spent a lot of time coloring, writing, play-acting, and daydreaming. I loved it when people told me stories, nursery rhymes, and fairy tales. I liked playing with toys that had personality, like dolls or animals. Because I was naturally gentle and sensitive, I was easily upset when other people became overly competitive, aggressive, or violent.

C

☐ 4
☐ 3
☐ 2
☐ 1
☐ 0

I was an independent child who appeared to be older than my years. I was an early talker and learned to read long before I started school. I asked a lot of questions and was never quite satisfied with an answer unless I could experience it for myself. I liked to play with chemistry sets, plastic models, magnets, magnifying glasses, puzzles, and construction sets.

D

☐ 4
☐ 3
☐ 2
☐ 1
☐ 0

I was a noisy, energetic, and freedom-loving child. Because I wanted life to be action-packed and fun, I did what I wanted to do when I wanted to do it. So it seemed like I was always getting into trouble. I liked physical contests and games, especially if they could be played outside. My bedroom was usually messy and cluttered with toys, clothes, and sports equipment.

Category 8: Youth

The following statements list the general characteristics of adolescent youth.

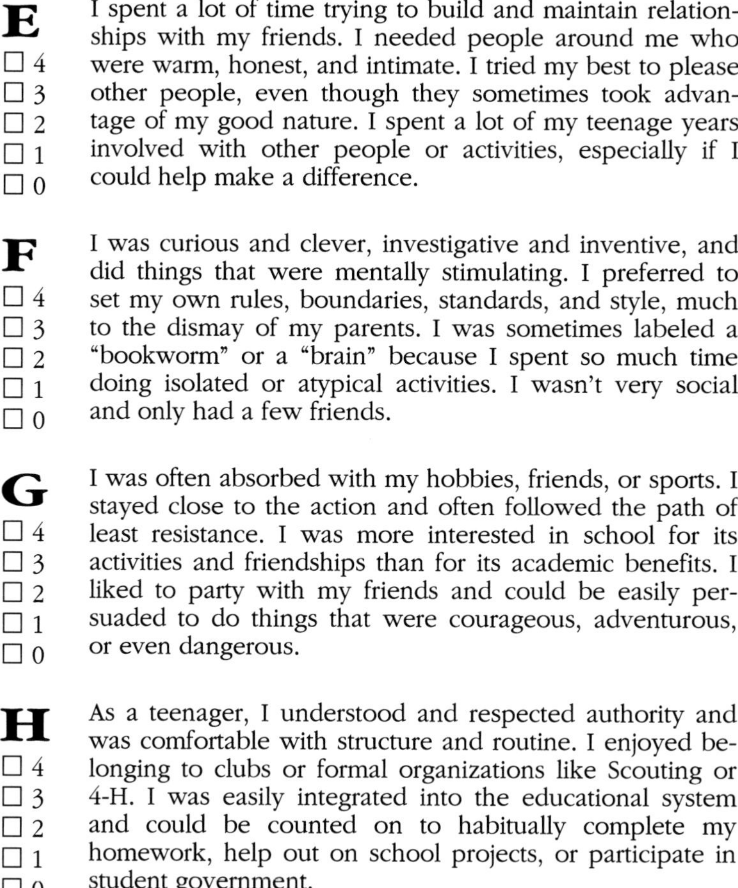

E
☐ 4
☐ 3
☐ 2
☐ 1
☐ 0

I spent a lot of time trying to build and maintain relationships with my friends. I needed people around me who were warm, honest, and intimate. I tried my best to please other people, even though they sometimes took advantage of my good nature. I spent a lot of my teenage years involved with other people or activities, especially if I could help make a difference.

F
☐ 4
☐ 3
☐ 2
☐ 1
☐ 0

I was curious and clever, investigative and inventive, and did things that were mentally stimulating. I preferred to set my own rules, boundaries, standards, and style, much to the dismay of my parents. I was sometimes labeled a "bookworm" or a "brain" because I spent so much time doing isolated or atypical activities. I wasn't very social and only had a few friends.

G
☐ 4
☐ 3
☐ 2
☐ 1
☐ 0

I was often absorbed with my hobbies, friends, or sports. I stayed close to the action and often followed the path of least resistance. I was more interested in school for its activities and friendships than for its academic benefits. I liked to party with my friends and could be easily persuaded to do things that were courageous, adventurous, or even dangerous.

H
☐ 4
☐ 3
☐ 2
☐ 1
☐ 0

As a teenager, I understood and respected authority and was comfortable with structure and routine. I enjoyed belonging to clubs or formal organizations like Scouting or 4-H. I was easily integrated into the educational system and could be counted on to habitually complete my homework, help out on school projects, or participate in student government.

Category 9: Education

The following statements list the learning preferences of each personality type. Reflect back on your own education history as well as current learning situations.

A

☐ 4
☐ 3
☐ 2
☐ 1
☐ 0

I learn best when course content is structured, clearly defined, and presented in a chronological and concrete manner, with timelines, diagrams, maps, and models. Rules and directions are a great help to me and help me know when I am on the right track. Traditional subjects appeal to me, such as history, law, political science, home economics, and business.

B

☐ 4
☐ 3
☐ 2
☐ 1
☐ 0

I learn best in an open, supportive, and interactive environment that is focused on the individual learner. Learning activities that appeal to me include small group discussions, creative exercises, and non-competitive academic games or contests. Subjects that appeal to me are social studies, creative writing, literature, drama, music, languages, arts, and humanities.

C

☐ 4
☐ 3
☐ 2
☐ 1
☐ 0

I am driven to understand the world around me. I learn best when I am exposed to the driving force or overall theory behind a subject. I am impatient with drill, re-view, and routine. I prefer to work independently on challenging subjects such as science, technology, mathematics, drafting, engineering, architecture, analytical writing, and vocabulary.

D

☐ 4
☐ 3
☐ 2
☐ 1
☐ 0

I learn by seeing and doing, rather than by listening and reading. I need physical involvement in the learning process and am motivated by my own natural competitive nature and sense of fun. I thrive in a dynamic, open atmosphere where I am free to move about. Subjects that are fun or practical appeal to me, such as physical education, vocational and industrial skills, art, music, and drama.

Category 10: Love

The following statements list the preferences of different personalities when it comes to love, mating, and other intimate relationships.

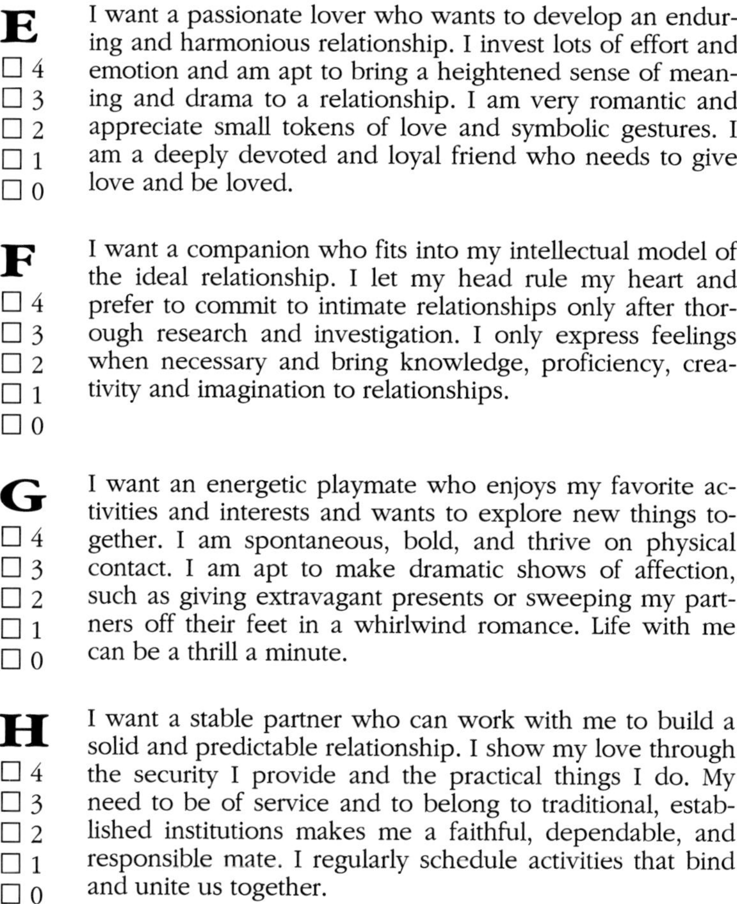

E

☐ 4
☐ 3
☐ 2
☐ 1
☐ 0

I want a passionate lover who wants to develop an enduring and harmonious relationship. I invest lots of effort and emotion and am apt to bring a heightened sense of meaning and drama to a relationship. I am very romantic and appreciate small tokens of love and symbolic gestures. I am a deeply devoted and loyal friend who needs to give love and be loved.

F

☐ 4
☐ 3
☐ 2
☐ 1
☐ 0

I want a companion who fits into my intellectual model of the ideal relationship. I let my head rule my heart and prefer to commit to intimate relationships only after thorough research and investigation. I only express feelings when necessary and bring knowledge, proficiency, creativity and imagination to relationships.

G

☐ 4
☐ 3
☐ 2
☐ 1
☐ 0

I want an energetic playmate who enjoys my favorite activities and interests and wants to explore new things together. I am spontaneous, bold, and thrive on physical contact. I am apt to make dramatic shows of affection, such as giving extravagant presents or sweeping my partners off their feet in a whirlwind romance. Life with me can be a thrill a minute.

H

☐ 4
☐ 3
☐ 2
☐ 1
☐ 0

I want a stable partner who can work with me to build a solid and predictable relationship. I show my love through the security I provide and the practical things I do. My need to be of service and to belong to traditional, established institutions makes me a faithful, dependable, and responsible mate. I regularly schedule activities that bind and unite us together.

Scoring Guidelines

To get your results, go back through the test and total all the points you gave to each letter. Write the number next to its letter below. Then, total the points in each row (Column 1 + Column 2) and write that number in the Total column.

Column 1	Column 2
B	E
A	H
C	F
D	G

Total	Color
B + E =	Blue
A + H =	Gold
C + F =	Green
D + G =	Orange

Fill out the table below with the colors in your spectrum.

1st Your highest or brightest color (primary): ______________

2nd Your next highest color (secondary): ______________

3rd Your next highest color (tertiary): ______________

4th Your lowest or dimmest color (quaternary): ______________

Try to commit this order to memory. This is an important piece of information to which you will refer throughout this book.

Personality Summaries

Let's recap what you just learned about yourself. Below are some simple phrases that summarize the salient characteristics of each of the four personality types. Do you agree with what it says about your primary color?

Blues

- ☐ Need to feel unique
- ☐ Look for symbolism
- ☐ Value close relationships
- ☐ Encourage expression
- ☐ Desire quality time with loved ones
- ☐ Need opportunities to be creative
- ☐ Compromise and cooperate
- ☐ Nurture people, plants, and animals
- ☐ Look beyond the surface
- ☐ Share emotions
- ☐ Make decisions based on feelings
- ☐ Need harmony
- ☐ Are drawn to nurturing careers
- ☐ Get involved in causes
- ☐ Bring unity to society

Golds

- ☐ Are dutiful and stable
- ☐ Need to be useful
- ☐ Want to be self-sufficient
- ☐ Value order and organization
- ☐ Desire punctuality
- ☐ Schedule their lives
- ☐ Make and keep commitments
- ☐ Measure worth by completion
- ☐ Prepare for the future
- ☐ Believe work comes before play
- ☐ Safeguard tradition
- ☐ Are responsible and dedicated
- ☐ Are drawn to respected occupations
- ☐ Enjoy positions of authority
- ☐ Bring stability to society

Greens

- ☐ Are innovative and logical
- ☐ Seek to understand the world
- ☐ Need to be competent
- ☐ Require intellectual freedom
- ☐ Push themselves to improve
- ☐ Are slow to make decisions

- ☐ Value concise communication
- ☐ Look for intellectual stimulation
- ☐ Are sometimes oblivious to emotions
- ☐ Are detached
- ☐ Believe work is play
- ☐ Are drawn to technical occupations
- ☐ Analyze and rearrange systems
- ☐ Focus on the future
- ☐ Bring innovation to society

Oranges

- ☐ Are free and spontaneous
- ☐ Are impulsive risk-takers
- ☐ Are active and competitive
- ☐ Are optimistic
- ☐ Commit fully or not at all
- ☐ Thrive on crises
- ☐ Are drawn to tools
- ☐ Like to be the center of attention
- ☐ Have great endurance
- ☐ Are drawn to action jobs
- ☐ Need variety
- ☐ Are dynamic, animated communicators
- ☐ Are generous
- ☐ Like to live in a casual atmosphere
- ☐ Bring excitement to society

Your Colorful Brain

Before we begin exploring each of the colors in greater detail, here is some information that might help you remember how the four colors are associated to each other.

Brain hemispheres

The human brain is a paired organ composed of two halves called cerebral hemispheres. Each hemisphere is similar in size and appearance.

In 1981, American neurobiologist Dr. Roger W. Sperry won the Nobel Prize in Physiology/Medicine for his experimentation on the functions of the brain's left and right hemispheres.

His research proposes that the left and right hemispheres each perform different, highly specialized functions. In most people, the left hemisphere is a language center while the right hemisphere processes spatial information. Most of us have an unconscious preference to the functions of one hemisphere over the other.

Furthermore, the logical, rational, sequential analysis of information that we call "thinking" is associated with left hemisphere dominance. The making of associations, insights that produce a new "big picture," and the free flow of creative ideas are associated with right hemisphere dominance.

Further research also indicates some functions are associated with different quadrants of the brain, as noted in the diagram below:

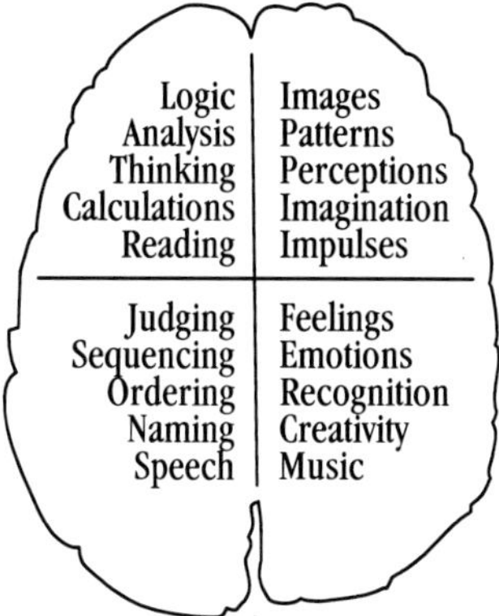

Notice anything special about the four quadrants? They're directly related to the four personality colors! The upper left quadrant features Green preferences, the lower left resembles Gold, the upper right appears to be Orange, and the lower right is definitely Blue.

Coincidence? Perhaps. Over the years, a lot has changed in the world of neuroscience. But many of Sperry's ideas are still in use today, and I'd like to continue using them to describe human temperament. Which is why the Insight logo is the way it is.

The Insight logo

If this book were printed in color, you would notice our company logo comprises all four colors. Green and Gold, the "left-brained" temperaments, are on the left. Orange and Blue, the "right-brained" temperaments, are on the right.

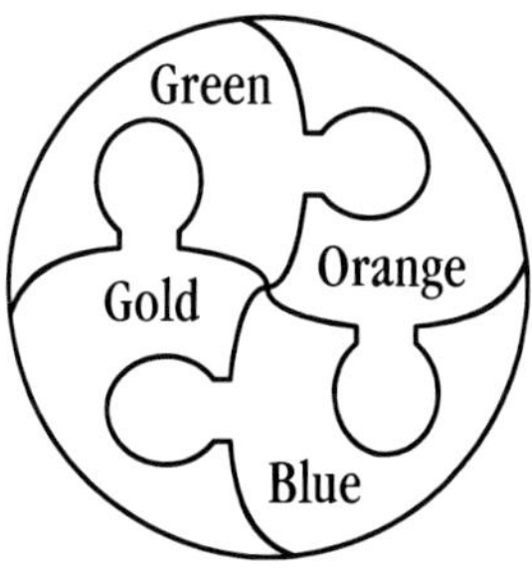

Our planet is well populated with puzzling people. But once we understand the role each person fills, the puzzle is solved. Therefore the logo is created from four people-shaped puzzle pieces, suggesting we can't understand the world until we understand how each color fits into the puzzle. It takes all four types to make the world run as well as it does. In fact, society would not exist as we know it without the unique contributions of each temperament.

The nexus

At the center of the logo is its *nexus*—the place where all four colors connect. If we truly want to be successful in our relationships, if we sincerely want to form meaningful connections with the people in our lives, we need to seek out and eventually establish residence within the nexus. The objective of this book is to teach you how to do this successfully and comfortably.

The next ten chapters examine each of the four colors as they appear in ten specific categories—the same categories as used in the Insight Personality Instrument: Values, Motivation, Communication, Work, Supervision, Recreation, Childhood, Youth, Education, and Love. By taking a long, hard look at each personality style in these categories, you will begin to see clearly how the colors think and feel, how they work and play, how they show affection to their loved ones, how they act as children and adults, and so on. Then, endowed with this knowledge, you will be able to make the changes you need to make as you move towards the nexus—and begin to interact with people the way they prefer to interact. Can you think of a greater way to eliminate concerns, confusion, and conflict?

CHAPTER 1

Values: Discovering the Real You

This chapter focuses on values—the set of attitudes and attributes each temperament prizes and strives to achieve throughout life. As people live up to their values, they experience joy and happiness; if they can't, don't, or won't, they experience misery and sorrow. One of the most important things we can learn in life is to understand and respect what people value.

Examining Values by Category

The four colors are like the four cardinal points on a compass. Steering in a particular direction will take you to a specific destination—a destination that's preferred over the others. The trick in life is to find out which direction you want to go, so you can get to the destination you desire. Then all you need to do is whip out your compass, find your bearings, set your course, and before long you'll get there.

But which direction do you want to go? What milestones will mark your journey? What road signs will you follow? What choices will you make along the way? By understanding your personality style, you'll be able to determine which attitudes bring you the most joy, which things you'll need to survive and thrive on your trip, and which actions will make your journey far more satisfying. To help you along your way, perhaps we ought to look more closely at what the various destinations are like. What does the ideal Blue world look like? What characteristics do Greens admire? What does a Gold treasure? What activities bring joy to an Orange?

Carefully examine the chart below. Here you'll find a summary of the core values of each personality type. I call these things "values" because a person attaches importance to them and prizes them above other attributes. They reflect a person's deep-seated, inborn preferences.

Values	Blue	Gold	Green	Orange
Advocate	Growth	Discipline	Solutions	Success
Appreciate	Uniqueness	Prudence	Innovation	Courage
Cherish	Intimacy	Traditions	Technology	Recreation
Collect	Relationships	Responsibilities	Data	Experiences
Desire	Comfort	Power	Efficiency	Victory
Enjoy	Communication	Completion	Mysteries	Challenges
Join	Causes	Organizations	Debates	Activities
Need	Harmony	Order	Time	Incentives
Provide	Empathy	Structure	Information	Excitement
Pursue	Meaning	Security	Understanding	Adventure
Respect	Integrity	Achievement	Genius	Talent
Show	Kindness	Dedication	Composure	Skill
Treasure	Acceptance	Appreciation	Autonomy	Freedom
Trust	Feelings	Authority	Analysis	Impulses
Want	Romance	Rules	Competence	Action

The chart identifies each temperament's top fifteen unique values—the values that aren't shared with other types. This is important information. Consequently, we'll spend the next few pages reviewing each item in greater detail. And since this information is a reflection of the heart, mind, and soul of each color, please handle with care.

The Blue Temperament

Advocate growth

The Blue temperament is fairly difficult to describe because the goals of a Blue are somewhat nebulous, even in the minds of Blues. You see, their purpose in life is to find their purpose in life. Consequently they're in a perpetual search for their true selves, trying to find the set of qualities and characteristics they want to define them. They're actively engaged in the act of growing, developing, emerging, becoming all they can be.

Blues fervently believe that they, and every other person on the planet for that matter, are endowed with the capacity to accomplish anything they truly desire. Nothing is out of reach for those who put their hearts and souls into it. As a result, they're often on the sidelines, cheering people on to their goals, encouraging them to reach for the stars and accomplish their dreams. As advocates of growth, they believe one of the most important things they can do in life is to nurture individuals one-on-one, particularly children and teenagers. This way Blues can help others discover their true selves too, and mature emotionally, spiritually, and artistically.

> "To be what we are, and to become what we are capable of becoming, is the only end of life."
>
> — ROBERT LOUIS STEVENSON

Appreciate uniqueness

Blues believe every person is a distinctive and extraordinary individual. Seeking out this being, carving it from the block of habits, customs, training, and responsibilities that life heaps up, is one of the larger goals of the Blues' existence. Each little step along the path must be watched over; hence expressions of individuality, such as choice of clothing and style of hair, are extremely important to Blues. A Blue won't be a number, but instead is defined by everything that makes him or her not just another number. Recognize these unique attributes by pointing them out, commenting on them, responding to them in some way, and you create magic for the Blue.

> "Uniqueness: The quality of being one of a kind, unmatched, unequaled, unparalleled, single in kind or excellence."
>
> — WEBSTER'S REVISED DICTIONARY

Cherish intimacy

Life, for a Blue, is something to share, feel, and experience with other people. Blues want to understand and they want to be understood. When a Blue finds a portion of his or her self, the ability to share it with a trusted other is one of life's most sublime opportunities. It's more than letting down one's guard; it's letting a treasure shine out of the hidden light within, inside the confines of career, a relationship, a boudoir. To a Blue, one of the best ways someone can show love and establish this degree of closeness and familiarity is to spend time talking, listening, and sharing feelings. To belong with someone completely, to be a significant part of that person's life, is their fondest desire.

> "Intimate relationships cannot substitute for a life plan. But to have any meaning or viability at all, a life plan must include intimate relationships."
>
> — HARRIET LERNER

Collect relationships

Whether they're at home, school, or work, Blues enjoy connecting with others. In fact, even the shyest Blue is seldom alone for long in new circumstances. Within a short span of time they begin to sniff out others with kindred spirits; soon they form a small community of close-knit associations. This is vital for Blues, as relationships are their lifeblood. Without others to talk and listen to, their own compass may start spinning wildly and they'll lose their bearings. As a result, their circle of friends and acquaintances is vast and is seldom big enough. If they want to find some new friends, they leave out the equivalent of a salt lick to attract wildlife. Plates of cookies, bowls of candies; these attract browsers and browsers are good for conversation. Or they might become involved in a variety of social events that attract people, such as block parties, athletic competitions, educational workshops, service projects, and so on.

Blues work extremely hard to establish relationships, often much harder than the other person. When that occurs, the Blue is apt to feel neglected, unappreciated, or even abused. But they get used to this over time, and eventually accept the fact that they may be the better half of any relationship they form.

> "Without relationships, no matter how much wealth, fame, power, prestige and seeming success by the standards and opinions of the world one has, happiness will constantly elude him."
>
> — SIDNEY MADWED

Desire comfort

Like most people, Blues appreciate the comforts and conveniences of life. An attractive home filled with comfortable furnishings, inspirational artwork, tasty food, and fragrant flowers is extremely desirable. But—and here is where Blues part company with others—these comforts cannot be obtained at the expense of more important things, like family and friends.

If a couple spends so much time earning money that they neglect each other or, heaven forbid, their children, just so they can afford nice things—this is unacceptable. If a child looks at you with pleading eyes and says he wants to go for a ride in the wagon—washing the car or mowing the lawn can wait until later. Or if a friend calls and needs to talk about a personal problem, even though you just settled down with a good movie and a bowl of fresh raspberry cobbler, you'll drop what you're doing and hurry on over. So, in a Blue's home, when the dishes pile up, or the toys aren't put away, or the shirts aren't ironed, it is okay—taking care of people is far more important than taking care of the house. A Blue can tolerate a little personal discomfort if it makes a loved one more comfortable.

This attitude is the result of the altruistic desire of the Blue to have peace on earth and goodwill to men. In a Bluetopia, everybody would be happy. No one would keep and hold the upper hand to exploit others, and no one would go without food, clothing, shelter, or friendship. In a word, we would all get along, and everybody would like each other. Beating swords into plowshares and spears into pruning hooks is no mere literary allusion to a Blue; it's a cherished goal.

But if people step on co-workers at the workplace to get a better salary, or cut down a tree from an endangered species just to have some pretty woodwork in their homes, this is going way too far. Perhaps this explains why Blues get so passionate about fighting injustice, inequality, and exploitation. It destroys their comfort level and they can't feel comfortable if they know someone else is miserable.

> "In all life one should comfort the afflicted, but verily, also, one should afflict the comfortable, and especially when they are comfortably, contentedly, even happily wrong."
>
> — JOHN KENNETH GALBRAITH

Enjoy communication

Blues have a magic power to draw you out in conversation. They can listen seemingly for hours. They can speak wisely about deep things. They can put you in touch with yourself. Part of this comes from the Blues' eternal search for self. They know the invisible paths of the mind and psyche, because they've walked them themselves. Thus, sitting for an hour in a garden corner with a Blue in deep conversation may be akin to taking a voyage to some undiscovered country, even if it's within the walls of one's own heart.

Their desire for understanding leads Blues to live in a world of symbolism and hidden meanings. They're sensitive to nuances and subtleties in gesture that are often imperceptible to others. Body language, for instance, that would escape other people is noticeable to Blues. They are masters of metaphors, similes, and imagery. Because of this, the added dimensions Blues add to communication are often lost on others.

> "Good communication is as stimulating as black coffee and just as hard to sleep after."
>
> — ANNE MORROW LINDBERGH

Join causes

Historically, Blues have sought ways to make their mark on the world. They've reached out to others, created literature, and sought out and joined causes that have a lasting significance or have shown themselves capable of helping to make the world a better place.

Blues have conceived of and supported many historical and contemporary social movements, such as civil rights, equal rights, and animal rights. They often have a sense of mission and use their creative talents to convert followers to their cause, whatever it might be.

> "The superior man is... eyes for the blind, strength for the weak, and a shield for the defenseless. He stands erect by bending above the fallen. He rises by lifting others."
>
> — ROBERT INGERSOLL

Need harmony

Blues love the part of the U.S. Constitution that mentions ensuring "domestic tranquility." They would love nothing more than to have guaranteed peace and harmony on the domestic frontier. Just imagine what the world would be like if you didn't have to confront the paperboy who consistently throws your newspaper into the flowerbeds. Or if you didn't have to join a health club because you couldn't turn down the neighborhood Girl Scouts when they asked you to buy a case of Thin Mint cookies. Not to mention the joy you would feel if you didn't have to constantly threaten your kids with the punishment of a lifetime because they can't stop fighting over a cool video game.

But here's the bottom line: Blues don't just desire harmony—they require it. Arguments, yelling, fighting, even disputes over who gets to be the banker in a game of Monopoly—all of these things cause internal angst to the heart of a Blue. For many it's not only emotionally disturbing but physically upsetting as well. It's intolerable and excruciatingly painful. No wonder they make excellent peacemakers, diplomats, mediators, and go-betweens.

It's no surprise, then, that most Blues aren't aggressively competitive. A competition implies someone has to lose, and a true Blue wants everyone to be a winner. Forced into a conflict, they'll be more concerned that everyone is satisfied in the end than that their side wins. Though they won't surrender their own deep-seated ideals, Blues will often let others have their way just to maintain some sense of harmony.

> "A family is a place where minds come in contact with one another. If these minds love one another the home will be as beautiful as a flower garden. But if these minds get out of harmony with one another it is like a storm that plays havoc with the garden."
>
> — BUDDHA

Provide empathy

"Walk a mile in my shoes" is a call to action for Blues. As part of conversing with, relating to, and growing closer to someone, Blues will often crawl into others' skins. The 1983 Woody Allen movie, *Zelig,* illustrated this ability. The movie depicts the condition of a man who was reportedly so sensitive that he could take on the style, manner, and appearance of the people he spoke with. Some Blues have this capability, rather like the old adage that a dog and its owner come to look alike, or two old married people come to resemble each other, only the Blues seem to do it in real time.

The ability to learn how others feel and then give as others need lends Blue's ministrations a particularly healing nature. As a result they're some of the best caregivers in society.

> "I want, by understanding myself, to understand others. I want to be all that I am capable of becoming."
>
> — KATHERINE MANSFIELD

Pursue meaning

In their quest for deeper meaning in their lives, many Blues have turned to personal meditation, prayer, yoga, or other forms of spiritual enlightenment. They don't believe the visible is all there is, so they try to see beyond the surface to discover what's inside. To do that, they rely on their sixth sense and intuitive spirituality for insight. The whole concept of group therapy that involves the open exchange of emotions is another example of a patently Blue activity. In fact, Blues largely started and attended the encounter-group movement, seeking greater meaning and intimacy in their relationships. They sought to find themselves and "get in touch with their feelings."

> "The true meaning of religion is thus not simply morality, but morality touched by emotion."
>
> — MATTHEW ARNOLD

Respect integrity

Integrity, honesty, sincerity—to a Blue these are particularly cherished virtues. If a person is true to his or her own beliefs, then that person will be true to others as well. Authentic, honest people are a rarity and important to Blues. It doesn't matter so much what the beliefs are, if a Blue senses they're held dear, it will engender a sense of confidence and trust.

> "We lie loudest when we lie to ourselves."
>
> — ERIC HOFFER

Show kindness

If there's any color that's known for its genuine, heartfelt compassion—not born out of a sense of obligation or duty, but out of sincere concern—it's the Blue. They're naturally kindhearted, caring not only about your personal well-being, but about the well-being of your spouse, your children, and your pet goldfish. They're gentle folks who understand the value of a tender embrace, a hand to hold on to, a shoulder to cry on, and a cushy lap to sit upon. If you're ever down-in-the-dumps and need a little tender loving care, find yourself a Blue. Then, when you're back to normal, don't forget to show appreciation—take your friend out for lunch, send a personal note, and be there when he or she needs a return on the investment.

> "This is my simple religion. There is no need for temples; no need for complicated philosophy. Our own brain, our own heart is our temple; the philosophy is kindness."
>
> — DALAI LAMA

Treasure acceptance

Blues are naturally inclusive. They hate to see neglected and dejected people standing off on the sidelines. They're the first to reach out to include them in their own circle, even if it might be a tad awkward. Consequently, they really detest exclusionary acts motivated by prejudice, bigotry, chauvinism, discrimination, and intolerance. Nothing quite peeves a Blue like those dastardly deeds. They argue that even if you despise the play, that's no reason to loathe the actor. They firmly believe that only by showing an increase of love can you ever hope to change negative behaviors. Consequently, the Blues are always there with outstretched arms, waiting to receive the wayward and soothe their wounded souls.

> "We cannot change anything until we accept it. Condemnation does not liberate, it oppresses."
>
> — C. G. JUNG

Trust feelings

Blues trust their feelings implicitly. The whisperings of their hearts have similar authority to any trusted and believable voice, whether it comes from a parent, teacher, sibling, or—most powerfully of all—peers. Blues are led by what they sense, judge by what they perceive, and direct their actions by what they feel inside. This results in a strange burden. A Blue can have adequate evidence that a given choice is good or bad, and reasonable experience in similar matters to back up the evidence, yet in a way unintelligible to those less inner-oriented, make a decision based on feelings that contradict these obvious guides. This makes Blues an enigma, because the only way to predict them is to know them, yet shaped as they are by their inner voices, it's hard to understand what will be their call to action. About the safest way to deal with Blues is simply to love them, which is precisely what they want.

> "All our reasoning ends in surrender to feeling."
>
> — BLAISE PASCAL

Want romance

Regardless of their gender, the path to a Blue's heart lies in the fine art of romance. More than most, they need to be wooed and courted in sentimental ways. Flowers, candlelight dinners, love letters and poems, music and love songs, artistic paintings and etchings on the apartment wall—all of these resonate in the Blue's soul. There's no substitute for these outward expressions of love, and unless they're present, the Blue isn't sure you have what it takes to win the heart.

You see, the longing for romantic relationships is deep within a Blue's breast. They seem to be like bookends or saltshakers, always in search of their soul mates and only half present without them. Offering small tokens of affection, performing little acts of love—these kinds of behaviors demonstrate a truth and faithfulness of spirit that engenders the deepest trust for the most intimate of relationships. Of course, once a relationship is established, the key to keeping the spark alive lies in repeating again the steps that lead to the relationship's creation. After all, a Blue can never be told too often how much he or she is loved.

> "We are all born for love. It is the principle of existence, and its only end."
>
> — BENJAMIN DISRAELI

The Gold Temperament

Advocate discipline

If any personality style is known for believing in the benefits of discipline, it's the Gold. Whether it's promoting a regimented training course that produces moral or mental improvement, or advocating firm punishment intended to correct misbehavior, the Gold believes a small, short-term investment in discipline will yield substantial long-term dividends in character. Like a refiner's fire burns the impurities out of precious metals, discipline removes undesirable traits from a person's character. Therefore, the more discipline you experience, the better you will become. This is why many Golds literally become the disciples of successful people, abandoning many of their own desires in order to follow their leaders, walking the walk and talking the talk, hoping they're on the road to success, hoping to earn what they do not yet possess.

> "Discipline aims at the removal of bad habits and the substitution of good ones, especially those of order, regularity, and obedience."
>
> — C. J. SMITH

Appreciate prudence

Prudence, Temperance, Chastity, Modesty—these are more than your great-great grandmothers' names to a Gold. Each is the name of a virtue that implies discretion, restraint, conservation, forbearance. Prudent people know how to conduct themselves with good judgment, common sense, and even caution, especially in practical matters.

One way Golds show prudence is to be prepared, just like the Boy Scouts. The easiest way to do this is to save a little, reserve something, hide something away for a rainy day. It's not so much that they're pessimistic prophets of doom—they just want to be prepared in case setbacks and unfortunate events occur. They tend to agree with Robert Burns that the best laid schemes of mice and men often go astray. Consequently, Golds will spend considerable effort anticipating problems and forming backup plans. For example, they will often begin making their retirement plans while in their twenties, or start college funds for their children the day each child is born.

Another way they practice prudence is to avoid the kind of excessive, loud, extreme actions and attitudes that would lead to spending all that one has, drinking or eating to excess, driving too fast. "Wanton waste makes woeful want," is a rallying cry to Golds. Toning down gestures, actions, even the volume with which one speaks, are Gold hallmarks of refinement.

> "An ounce of prevention is worth a pound of cure."
>
> — HENRY DE BRACTON

Cherish traditions

As Tevye sang in *Fiddler on the Roof,* one of the Gold watchwords is *tradition*. They have a strong interest in tradition, and it often grows more important to them as they become older. Gold members of families, clubs, churches, or companies are those who want to observe traditions and do things the way they have always been done. If there aren't any traditional ceremonies or celebrations, they will create them and then seek to maintain them. To the Gold, traditions bring a feeling of stability, security, and order.

Golds will have misgivings about anything that fosters change. They know change is inevitable and sometimes desirable, but for a Gold, change must come slowly and cautiously. They will react in horror to anything that would do away with "tried and true" ideas. The lessons of history should always be considered when making decisions. They're strong advocates of the fundamentals of institutions and society (though certainly not all Golds will agree on what these fundamentals are). They may support societal evolution, but they're normally the enemies of revolution.

> "America, do not abandon the great traditions that stretch to the dawn of our history, do not topple the pillars of those beliefs—God, family, honor, duty, country—that have brought us through time and time and time and time again."
>
> — BOB DOLE

Collect responsibilities

By their natures, Golds feel obligated to take on responsibilities. In fact, it's almost against their moral code to refuse additional responsibilities, especially when asked by a trusted supervisor. Regardless of how busy they are, all it requires is a bit more planning, organization, and hard work to pull it off. Furthermore, they firmly believe in the truism, "If you see the need, the job is yours." Besides, if they don't do the job, chances are it won't be done correctly, promptly, or under budget. To have responsibilities—and fulfill them—shows the world you're a dedicated, accountable person. And if you can be trusted with a few assignments, then more trust will follow, and with it greater responsibilities.

> "Success on any major scale requires you to accept responsibility... in the final analysis, the one quality that all successful people have... is the ability to take on responsibility."
>
> — MICHAEL KORDA

Desire power

Power, in a Gold's mind, is the ability to exercise control in order to get things done. And power should only be vested in those who have shown themselves worthy of it, in those who are capable of exercising power judiciously and righteously for the good of the whole. Obviously not just any Tom, Dick, or Harriet is qualified to have power—only those who have earned it through an established pattern of hard work, self-discipline, and performance.

Someone needs to have the power to lead and make decisions. It can be a terrible burden, because the first decision carries the seeds of the second through the last, and yet indecision and waiting will steal the opportunity to choose. Golds sense this, and hence are driven to look at the information, sift the reliable from that which is not—usually by obtaining the opinion of a trusted expert—and then deciding and acting upon it in a timely manner. Golds are fit for this kind of executive role because they understand the need for the greater good, they know their limits in terms of information gathering and processing, and they love, even crave, getting things done.

Empowered Golds speak up when they see a mess forming that will take more than the resources of the mess-maker to fix. Public expenditures, perhaps even the Gold's own efforts, will be needed to set things right once the error has run its course. So the time to act is now, and Golds usually do, probably making the world better for everyone.

> "I really believe my greatest service is in the many unwise steps I prevent."
>
> — WILLIAM LYON MACKENZIE KING

Enjoy completion

Every task completed is an accomplishment, and every accomplishment is one more line in the Gold's case file that, when all is said and done, establishes that he or she is living a good and serviceable life.

To keep track of their progress, Golds often keep to-do lists. These lists can become a significant driving force in their lives. They enjoy the satisfaction of planning a task and seeing it completed. When Golds do something that isn't on the list, they will often add it to the list so they can check it off, showing they have accomplished that particular item. To complete something, for a Gold, is like putting out a fire or scratching a fierce itch.

This also applies to long-term projects. Golds often shape their lives around long-term goals that require extended effort and sacrifice. Achievements that require effort over time—college degrees, children successfully reared, mortgages paid off—point out ways in which the Gold has shown diligent effort in the past, and may point as well to ways in which the Gold is likely to be serviceable and useful to society again.

> "The reward of a thing well done is to have done it."
>
> — RALPH WALDO EMERSON

Join organizations

The Gold desire for belonging and being useful is often shown in their inclination to join and support business and service organizations, PTAs and PTOs, church auxiliaries, lodges, and municipal or political organizations. They sometimes join just for the personal associations and networking opportunities these groups provide. Other times, they join because they feel the potential for accomplishment is multiplied if people are organized.

The organization also provides a statement of purpose and sense of history, usually replete with the traditions and rituals that Golds find so reassuring. They also perceive within the companionship of like-minded individuals a certain security, either for themselves, the ideals the group promulgates, or perhaps for society at large. The goals of the group form a focus that can galvanize the organization into action, thus giving Golds a chance to belong, protect and preserve, and get things done, all at the same time.

> "An empowered organization is one in which individuals have the knowledge, skill, desire, and opportunity to personally succeed in a way that leads to collective organizational success."
>
> — STEPHEN R. COVEY

Need order

The Gold personality sees life as something to organize and arrange. Everything should be in its proper place and follow the correct sequence. If you look in the closet of a person who is extremely Gold, everything will be organized by type. Pairs of shoes will be neatly arranged in a specific location. Clothes on hangers will be facing the same way, maybe even sorted by color or arranged by day of intended wear. To a Gold, putting clothes in a closet in a disorganized manner would be as bad as throwing them on the floor. Most Golds believe that if something is to be done at all, it should be done right. They often view things as either black or white and believe there is only one correct way to do each thing.

Another way Golds can order the world around them is by scheduling their lives. To help them effectively manage their time, they zealously use day planners, pocket calendars, and appointment books. Count on the Gold to remember important meetings, appointments, anniversaries, and birthdays.

Furthermore, they will be punctual to their appointments. Punctuality is a not just a sign of respect for others, it also demonstrates the Gold's dedication to an obligation. They will do whatever it takes to be on time because they view themselves as capable, responsible individuals. As such, they feel they should be able to control their own lives to satisfy the requirements of their commitments. This belief causes Golds to be impatient with tardiness and absenteeism in others as well.

Even though their practical natures may lead them to dislike unnecessary red tape and inefficiency, Golds are often involved in maintaining systems that require multiple "checks and balances." Completing forms, maintaining logs, writing progress reports—these detailed tasks that other colors might call trivial may not really be enjoyed by the Gold, but they're accepted and completed with the understanding that they're part of maintaining a sense of order.

> "It is not enough to do good; one must do it the right way."
>
> — JOHN MORLEY

Provide structure

Golds promote and defend structure in the home and workplace. Because of the Golds' appreciation for organization, they establish hierarchical structures—with someone in charge and others positioned throughout a clear chain of command. Golds value respect for authority and exact obedience to those in higher positions; they set up rules to govern the conduct of every member of the organization. The result is that resources are easier to share, with greater disbursements to those who need them.

As needs are met, resources are made available, and clear lines of authority are set up, more and more effort can go towards the accomplishment of the mission, with less time and effort spent dealing with internal frictions. This leads to conservation of resources against hard times, and also to the creation of rituals and traditions within the ranks. The result: a more structured and harmonious environment, courtesy of Golds.

> "When liberty destroys order, the hunger for order will destroy liberty."
>
> — WILL DURANT

Pursue security

The word *security* means a lot of things to a Gold. At its heart it means that they, and their loved ones, will be free from needless risk or danger. Golds would love nothing more than to live in a world were they didn't have to worry about the future. However, since that isn't practical, they seem to spend a great deal of their time trying to fashion adequate remedies in the name of security.

Security means having a good-paying career at an established institution that fosters positive societal standards. Something in the education, business, banking, military, medical, or civil service industries would do nicely.

Security means putting aside something from every paycheck, no matter how tight money is at the moment. It means paying off any necessary debts as soon as possible. (Golds won't go into debt willy-nilly. Only a mortgage or a student loan would qualify as necessary—definitely nothing so frivolous as an entertainment system or living room furniture.) It means owning your home free and clear. It means having at least a year's supply of food, water, and fuel. It means knowing how to survive in the wilderness in case a frenzied mob drives you from your home.

Security also means making contingency and disaster plans. It means having fire extinguishers, fire detectors, carbon monoxide detectors, rehearsing fire escape routes with your family, having a laminated list of important phone numbers, and an up-to-date video inventory of all your household possessions. It means having a will, an executor of your estate, and a trusted attorney. It also means having more than adequate insurance. By the way, it's no surprise that the insurance industry was created by Golds for Golds and people who "should be" more Gold-like. There's nothing like a good double-indemnification life insurance policy to give you peace of mind.

Security also means protecting your family from enemies—both foreign and domestic. It means having a home security system to detect intruders, a can of pepper spray in your purse, and a great big guard dog or other equally nasty weapon. Golds are fiercely protective of their families and won't hesitate to use force, even lethal force if necessary, to protect them. Perhaps this explains why so many soldiers and militia members are Golds who aren't afraid to stand up against tyranny and oppression. They seem to be the natural defenders of truth, justice, and liberty.

Nothing is quite so disturbing to a Gold as seeing what should have been a sure thing slip away through no fault of their own. That's why they're so opposed to many entrepreneurial enterprises and other unpredictable, uncertain financial ventures. They tend to stay away from high-yield, high-risk stock investments, preferring instead the slow but steady bond and T-bill markets. This also explains why they're such sticklers for letters of intent, formal proposals, written agreements, and official-looking contracts that are signed, sealed, and delivered—in triplicate. They want all the I's dotted and T's crossed, so they can minimize the element of risk.

> "The superior man, when resting in safety, does not forget that danger may come. When in a state of security he does not forget the possibility of ruin. When all is orderly, he does not forget that disorder may come. Thus his person is not endangered, and his states and all their clans are preserved."
>
> — CONFUCIUS

Respect achievement

Golds believe in the law of the harvest: you reap what you sow. So if you're interested in the things that money can buy, and you work harder and smarter than most people, you should be entitled to more benefits. Likewise, if you sit back on your haunches and expect good fortune to drop in your lap, then you deserve whatever morsels you can scrounge up. The same holds true for other things as well, not just those that you can buy with money. If you study hard, you'll pass the test. If you exercise, you'll get healthier. If you convince enough people to vote for you, you'll win the election.

Golds are forever looking for benchmarks they can use to judge and measure their world. They're not doing this to be cliquish, snobbish, or prejudiced—this is how they make sense of the world. They're compelled to compare and contrast in order to understand. And a person's status or condition is a way of making that judgment. Therefore, if you have the signs or symbols that indicate you're successful or qualified—which are conditions the

Gold respects and values—then they can make the necessary judgments and deal with you accordingly.

> "Happiness is that state of consciousness which proceeds from the achievement of one's values."
>
> — AYN RAND

Show dedication

Loyalty, perseverance, devotion, enduring to the end—all of these describe values that are highly prized by Golds. Sticking to the task until the task is through. Staying married to someone even though the going gets rough. Remaining with your long-time employer even though a competitor has offered to double your salary. Staying at work past midnight to get the proposal finished. Going above and beyond the call of duty. These are touchstones every Gold seeks. Therefore, they tend to be a dedicated lot that you can count on to keep their word when push comes to shove. As a result, they end up being models of dedication, sometimes without even trying.

> "The person who makes a success of living is the one who see his goal steadily and aims for it unswervingly. That is dedication."
>
> — CECIL B. DE MILLE

Treasure appreciation

After working so long and hard, Golds take delight in knowing they have done well, whatever the task, and that you appreciate them for it. However, most Golds won't indicate they need special recognition, arguing they were only doing what they said they would do, and people ought not to be thanked for doing their duty. In fact, this sense of obligation will probably keep them serving even if people are consistently ungrateful for their efforts. With that said, it's still important to offer Golds regular, sincere, appropriate tokens of appreciation. A thank-you card, a certificate of appreciation, an acknowledgement in the company newsletter, an extra day of paid vacation, an advancement in position or salary, a reserved parking space, or a name on a plaque where everyone can see it—these things will go a long way to recharge a weary Gold.

> "Men are rich only as they give. He who gives great service gets great rewards."
>
> — ELBERT HUBBARD

Trust authority

Golds believe most people in authority have, for one reason or another, earned the right to be there. Whether they climbed the rungs of the corporate ladder, jumped through the required hoops, won the votes of the electorate, placed a sufficient number of certificates or diplomas on their office walls, wrote the book on the subject, or simply kissed the right number of toads—their authority comes from the fact that they have followed the rules previously established by other authorities. Therefore, they deserve our respect and trust.

When it comes time to making decisions, Golds will consult the appropriate authority to make sure it's the correct choice. The authority's assistant probably isn't good enough—they need to hear it from the source or read it from the official reference manual. These are the folks who, in order to make proper judgments, will actually spend time to read the guidelines, instruction sheets, rulebooks, and user manuals. Then they'll normally follow the instructions to the letter.

Again, the issue is more about doing the right thing, rather than doing only what you can get away with. If your teacher says you must write a five thousand–word paper to get an A, then you'll write a five thousand–word paper—you wouldn't even consider turning in a shorter paper that would result in a lower grade. Or if your boss says to follow a certain procedure when making widgets, you wouldn't think about doing it differently, even if there were a more efficient way. Until the system is officially changed, you'll support the established process.

> "Don't think of me as the boss. Think of me as a co-worker who's always right."
>
> — BOB THAVES

Want rules

Golds place a great deal of value on rules and regulations in all aspects of life. Before participating in any activity, they will want to know what the rules are so they can know how to behave. When starting a new job, Golds often look for an explanation of company rules and procedures. When playing a new game, they study the rules before beginning. When joining an organization, they learn what rules will govern their behavior. No matter the activity, Golds want to know the "right" way to behave.

To a Gold, rules are like the string on a kite. Without a string to control its movement, a kite will quickly fall to the ground. Likewise, if people don't have rules to control their actions, they may fail to be useful. Golds feel society exists because of rules, laws, standards, guidelines, and restrictions. If people routinely disobey these regulations, society will collapse. As a result, not only do Golds earnestly try to follow rules, they also want everyone else to follow them. Golds take the "rights" and "wrongs" of their culture seriously and strongly disapprove of wrongdoers. While they will make allowances for those who are truly penitent, Golds won't be sympathetic towards those who repeatedly disregard the law.

> "Law is order, and good law is good order."
>
> — ARISTOTLE

The Green Temperament

Advocate solutions

For Greens, the purpose of life is to find the solutions. Unfortunately, they aren't always sure what the problems are. And that's what makes life so intriguing. To get to the solutions, you have to first uncover the problems, and golly, just take a good hard look around and you'll find more than enough prospects.

So the first step is to limit the field and refine the search. Here is where a Green starts to choose just what it is she or he wants to understand. Rather than trying to solve all the world's problems, the Green will stake out a general area, say science, and whittle it down a bit until a narrower area of problems appears—say biology. Then genetics. Then the human genome. Ultimately, after getting more and more specific, the Green decides to analyze deoxyribonucleic acid to figure out which pairs of adenine and thymine or cytosine and guanine cause diabetes. Then poof, sixty-one years later, while studying the 9,131,966th pair, the Green dies.

When you go through his or her logbooks, you discover that the Green never did isolate the right base pair. However, you also learn, among other things, that this person wrote a best-selling book revealing the mating habits of the African tsetse fly, developed a way to mass-produce scratch n' sniff playing cards, collected 8,547 specimens of bat guano, created blueprints for a hand-powered ice maker that makes five pounds of ice in less than two minutes, and climbed Mt. Fuji backwards because a laboratory technician said no one had before. You see, while looking at base pairs, the Green had a stray thought, which took her off on a fascinating tangent, which led to another departure, which ultimately made her an expert in much more than DNA. And so it is with Greens, always in search of solutions to every problem they encounter, uncovering new problems with every twist and turn.

> "All progress is precarious, and the solution of one problem brings us face to face with another problem."
>
> — MARTIN LUTHER KING JR.

Appreciate innovation

The status quo isn't good enough for Greens. Just as nature refines and improves over generations, allowing that which is better to reproduce faster than that which is merely good, so Greens tinker and twiddle until they design something better. Sometimes the improvement is incremental, with little refinements based on ever more careful observation and ever more refined adjustments. Other times, usually the best times, whole new sciences evolve, new panoramas of knowledge unfold, and new fields of inquiry emerge. To a Green, this is the same sensation as feeling the wind rush through one's hair in the pilot seat with Orville Wright over the beach at Kitty Hawk. New ideas! Going where no mind has gone before!

> "The best way to predict the future is to invent it."
>
> — ALAN KAY

Cherish technology

Gadgets and gizmos that bend nature in new ways have irresistible appeal to Greens. Wristwatch cell phones, cars with radios, boxes that show moving pictures and sound right in one's living room—these wonders and the technologies that enable them are part of Greens' playground. Holding up a small device that does something that hasn't been do-able before and explaining how it works allows the Green to stand on the cutting edge of what is known and done. Even vicariously, such things give a Green thrill. A piece of an audio tape that had been in an astronaut's space capsule used to sit in most NASA engineer's wallets; a chunk of hologram decorated many physics professors' desks. Technology is an indicator of human progress to Greens, and they often celebrate its artifacts. What's more, technology is just plain fun.

> "Any sufficiently advanced technology is indistinguishable from magic."
>
> — ARTHUR C. CLARKE

Collect data

Like a computer without software, Greens are virtually stymied without resources to tap. They need input—new facts, new data, new theories. Sometimes Greens can even become information junkies—addicted to acquiring fact after fact, forever learning and never quite understanding. For these individuals, to be placed in a world without information to assimilate is a fate almost worse than death.

Facts are the beginning of knowledge, and Greens need to know where the facts come from. In the days of the Internet and digital TV, it's easy to read pages and pages off the Web and its newsgroups and see dozens of informative programs each month. In the days before the Internet, it was a little harder to stay connected, but books, newspapers, magazines, newsletters, and the trade journals helped. Before that, there were always libraries. Without these, Greens would likely start poking sticks into the ground to track the sun, at the same time keeping their ears glued to a radio.

An interesting, seemingly contradictory sidebar is that Green prisoners of war seem to survive for quite a long time without resources—longer than non-Green internees. This is primarily because they normally live in their brains—and you just can't keep a good brain down. So a Green can live quite well, replaying events of the past, devising new strategies, creating imaginary worlds to live within—all without uttering a syllable. They occupy their time with reprocessing, regurgitating, and reinterpreting the data they have already collected and stored up for just such an occasion. Of course, new data to chew on is still highly desirable, and more satisfying than a succulent filet mignon dinner.

> "It is a capital mistake to theorize before one has data. Insensibly one begins to twist facts to suit theories, instead of theories to suit facts."
>
> — SIR ARTHUR CONAN DOYLE

Desire efficiency

To a Green, efficiency isn't coming up with a solid organization, backup plans, and checks and balances to make sure something comes off effectively—it's simply doing something successfully with as little energy as possible. Efficiency has everything to do with competence, know-how, and ability. A person is far more likely to be efficient if he or she thoroughly understand the process and comprehend the technicalities.

Efficient bread bakers understand the science behind yeast compounds, so they can take a recipe, tweak it, and create something that's faster, better, or easier for others to replicate. Efficient house painters don't guess at how much paint they might need—if they ran out of paint they would have to return to the store to buy more, hoping they could match the tints in the process. No, efficient painters take a few measurements, factor in the porousness of the surface to be painted, identify how thick the layer of paint should be, then whip out a pocket PC to plug this data into a spreadsheet. Now they know exactly how much paint they will need, plus a predetermined percentage to compensate for accidental spillage. That way, they simply need to make one efficient trip to the store, saving a couple of hours. Of course, they probably spent several weeks creating the spreadsheet—but look at how efficient they are!

That leads to a common pitfall for Greens—sometimes their improved solution takes more effort to develop than they would have spent implementing an established procedure in the first place. However, the point is to make things better, more precise or accurate, and less wasteful for those who follow. Greens recognize they may never see the fruits of their labors, but that isn't nearly as important as the long-term effects that may be realized by their successors who will almost certainly praise their ingenuity posthumously for generations.

> "Efficiency is intelligent laziness."
>
> — DAVID DUNHAM

Enjoy mysteries

Among the people Greens admire are those clever men and women who see things that are often overlooked and are able to deduce the solution to a grand mystery.

Even though they are fictional, sleuths such as Hercule Poirot, Jane Marple, Sherlock Holmes, and Jessica Fletcher represent Green ideals remarkably well. They gather information, form hypotheses, test their assumptions, and evaluate the results until they're able to reach an accurate conclusion, which is often surprising and defies sensibilities until it's patiently explained to the dumbfounded masses. To be at that level of cognition, to be able to bewilder and amaze others, is a secret desire of most Greens. Perhaps this is why most Greens identify the whodunit mystery as a favorite genre of literature and cinema.

Unfortunately, over the centuries, when Greens have used their abilities to accomplish things that were seemingly impossible or have redefined the way people saw the world, they were often labeled heretics, sorcerers, or witches. If they weren't cast out of the village, they were often put to death. Fortunately, our society now pays a great deal of homage to people who are able to amaze us or suspend our disbelief. Some of the most successful people in the world are Greens who have pioneered high technologies that appear magical to the uninformed. For instance, the entire entertainment industry relies heavily on Green innovations to make thrill rides more thrilling, special effects more special, magic tricks more magical, and mysteries more mysterious.

> "To me there is something thrilling and exalting in the thought that we are drifting forward into a splendid mystery—into something that no mortal eye hath yet seen, and no intelligence has yet declared."
>
> — E. H. CHAPIN

Join debates

Because they live in the world of ideas, many Greens enjoy debate and structure compelling, logical arguments. They tend to stay emotionally detached from a position and may be able to defend either side with equal intensity. In fact, in casual conversations, Greens often take the opposite viewpoint just to keep things interesting. Sometimes this makes them appear to be antagonistic or contentious, especially if they're talking with a more sensitive individual. But this is seldom their intention. They're simply discussing information in their natural, challenging style.

> "To repeat what others have said, requires education; to challenge it, requires brains."
>
> — MARY PETTIBONE POOLE

Need time

Time is a resource that's highly valued by Greens. Given enough time, they can solve any mystery, master any subject, or find any bug. They need time to identify and analyze the pros and cons, to test the product and pinpoint its weaknesses, to process any new data that may have just turned up, to make just about every decision. There is never enough time, especially if you're engaged in your work from tip to toe. Remember, Greens who enjoy what they're doing will do it ad infinitum. Eating, sleeping, bathing, changing clothes, socializing, writing progress reports—Greens often meet these "necessities" with irritation or contempt. Perhaps this is why many Greens seem to have a hard time managing their time. A project will invariably take as much time as available—often winding up just moments before it's due. This isn't due to procrastination, but to the desire to make it as good as it can be. So Greens will keep fine-tuning and improving their work until the last possible moment. After all, the product is a reflection of their own competence and ability; if it's merely mediocre, then so are they.

> "Time is the most valuable thing a man can spend."
>
> — THEOPHRASTUS

Provide information

Greens are founts of information. Most of it's highly reliable, although sometimes it may be too obscure to be useful. For example, they love to impart little known factoids. Did you know that 111,111,111 x 111,111,111 = 12,345,678,987,654,321? Or that the name "Wendy" was made up for the book *Peter Pan*? Or that when Heinz ketchup leaves the bottle, it travels at a rate of 25 miles per year? After all, you never know when you'll need to inform someone that a standard computer byte is composed of two nibbles, and that there are normally four bits in a nibble.

Greens are, for the most part, open books, despite their often enigmatic, distant appearance. Normally shy and reticent, they hesitantly divulge little about themselves. Yet, if the request is for information about one of their proficiencies, they'll sing like canaries on steroids. You see, even more than knowing, Greens like to be seen as being knowledgeable. Start Greens talking about their interests with a feather, and you may have to shut them up with a hammer.

> "I'm very well acquainted too with matters mathematical, I understand equations, both the simple and quadratical, About binomial theorem I'm teeming with a lot of news—with many cheerful facts about the square of the hypotenuse."
>
> — SIR WILLIAM S. GILBERT

Pursue understanding

"Why is there air?" was one of comedian Bill Cosby's famous questions. The practical answer—to fill up volleyballs—provides little satisfaction to dyed-in-the-clover Greens. Why air, why not a more viscous fluid? What would happen if the air suddenly turned into such a fluid? Given time, could humans sprout gills? If the new liquid were heavier than water, would people have to become deep-sea dwellers to breathe?

Greens are driven to ask questions about their world. To understand not only how things are put together, but to know how to do things—this brings joy to their souls. Even from an early age, Greens want to understand how things work and the reasons behind everything. They may take things apart to see how they work or read extensively on a subject of interest. From the time they can form the questions they want answered, learning and thinking are constant preoccupations. In fact, the stream of questions is never-ending.

Because of their questioning nature, Greens are the innovators of the world. They bring progress to society. They expand the intellectual horizons. They're the ones who explore new ideas and add to humanity's understanding of the universe.

> "The important thing is not to stop questioning."
>
> — ALBERT EINSTEIN

Respect genius

Genius comes in many different forms. Whether it's intellectual, physical, emotional, social, or financial—a genius is someone who has an extraordinary advantage over others, an inborn ability or talent that's far above average. Everyone has a spark of genius and it's each person's job to find it, add tinder to it, and start a fire that illuminates the world. They reason, "The light of knowledge you bring into the world may be the torch by which I may better read. Therefore if you have an intellectual gift, I will stand back in awe, drawing from your insights to help me form conclusions in my own field of expertise." Thus it is that Greens give each other deference. When one's gift is made manifest, and it may come suddenly or in a field one hasn't studied (or better yet, in a field no one has studied), then one is allowed to take his or her place with the elders of the tribe. When one gifted in another area rises to speak, the others sit to listen. Greens thus trade access to knowledge as others might trade fine art or baseball cards.

> "The greatest happiness for the thinking man is to have fathomed the fathomable, and to quietly revere the unfathomable."
>
> — JOHANN WOLFGANG VON GOETHE

Show composure

Greens prize their ability to stay calm in an emergency. When others are off being emotional, they remain in absolute control of their faculties. It's illogical when, at the moment of crisis, some people disengage their brains and let their feelings run amuck. Yes, little Johnny may have cut off his thumb, but that's no reason to wail and bop around like a decapitated turkey. So the unflappable Green quietly takes charge, sends someone to phone for help, has Johnny lie down with his hand up in the air, then applies a tourniquet created from Johnny's shoelace and a toothbrush. Meanwhile, the Green has directed another bystander to locate the emancipated digit and place it in a plastic bag on ice. As Johnny's weepy father is rambling on about how Johnny will never be able to hitchhike again or save a gladiator's life, and how he would gladly sacrifice his own big toe if the surgeon can't reattach Johnny's thumb, the Green is speaking calmly to Johnny and adjusting the tourniquet at regular intervals.

Of course this calm demeanor doesn't only surface during emergencies. This is a Greens' normal operational status. They prefer to remain as cool, calm, and collected as possible. Even if they just discovered how to turn lead into gold, they might be as giddy as a schoolgirl inside but as cool as a glacier on the outside. They have learned to keep their emotions under wraps so feelings don't interfere with their objective analysis.

> "Always behave like a duck—keep calm and unruffled on the surface but paddle like the devil underneath."
>
> — JACOB BRAUDE

Treasure autonomy

One of the most basic Green needs is intellectual freedom. They must have the freedom to pursue their thoughts and are repulsed by anything that would restrict their ability to examine and question the world around them. They don't believe that "there are some things that shouldn't be questioned." They're definitely not interested in having others think for them. Given an issue, Greens will fight for the right to take it apart and analyze it themselves. This is part curiosity, part intellectual honesty, and part stubbornness.

Often, when the facts of a matter lie discovered and arranged on the table, their meaning remains an issue. Once again, the Green will not be led. Conclusions are serious business, and thoughts will not be rushed.

To work at his or her peak, a Green will require a curious mixture of intellectual companionship and intellectual isolation. This may defy the structure of the organization in which the Green serves, but chances are this is okay. The Green has likely been walking a lonely highway anyway. A little bit of corporate turmoil is pretty much the price one pays to be Green or to have a Green around.

> "The mind is an attribute of the individual. There is no such thing as a collective brain. There is no such thing as a collective thought. An agreement reached by a group of men is only a compromise or an average drawn upon many individual thoughts."
>
> — AYN RAND

Trust analysis

Greens believe in the power of analytical thinking. Therefore, in important matters that affect them, they prefer to be allowed to make the decisions or at least audit the decisions made by others. Few things escape the rigorous examination process Greens provide. Simple questions and answers often resemble interrogation sessions. Casual explanations often end up drafted on whiteboards or napkins, dissected for any flaws in approach or logic. This process can go on and on and on. Even when it seems to be complete, it can start up again if a new fact or figure surfaces that might nullify the whole conclusion.

Curiously, once they find the path to the answer, Greens prefer moving on to another problem rather than sitting through the dreary details of actually implementing the solution. The exercise has yielded its pearl. The Green's job is finished. He or she can delegate the implementation to others. Seeing the solution through to the end would be trivial and possibly tedious—both painful states for a Green.

> "There are three principal means of acquiring knowledge . . . observation of nature, reflection, and experimentation. Observation collects facts; reflection combines them; experimentation verifies the result of that combination."
>
> — DENIS DIDEROT

Want competence

The major source of self-esteem for Greens is competence. To feel good about themselves, Greens must be competent and capable. They not only value expertise, they fundamentally require it. They constantly monitor their own progress and push themselves to improve.

The focus of individual Greens may differ, but in all cases it's important for them to master understanding of whatever fields they stake out as their areas of competency. The more extreme the Greens, the more exacting and demanding they will be to acquire skill and knowledge. They will settle for nothing less than competence in whatever areas they choose to pursue. They're constantly accumulating mental lists of things they should know and should be able to do. They can become perfectionists and are often frustrated at the inability to reach perfection.

If you examine your Green acquaintances, chances are you only see their competencies and not their weaknesses. They really seem like rather sharp, talented people, don't they? But if the truth be known, they have a side that isn't quite ready for prime time. They're extremely reluctant to let all but those closest to them see this bungling, clumsy, untrained side. This part of their character is a work in progress, and only the artist needs to know how many mistakes were made before the work was completed. It's humiliating for Greens to have others witness errors in their work, especially errors in logic. So you'll never know how many hours they spent learning and honing their latest skill. And that's precisely the way they want it.

Once Greens master a technology or field of interest, they're likely to move on to other challenges. Once they have conquered the theory and developed the necessary skills, a field may no longer hold their interest. Too many things remain to be explored to spend much time on only one area. But even after moving on to new challenges, Greens expect to improve competency in every area, new and old.

> "Competence, like truth, beauty and contact lenses, is in the eye of the beholder."
>
> — LAURENCE J. PETER

The Orange Temperament

Advocate success

Because of their optimistic temperaments, Oranges are convinced that success is always right around the corner. All that's needed is the right combination of luck, skill, and perseverance. Of course, nothing breeds success like success, and Oranges have no objections to starting the cycle with their own victories to show it can be done. Oranges are happy winners, often willing to share in the spoils. It's likely their native ability to land on their feet translates into their vision of potential success all around in most any enterprise.

> "There is only one success—to be able to spend your life in your own way."
>
> — CHRISTOPHER MORLEY

Appreciate courage

Oranges are motivated by the thrill of performance, enlivened by the act of execution. Not every life is an ice rink, not all the world is a stage. One universal testing ground, however, is the measure of how you stand against bad odds, how you proceed without flinching into situations of peril and risk. The ability to do what needs to be done when your knees are knocking is called courage, and Oranges respect it.

Regardless of their situation, Oranges appreciate people who stand up to their fears. It may be asking for a raise from a tight-fisted supervisor, proposing marriage to your sexy sweetheart, standing up to the beefy bully from down the street, informing your parents you just totaled their classic Corvette, bungee-jumping off a one thousand–foot bridge for the first time, or deciding to streak naked through the next stockholder's meeting. These things take guts, pluck, nerve, chutzpah.

Oranges' madcap adventures usually have their roots in the attempt to face fear and confidently show their bravery. To an Orange, there's nothing worse than being a lily-livered, chicken-hearted, weak-minded, cowardly nidget, who is unable to say "boo" to a goose.

> "Courage is not the absence of fear, but rather the judgment that something else is more important than fear."
>
> — AMBROSE REDMOON

Cherish recreation

When Oranges have occupations that are less than ideal for their personality styles—jobs where they do sedate things for most of the day—it's no surprise that when they reach the end of a workweek, they're off like a rocket. Of course, even if an Orange does have a thrilling, fast-paced job, by the weekend he or she is still ready to cut loose and seek amusement with as many stimulating activities as possible.

Each color has a different idea of what fun is, and to an Orange, it's doing something engaging, enjoyable, or entertaining. However, rather than picking one or two activities to keep them busy for a day, Oranges prefer choosing from a smorgasbord. They'll do a little of one activity until they get bored and decide to move on to the next, then the next, and so on. Few activities take more than an hour or two, which also means they take their recreation seriously and with gusto, even if that means they take the risk of injuring themselves now and then.

Activities may involve other people as long as they don't get in the way or hold the Orange back. But activities may also involve being by themselves—even Oranges need a little alone time every so often. Even then, chances are they will be doing something active if they're physically able to do it. They just don't prefer to plop down in front of the TV and watch an endless parade of inanity hour after hour. Watching an occasional action-adventure flick, comedy routine, or athletic competition is fine, but a couple of hours are more than enough before it's time to get up and do something different.

By the end of an ideal play day, Oranges will have spent nearly every drop of energy on an impressive number of nerve-racking, bone-jarring, blood-pumping activities. Of course, they also keep a little stored away just in case they're able to woo a loved one into something more arousing—but that's another story (see chapter 10).

> "If life doesn't offer a game worth playing, then invent a new one."
>
> — ANTHONY J. D'ANGELO

Collect experiences

Oranges seek to sample all that life has to offer. They're really living when they're able to feel, taste, smell, listen, and see the environment around them. When the wind whips through the hair, the parachute pops open, the pedal hits the metal and smoke comes off the tires, the water smacks like a block of ice, the snow blows up your parka—these are moments when Oranges are feeling alive. When off duty, Oranges act, move, play, sit, and stand in such a way that they can see and feel things. It's as if they sense innately that life in a corporeal body is finite, and they want to make sure they wear out rather than rust.

As a result, Oranges collect experiences the way others collect knowledge, relationships, or responsibilities. They must live through something for themselves—living vicariously through someone else is unfulfilling. Perhaps this is why they seem to be always on the go, because there is always something more to experience. Life is simply too short to waste time studying, worrying about the future, or thinking up thoughtful things to say to your loved ones. Life is meant to be lived! If you aren't experiencing what it has to offer, then you're not living at all.

Most Oranges, if they survive to old age, would like nothing more than to amuse their grandchildren with tales about their wild exploits and adventures. By now, the stories have probably grown more interesting and exciting than they originally were, and certainly more colorful. Their objective isn't only to amuse their progeny—although amusement is nice—it's to inspire them into waking up and experiencing life for themselves—to seize the day and make their lives extraordinary.

> "I think that, as life is action and passion, it is required of a man that he should share the passion and action of his time at peril of being judged not to have lived."
>
> — OLIVER WENDELL HOLMES, JR

Desire victory

Whether it's defeating an enemy in battle, an antagonist in a contest, or simply gaining the upper hand in a struggle or competition, Oranges desire victory. While everyone wants victory to some extent, Oranges seem to want it more. They crave it, yearn for it, and come to blows for it. After all, the opposite of victory—defeat—is utterly intolerable. Only losers, wimps, failures, and weaklings are suited for defeat.

This fervent desire is pretty obvious in athletics and other physically demanding activities. But it's also evident in every other aspect of their lives. Oranges enjoy competition and are aggressive in their desire to win. They're eager to demonstrate their talents and skills and prove their capacity to endure and succeed. Of course, they don't have to be picture perfect in their execution; they just have to outlast their opponents. After all, victory goes to the player, the soldier, or the gladiator who makes the next-to-last mistake.

> "Far better it is to dare mighty things, to win glorious triumphs even though checkered by failure, than to rank with those poor spirits who neither enjoy nor suffer much because they live in the gray twilight that knows neither victory nor defeat."
>
> — THEODORE ROOSEVELT

Enjoy challenges

Internal or external pressure to be victorious causes the Orange to not only face most challenges head-on, but to seek them out enthusiastically. If Oranges don't have a mountain to climb, a record to break, a game to win, or a test to pass, they'll turn something—anything—into a challenge. After all, nothing is as fun to do as a thing that cannot be done.

Oranges are masters at reframing situations to take into account only what is real and now and not what is traditional or "known." Thus an Orange can ride to victory on a wave of success, taken when no one expected the tide to turn. Dealing with the real rather than the imaginary or customary frees up many resources, as well as cuts a few corners and steps on a few toes. However, the unqualified success that comes from pulling something off more than makes up for the times when an Orange splats terribly and has to creep off to lick wounds.

From childhood, Oranges readily respond to the "I Dare You" challenge. Many an Orange has been the first among his or her peers to jump off the high dive, smoke a cigarette, walk into the wrong locker room, say the first swear word, or throw the first spit wad at the brainiac on the front row. It's not that they're overly susceptible to peer pressure, it's just that they don't want to resist a challenge. Are they courageous enough? Are they bold enough? Are they daring enough? These are the characteristics they prize and value. Naturally they seek out opportunities to prove they possess these attributes.

A common mistake made by many parents or teachers of Oranges is to say, "These rules are unbreakable." Well, if you make that blunder, you've just thrown down the gauntlet, and any Orange worth his or her salt will take up the implied challenge and test you, and test you again, until they emerge victorious. To an Orange, barriers are meant to be overcome, borders are meant to be crossed, chains are meant to be broken, and walls are meant to be scaled. This could be good if the wall is the Iron Curtain—but not so good if the wall surrounds Fort Knox. The trick is to channel an Orange's "rebelliousness" into doing something more constructive than destructive.

> "The greater the difficulty the more glory in surmounting it. Skillful pilots gain their reputation from storms and tempests."
>
> — EPICURUS

Join activities

Oranges seek out things to do. They make and take action, and their native flair allows them to join in without looking out of place. Popping between parties and events with ease and fluency, they add sparkle wherever they go. In the world of sports, they tend to join games easily. On the trail or by a stream, if they can rustle up some gear, they can pitch in and make do. Flexibility is their hallmark; their natural likeability and ready smiles get them into places and opportunities most others just dream about.

Of course, Oranges don't join all activities—only those that speak to their values and interests. When activities start to get more formal or structured, such as organized team sports and competitions, then they'll hang back a little bit, until they sense there is some fun to be had in spite of the people who wander around spouting rules, schedules, procedures, and release forms. But if they see an activity that's already in full swing, full of life, entertaining, and gives them the opportunity to either practice a skill they desire, learn a new one, or show off their expertise—count on the Orange to join in wholeheartedly.

> "The game of life is a lot like football. You have to tackle your problems, block your fears, and score your points when you get the opportunity."
>
> — LEWIS GRIZZARD

Need incentives

Left to their own devices, Oranges will find something to do. It may not be approved, wise, or safe, but it's likely to be entertaining enough to fill the needs of the moment. To entice an Orange away from whatever trouble they have stirred up, one has to use an incentive.

Orange incentives are things they value above all others: adventure, boldness, competition, danger, excitement, flexibility, generosity, publicity, impulses, jackpots, etc. If they can get these things in exchange for a little bit of performance, then you'll probably be able to keep them in harness long enough to accomplish a specific objective.

More than the other colors, however, these enticements need to be tangible, practical, and distinctive. In the workplace, for example, Oranges need something more than a regular paycheck, a pat on the back, or the satisfaction of perfecting a process. They need a bonus—something extra special that most people don't get. A cash bonus, a free round of golf, a gift certificate to a popular restaurant, tickets to a movie, an extra week of paid vacation—these things are acceptable incentives, but an employer could do better. Perhaps skydiving lessons, a glider ride, scuba diving equipment, an annual pass to the gym, season tickets to a sporting event, a home theater system—these things reflect Orange values.

> "Every man without passions has within him no principle of action, nor motive to act."
>
> — CLAUDE A. HELVETIUS

Provide excitement

If you ever want to conduct an interesting experiment, put a vibrant Orange into a room with a bunch of other colors, stand back, and observe what happens. It's like putting a tablespoon of baking soda into a cup of vinegar—you'll get an immediate reaction which is rather messy and smells funny. Next, put a bunch of Oranges into a room together. Please be sure to take cover, because what you'll see is akin to atoms colliding in a nuclear reaction. You see, Oranges want a bang out of life. So if they're dropped in the middle of Dullsville, they have no choice but to stir things up a bit, creating a crisis here and a quandary there—all in the name of making things a bit more exciting. And when Oranges have other Oranges to feed off of, the excitement level rises exponentially. The whole becomes radically more than the sum of its parts.

Oranges are the sparkling, minty little things that restaurateurs bury in hand-mixed ice cream. They're supposed to go off noticeably. If a true Orange is a heads-down, keep-to-it, hoe-to-the-end-of-the-row worker, then he or she is clearly acting the part. After five o'clock, follow the little red sports car that rolls out of the parking lot and roars down the street, and watch for action to happen. The spouse or organization that knows how to harness them without cramping them will be in for the ride of a lifetime.

> "It is vain to say human beings ought to be satisfied with tranquillity: they must have action; and they will make it if they cannot find it."
>
> — CHARLOTTE BRONTE

Pursue adventure

Ah, to travel around the world, visiting unusual locations and boldly going where no one has gone before. To climb thousands of feet up the side of a sheer mountain cliff without ropes. To float down the Amazon, explore its primordial jungles and its native inhabitants. To hitch a ride on the top of a huge container of highly explosive fuel called the Saturn V rocket and become the first person to step on the moon. These are the adventures that capture the imagination of an Orange.

But adventure isn't just found in exotic locations—it can be found at work or home. Perhaps it's found in rescuing an infant from a burning building, chasing down an escaped convict, imploding old buildings with tons of dynamite, or taking over an existing business and making it profitable. It can also be found in eating an unusual food in a new restaurant, starting a new relationship, buying a new car, exploring a new hobby, even being the first person on the block to see the latest James Bond flick. Oranges find adventure in unusual, unpredictable, unknown, unfamiliar situations, which they try to survive. Of course, the greater the risk, the greater the thrill and the greater the adventure.

> "Adventure is the champagne of life."
>
> — G. K. CHESTERTON

Respect talent

An Orange loves a virtuoso, especially if he or she is the exceptional talent. This likely stems from the Orange penchant for movement. A virtuoso will rise above all others in a group through natural talent even if each practices the activity identically. The virtuoso is the one who, by dint of inner character, masters physicality in a given activity. The exceptional movements, whether in dance, battle, house painting, chicken plucking, joke telling, or playing a saxophone are a form of performance poetry. Nothing is wasted and extra meaning is carried by nuances.

> "If you have a talent, use it in every which way possible. Don't hoard it. Don't dole it out like a miser. Spend it lavishly like a millionaire intent on going broke."
>
> — BRENDAN FRANCIS

Show skill

To perform well and look good doing it. This is the Orange trademark. It's not enough to succeed; to succeed and make it look easy—that's the goal. There are two ways to achieve this level of virtuosity—endless practice, or being blessed with panache. Oranges would rather go for the panache; as a result they soon look like they know what they're doing. With this good presentation comes consumer confidence and soon prosperity. It's usually just one more facet of the Oranges' ability to roll with the punches, and their uncanny ability to land feet first, even when jumping from moving objects.

> "Every success is built on the ability to do better than good enough."
>
> — AUTHOR UNKNOWN

Treasure freedom

"I got no strings on me!" sang Pinocchio, the wooden puppet miraculously transformed into a real boy. Similarly sings the Orange soul. They treasure the ability to live life freely and commitments seem to tie them down. Of course, like everyone else, Oranges have relationships and goals that require some degree of commitment, but the difference is that there are fewer of them and they tend to be more tentative. An Orange with ties that are too numerous or too binding is likely to become restless and may experience an overwhelming urge to run away.

Free-spirited, a will-o'-the-wisp, an Orange is simply not well adapted to physical or emotional confinement. Any attempts to fence in an Orange, with the possible exception of financial bonuses and meaningful rewards, will likely result in the Orange leaving rather than being tamed. True, most successful Oranges have learned that to get by it's usually best to "do what you have to, so you can get what you want." However, this doesn't cancel out the inner call of impulse. Even established Oranges may suddenly hear its whistle, and be led off. One hopes they'll be back by suppertime.

> "Live free or die."
>
> — NEW HAMPSHIRE STATE MOTTO

Trust impulses

The internal clock for Oranges is impulse, flash, and the craving to fulfill the idea of the second. To be impulsive is to be alive. Some Oranges may even feel guilty if they don't have impulses. Everyone occasionally feels the sudden urge to do something, but most people ignore these urges in order to achieve more distant goals. To Oranges, doing this would make them feel bound and confined. A life of action without long-term goals or plans is life at its freest and most intense. "I came. I saw. I conquered ... then they threw me out, but not before they had me sign something about paying restitution for damages."

> "One can never consent to creep when one feels an impulse to soar."
>
> — HELEN KELLER

Want action

The Orange personality style is one of high energy, and therefore Oranges often have a difficult time sitting still. They detest long meetings—even if the subject is important to their personal welfare. They would rather get up and do something than sit down and talk about it. Action is what motivates Oranges—action is an end in itself. Oranges may not object if their acts contribute to the purposes or goals of others, but that's not their motivation for doing them. They act because they have the impulse or the whim. More than the other colors, the Orange has a hunger for action without constraint—exploratory action without rules or practice.

> "Do not be too timid and squeamish about your actions. All life is an experiment. The more experiments you make the better."
>
> — RALPH WALDO EMERSON

Color Reports

As you've read through the preceding descriptions of each temperament, you've probably identified with a few values from each of the four colors. That's perfectly normal. Remember, we are all a blend of the four styles. However, most of us have one color that's stronger than the others—your *primary color*. There aren't many people in the world who are 100 percent one color. In fact, I've only met a handful of people out of thousands who don't have a four-color spectrum at all. I've asked these unique individuals to help create materials for this book, so you can see exactly how a person with a solid color views the world in a variety of situations. Below is what they wrote when they were asked to describe themselves in 250 words or less.

Blue

I truly believe every single person is on this planet for a purpose and that everyone has a unique role to fill. It might be nurturing a child, rescuing someone in distress, easing someone's pain, correcting an injustice, protecting the innocent, or even saving an endangered species. My job is to find a mission—then I can put my heart and soul into accomplishing it.

My searching has made it easy for me to see subtleties and nuances others sometimes miss. As a result, I often communicate on several levels at once, regardless of whether I'm writing, speaking, or listening. I also express my uniqueness through my music, my art, my pet projects, my social causes, even my clothing styles.

Those with whom I connect get a tremendous amount of my time and energy, because I'm always searching for good friendships. I should probably use my head more and my heart less in relationships, but I always see the good in everybody as I try to help them realize their potential. I seek to be as genuine and as honest with them as possible, and that means no airs or false fronts.

Above all, I want everybody to be happy and comfortable with each other. Consequently I'm often a peacemaker or a consensus builder. I'd much rather see people work harmoniously toward a common goal than seek out their own superficial self-interests. What a wonderful world it would be if we all joined hands and worked together!

Gold

I strive to pull my own weight and lend a hand in everything I do. I believe everyone should do the same. Call it service or call it duty, I can be counted on to finish my tasks on time and under budget. In fact, I can't rest comfortably until I fulfill all my responsibilities and do whatever needs to be done.

Things run the way they do for good reasons. I believe that doing away with established systems, procedures, rules, or standards will cause things to fall apart. My motto is "if it ain't broke, don't fix it!" Someone in authority decided that's the way things should be and it's my job to do it, even if I don't agree with it.

I usually have a plan in place before I start a project and try to follow it to the letter. I am careful, cautious, thorough, and accurate in all I do. Structure, order, and discipline aren't strangers in my life. My closets are organized and neat. I arrive at my appointments on time and prepared. I make lists and check off items as I finish them. I figure out what I want in life, set my goals, and take the necessary steps to reach my objectives.

I'm also prudent and want to be prepared for the future. I believe in getting a traditional education, securing a respectable job, saving as much money as possible, taking care of my possessions, and maintaining an adequate supply of food, water, and fuel. It's important to always keep something laid aside for a rainy day because, like it or not, it will rain!

Green

More than anything, I want knowledge—how things work, how to do things, what is going to happen next, how to make it happen, and so on. It has always been this way. From the moment I took apart my alarm clock as a youth or built my own ham radio and stereo set-up, I've craved accumulating information and technical proficiency.

So there are no unpleasant surprises, I do my own fact-finding. I don't inadvertently take in information, think about it, analyze it, and work out a solution only to have an overlooked fact change everything. I suppose this means I appear slow to make decisions, but as I see it, a slow, good decision is always better than a quick, bad decision.

I really enjoy an intriguing discussion, but please don't bore me by stating the obvious or becoming emotional. Spit out your facts, let me verify them, then let's move on. If you ask me a question, give me a chance to think about it for a second and then you're likely to get a concise and accurate answer. If you really want to know the nitty-gritty details, I can give those too.

I am rarely satisfied with the status quo. There is always something else I can learn. If I can read faster or master another language, I can soak up information more quickly. At work, I get carried away when it's interesting, even lose track of time. When I am learning, investigating, inventing, or reasoning, work becomes play.

Orange

I bring excitement, energy, and adventure to most gatherings. I'm kind of a natural performer and have that "star" quality that attracts people. I am often right in the thick of things, since it's extremely hard for me to sit still and watch things happen. I rarely worry about getting hurt or embarrassed. I take risks all the time at work, play, in my relationships—I just don't seem to worry about the consequences. I've had a few really bad scrapes, but my optimism allows me to get through setbacks that might shut down others.

I like using tools that roar, chop, or cause things to tremble, and operating vehicles that speed, climb, or soar. I like doing things that keep me on the go—building, painting, creating, planting, hammering, bull-dozing, climbing, performing, running, wrangling, negotiating, dancing, partying. Even if I don't enjoy a task, I usually turn it into some kind of game so I can have fun doing it. And if I'm having fun, I can just go on and on doing it after everyone else quits and goes home.

I like challenges, contests, and competitions, especially if they require talent, skill, and adrenaline. I stretch the limits and set new records. But if there is anything I truly need, it's freedom to be me—which is being spontaneous, free, alive. I focus on the here and now. I want to experience all that life has to offer, and I do it with gusto.

Poster Power

Below is a sample of some posters created by groups of people who share the same primary color. Notice how strikingly the posters differ. We'll examine these differences further in the next section.

Blue

The Blue poster is "soft," with a greater likelihood of flowers, happy faces, and pictures. It's often written in script or informal print, with most of the words reflecting their relationships.

LOVE SENSITIVITY FAMILY
CHARITY BELONGING
PASSION CARING SERVING
AFFECTION PEOPLE PERCEPTIVE
ROMANCE
INTENSE INFLUENTIAL HELPFUL
PEACE DRAMA NURTURING
HARMONY EMOTION EMPATHIC
LISTENER MUSIC CREATIVITY
RELATIONSHIPS CANDLES HAPPY

Gold

The Gold poster is usually neat, in columns, devoid of mark-outs, with items that are often numbered or bulleted. The list may even be sorted from most important to least important.

✓ Organization	✓ Stability
✓ Security	✓ Discipline
✓ Leadership	✓ Family
✓ Success	✓ Preparedness
✓ Tradition	✓ Planning
✓ Perfection	✓ Consistency
✓ Goal Oriented	✓ Conservative

Green

Green posters look functional and are only as neat as they need to be. There's usually some kind of pattern or system that has been built into the sheet—notice the diamond shape. It often has just a few words, since Greens are normally succinct.

$E=MC^2$ CALM ???
COMPETENCE
CURIOSITY LOGIC
CALCULATIONS LEARNING
SELF-DIRECTION SKEPTICISM
ANALYSIS INGENUITY
INDEPENDENCE
SPACE & TIME
DATA

Orange

More often than not, the Orange poster will be a mass of words, pictures, diagrams, and whatever else the Orange person feels like putting on the sheet. The words reflect their fun-loving nature and are often a tad risqué.

Primary Differences

Now let's take a look at how the personality types differ from each other. The easiest way to begin this analysis is to examine the diagram below.

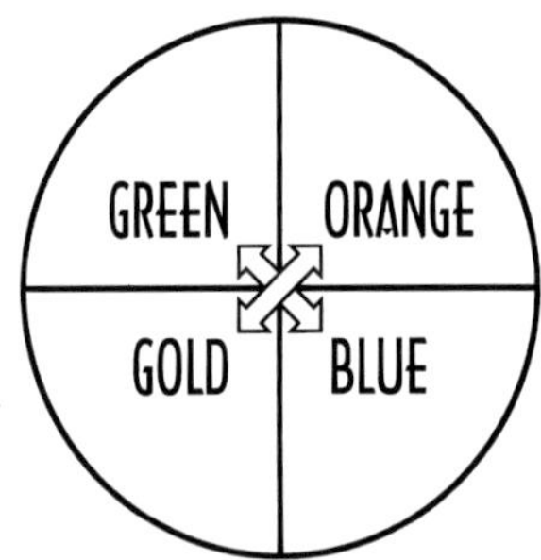

Notice the diagonal opposites. Blue and Green are opposite each other, as are Gold and Orange. This is because in order to make decisions, each color prefers to process and filter information in entirely different ways. To illustrate this opposition, let's start with the Blue and Green pair.

Blues prefer the "feeling" process. Their feelings and emotions affect their decisions. They will often ignore facts in order to accommodate their feelings. On the other hand, Greens prefer the "thinking" process. They evaluate information in a careful, logical, cerebral manner. They will regularly ignore their feelings in favor of the facts. Notice the opposition—the battle between heart and head. But feeling and thinking people are also opposite in other ways as well:

Blue	Green
Subjective	Objective
Personal	Private
Sympathetic	Neutral
Imaginary	Factual
Friendly	Reserved
Emotional	Calm
Tender-hearted	Tough-minded
Intimate	Detached
Humane	Fair
Tactfulness	Truthfulness

Besides the feeling and thinking processes, there are two other ways people prefer to process information. These are called the "judging" and "perceiving" processes. Golds prefer judging and Oranges prefer perceiving.

When given the choice, Golds choose to live in a planned, controlled, and organized manner. As they're faced with a new piece of information, they judge it to see where it fits within their ordered lives. They weigh it against their historical experiences and internal standards. Then they decide what they ought to do with it, and make a plan to do it. Oranges on the other hand, just want to do something with the information. They want to put it to use immediately, in a spontaneous and flexible manner, adapting it to meet the needs of the here and now. They desire to have as many experiences as possible and not miss out on anything life has to offer. Notice how these temperaments are opposite each other in other ways as well:

Gold	Orange
Scheduled	Spontaneous
Definite	Tentative
Formal	Relaxed
Planned	Adaptable
Constrained	Unrestrained
Established	Negotiable
Structured	Impulsive
Serious	Light-hearted
Restricted	Liberated
Resolute	Flexible

The following pages examine in greater detail the nature of these opposites. This will increase your understanding of why tempers sometimes flair between different personalities, and give you greater insight into why people are ostensibly poles apart from each other.

Blues vs. Greens

Sociability

Blues and Greens appear to be opposites in many respects. One key reason for this is that Blues are people-centered, while Greens are idea-centered. This makes Blues appear more sociable than Greens, because sociality is their element. Most Blues are typically outgoing and good-natured. They're comfortable in small group settings, where they can more easily observe what others are feeling and share their own impressions as they work on building new connections. Blues derive strength from others. Being around people charges their batteries. They fully involve themselves in conversations, enthusiastically participating and effectively tuning out the rest of the world.

Greens, on the other hand, tend to be more introverted and often avoid social situations. When they do attend, and can't get away with being a loner, they prefer to hang out on the sidelines with one or two like-minded associates and talk about common interests, issues, or problems. Even then they appear to be somewhat reserved and unapproachable. It isn't that they're unfriendly—it's just that they often get tongue-tied, not knowing the precise thing to say or the most effective way to say it. You see, it takes time to formulate a competent or clever response, and by the time Greens have chewed their mental cud and have thought up something to contribute, the subject has invariably changed. As a result, they often remain silent while more extroverted types carry on the conversation—making the Green appear to be shy, inhibited, or unsociable.

Need for people

As mentioned, Blues are charged-up by people, while people wear Greens down. Blues derive their strength from the presence of others because they're genuinely glad to see them. Visiting with people is an uplifting, inspiring, and enriching activity to a Blue—a fundamental source of positive energy. Greens, however, often prefer to be alone, especially when they're in the middle of a rigorous problem-solving session. Because to give attention, discuss, debate, and offer points of view, Greens must divert their full concentration from the problem at hand. Too much of this type of diversion is extremely frustrating and quickly drains their energy, thwarting their progress. Hence, avoiding or escaping the "madding" crowd is a high priority for many Greens.

Decision-making

Blues make decisions emotionally, by listening to their impressions and heartstrings. No matter what their heads—or their friends and family—say to them, a Blue won't go forward without an internal okay. It's as if an alarm bell rings out when they get too far away from their center. Greens make decisions with their heads. They demand unadulterated logic in their planning. Fuzzy thinking caused by emotionalism may cloud their judgment, and would be insufferable.

Role of emotion

Blues respond to inner calls, and what stronger call can there be than the emotions within one's own heart? Therefore, Blues ride the waves of their emotions, feeling the highs and the lows with equal seriousness, and regard seriously the emotions that drive and influence the actions of others. If a partner is having a bad day, that is enough for a Blue to cancel his or her own plans. Greens, on the other hand, are sometimes oblivious to emotions, both their own and others. They respond to the order in the universe. Just because their own feelings are swelling up inside is no reason to let outward performance suffer. Greens can usually compartmentalize their lives in such a way that their emotions run on a separate track, with the volume turned down. Similarly, if someone in their lives gets overly emotional, a Green is likely to regard it as a momentary aberration. They may refuse to take anything that person says or does seriously until the person gets back in control.

Communication styles

Blues talk about anything and everything. They sometimes seem to listen by speaking. Thinking by hearing requires them to be verbal about everything, and vocalizing their inner depths helps them to understand themselves better. Communicating is also a form of openness that allows others to grow closer to them.

On the other hand, Greens like succinct and relevant conversations. Like the most powerful computers, the Green's thinking time is expensive. It must not be wasted on trivial matters. This compels them to encourage those around them to avoid speaking the obvious. Also Greens judge themselves and others based on what they say. The quality of the information spoken, hence an analysis of the merits of the speaker, can be inferred by listening. Therefore a Green is likely to listen critically to size up other people in conversations, as well as thinking much and saying little on his or her own part.

Sharing and openness

Blues like to talk about their troubles. The challenge of life and its intricacies and mysteries—what a marvelous adventure! How can one fully appreciate the journey and discover life's meaning if one doesn't share it with others? And if friends aren't nearby, perhaps a new one can be found. It might even be easier to talk to a complete stranger than to someone a Blue knows particularly well.

Greens, however, usually prefer to keep problems to themselves. A problem is something in life that a Green hasn't solved. It wouldn't do to have too many of those hanging around, would it? Not knowing the solution might reflect poorly on one's competence, and that would be a hard thing for a Green to abide. Better to go back and think some more, try a few new solutions, maybe read up on it, than to expose one's weakness by talking about it.

Interpersonal warmth

Blues tend to be warm and friendly. The world is filled with more people than you could ever meet, yet that special someone—perhaps a soul mate or a new best friend—may be just around the corner or sitting next to you on the subway. How will you find out without approaching them? And who knows, the poor dear may have some gnawing inner problem. Better to be open and warm to all than to miss the opportunities that come from being yourself.

In contrast, Greens tend to be cool and reserved. Their thoughts are their own. Their ideas are their identity. Carelessly voiced, they could be snapped up by someone and plagiarized. Perhaps worse, they may end up being wasted on someone who cannot appreciate them. Greens will know if you're the right stuff for them by and by. In the interim, they may choose to keep their distance.

Conflict

Blues avoid conflicts and arguments. There are no winners in a fight. Even bullies have tender moments when they need support. If there were more caring, maybe there would be fewer conflicts. After all, how can anyone be angry if they know they're loved? Blues want to provide that unity and accord, and the peace it brings.

Greens, on the other hand, don't view conflict as being all that bad. After all, ideas are like knives with which you cut through the jungle of obscurity, and ideas get sharper as one rubs them against the stone of reason. How better to sharpen one's ideas than discussing or debating them?

Nurturing

Blues get caught up in causes. Ever the comforter, Blues are like emotional medics trailing after the crusaders, binding their wounds, strengthening and cheering them on. Occasionally a Blue will make some daring move out of passion and join the fray directly, even if he or she is poorly equipped or hopelessly outnumbered. It's more important to do something to help the helpless, no matter how futile it may seem, than to do nothing at all.

Not so with Greens, who remain objective and detached to the end. Team spirit and enthusiasm are not big items for Green. They seek the keen edge of strategy as their ally. Jumping to the chants of onlookers may fire up others, but a Green wants to hang back, and see the bigger picture before committing to action.

Clothing styles

Blues shop for style, comfort, and flair. "Clothes make the man," and reveal the inner person. At the same time, it's no good being too formal, to the point of making others uncomfortable. Life is for giving. A secret pocket for a hankie or an emergency cough drop is a nice addition to any clothing item.

Greens, however, waste little energy on style sense. They shop for functionality and efficiency. Mao's pajamas, sailor's dungarees, mechanic's overalls, and nondescript t-shirts and jeans are fairly common choices. Clothing is meant to keep you warm and cover up body parts. Decorations and frills add little value, increase the cost of the garment, and complicate cleaning.

Trend following

Blues, as they strive to be the most attractive they can be, tend to follow fashions and trends. By dressing like the crowd they can be "one with the people." They can show they're "in touch" by wearing the latest trends. However, they also have a strong sense of personalization, and whenever possible, they will accessorize with something that reflects their individuality or connects them to a loved one.

Greens tend to ignore current fashions and trends, often laughing them off as small-minded manipulations designed to sell more clothes. A closet full of whatever served them well in prep school or college will be just fine, thank you. Preferably, the colors should all be interchangeable as well. Whatever authority determines this year's neckties should be wide or skinny, or that skirts should be short or long, gets little attention from Greens.

Reception to instruction

Blues "know how much you care" instinctively. If your heart isn't in tune with them, why should they listen to what you have to say? Blues need to know you're truly looking out for them when you give instructions or try to convince them about something.

Greens, on the other hand "care how much you know," and the attention and heed they provide is proportional to their assessment of your aptitude. Show Greens your expertise, and you will earn their attention.

Golds vs. Oranges

Need for structure

To Gold people, getting things done requires a methodical, well-thought-out approach, so Golds love structure and organization. If the job, and more importantly, the results, can be sized up quickly just by looking (boxes packed, bales shipped), then Golds can quickly reassure themselves and others that work is proceeding forward. In fact, Golds tend to be so organized and regimented that even if the work is going poorly, one might never know it by looking.

Oranges, on the other hand, seek freedom. Doing, not getting done, is top priority for Oranges; hence they may shortcut the busy work—filing, sorting, stacking, putting away, cleaning up—so as to take less time from the movement of doing. This is a good thing in a way. After all, do you really want a firefighter stopping along the way to your flame-filled apartment to fill out paperwork? By instinctively focusing on what's most important, and likely what's the most fun or challenging, Oranges get the impossible bits out of the way before tackling the boring ones.

Consistency

Golds like consistency. They tend to make minor, incremental improvements in whatever they do, so after a while, whatever task they're doing is getting done just about as well as it can be. Any radical changes would require significant alterations in the preparation, clean up, or delivery, thus Golds resist any such tinkering with their well-oiled machinery.

Oranges, on the other hand, enjoy the flexibility that comes with new and unpredictable situations. They love to start with clean pieces of paper and be told what results to shoot for without being told how to go after them. Doing something new is a joy to an Orange, although doing it again enough times to perfect the process is usually boring. In fact, if they become too familiar with the routine, they're likely to spice things up by incorporating mistakes, just for the thrill of overcoming them.

Punctuality

Golds are impressed by punctuality, not only because it shows respect and appreciation for the time of other people, but because it shows that one is in control of his or her life and environment. Controlling and regulating come naturally to Golds, just as family dogs with sheep-tending in their pedigree sometimes "herd up" children and other family animals. Non-compliant sheep earn a bark or growl, and the same sometimes applies to people who aren't where they're supposed to be. Also, minor inconveniences and irregularity can throw off larger schedules.

Oranges, for their part, are less concerned about time and its measurement. What happens, happens, and the spirit of the moment outshines the tyranny of the clock. An Orange means no disrespect by being late. In fact, he or she probably wasn't late, the other people were just early.

Tolerance of risk

Golds, more than most, appreciate sure things. The world is a precarious place in which things often go wrong, and it takes hard work to anticipate and overcome problems. Golds feel better when they know someone has gone before them to organize and check things out, pointing out the pitfalls and hazards.

Oranges, however, don't avoid risk—they seek it out. The daily grind is oh-so-much more exciting if the results are life and death. And if something isn't really life or death, then at least one can drive fast, jog to appointments, or do anything to create a sense of enthusiasm and urgency. Faster, further, louder, all without a safety net—these are tools Oranges use to keep life exciting.

Attention to instruction

Golds can sit and listen. A Gold can visualize processes, so telling a Gold what to do and how to do it is a perfect training situation. They know their productivity will depend on what they hear, so Golds pay attention. When the time comes to act, they act in line with the instructions.

Oranges get bored sitting and listening. Their minds are so full of fire that mere words, whether in lecture or printed in books, rarely overcome the internal roar that is Orange. When it's time to move from learning to doing, Oranges can get lost in the shuffle. Let them watch, however, and better yet, practice, and they will be off and running.

Planning and forethought

Golds like to plan. Nothing makes less sense than spending time doing a job that can't be finished, and even worse is the simple failure to have the needed supplies on hand. Golds hate to stop the works and lose the momentum, so they tend to plan, check, and double check. The science of logistics is their forte.

Oranges will do many things on a whim. When the endless collage of life suddenly presents them with a pattern, they jump right in and seize the opportunity, often moving with cat-like grace into new and uncharted territories. Most of what the Orange pulls off cannot be planned anyway. The opportunities are only visible when one is "in the moment."

Outlook on life

Golds sometimes appear to be gloomy. Enough has gone wrong before to allow Golds to predict with certainty that something will go wrong again, so they tend to be realistic, even pessimistic, about how things will turn out. Yet this attitude seems to spur them on to develop countermeasures. Then, after the unplanned, undiscovered, and undocumented wrinkles work their worst, a Gold will emerge unruffled, because he or she likely has a bit of reserve laid up against just such a thing.

Oranges, by contrast, are normally upbeat optimists. They think, in fact expect, everything to work out. They see in most situations great capability to adapt and make things work, if the people involved are just willing to look at things in new, fresh ways. This is where the Orange's belief in a sunnier tomorrow shines—things can't be all bad, and they will surely become better soon.

Seriousness of purpose

As just mentioned, Golds tend to be more serious-minded as they worry about the worst and spend much of their waking hours fighting and preparing against it. Their core values drive them to serve while others are off relaxing. With the weight of important duties and responsibilities squarely on their shoulders, it's no wonder they often appear somber and solemn.

Oranges tend to be more jovial and lighthearted. They will cope with tomorrow's troubles tomorrow, or maybe even the day after, if there is still a need. In the meantime, there are jokes to share, stories to tell, contests to win, lovers to woo.

Ritual

Golds don't like their routines upset. They arrange their lives like fine watches, with every thing working and staying that way because every part functions as and when it's supposed to. Every item on a Gold's agenda has its designated time, and to divert one's attention to something gone amiss is to risk leaving another thing undone.

Oranges thrive on crises. Reacting to unplanned events, adjusting to sudden, even overwhelming changes, adds zest to their lives. For instance, discovering that the jack is no longer in the auto would be extremely upsetting to Gold. Oranges take it in stride. They deal with what is, not with what should be. "No jack? Got to be something else that we can do. Here's a big rock, here's a big branch lying on the ground. You sit here and try not to fall off and drop the car on me; I'll pull off the tire—Oh shoot! No lug wrench either. Now this gets interesting...." With this troubleshooting philosophy, Oranges often rise to the top in times of tribulation.

The future

Golds think of the future and plan for it. Golds know their own energies may diminish someday, as they've seen happen with so many who have gone before. The only way to avoid being a burden is to lay aside a little against that unfortunate day. Besides, really great accomplishments require the labor of today as well as stored energy from the past. The only way one can access past energy is to store it up when one has the opportunity, usually in the form of food, fuel, or money, such that these things are taken care of when the need arises.

Oranges blossom in the moment. The morrow is a long way off. If there is a resource, it had best be consumed with glee, and sucked of all its hidden worth, so one can maximize one's power in the present. And why not? After all, who knows what tomorrow may bring? The future will take care of itself.

Tradition

With their eyes on the future and a healthy worry for it, anything that reminds Golds there is still time and certainty makes them feel better and less exposed. Accordingly, Golds take joy in traditional things, crowding around themselves family, friends, and totems of status, to remind themselves that many united shoulders can carry almost any weight.

Oranges are quick to abandon traditions so they can explore new horizons. In the new, one must employ every sense. Hence, to live on the cutting edge is to be the most alive. No boring rituals or predictable customs will suffice for the Orange; rather, dashing and bold actions carry the day. In fact, many Oranges may decide not to participate in conventional activities simply because they're traditional—the Orange has already been there and done that.

Formality

Golds have a formal nature. They honor that which has gone before, dignifying the works of their forebears. Demonstrating reverence by a sense of formality has two purposes. First, it lets others demonstrate their allegiance to the same set of ideals. Second, it demonstrates familiarity with the customs and traditions that are held dear.

Oranges live in the present, and tend to let the past take care of itself. Conforming to prescribed behaviors, least of all to formality and ritual, is unnatural to Oranges, who recognize the power of the moment more than the goals of the past. This is why Oranges counter stiff formality with its natural opposite—a casual, relaxed, even colorful nature as compared to the formal, proper, conservative, reserved nature of the Golds.

Secondary Differences

Neighboring differences

Having looked at how the four colors are different in regards to their opposites, now let's examine how they're unlike their neighboring colors. Each color has two neighbors. Blue (Gold and Orange), Gold (Blue and Green), Green (Gold and Orange), and Orange (Blue and Green).

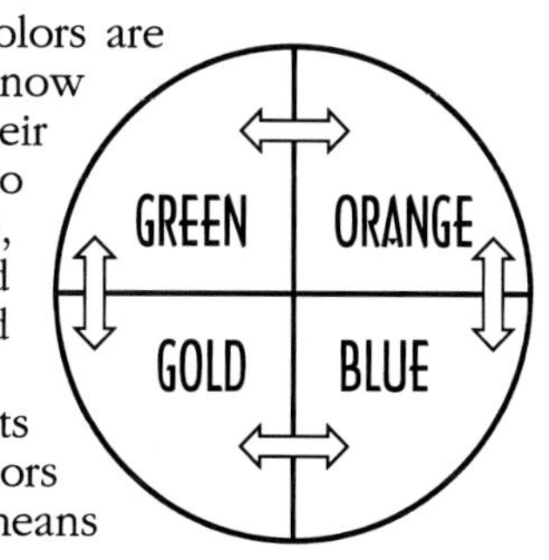

Take a look at the following charts to see some of the ways these neighbors are different from each other. By no means are these lists complete.

Blues	**Golds**
People come first	The organization comes first
Do things with people	Do things for people
Seek uniqueness	Seek conformity
Abandon goals if they feel like it	Are driven to reach goals
Are naturally passive	Are naturally assertive
Serve out of compassion	Serve out of duty
Avoid confrontation	Confront problems head-on
Take the easy road	Take the right road
Unify and cooperate	Divide and conquer
Seek consensus from peers	Seek counsel from authorities
Bend rules to situations	Rarely bend rules
Easily express feelings	Show feelings when appropriate

Golds	**Greens**
Seek to belong	Seek autonomy
Believe in controlling thoughts	Believe in freedom of thought
Can't easily visualize concepts	Visualize concepts
Can't stand disorder	Don't mind disorder
Set and obey rules	Question the need for rules
Establish procedures	Tweak established procedures
Trust authority	Challenge authority
Dislike altering planned course	Make mid-course corrections
Promote completion	Promote evolution
Want conclusions, finality	Want progress, advancement
Are grounded in the present	Dwell in the future
Rigid deadlines and timeframes	Flexible deadlines and timeframes

Greens	**Oranges**
Prefer to be calm, composed	Prefer to be excited, animated
Are cerebral	Are physical
Cultivate their minds	Cultivate their bodies
Take calculated risks	Take perilous risks
Avoid the spotlight	Like the spotlight
Like to sit and ponder	Like to get up and go
Rather learn than do	Rather do than learn
Make few friends	Make many friends
Use their minds to intimidate	User their bodies to intimidate
Say punny things	Say funny things
Prefer to interact with few	Prefer to interact with many
Enjoy being nerdy and enigmatic	Enjoy being hip and charismatic

Oranges	**Blues**
Tend to use people	Tend to be used by people
Like to compete	Like to compromise
Like physical tokens of affection	Like symbolic tokens of affection
Think about the effects on self	Think about the effects on others
Objectify persons	Personalize objects
Rely on their five senses	Rely on their sixth sense
Want to stand out in a group	Want to fit in with the group
Forcefully express emotions	Creatively express emotions
Enjoy pandemonium	Enjoy tranquility
Thrive on conflict	Thrive on harmony
Set trends and fashions	Follow trends and fashions
Desire sizzling passion	Desire tender romance

CHAPTER 2

Motivation: Why People Do the Things They Do

Understanding what drives each personality type is a key that will open many locked doors in your relationships. The valuable information in this chapter will explain what inspires different people and how to use that information to motivate yourself and other people.

Understanding Motives

There was a time when many psychologists avoided discussing motives. Motives were difficult to observe, describe, and predict. There was an awful lot of guesswork involved. Better, some thought, to reach into a textbook full of one-size-fits-all principles than to try and guess exactly why people do the things they do.

Why? What makes it better to ignore the four basic temperaments and use a boilerplate template to read people? What could be more natural than forming an educated guess about which one of four styles someone prefers, and then refining that guess—all the while paying sincere and careful attention to the person you're watching? Behavioral science is wonderful, but sometimes its proponents seem to forget that they're dealing with people, and that in most cases healthy people are more than willing to engage in self-disclosure if the audience is open-minded, empathetic, and genuinely interested.

We can gain a world of information by trying to work out motive. Why is he doing this? What's she trying to get from doing that activity? Answering these questions is far easier once you know, or have formed an initial guess, at a person's primary color.

To illustrate, suppose one of your friends, whom you had once considered to be a genuinely nice guy, suddenly announces he is running for an open city council seat.

Why do people become involved in politics? Blues may do it to champion the underdog and help those who can't help themselves. Golds may do it to show they're responsible citizens, for the chance to set the policies and preserve traditions. Greens may do it to solve problems and make the system more efficient. Oranges may do it for power, notoriety, or just for kicks—to see if they can do it.

So what color is your friend? Does the reason fit? Can this lead you to knowing more about your friend? Will finding this out help your relationship?

Here's another scenario. Your formerly sedentary business partner suddenly aspires to become a Buff Meister—someone who gets in shape in order to begin a reign of intimidation over their flabby coworkers and associates.

Why would people choose to go to a gym and lift weights? Blues might be trying to get the type of body that would make them or their significant others feel better. Golds may be trying to get their money's worth out of a club membership or as part of an established fitness routine. Greens may be trying to master new techniques or test a hypothesis on muscle growth. Oranges could be engrossed in pushing their physical limits or in building an eye-catching body.

Not willy-nilly

Obviously, the first step in understanding motives has to do with identifying someone's temperament. And, unless they've already read this book and are walking around with a t-shirt that says, "It's not easy being Green," you've got to rely on less dependable methods—like guessing.

Fortunately, the purpose of this book is to empower you with the ability to make more accurate guesses. In chapter 1 you learned what each color cherishes most in life—perhaps the most important information to learn about someone else. This chapter will focus on how to motivate each temperament using the things they value. And the rest of this book will build on that foundation and focus on what each color looks like in a variety of real-life settings. After all, the better you understand each temperament, the easier you'll recognize classic characteristics and behaviors, and the more accurate you'll be in guessing someone's spectrum.

I might as well pop your bubble a bit while I have your attention on this matter. You will be wrong now and then. Even after you have the first color nailed down, the rest of the spectrum awaits your discovery. Observing someone's behavior or actions doesn't necessarily reveal a person's personality type, and knowing a personality type doesn't always provide the clues to motivation. After all, most people can learn to do things that we would normally associate with a specific color. Further, every action or activity can be performed for any number of motives. As a result, there will be times when you miss your mark completely.

But that's okay. Even if you have to back up and try again a few times, the result is that you may end up knowing some people better than they know themselves. And you will be giving them a high form of flattery, because most people love to have that kind of attention paid to them.

Motivating by Color

When one is new to motivating by colors, one of the most difficult habits to form—but one of the most rewarding—is to realize that people don't view things the way you do.

Most of us with a strong primary color tend to walk around viewing the world through the perspective of that color. It's as though we had on a pair of eyeglasses fitted with Blue, Gold, Green, or Orange lenses. Everything we see is tinted with that hue. However, after we've worn the spectacles long enough, we don't even realize the tint exists. Not until we take them off do we see things as they really are.

To communicate with people in a meaningful way, particularly if you're trying to provide motivation, you need to thoroughly appreciate their perspective. The easiest way to do that is to put on a pair of their glasses. Only then can we broaden our vision and see things through the eye of the beholder. If we have sensitivity for the other person's point of view, and are able to speak to them in language that's meaningful to them, we go a long way towards increasing our power to enthuse, excite, and motivate—to build fires in others that stay lit.

Motivating secrets

There are a number of strategies proposed by myriad authors about how to get people to do what you want them to do. Most of this advice is good, but nearly all of it's designed for a single-color audience. You now know that the world consists of four colors and some blends, so mono-colored suggestions are not going to be adequate anymore.

The problem with using non-color-appropriate techniques for motivation is that they often just don't work. You end up not only ineffective, but frustrated besides. If you're not careful, anger sets in, and then you have taken a situation that was merely not working and turned it into a sizeable problem. Better to bone up on the motivation techniques that are most likely to fit the bill for each color.

One of the most treasured pieces of advice on human relations is known as *The Golden Rule.* It appears in the teachings of nearly every world religion and philosophy. In the New Testament it's recorded as, "Do unto others as you would have them do unto you." Unfortunately, this is taken wildly out of context too often. It's precisely the reason that each year there are still many women who get chainsaws, fishing poles, and horribly embarrassing nighties for their anniversaries. The advice is perfectly sound in its context, delivered to a people under military occupation from what was then the most powerful nation on the planet. "Do unto others..." was a way of encouraging the early Christians to avoid inciting their occupiers by attempting poorly considered violence, and to mollify their occupiers away from carting off their wives, or killing their children for sport. Today, a more fitting rendition of the passage may be, "Do unto others, by caring enough and knowing enough about them to meet their needs and wants as you would want to have yours met."

The following are a number of practical suggestions for motivating others in ways that make sense to them.

Motivating Blues

Praise their contributions

Blues pride themselves for wanting to make a difference in the world—for going beyond the call of duty to bring a little comfort, a little peace, a little bit of heaven to earth. Acknowledging their contributions is a way of telling them how much you appreciate having them around. If you regularly stop by their desk, office, or assembly line and indicate—in a sincere manner—how much you appreciate them, they'll eat out of your hand. More than the other colors, Blues need reassuring strokes to keep them cheerfully engaged in a good cause.

Acknowledge their significance

A Blue will matter. He or she will be part of your fabric either by direct contribution or by social interaction within your ranks. And they're so loveable that it's hard to set them right without upsetting half of the people in their sphere of influence, which is likely to be bigger than you ever imagined. In fact, if you were aware of all the things that a Blue did or influenced, you would acknowledge their significance constantly. Tell them something like, "You sure made Mary feel better after Bob said what he said," and a Blue is likely to glow for hours.

Support their intuition

A Blue can spot sadness like a narcotics dog can find illicit drugs in a plastic baggy in an envelope in a shopping bag in a suitcase on a moving conveyor belt. Blues can be the distant early warning system for trouble and disaffection in the ranks. Let them know you value their sixth sense. Assure them you respect their need to keep confidences, but assure them it's important that if another employee or teammate is unhappy then you want to address the situation early while it's still a whimper. Empowering Blues to help you in this task makes them feel needed, and that makes a Blue feel good.

Give personal attention

Don't try to give a Blue praise by bulk mail. They give personal attention to people around them constantly, perhaps to a fault. Therefore, when they receive attention, they need it to be genuine, positive, and directed especially to them. Noticing a positive action and praising them for it may be a more powerful corrective than mentioning you noticed a negative. Most of the colors are likely to self-correct if their negative actions threaten a source of positive acknowledgment.

Encourage creativity

When a Blue does something imaginative or inventive, consider it an honor. You have made that person feel comfortable enough to experiment and think outside the box. Many long-lasting improvements are engendered out of such creativity. The tendency to compare every effort to what is required in the manual can create a straitjacket for Blues. If a strategy is not compromising life and safety, let it stand—moreover, encourage it. Blues enjoy contributing to distinctive, one-of-a-kind projects.

Promote social activities

Blues love a multi-faceted relationship, mixing home into the office (cookies, decorations, and pictures) and the office into home (sporting company logos on their cars and putting a company coffee mug on the mantle). Facilitate this merging of identities by sponsoring a company bowling team, fielding or sponsoring a softball team, or adopting a stretch of highway. Around the home, make it a family project to clean the gutters for the widow down the lane, or keep the snow off someone's sidewalk, preferably as anonymous helpers. And by all means, plan barbeques and casual get-togethers. Devoted Blues can be your best ambassadors if you feed them on their many levels.

Recognize their individuality

Give Blues the leeway to express their individuality in meaningful ways. Perhaps it may be allowing them to decorate their workspace, bedroom, or uniform in a distinctive manner. Or let them customize the way they tackle their workload. Or simply recognize them as rare, irreplaceable individuals that make life worth living. Individuality in Blues is a by-product of their quest for knowing self. Displaying that individuality is a public acknowledgement that they're getting somewhere in their pursuit. Thus, to be different is to be. A policy that attempts to smother Blues, especially if it's applied unfairly, is a swat on the nose. You really don't want to injure them. For all their benevolence, Blues can cause a bit of damage if they explode. They have tentacles that extend throughout your organization, and can trigger repercussions for ages. Make peace, or better yet, don't step on them in the first place.

Reward with sincere appreciation

Be utterly sincere. A Blue may easily pick up on insincerity and may end up feeling used, while heart-felt gratitude may cause this same individual to go to amazing lengths to please. If you don't think that a given incident of service and caring is noteworthy enough to single out, then don't try. Find another Blue to deliver flowers for you and offer up your good words.

Motivating Golds

Praise their judgment

As a Gold, the decision to go left or right, hold or sell, spend or save, invest or decline, will be valid only if it works. Golds give few points for process and high value for results. This means they must "win" in order to feel good about themselves. It's a hard burden to carry, and the safest path is to stick to the conservative, tried procedures that have got the family, organization, or company to the point where it is.

Golds can pine for bigger things, newer things, better and more powerful things, as can any other color. But, loyal to the tried and true, they're not as likely to act on these desires as are the more impetuous Blues and Oranges, or those more ready to forgive themselves if things go wrong as long as they followed a logical process, such as Greens.

"Better to be safe than sorry." "If it ain't broke, don't fix it." These phrases comfort Golds in those lonely hours of sticking to their knitting when the sky seems to be the limit. Mention their willingness to keep on the safe path, praise their steadiness, point out how successfully they did nothing and what they have to show for it, and Golds will feel vindicated.

Recognize their dependability

There is an old story about a man who blew the mill whistle at noon, and another man who set the town clock based on the mill whistle. The story goes that both did their jobs diligently for years, and only years later did each finally meet the other. Both were shocked to discover their long interdependence. Interestingly, the story never ends by both parties discovering that the town had ended up out of sync with the rest of the world. The punch line, hidden and understated, is they had depended on each other, and that neither ever let the other down, even though they had not met; that is, their service went unsung. That's quintessential Gold, dependable through and through.

Place them in charge

As the "color most passionate with things turning out okay," Golds have a lot of experience in avoiding problems before they happen. Many Golds hone their social skills to the point where they can quietly manipulate a situation in such a way as to keep it running without embarrassing other individuals who need a hand. Other Golds either don't learn this, or don't seem to care, earning the entire temperament a reputation for "being bossy" and "always stepping on toes." Truth is, almost any Gold with life experience can work through complex logistics as second nature. Remove the social barriers by letting them run things. The Gold will be less frustrated, and the affair will probably come off just fine.

Involve them in planning

If you're uncomfortable placing a Gold in charge of something, say because there's a question of experience or social pressure against it, you can at least involve the Gold in planning. In the first place, it will give the Gold a chance to learn more about the culture of the group. Second, they earn the stature that comes from being on an executive team, even if they're a junior member. And finally, they're amazingly good at it—planning is an instinctive reflex for most Golds.

Give them responsibilities

It seems to be an oxymoron to most of us, but you can effectively motivate Golds by giving them more work to do. Responsibilities are an indicator of earned trust—the kind that can only be achieved by consistent effort over time—which is what Golds pride themselves at doing. So, by giving them an extra clock to wind, an extra fish to feed, an extra committee to sit on, or an extra board to chair, you affirm to the Gold that he or she is worthy of such responsibility. All responsibilities are taken seriously and none will be neglected. The truism, "If you want something done, give it to someone who is busy," was almost certainly written to describe a responsible Gold.

Give consistent feedback

You can actually drive a Gold nuts by giving inconsistent feedback in similar situations. As oriented as they are to learning the ropes, introducing ambiguity in those ropes is just about enough to melt a Gold down. Instead, consider setting up a ritual around giving and receiving feedback. It will become a sanctified hour for the Gold, in which he or she learns the worth of the activities between this review and the previous one. It should not be a haphazard meeting, but one conducted quietly, without interruption (preferably tell a secretary to hold all calls and tell visitors to wait, maybe even doing so within earshot of the Gold). Sit in the same chairs every time, with elements of office décor in the same positions. The Gold will feel special for having received such attention. It need not be a protracted meeting—a concise, to-the-point review will suffice—but the element of ritual brings stability to a striving Gold that can be most reassuring.

Let them organize things

If you're not strongly Gold yourself, you need one in your life to set things up. They can see at a glance what's needed and what's superfluous, and can set in order what you've got and create shopping lists for what you've not, usually before you're through with your morning coffee. What's more, when they're finished, it will be running right, whatever it is. Curiously, the Gold will be happier for this, because whatever was out of kilter was likely an irritant anyway.

Reward with public recognition

The reward for all these good efforts—and strong Golds usually produce first-rate efforts—is smooth-running, well-oiled machinery. A Gold is uniquely incapable of asking for acknowledgement for such efforts. A pat on the back in the hallway may be enough for say, a Blue, who values the relationship with you, but Golds require public acknowledgement that they have arrived at a certain level of distinction due to their performance.

Motivating Greens

Praise their insight

Greens often feel as if they're the lamp on the front of a powerful locomotive. Others, Golds mainly, keep the train running smoothly up hill and down and blow the big horn; but as far as seeing what's around the next bend, that's Green's talent. The hard thing about predicting the future is that it requires one to create and follow multiple scenarios and update each when new information rolls in. When the time comes to report, most leaders want only one's best guess of what's going to happen. All the real work—the reasoning, the analysis—gets left on the cutting room floor. All that remains is an educated guess as to what comes next, and the penalty for getting it wrong is that everybody laughs at you.

Greens need their shoulders rubbed just like everybody else. For the most part, they take their responsibilities seriously. Look over a Green's office, notes, files, piles, and whiteboard, and comment about how much effort it takes to keep track of so much data. Also, marvel a little about their ability to distinguish what is trivial from what is critical. Likely, you'll soon see red cheeks on your Greens, and an admission that they just do what they do and the answers present themselves. "Anybody could do it," they'll say. Truth is, working with data so much that it speaks to you is a special trait indeed. It's a big part of being Green.

Recognize their expertise

A Green gathers his or her skills at considerable expense. They often appear pale because they're so busy working and training that they don't get to see the sun. When they can finally bring those skills to bear, it's a moment of great vindication, a time for them to tell themselves it was all worth it. Recognize the Green's efforts to master a discipline, and you've validated a most highly prized value.

Involve them in decisions

It's amazing to Greens and also to many bystanders that so few teams involve their Greens in major decisions. True, most enterprises must operate at faster than Green time. There aren't enough hours to analyze all that a Green would analyze. But remember, the question is not always to determine the one right course. There is plenty of value in avoiding the wrong course. Even though it may take Greens a while to pick the right route out of infinite options, they can be extremely fast at detecting options that look better at first glance than they will end up being. Involving your Greens from the beginning is much better than inviting them to help you pick up the pieces after it all goes astray.

Explain the overall picture

Greens move from whole to part. The big picture is important to them if they're to appreciate the value of their particular task. "Wherever thou art, act well thy part" is a test of faith for Greens. They want to know where they are, where you are, what the goal is, and the lay of the land in between.

Support their ideas in public

"Jones here says we need to move ahead in the bio-tech sector because our new process technology will dramatically cut costs and we want to be in prime position when the time comes. Jones also assures me that if bio-tech doesn't swing our way, we'll still be able to capitalize on our developments in the oyster oil sector. I'm glad to have a fine young engineer such as Jones on board. Does anybody else think so too?" (Cheers from the crowd.) Jones is having a very pleasant daydream. It need not be just a dream, however. When you hired Jones, you got a brain for free. Let Greens contribute from their strengths, and they will shine.

Encourage new ideas

Doing things the same old way, from cooking to lovemaking, is anathema to Greens. There is room for constant variety in all activities. Who knows? Some new approach or principle may present itself if one but takes the initiative to try things a different way. Give the Green the opportunity to think outside of the box, or better yet, design a new one with seven sides.

Appreciate their uniqueness

When a Green enters the planet, the night sky gets a little darker. Not really, but it might seem that way to a Green. Greens feel most of the time as if they have an open viewport, a window on the world that allows them to see cause and effect, absorb lots of information, pick up technical topics quickly, and tell truth from error. When the world behaves illogically, it can feel like washing one's hands in a bucket of broken glass. Greens need a surprising amount of reassurance from non-Greens that their unique skills are appreciated and admired. Tell them you noticed how quickly they picked up on the inconsistencies in the new nuclear proposal. Let them know that it might have taken months before the administrators noticed the problems the Green noticed in the picker/stacker system. Appreciate them for what they can visualize in their mind's eye.

Reward with independence

Having either been blessed or cursed with the ability to see certain things quickly, Greens tend to exhibit a smidgen of impatience with persons of lesser aptitude. Instead of penalizing and stultifying (a cool Green word) a Green by asking him or her to sit quietly while the rest of the group completes its work, send the Green on a mission elsewhere. In school, for instance, nothing will keep them as current in their studies as sending them to the library to do independent research during class time. Independence, or being excused from rituals, will form a high incentive to the Green.

Motivating Oranges

Praise their achievements

Oranges aspire towards virtuosity, which can be defined as doing the extraordinary while making it look easy. Unfortunately, to get continuing value from their exploits, they must either repeat them or recount them. Repeating the deed is likely to be difficult, as many of the tight spots in which Orange shines occur as a result of exceptional, often dangerous circumstances. Telling their own tales is full of pitfalls, since there's an overwhelming temptation to embellish the facts a trifle, turning true-life events into fanciful fiction. A great compromise is for you to set them up—"Oh, Darrell, tell them about the time that you...." You can create some of Oranges' finest hours by re-heating and serving some of their finest moments.

Recognize their performance

Oranges, from the moment they start to walk, are off and running. Many of their accomplishments are noteworthy, and a lot are notorious. Giving them praise when they do something positive may guide them towards contributing more in ways that benefit your organization, or at least don't involve a jury of their peers.

Offer tangible rewards

While Oranges appreciate their names on plaques or on trophies in a case, approbation within the group is not their strongest motivation. Oranges are stars, not necessarily team players, so rewarding them by saying you love them for their contribution is not as big of a hit as telling them their performance is out of sight and over the top.

But there is a further caveat. Oranges are quick to figure out that the name on the plaque is an honor only if they're not on the outs with the people who put the plaque there. With free-spirited Oranges, that's never a guarantee. Therefore, a more tangible reward, like an envelope with cash in it or gift certificates—these make honorable mentions much more honorable from the Orange point-of-view.

Focus on finished products

You will notice that some colors are better at following through with obligations than others. Greens are notorious for starting balls rolling by designing the plan, but then leaving others to execute it. Oranges too are notorious for beginning brilliantly and then quitting abruptly. Oranges can abandon projects for a variety of reasons. One thing that can keep Oranges from showing up is if the project becomes horribly mired, making it difficult to maintain their virtuoso image. Interestingly, a Gold may be called in to pick up the pieces and start it over, but a true masterstroke would be to call in another Orange to clean things up. Oranges are natural troubleshooters. This requires that your praise and reward structure focuses on jobs that are finished. Although you will still have to applaud the bold strokes you see, you can make sure the Orange knows that to the victor go the spoils, but the job isn't over until the paperwork is done.

Appreciate their skill

Be in awe of Oranges. Act a little bit reverent, as if they're some special creatures masquerading as normal humans. Laud their ability to jump high, talk fast, remember 10,000 jokes, and know the way to every Denny's in sixteen states. In so doing you're making tacit note of their accomplishments, as well as acknowledging their skills.

Give opportunities to perform

If they shine, let them glow. That's a sure way to win the heart and motivation of an Orange. "C'mon Nick, show us the zipper trick; do it again, like you used to." Giving Oranges the stage and top billing makes them feel great, and makes you look magnanimous.

Give immediate feedback

Who knows how many Oranges have been de-motivated by having to wait nine weeks before the accounting/management machine acknowledges outstanding performance. Even if your bean pushers can't grind out a check for a performance bonus faster than a glacier races, even if you can't push through a promotion or a raise or a medal faster than rust, at least print up some kind of certificate and rattle it around the organization. "Watch me! Watch me!" is the gifted Orange's call for attention. Scratch that itch to harness that force.

Reward with physical freedom

When an Orange starts to show signs of boredom, it's time to send him or her away on a trip. Far away. As mentioned, Oranges will introduce entropy into a system just to make it more interesting. You need to keep these organizational pyromaniacs away from the dry sticks and out of harm's way. Fortunately, your Orange will probably have some good results stored up, which you can reward with two weeks in Fiji, immediate departure. When he or she returns with a tan and some scars from reef diving and eel bites, you can relax, grateful for what you've been spared. If a trip is not in the works, then you can always do the next best thing. Give the Orange a company car, and a week off. Monitor the results and turn a blind eye to the means. You probably don't want to know anyway.

Selling Styles

During the course of teaching temperament theory to groups of people, one of the first things they want to know is how to apply this information to specific, real-world problems. Therefore the rest of this chapter will move away from general purpose motivational strategies and focus on how to solve a problem that all of us occasionally experience: how to get someone to buy from you.

At some time or another, all of us put on the hat of a salesperson. Regardless of whether you're trying to sell someone on an idea, a product, or even yourself, the persuasion process is normally the same. You first have to gain the person's attention, build a relationship of trust, deliver the required information in a palatable, attractive manner, then finally make a compelling invitation that closes the sale. Every step in that process can be enhanced with an understanding of personality styles. In fact, if you don't take temperament into consideration your chances of success are diminished dramatically.

Any individual can do well in the art of persuasion if they have the desire and skills to succeed. No particular color has a corner on the seller's market. However, it's beneficial to realize that different personalities are naturally endowed with a set of strengths and preferences that colors their approach to life, including their approach to sales. For example, if Shelly, a Green seashore-based seashell seller only sells seashells on the seashore the way she seeks to sell, in Shelly's selling style, she is simply succeeding with shoppers that share similar Shellyish stances—her Green buyers. This completely ignores the Gold and Orange buyers and possibly offends the Blues. Therefore the key to sales success is to recognize and capitalize on your strengths, then adopt the characteristics of other personality types to meet the demand of a particular sales situation.

Blue salespeople

One of the greatest strengths of Blue salespeople is the ability to project an aura of genuine concern for their customers. Perhaps it comes from their contagious cheery dispositions, their peaceful countenances, or their willingness to chitchat. Whatever it is, they have the talent to build relationships of trust faster than any other color. Their demeanor shouts, "You can trust me. I'll personally look out for your interests." Thus, they sell themselves first.

When getting to know a customer, Blues prefer to move quickly past the formal introduction stage and adopt a more casual posture. They call people by their first names, and, if possible, a nickname. Their hearts might even skip a beat when a customer says, "You can call me Robert, but my friends call me Bob." Here's an open invitation to start a new friendship, and what could be better than that, both personally and professionally?

Blues are ideally suited for selling situations where they need to preserve a long-term relationship with a customer. This is something they can do in their sleep, and no one can match their ability to build and maintain these associations. Because they categorically believe, "the customer is always right," Blues strive constantly to be in touch with the desires and needs of their customers. They're empathic listeners who hang on every word and pick up every nuance. They'll go to great lengths to get inside someone's heart and head to discover their feelings and perspectives. Often, Blues will know the names, ages, and interests of the customer's family and keep track of birthdays and anniversaries, make well-wishing phone calls, or send out cards and simple gifts.

Since Blues are naturally friendly and agreeable, it's hard for customers to turn them down. On the other hand, Blue salespeople also have a hard time turning down an offer or counteroffer, especially if it comes from a despondent customer. In some cases, charitable Blues have paid for an item out of their own pockets and given it away to a particularly needy customer. In a like manner, many Blue salespeople have a tough time pressuring a customer into a decision, especially if the customer seems concerned or confused. This can lead Blues to premature negotiation or deal sweetening. Badgering an obviously anxious client is a painful experience for most Blues, who would rather crawl under a rock and die mercifully. Over time, the salesperson may learn how to deal with this situation, but until that happens, it's probably better if the negotiation or "hard close" duties be delegated to a non-Blue teammate so the Blue can focus on what he or she does best.

One might think that Blues become salespeople to make money. But that isn't their central objective at all. They're in sales to help people. If occasionally they sell something that makes life better for someone, then hooray, they've earned a few coins. But if what they're selling might make someone's life worse—such as driving a person nearer to bankruptcy for an extravagant item—well then, they're now facing a huge dilemma. Do they encourage someone to do something that might have negative ramifications, or do they just turn away from their hearts and think about their own pocketbooks? Nine times out of ten, the customer-centric Blue will sacrifice the sales commission. For example, after running a credit check and discovering that a customer has already maxed out a few credit cards, a Blue might say, "Yes, the Acme 4000 is wonderful machine. But to be honest with you, our profit margin is extremely high on this model. You can get the exact same features for far less money with last year's version, the Acme 3000." In some situations, much to the chagrin of their supervisors, Blues have volunteered quietly that the same item can be found for less money at a competitor's store.

Blue Salespeople

Are customer-oriented
Sell themselves first
Are helpful, nurturing consultants
Listen carefully and show empathy
Take the sale personally
Are concerned with relationships
Pay close attention to the customer
Aren't pushy or offensive

Gold salespeople

Meeting the goals of the company is an extremely high priority for Golds. If a supervisor asks every salesperson to commit to selling twenty units by Friday, they'll do it, even if it requires an additional investment of time. While other colors might grumble loudly, Golds fully realize that the company can't move forward unless everyone shoulders individual responsibilities and fulfils specific quotas. Golds reason that if the company goes down in flames, so do their careers.

It's not surprising then, that Golds sell their company first. They judge that once people develop confidence in it, they'll keep on buying its products and services, regardless of what's being sold or who's doing the selling. For example, they'll say things like, "We're IBM. We've been making reliable products for more than a century. We're one of the most stable companies on the planet. You can depend on us, just like your predecessors did."

Golds are serious about sales. It's a business that requires planning and preparation, as well as discipline and diligence. Consequently, they prefer settings where they can control as much of the sales process as possible. That way, they can plan their work and work their plan. They would rather set appointments than deal with sporadic walk-ins. They prefer to deliver a formal sales presentation instead of a constantly changing, shoot-from-the-hip sales pitch. When possible, they'd prefer to make the presentation in their own facility, where they can control the environment, where they're free from interruption, and where they have essential resources on hand.

After touting the benefits of their company, the focused Gold will launch into a well-developed and organized sales presentation. Information is presented in an orderly, commonsense manner. If appropriate, they'll whip out a few professional-looking brochures, charts, or graphics to illustrate their information. Or perhaps they'll use a computerized presentation to systematically draw attention to specific points. It's obvious to observers that the Gold has rehearsed and refined this presentation to make it so polished and classy. Most people walk away from a Gold presentation appropriately impressed, ready to sign on the dotted line.

Sometimes the Gold can become so focused on delivering the message that he or she turns this asset into a liability. After Golds get on a track, it's hard to throw them off, even if there's a dismayed person standing on the track in front of them waving his arms wildly, trying not to get crushed. Consequently, Golds also need to remember to focus on the audience, making unplanned course corrections if warranted.

Gold salespeople have a wonderful ability to bring things to closure—to get the contract signed and the deal put to bed. However, this can also mutate into a liability, especially when the prospective customer doesn't do what's expected or can't make a decision. Some Golds, too eager to close the sale, adopt an attitude of "It's my way or the highway." They become impatient, pushy, or argumentative, effectively alienating their audience.

More than any other color, Golds are goal-oriented and need to see a series of well-defined steps that will take them to the objective. When they have a clear path to follow, they'll stick to it with every ounce of strength they possess. They'll monitor their own progress, dotting every I and crossing every T. Of course, they like to receive recognition for the fine work they do, so an occasional pat on the back, award, or advancement is a good incentive to help them stay on course.

Gold Salespeople

Are company-oriented
Sell the company first
Are well-prepared and organized
Are professional and focused
Pride themselves on punctuality
Are detailed and exact
Demonstrate dependability
Are reliable

Green salespeople

Greens have a difficult time selling something they don't completely understand. Naturally inquisitive and skeptical, they'll take an idea or product and dissect it, examine it from every angle, and try to find its weaknesses. In the end, if they don't find any fatal flaws, they'll wholeheartedly endorse it to others. Moreover, this independent investigation has made them self-taught experts, who are now capable of constructing some mighty persuasive arguments for buying the item. As salespeople, this in-depth knowledge of the product line is perhaps their best asset.

In a perfect world, Green sellers wouldn't have to do any selling—at least not in the traditional sense of sweet-talking or pressuring people to buy something. They'd rather position themselves at the far side of the room in the information booth where prospective buyers could flock for answers, much like the ancient Greeks approached the Temple of Apollo. And like the Oracle of Delphi, the Green expert would adroitly answer just about any product-oriented question. Of course, this isn't a perfect world, so Greens reluctantly meander through the room, striking up token conversations, hoping that people have problems for them to solve. Their employers hope they won't appear arrogant or so preoccupied with their thoughts that they push away customers.

When asked, they'll tout the item's inherent qualities and its superiority to the competition. They'll explain how many years it took experts to design it, and how many meticulous steps it took to manufacture it. They'll refer to the reviews and recommendations that were listed in the trade journals. They'll say that if you take a long, objective look at it, you'll decide, as they have, that this is the finest model available. It may not be as big, inexpensive, or attractive as others, but it's the better choice by far.

Greens prefer selling solutions to problems, or selling things that are new and innovative, which is why you'll find so many in the technology sector. Demonstrating the strengths of a high-tech gizmo is actually a veiled opportunity to play with it, discovering all those intriguing intricacies and details. Undoubtedly, as soon as they master the device, a new and improved model comes out, demanding new research and investigation. In fact, some Greens enter the sales arena just for the chance to play with the latest and greatest innovations; selling is viewed as a necessary evil—a way to placate the boss.

If their brains become disengaged for long periods of time they start to get restless, which is why repetitive activities, such as door-to-door sales, don't hold Greens' interest for long. There are only so many door approaches to concoct. They'd much prefer to tackle a sales job that is intellectually challenging and requires constant improvement or analysis.

Green Salespeople

Are product-oriented
Sell solutions to problems
Sell the product first
Are knowledgeable and competent
Like new and innovative products
Are good with technical details
Talk about ideas and possibilities
Are logical and practical

Orange salespeople

Because of their natural wheeling, dealing dispositions, Oranges make sensational salespeople. In fact, if you ask the parents of an Orange, they'll likely say their child has always been a huckster at heart. From their earliest years, Oranges seem to master the art of manipulating people to do what they want done. On more than one occasion they have talked their way out of a punishment into a bowl of ice cream topped with hot fudge, whipped cream, and a cherry. Like Tom Sawyer, they have an uncanny ability to entice people into doing something normally undesirable, like trading prized possessions for the opportunity to whitewash thirty yards of a nine-foot high fence.

Oranges are keenly aware of the bottom line—if they can't see how a sales activity will stimulate their bank accounts, they'll resist doing it. Given the choice between receiving a modest but reliable salary and a generous sales commission, they'll choose both. And if their negotiation skills are as good as they say, they'll probably get both. The bigger the payoff, the greater their involvement—which is why they're highly motivated by sales contests that feature huge prizes or bonuses for being on top.

Playful Orange salespeople don't sit around waiting for sales opportunities. Whenever possible, they'll take the sales job out of the office and gravitate towards places that are filled with activity. Restaurants, taverns, malls, golf courses, amusement parks, casinos, hotel lobbies, rock concerts, carnivals, backyard pools, conventions, ball parks, fashion shows, demolition derbies, nude beaches—these are prime places to meet and influence people.

Orange sellers really know how to pour on the charm. They have a way of making the customer feel like the most important person in the world. This flattering attention definitely gives the Orange the upper hand and sets the mood for the forthcoming interchange. Smoothly, deftly, they'll try to keep the customer engaged in conversation. They'll start off with, "So what can I do for you?" They'll listen for a second to get a feel for the direction they should go, then launch off towards a particular product. They'll immediately demonstrate or tout its more exciting features and benefits, trying to get the customer to experience or test-drive the product as much as possible. If the customer has questions, they'll immediately toss out credible answers, even if they aren't entirely accurate. They don't improvise or embellish the truth maliciously; they're just trying to keep the momentum going. If the customer doesn't seem overly thrilled, they'll bring up options and alternatives, opening up new avenues as necessary. Perhaps they might be too adaptable, providing so many options that it just confuses the buyer. Some extroverted Oranges tend to talk too much, too fast, or too loudly for their more introverted cousins.

When Oranges are placed in situations where they have a sales manager who likes to set up hoops to jump through, you can predict that they'll rebel a bit more than other colors. Filling out paperwork, building contact profiles, maintaining logs, writing sales reports, setting weekly goals, entering information into a database—all of these are angst-inflicting duties.

Orange Salespeople

Are action-oriented
Sell the immediate benefits first
Are good at improvising
Are flexible and fast-paced
Are smooth and persuasive
Enjoy the thrill and challenge of the sale
Make an impact on their customers
Are enthusiastic, energetic, and playful

Buying Styles

While I'm writing about the selling process, I might as well throw in a few pages to describe the way each temperament prefers to buy. Like most everything else in life, an individual's buying style is determined largely by his or her personality style. Different personality styles are motivated to buy for different reasons. They expect different things from salespeople. Consequently, when deciding how to make your sales pitch, you should consider the preferences of the buyer.

If you don't know someone's personality style, make sure your sales pitch includes something for every color. Phrase it in such a way as to touch the heart of every Blue, inspire confidence in the Golds, challenge the Greens, and excite the Oranges. Watch to see which approach draws the greatest response, then shift the balance of your presentation to reflect that color.

Blue buyers

Blues are inclusionary people who, as expected, have a broad open-door policy. Whether at home or at work, if you have something to say, count on Blues to let you inside and take the time to listen to your pitch. They'll even appear to be good-natured, even if they'd rather have their eyes poked out with a rusty spike than continue listening to you. Throughout the history of humanity there has never been a well-adjusted Blue who slammed the door on an irritating door-to-door salesperson or cut short the oft-repeated spiel of an annoying telemarketer. Under no circumstances would they contemplate being this impolite, hoping in their heart of hearts that the poor salesperson is merely trying to earn enough money to buy his disabled child a set of leg braces and abhors acting annoying anyway. So rather than being filled with wrath, the Blue is filled with compassion and acceptance.

Don't confuse this openness with naiveté. Most Blues readily recognize when they're being hustled by a slick snake-like solicitor. Their sixth sense generates alarm bells that ring out whenever it perceives the slightest scent of phoniness and deceit. While they'll still take the time to politely listen to the opening portion of your pitch, they've already intellectually dismissed the message and its messenger and are simply being tolerant. As soon as it's appropriate, they'll tender an excuse, escort you to the door, and return to the task they were engaged in before being interrupted.

But, if they perceive you to be agreeable, honest, and sincere, you're one step closer to winning over a new customer, for Blues are reluctant to turn a pleasant straight-shooter away. It's not the pitch that makes the difference, but the personal warmth and authenticity of the hawker. In fact, if they're wary of you, Blues won't even dream about buying your wares.

Presuming you've passed the initial good-character litmus test, now's the time to get familiar with your customer. Most Blues enjoy talking about their relationships, so spend a brief moment or two chatting about their family, friends, or mutual acquaintances. They also like talking about their surroundings, especially if they've made contributions to them, so notice and mention the décor, the landscaping, the handmade crafts. Mention how you feel comfortable in the room; how it's filled to the rafters with good vibes. Of course, this patter mustn't be forced or insincere in the least, but natural and heartfelt.

As you communicate, make comfortable eye-to-eye contact and smile pleasantly. Assume an amiable listening position by standing or sitting near the customer, preferably side-by-side. You can also lean up against the wall or doorframe to put your listener at ease. You don't want to directly face the customer, which may be perceived as aggressive, or cross your hands, arms, or legs, which, according to body language experts, implies you're erecting a barrier or exhibiting a close-minded attitude. Blues like this cozy, warm exchange with an attentive listener. Don't launch immediately into your pitch unless you perceive they're growing weary of the laid-back repartee. Keep in mind that at this point, the primary objective is to establish a relationship filled with trust, respect, understanding, and thoughtfulness.

When it's finally time to make your pitch, Blue buyers like to know how the product or service is going to benefit, in momentous ways, their lifestyle and interactions. They care little about statistics, warranties, and technical specifications, so don't dwell on those. Focus instead on how it makes life better, easier, or more comfortable. A phrase such as, "You truly deserve this..." validates their unspoken feelings and soothes their consciences. Explain how it will make them or their loved ones happier, less stressed-out, and more contented. Tug on their heartstrings, for that is their most influential decision-making organ. If it feels good emotionally, they'll probably swallow your arguments. While not quite as impulsive as their Orange cousins, Blues are still prone to act on their impressions, and act sooner than later.

Because of their willingness to listen, you need to make a soft close early on to assess their commitment level, else you might end up having spent 45 minutes merely making a new friend. "You've seen our TV commercials, haven't you? You know about our reputation for killing bugs. You'd want your garage treated, right?" After you've asked a question, don't forget to stop, look 'em straight in the eyes, and wait for an answer. You need the feedback to gauge their degree of buy-in.

If Blues don't feel quite right with making a decision on the spot, don't try to force it. They have an aversion to aggressive situations, probably since they know they tend to cave under pressure rather than becoming combative. If you succumb to the temptation to use that weak spot against them, you'll instantly quash the sale at hand and burn the bridge to future sales. You don't want to get on their bad side, because most Blues have a special place in their long-term memories for malevolent users and abusers. It's best to pull back and try to resolve their concerns in a friendly way. They'll eventually make a decision when they feel the time is right.

Blue Buyers

Have an open-door policy
Are reluctant to turn someone down
Talk about relationships and people
Prefer cozy, warm communication
Don't like to be pressured
Make decisions with their hearts
Easily detect insincerity
Enjoy personalized attention

Gold buyers

Gold buyers are bound and determined to be in control of the entire sales process. Like most activities in their life, they prefer it to happen on their own terms and within their own timeframes. When an unsolicited salesperson approaches, a Gold will dismiss the misguided individual promptly, but politely. In fact, Golds meet most intrusions into their schedules with palpable disdain. While most people who can't say, "No," often put "No Soliciting" signs on their front gates to warn off door-to-door salespeople and other interlopers, the Gold does it as a matter of policy. It's best to adhere to such counsel, unless you're looking for a little reproach to add zing to your day.

Another reason Golds dislike unsolicited sales opportunities is because purchase decisions shouldn't be made arbitrarily. Money is a precious resource and must be conserved carefully and used wisely. Both big- and small-ticket items are usually budgeted for in advance, and only after they have been scrutinized and deemed necessary. Any impulse purchase must be avoided because it has long-term ramifications for their carefully planned budgets. To do otherwise is the mark of fiscal frivolity and flies in the face of their fundamental philosophies.

Knowing that an unasked-for product purveyor is simply wasting his or her time with a Gold, let's now assume the Gold is ready to participate in the sales cycle. He or she is willing to consider a purchase and has summoned a salesperson. What do Gold buyers seek?

Golds expect professionalism, punctuality, and precision. They want to know they're dealing with a businesslike salesperson who won't waste their time by being late or long-winded. The presentation should be well-conceived, well-rehearsed, and well-delivered. The presenter should be well-groomed, well-organized, and well-behaved. In short, the presenter should look and sound and act like a responsible Gold, even if he or she is a luminous Orange.

Preferably, you will use a professional-looking presentation binder or computer slideshow to step through your sales pitch. This should include your company name, logo, license, patents, goals, statistics, and guarantees—all interlaced with full-color photos. If the materials are in a binder, make sure they're laminated—this is evidence of permanence. If the customer wants a handout that summarizes the salient points in order to avoid unnecessary note taking, don't distribute it at the outset unless you want to give the customer an excuse to cut the meeting short. Bring out the handouts at the end, and leave them with the person so he or she can later peruse the important tangential facts, procedures, and policies. During the presentation, give the customer plenty of credible incentives for making the purchase. Along with the advantages, you should disclose and discuss the disadvantages. Honestly explaining that, "We're not a miracle service, you know," will make potential buyers trust you more. In fact, it's best to lay all your cards out on the table—Golds hate guessing games and surprises, especially when it affects the pocketbook. Be as forthcoming and truthful as possible; this will only increase your trustworthiness—a solid Gold characteristic.

Assume Golds have already thought about making a purchase. Say something like, "I'm sure you and your spouse have talked about getting this service." A Gold will probably readily nod his or her head in agreement; otherwise, it indicates inadequate planning.

If a Gold is nearing a commitment, but isn't quite there yet, you can always make an appeal to his or her values. What do Golds value? For starters, how about protection, security, and dependability? Play up to those values and incorporate them into your dialogue. "So, you want to keep your family safe while you're on a business trip, don't you? It would be awful if something happened while you were away. What if the power went out and a street gang started looting the neighborhood? Well, the

Snoozing Guard 2000 Home Security System is just what you need. For pennies a day, we'll monitor your house 24/7. No one will get in or out without our knowledge. In fact, we can have an elite squad of military-trained commandos at your home in less than five minutes, in case deadly force is needed. We guarantee it." Furthermore, don't forget to sell the stability and reliability of your company with phrases such as, "We've been serving homes like yours for more than seventy-five years! We've never had a complaint filed against us at the Better Business Bureau."

The presentation should be short and sweet, with plenty of time reserved to resolve concerns. If Golds want the meeting to run overtime, let them make that determination. By keeping focused on the bottom line and steering away from hype, you're more likely to gain their respect—and their business.

Gold Buyers

Don't like their time wasted
Don't like surprises or games
Need a reason for buying
Are motivated by duty and guilt
Like responsible, trustworthy people
Want to know the pros and cons
Focus on the bottom line
Expect polite, well-planned presentations

Green buyers

Most Greens are rather disenchanted with the whole buying and selling process. They view it as an outdated and inefficient way to acquire merchandise. Imagine having to spend time and fuel to travel to a distant location where items are displayed and warehoused, then having to hunt for the exact item you want while fending off annoying salespeople, followed by standing in a long line with other aggravated shoppers while a cashier leisurely scans in barcodes, takes your money, and makes change. Worse yet, there are some goods and services that can only be purchased after long periods of dialogue with a sales rep whose sole purpose is to convince you to purchase something you didn't know you wanted. It's such a waste of limited resources—resources that could be spent in more worthwhile endeavors.

If Greens could design an ideal system, they'd probably devise a way they could sit at home in a comfortable chair, look at a full-color picture of a product, press a button to find out as much information about it as they wanted, press another button to find the lowest price on the planet, and finally press another button to purchase it. The next morning, the product would be sitting in a box on their front porch. If only such a system existed! What a perfect world it would be! Perhaps the Internet comes close, but those days of waiting for the purchase to arrive could be shortened (and not by the current additional shipping cost).

So as long as Greens are placed in the position of having to purchase things at a store or through a salesperson, they will continue to be dismayed and a bit irritated at the whole procedure. Thus, when approached by a peppy sales staffer, they'll probably respond with a scowl and a mumbled reply. It's best to leave these Greens alone. If they need help or advice, they'll seek it out. Otherwise, they don't want anyone to impede their investigation. Of course, this doesn't describe all Greens. A few truly enjoy shopping and interacting with salespeople. But these individuals are mutants.

Greens approach shopping much like they solve a whodunit mystery. They determine what went wrong, identify the suspects, examine alibis and motives, and through the process of elimination end up with the guilty perpetrator. In this case, let's suppose a 36-year-old Green bachelor's dishwasher stopped working and he needs to find a replacement quickly since he's now out of clean dishes. So he's off to the department store to find a replacement model. If he weren't so hungry and had more time, he'd first rifle through a stack of *Consumer Reports* and review the favored makes and models, or he'd boot up his computer and surf the Internet to dig up and compare manufacturer specs. But since he's in a hurry, he's opted to go to a store where he still has credit. Now here's where the fun begins.

As soon as he arrives at the appliance section, he goes straight to the dishwashers and starts poking around. A salesman quickly arrives and strikes up a conversation, but is just as quickly rebuffed. The aloof Green is not interested in casual chitchat. When he has questions, he'll ask them; so until then, the salesman should just go away. The dejected salesman goes back to his end-of-the-aisle workspace where he steals periodic glances at the Green to make sure nothing's afoot.

Meanwhile, the Green continues the investigation. He'll read the labels, slide the latches, push the buttons, and browse the user manuals. He's looking for data to absorb, and that takes time. He won't be rushed into making a hasty decision. Once he's acquired enough info, he makes a few pre-emptive strikes to narrow the field down to two or three finalists.

Finally, he calls the salesman over. Our Green has a few questions about installation. Which one is the easiest to put in? Can he install it himself, or does it require a pricey plumber? How is it installed? What are the pitfalls? What tools are required? Are all the couplers and tubing provided? The Green probably has uncovered the answers already, but now he's proving his hypothesis with a secondary source. He's also making sure he hasn't overlooked any flaws or limitations.

At the end of the interrogation, the Green takes a moment to process the information and form a conclusion. Then, without further ado, he whips out his credit card and makes the purchase. He declines paying extra for a service contract, of course, makes arrangements for delivery, hops back on his scooter, and goes home. Mission accomplished. Case closed. Tomorrow he'll eat off clean dishes.

Notice how our bachelor handled the sales process. Employing a typical Green stratagem, he remained completely detached from it, not letting the salesperson interfere at all with his analysis. He only spoke when he needed to get facts and figures and when he was finally ready to make the purchase. Greens don't need salespeople—they need answers. Preferably objective answers, without the biases of a loquacious commission-driven salesperson skewing the data. Greens won't be rushed into making a decision, nor will they tolerate traditional "buddy-buddy" sales tactics. They're in the store to buy, not to chat away the day with a stranger who suddenly wants to be their best friend. To make a purchasing decision, all Greens need is access to a knowledgeable expert or database and a little space and time to formulate a conclusion. Nothing more, nothing less.

Green Buyers

Ask a lot of questions
Meet to learn and gain wisdom
Can't be rushed into a decision
Look for loopholes and flaws
Appear cool, aloof, and skeptical
Want data, facts, and figures
Want to see the "big picture"
Dislike redundancy and small talk

Orange buyers

While a few Oranges don't enjoy being a customer, most do. There's something wonderfully appealing about being the center of attention and having salespeople fawn all over you, trying to get you to buy their wares. Sure, you know it's a bit phony, and probably just a well-rehearsed act, but it's entertaining nonetheless. It's also more amusing than sitting around on your keister watching your money earn interest in a savings account—although lots of Oranges wouldn't have such a critter in the first place. Besides, spending money is genuinely fun.

It's also fun—albeit a tad cruel—to saunter into a store with a few buddies, act as though you were rich and famous, try on or try out a wide variety of the most expensive merchandise, cause the sales staff to drool in anticipation of their commission checks, then leave abruptly, empty-handed, muttering something to your entourage about how you left your money in the limo and will be right back—even though you have no intention of returning in this or any other decade. Later you meet up with your pals to laugh about the reactions of the dismayed store employees who, just in case you came back, stayed on for another shift—without pay.

Of course, this is just one of the many exploits that Oranges routinely pull off in shopping malls across the world, especially when accompanied by friends. Shopping is a game—much like a high stakes game of five card stud, where bluffing and conning lead to the jackpot. If you don't have a strategy or don't play your hand correctly, you'll lose every time. So Oranges enter an establishment with a flexible plan of attack and a poker face, looking for action.

What they really want is a salesperson who'll play with them, and not some tightly wound fuddy-duddy. They prefer someone who'll appreciate and reciprocate their light-hearted humor and good-natured bantering; someone who wants to turn a potentially dull encounter into something they can go home and tell their family about; someone who wants to have a rip-roarin', lip-splittin' good time. Of course, if they can't find that type of person, then they'll probably kick their exuberance down a notch and quickly get the deed done or they'll move on to another store.

Oranges don't like to listen passively to a sales pitch; they prefer to do something that requires action. Whether it's walking around a car lot kicking tires or looking under hoods, whipping out a loaf of bread and testing a line of toasters, or booting up a row of computers and testing out a memory-hogging video game—they want to do something while the salesman is rambling on and on.

In fact, they don't really care about technical specs and particulars, they mainly want a clear, brief overview, and perhaps a rundown of the key benefits and features, especially the features that make the product bigger, newer, faster, better, shinier, or sexier that its competitors. They like being the first one on the block to have the latest and the greatest, even if it turns out to be a Ford Edsel.

Bells, whistles, flashing lights, and nudity attract Oranges like mosquitoes to a backyard bug zapper. They like a little risk, a little adventure, a little spice. If hype is good, sensationalism is even better. Nothing is quite over the top. Remember, Oranges like to be entertained, engaged, and kept on the edge of their seats, like a kid watching *Raiders of the Lost Ark* for the first time. They follow their instincts and often make decisions on the spur of the moment, even for fairly expensive items.

When it comes time for the hard close, Oranges like to haggle, even if the price is clearly marked and not subject to negotiation. A savvy salesperson might sense this and artificially inflate the charge on an ancillary service, then after a fair amount of wrangling, lower it in "defeat." When Oranges feel like they've won the game, then they're more than happy to return to the store in the future, in hopes of making another big score.

Orange Buyers

Are willing to take risks
Want a clear, brief overview
Need to see the immediate benefits
Like to be kept on the edge of their seats
Make decisions on an impulse
Like new, different, and bold things
Like to haggle and negotiate
Like to be the center of attention

What Advertisers Don't Want You to Know

If it's still a secret to you, then let me be the first to clue you in. Advertisers have your number. At the turn of the century (the last one, with the nines in it), it may have been enough to hit you with ad frequency, hoping that many repetitions would make their name stick so you'd reach for their brand. These days, marketers scientifically poll the populace to determine who is likely to buy for what reason. They plot your economic level, your level of education, and your geographic and ethnic preferences to develop efficient campaigns that are the most likely to produce the desired outcomes—then they hit you with ad frequency hoping to make their names stick.

Hey marketers—over here! Save yourself a ton of money by keying your advertisements to the personality styles of your audience. Instead of going after the percentage of females aged 22–37 with children in the home, think Blue. Need to hawk some antacid? Come up with something to appeal to Golds. Have a line of technologically solid but ugly, boxy, cars? Appeal to my Green side. Selling a product that makes timid folks jump up on the stage and do what needs to be done? Orange me—or show me Swedish bikini models—same thing.

Now the sinister part. The advertiser's job is to mess with you. They may be pleased at some level that your babies have tidier bums now that you use their disposable diapers, but they're far more excited that they need to order up extra pallets and forklifts to ship them to you. The sad truth is, not all products are equally good; not all companies are equally friendly to the environment, or equally diligent about sending part of their profits to help rehabilitate Amazonian tree frogs injured in logging accidents. And the scary secret is that it's often more costly to remedy some of their products' deficiencies than it is to pay for a bigger advertising campaign to get you to buy more of them.

Eyes open? You're a market. And all the commercials and advertisements and to a certain extent propaganda are chosen for their likelihood to stimulate sales or action. Since all of us together are a big monolith, advertisers and opinion makers use techniques to divide and conquer—they segment the market and work out their appeals to each portion. The ultimate segmentation is personality temperament. Understand which color buys into which argument, and create the opportunity to persuade them.

Now that you're aware of it, think back over which TV and radio commercials grab you and which you tune out, sitting passively until something you find more relevant comes on. Chances are, the advertisements that mean the most to you are in line with your native color spectrum.

Not to put too fine a point on it, but a part of every advertisement is there to get you to do something. It may be to buy a product, but it also can be to influence your opinion, or create in you a favorable impression about a product, company, or politician. Many software manufacturers have taken the art of advertising persuasion to new heights, creating elaborate commercials to remind you of the advantage of software products that are not yet available.

Often, the message and the way it's conveyed are acutely incompatible. How many advertisements for heavily sugared soda pops and adult beverages feature beautiful and athletic men and women doing high-speed, ultimate-thrill sports and activities? Conduct an informal survey of your community by looking for opened bottles of these beverages and observing the condition of whomever has hooked up to them. There is an obvious disparity between fantasy and reality. But associating a product with something that is important to the values of the target market segment can stimulate sales, even if the relationship is ridiculous. Are you a little bit too heavy to freefall on a snowboard onto a slope with eight feet of fresh powder? No problem. Have a high-carbohydrate sports drink. It's the next best thing.

CHAPTER 3

Communication: Talking and Writing with Color

For communication to be effective, the speaker and the listener must be able to interpret accurately what the other is saying. Because each personality style interprets information in different ways, we need to alter our communication style to accommodate the preferences of the person to whom we are talking.

Conversing in the Nexus

These days, it seems like there's a rush to get connected. We strive to be connected technologically through the Internet, cellular phones, and personal digital assistants. We attend meeting after meeting in an attempt to stay connected with our staff members about various business issues and to stay on top of the newest information. We have an insatiable need to be connected to our schedules, to our customers, to our employees, and to our friends and family.

What are the benefits of developing all of these connections? For starters, we may feel more able to conquer the tasks of the day successfully. We may be able to build a stronger business by offering customer service options in ways that are more convenient for the customers. We may feel closer to our families even when separated by far distances. In short, we use our connected status to serve our own purposes—to meet our individual, personal needs. Those needs are what we, as individuals, value.

When we talk about understanding and working with people of other temperaments, this need for connection becomes even greater. In order to communicate effectively with others—sometimes even with people who share our primary color—we need to be able to speak in terms of their needs and values. That's what this chapter is all about—empowering you with the ability to express your message effectively to anyone, anywhere, regardless of the colors involved in the process.

In the introductory chapter of this book, I wrote briefly about aspiring to live in the "nexus." The word *nexus* is literally defined as "a means of connection; tie; link." In our temperament vernacular, that translates into creating a connection, or link, between yourself and the person with whom you need to communicate. When you consciously strive to build this connection or link, you are "in the nexus."

Understanding the values and motivations of all four colors is an immeasurable help when moving towards the nexus. As you read this chapter, you will discover some words, phrases, body language, and communication tips that will also help your nexus quest. As a result you'll be able to build yourself—and those around you—a well-connected communication bridge!

> "To effectively communicate, we must realize that we are all different in the way we perceive the world and use this understanding as a guide to our communication with others."
>
> — ANTHONY ROBBINS

Signature Analysis

In Pacific Beach, Washington, a sleepy seaside hamlet drenched by drizzle and covered by trees and ferns, sits the Pacific Beach Naval Facility. Its white board buildings and asphalt walks poke starkly from the lush green grass that grows perennially around them. The entire facility is smaller than most junior high schools, and if you didn't know where to look for it you probably wouldn't find it.

The PacBeach installation was astoundingly secret for years. If you asked too many questions, the sailor you were speaking with would give your name to his Chief Petty Officer, and you might get a visit, likely an "invitation" to take it easy on his personnel by backing off on such queries.

The facility kept peace with its neighbors by opening its doors a few times a year for community functions (the base has its own bowling alley, quite a treat in such remote, wet country). The base for years operated one of the only ambulances within fifty miles. In return for these nods to the community, no one much bothered the Navy technicians working there.

The base's "official mission" was, and probably still is "oceanographic research," although most literature now lists it as a recreational facility. When you check nautical charts, however, you notice large sections of seabed are off limits for dumping metal of any kind. When you look at a larger chart of the same area, you see that USNS PacBeach sits less than one hundred miles from most of the major ports on Washington's coast, including the entrance to the straits of Juan de Fuca, the water gateway between the United States and Canada and portal to Seattle, which is more than a day's journey by water from the sea.

What does the little series of white cottages and a bowling alley do? Natives quietly whisper that it listens. The marvelous passive sonar technology that rides along on today's nuclear submarines has its roots in the work of PacBeach, and doubtless several similar facilities. Each ship that plies the ocean has a unique sonic footprint, a unique combination of the sounds made by its screws, rudders, propulsion system, overall construction, maybe even to some extent its cargo. Capturing these sound patterns into an acoustic database, and linking the patterns to the names of vessels, gives Navy subs the means to recognize thousands of ships by their sounds alone, using an exotic technology called *signature analysis*.

We humans can learn a lot from nuclear submarines. We can perform our own form of signature analysis by listening carefully to people as we speak. Doing so gives us the ability to pinpoint the color spectrum of someone we are meeting, dealing with, maybe even going on a blind date with. While at its roots, listening seems the easiest thing to do in the world, in truth there is much more to it. Unlike the Navy, however, we don't need to keep these techniques secret. In fact, you'll uncover them if you keep on reading.

Beware the undertone

If you've ever been to a snooty French restaurant, you'll recognize immediately what I mean by *undertone*. In nearly every language, there are certain tones and dialects reserved for communicating with underlings and subordinates. Similarly, many languages have higher forms reserved for speaking with elders, teachers, and sometimes God.

English is much more egalitarian, at least on the surface. True, if one looks hard enough, one can still locate the "thee," "thou," and "thine" of earlier centuries. By and large, however, English, especially American English, tends to treat all speakers and listeners as being on the same social plane, likely an artifact of George Washington's refusal to be crowned king.

This is not to say that such differences don't exist, they're just well hidden. Seeking them out is the first step in identifying the color spectrum of the person you're talking to.

Give me attitude

The reason for differences in tone is straightforward—the speaker is presenting his or her attitude about us. The nouveau riche, looking down on the little people from their Lear jets may let slip, from time to time, some of their appreciation with what they have achieved in life. This satisfaction, warming their souls, may occasion them to look fondly, or with a little disdain, upon their fellowmen. Haughtiness, although never in good taste, can color speech. Hence, you can often obtain a second key to speakers' mental and emotional whereabouts by listening to what they say and to whom they say it. Of course, the message screams loudest when we hear what they say about someone or some group that isn't around.

Marker words

Finally, the words with which we speak tend to reveal a great deal about our personalities. You can analyze people by listening when you monitor for certain verbal markers. How frequently these key words are heard in speech provides a strong fix on the identity of our target.

For example, Blues express in speaking the unification and relating language that guides their lives. They imbue their language with embracing, encompassing, empowering words such as *associate, collect, combine, fuse, integrate*. Blues also describe the world in terms of emotions, like *harmony, mystical, wonder, care for*, or of relationships, including *love, marry, feel, attract, clasp, bond*.

As you might expect, Gold speech often includes short, imperative command words, such as *check, keep, lock, do, go*.

Golds also reveal their fondness for rules and procedures through frequent use of words such as *proper, regular, regulate, right, comply, organize,* and their motivation to higher causes by words such as *duty, honor, sacrifice, protect, serve.*

Greenspeak carries with it a detached air of analysis, with judgment getting closer, but always reserved in case more data comes in: *analyze, measure, inspect, look it over, test.* Greens also use words that indicate intellectual processes: *critique, classify, arrange, sort, sift,* as well as terms dealing with discussion, such as *debate, argue, question, challenge, prove.* And of course, *think about it.*

Orange speech, on the other hand, tends to focus on what can be sensed, with words like *explode, fly, feel, see, ride, float.* They pepper their speech with enthusiastic verbs, such as *create, set up, dream, envision, cause, liven up,* and words that have a tinge of hope, such as *believe, imagine, hint, wonder, suspect.*

Some words are so common in the speech or writing of a particular color that they "mark" the person as a particular temperament. These are the special marker words that create a near-dialect of the English language for each color.

Special verbal markers

Special words permeate the speech of each color style. The Gold style, for instance, tends to be imbued with the business jargon of the day, *upsize, turbo, downsize, margin call, recession,* and so on. Greens tend to lace their language in similar ways, except that Green's speech usually has a more acerbic edge to it—*dot.com, dot.bomb, dot.gone,* etc.

There are also a few special words that dangle around the lips of strong personality types like bees buzz flowers. Blues use the word *we,* Golds use *should,* Greens use *perhaps,* and Oranges use *could.*

Also, don't forget that in speaking, "One man's ceiling is another man's floor." Thus, words that ring true of motherhood and apple pie to one color often end up as hisses on the lips of their opposites. For example, the word *duty* is spoken by both Golds and Greens; *responsibility* is spoken by Golds and Oranges. "Pay cash," however, usually makes sense in any color.

Deciphering Dialogue

Now that we know what to listen for as we communicate with the different temperaments, let's examine some actual dialogue and see if we can't dissect it a bit more.

Blue dialogue

> "And so I told him, 'If you think your sister shouldn't treat him that way, then couldn't you just tell her to sort of wise up or she will be missing out on a good thing, you know? I mean, there are plenty of girls out there who don't have her 'little problem,' and, I mean, he's okay with it, right? So, everybody has to overlook something, right? And in today's world, you can't be so sure. So if you ask me, this would be a good time for her just to forgive and forget. It makes me so angry. I wish they could get past this. What about you?"

The Blue speaker needs a lot of space to unwind the emotions and reactions of the day. Because Blues concentrate on intangibles, such as relationships between individuals, their language also tends toward the intangible. Literary devices color the speech. The importance of body language as a conveyor of nuance increases. Exchanges tend to be longer and more complete than Green, with periodic calls to see if the listener is still on the same wavelength, and often a summary that relates to how the message is felt on an emotional level.

One trait about Blue speech that drives others batty, particularly Greens, is their frequent use of pronouns. "He," "she," "them," all stay put for Blues. Greens would love the convenience of such casually assigned vocal variables, but could never tolerate the prospect for error their use might cause.

True Blues also are in short supply, so when one puts them together, their conversations tend towards the intimate. This makes Blues the subject of a lot of potentially embarrassing situations—things right out of *I Love Lucy,* such as the time Lucy tries three times to shout to her band leader husband Ricky that she has just learned that she's with child. The first two times Ricky can't hear her because the band is playing a loud passage. The third time the band suddenly drops to a pianissimo, just as an exasperated Lucy shouts, "I'm pregnant!"

Similar situations stain carpets in offices all over the country. Just as a supervisor, slurping a big mug of coffee, enters a cubicle occupied by two Blues, he overhears one Blue whisper a furtive question to the other, "Do you think the boss knows his assistant's pregnant with triplets?"

It's not that Blues mean either to talk regularly of such intimate details or to appear to gossip. Their mental makeup revolves around the private, the personal, the intimate. When they talk about it, it's as if the rest of the world is always taking it out of context.

Gold dialogue

Here's a passage from a speech delivered by a Gold schoolteacher. Can you spot the use of Gold signature words? Notice the general tone and attitude.

> I propose that there should be a means to insure better compliance with lunchroom rules. I mean, for Pete's sake, this is basic health and nutrition! It is something these children will be doing every day for the rest of their lives.
>
> A few years ago it was much more structured. We used to make the students wash their hands. Remember the powdered soap we kept in those heavy cans? Mrs. Kinsey had a nailbrush, too, and she made them use it, and let me tell you those tough boys from Mr. Schmalzel's auto mechanics class used to hate that. Of course that's all gone now. Along with manners. Sneezing, snorting, wiping their noses on their sleeves ... did you know I caught one of them licking his fingers and sticking them up into the shaved ice machine? Do you think he washed up first?
>
> There was a time when there was a little respect, a little common courtesy. After all, lunch didn't used to be a right. One purchased it, one enjoyed it, and it was good for you. And if you couldn't afford your lunch, no one just gave it to you. You worked. You helped cook it or serve it, or clean up afterwards. Everybody who wanted a meal could get one. But it wasn't free. There was no entitlement. Much better back then if you ask me. What will happen when they leave here? Who's going to feed them then?
>
> And it just seemed to mean more back then. It was more social. Some of the other girls and I—I had seven brothers and two step-sisters, and I was one of those that worked for my lunch—we used to spend hours trying to talk Mrs. Martin out of her recipe for Peanut Butter Pie. She made it every other Tuesday. Now these students consider lunch to be their privilege, after a hard morning of, what, watching videos? Playing computer games? Surfing the net?
>
> Oh it would do these children so much good to see it just once as it used to be. It would take some discipline, but we could still do it. Well, maybe not. Now, the new teachers seem to be as much part of the problem as the solution. Thank heavens this is my last year!

Notice that Gold speech tends to look backwards, unless the purpose of the conversation it to detect and eliminate potential errors. Note also that Golds are occasionally negative in their approach. Society is in decline, and they're watching it crumble. (Likely this stems from Golds' desire to pass on society's values to following generations. The difficulty of that process leads to permanent frustration).

Operating as they do on shared ideals, Golds can inadvertently slip into conspiratorial tones when speaking to those with whom they may feel an allegiance.

> "It's been months, and he still hasn't got the numbers up."
>
> "I know. I was watching the folder get closer to the top of the pile in finance. It's going to come back to bite him."
>
> "And you'll be right there to...."
>
> "Oh, no. Not me. He did this to himself."
>
> "And he really had it coming. Do you think...?"
>
> "He knows? Has to. We all do. It's just a matter of time."

Green dialogue

Greens have a unique speaking style that may seem almost cryptic at times.

> "I fired up my new 12-40 board last night."
>
> "How was it?"
>
> "Great rendering, texture mapping real fast. Shading looked good. I put a fan on it."
>
> "Graphics card?"
>
> "Yeah, there's this new fan that uses engineering instead of horsepower. Got some wicked looking fins on the fan cowl. Anodized metal that directs the air and wicks away the heat. Holds the fan in position too, of course."
>
> "Really?"
>
> "At first, I thought, 'No way, man, what a gimmick!' But then I checked the sites, and some dudes who got beta units say it really does eject the heat. Maybe allows a whole frame per second faster."
>
> "Awesome."
>
> "And then Dad was having a problem with his machine, so I went in an booted it up to see if he'd messed up the CMOS with his new 21 Gig drive."
>
> "The one that... ?"
>
> "That's right. Anyway, I'm just waiting for his machine to boot and it's like, 'Hello, anybody working in there?'"
>
> "Slow, huh?"
>
> "Not really, but it sure seemed that way. I mean, if he only knew how slow his box was by today's standards. Mr. Accountant! Big spreadsheet! Woo-ooo-ooo. Sixteen colors!"
>
> "If he only knew...."

You may notice that Green speech, contrasted with the others, is often shorter, punchier, although often laced maddeningly with jargon and occasionally awash with details. Greens also tend to use mental placeholders, stubs of conversations left over from previous ones and referenced by keys. They also eschew the obvious. The result is often a sensation on the part of the listener of being completely inside or outside of the loop. In more formal speech, the Green is likely to gather all the resources and make reasonable citations so the listener can come up to speed, often by using appositives, so the narrative can be uninterrupted. Unfortunately, if that happens, the words can run long. This is a function of Green's urge to be unambiguous and precise. Greens also frequently compare the way things are to the way they sense things logically should be. The result is an overarching sheen of apparent arrogance that causes them much grief, although it's likely not something Greens do intentionally.

A subset of Green communication occurs when two Greens, familiar to each other, are speaking of a project or problem with which they're both familiar. The conversation sinks, or rises, depending on one's point of view, to what in extreme cases can become a "Grunt and Point" mode.

> "Howzzit work?"
>
> "Great."
>
> "32-bit mode?"
>
> "Not that good. Better in 64."
>
> "Hmmpf."

If an outsider were to interrupt to ask about this conversation, he or she would likely encounter one of two reactions. The first might be mild shock, caused by bringing both Greens up suddenly from their shared mental space. The outsider might take the expression on their faces to read, "Who is this little person, and why is it speaking to us?"

The second reaction might be one of sheer exultation. The relatively small number of Greens can mean that they spend a great deal of their time feeling isolated. When another candidate for a mind meld comes by, it's a treat to be in that mode, and quite a thrill to finally be witnessed within one's element.

Orange dialogue

Oranges, on the other hand, may stage just such a conversation in an attempt to shock the heck out of people. Oranges like impact. They make it happen. Changeable, quick, adaptable, funny, Oranges cause explosions wherever they go. Therefore, the Orange marker words are likely to be short terse verbs.

"It was hot that afternoon, and I was wearing my blue mini, you know the one—short! I didn't say much all the way out there, right until we got up to the bend, and then I just asked, "Could we stop here? I have to do something." Then I just popped out of his car and went off into the bushes.

"What'd he do?"

"What could he do? He sat and waited. I took a good long time, and then I walked back into the car sort of dangling my wrap over my shoulder and smiling. I got him thinking."

"What happened then?"

"We drove to the lake, got out the food, and the blanket...."

"Oh my goodness! No!"

"I'll never tell. I will say that I 'forgot' to pack one part of my swim suit."

"Did you...?"

"Go skinny-dipping? Of course not! I had the other piece."

"Why, you wicked...."

"Let's just say he wasn't in a hurry to drive home that night."

Of course, the Orange's exploits can be merely the stuff of fantasy. For an Orange, there is as much joy in the telling as in the act. It's far more likely that the tale above related just a dreadful evening, involving poor preparations, improper instructions about dress, and an unscheduled stop at a roadside restroom. But you would never know it from listening to an Orange. If the story gets better with each telling, however, it might be a sign that the Orange is looking for shock value at the expense of the facts.

Oranges who know each other tend to talk in shorthand as well, but the shared experiences seem often to be about common threats from authority figures, something many Oranges have experience with.

"He see you?"

"Nah, It's cool."

"Close one, though."

"Too darn...."

"Keep it cool."

"Later, Bro'."

Once your ears are tuned to attitude, tone, and marker words, you can perform your own signature analysis on the people around you. If you want, you can even do it in stealth mode. Act nonchalant. Hide behind a newspaper. Set yourself up in a secret listening post. Make it a game. No one will ever know.

Speaking Colorfully

It's relatively easy to communicate one-on-one, especially when you know the temperament of your listener. To communicate successfully, all you have to do is to set aside your own colorized preferences and accommodate the predilections of your listener. Sounds like an impossible task, doesn't it? But it's really not that tough, especially if you take the time to practice your skills on a few insignificant others. Before you know it, you'll be wooing and wowing your audience like a silver-tongued devil.

Of course, you need to know a bit more about those preferences. The following pages list a few tips and techniques that will help you express yourself in meaningful ways with each temperament. Tattoo these trouble-free tips on your brain, because it's far too easy to revert to our own style and forget these guidelines, especially when we're in the midst of a heated conversation.

Conversing with Blues

Be genuine and sincere

Don't be superficial or insincere—Blues can instantly detect a phony. Instead, be authentic and honest. Keep in mind, however, that most Blues agree with the motto, "If you can't say something nice, don't say anything at all." So while they want honesty, they don't want brutal honesty. Lies and deceit are easily observed as well, so avoid those.

> "When the conduct of men is designed to be influenced, persuasion, kind unassuming persuasion, should ever be adopted. It is an old and true maxim that 'a drop of honey catches more flies than a gallon of gall.' So with men. If you would win a man to your cause, first convince him that you are his sincere friend. Therein is a drop of honey that catches his heart, which, say what he will, is the great highroad to his reason, and which, once gained, you will find but little trouble in convincing him of the justice of your cause, if indeed that cause is really a good one."
>
> — ABRAHAM LINCOLN

Be sensitive to body language

Most Blues have excellent observation skills. They see things that many people don't. They take in all aspects of how information is delivered, noticing body orientation, posture, gestures, vocal inflections, and facial expressions. Not only will Blues hear the message, but they will see it and perceive it as well. In fact, the delivery method may carry more weight than the message itself.

Learn to use these subtle things to clarify and strengthen your conversations. Be careful not to send mixed messages or become overly concerned when Blues misinterpret your inadvertent signals.

Focus on people and events

To Blues, people are more important than things. Consequently, focus your conversation on issues that involve people. Talk about each other, mutual acquaintances, or celebrities. Talk about past, current, and future events. Talk about issues that Blues are interested in, such as the effects of specific government policies on people, the plight of the homeless, or the conservation of natural resources.

For example, a perfectly acceptable animal to adopt is the manatee. These gentle behemoths look like a cross between a big seal and huge slug, and have the disposition of ... well, they may not have any disposition. They seem to eat by opening their mouths and letting food drift in, and they spend their time floating in the Florida Everglades. Basically, manatees aspire to little. They are just themselves.

Which makes them irresistible to Blues. Unlike saving the whales, which has become a battle cry with political actions attached, manatees offer little commercial interest. Other than being an attraction at a few marine theme parks, they just hang out and float. Their biggest enemy is humans, who constantly run into them with their speedboats. This has spawned an animal rescue movement regarding the manatees that has seen good results.

Perhaps it's their inoffensive, non-aggressive, non-energetic nature that makes the manatee so adorable. They're so ugly they're cute. By and large, if you mention that you're a friend to the manatees, and can tell a bit of their story, you're going to go a long way towards getting close to a Blue.

Express feelings and emotions

Blues communicate with their feelings and use them to express certain messages that words cannot convey. Learn to anticipate and recognize these feelings and then respond with some of your own in as clear a manner as possible. Don't suppress or try to disguise your emotions, unless they're inappropriate or out-of-control. Blues need to know how you feel about issues and can only infer a limited amount from your words alone. What you say isn't nearly as revealing as how you say it; thus style supersedes substance.

Listen intently

When talking with Blues, be sure to listen intently to the words and phrases they use. Blues love language and generally choose their words carefully. Make sure you hear and understand what they're saying before you respond. It may be helpful to restate what you think you heard. Keep in mind that listening to a

Blue involves more body parts than mere ears—it takes a willing heart, an open mind, a gentle touch, and a warm smile. You won't last long without these attributes.

Maintain eye contact

Between your forehead, eyebrows, eyes, eyelids, mouth, and chin, your face can contort to express thousands of different emotions—and do it in a split second. You can't pick up on those revealing facial expressions if you don't maintain eye contact. Reposition yourself so you can directly face the Blue, or at least sit side-by-side. Communication specialists have long maintained that meeting someone's glance with your eyes indicates you're interested and involved. To do otherwise signals a desire to avoid contact. On the other hand, you don't want to stare them down—that indicates dominance. Just try to maintain comfortable eye contact. And if this is a personal or intimate conversation, don't hesitate to respond with an appropriate touch, pat, or stroke.

Avoid debate or conflict

Blues avoid confrontation. They always meet argumentative attitudes and actions with dismay. If Blues are dragged into a conflict, they have a hard time remaining objective and logical, especially if it regards a personal issue. Try to steer away from debate or conflict whenever possible. However, if a conflict must take place, remain as neutral, deferential, and unemotional as possible. You don't want to intensify their irritation. Like a mirror reflects an image, Blues reflect emotions—so if you get upset, they'll get upset; if you're calm, they'll remain calm.

Show empathy and concern

In a similar vein, sometimes it's helpful to reflect the Blue's emotions—if they're happy, be happy; if they're sad, be sad. This shows that you emotionally and intellectually identify with what they're saying. Be compassionate and reassuring. Share relevant personal experiences. Without saying, "I completely understand," let them know that you do.

Conversing with Golds

Appreciate their time

Time is a precious, limited resource for most Golds. They govern their lives with schedules, clocks, and calendars, so make sure you're on the agenda and don't take more time than was budgeted. If you're not sure how much time you have to talk, ask them—they'll let you know. As you talk, explain how much you appreciate their time. Therefore it's imperative that you don't waste it. Make certain your message is worthy of their investment.

Then, at the end of your time together, thank them for listening to you or for giving you advice.

Stay on task

Golds are focused and task-oriented individuals. As you talk with them, try to have an objective in mind. Decide what the point of the conversation is and then don't stray off on tangents. In fact, as you begin talking, explain your purpose and determine if they have any objections. Of course, this doesn't mean that Golds never like to engage in casual conversations. They do—if they know that's the objective.

Be courteous and polite

Nothing turns a Gold off faster than someone who is ill-mannered, vulgar, impolite, or uncivilized. Try to be as courteous, refined, polished, and polite as possible. Don't use coarse, profane, or obscene language, and remember to avoid being loud, obnoxious, or arrogant. Be alert and attentive to the verbal and non-verbal messages of your audience.

One salesperson I know has raised color matching to an art form. When he approaches a Gold client, he strictly controls the presentation. He has even ordered associates to sit in the lobby if he feels they can't measure up to his Gold client's needs.

On the other hand, when he visits an Orange client, his demeanor is incredibly relaxed. Off goes the jacket, the tie gets cursed and loosened. Often as not you may soon find him leaning back in his chair, idly twirling another chair he has tipped up on one leg—and this while his client is talking. In the presence of Golds he exhibits rapt attention by locking on with his eyes. While with Oranges, his eyes wander, he yawns and stretches as needed, and he signifies acknowledgement by mumbling "unhh-huh… yeah."

He must have cracked the code. I've never known him to earn less than a six-figure annual income, or to own and operate less than two businesses at the same time.

Be direct and professional

In general, Golds are a conservative group of people who associate with others who reflect conservative values. Because Golds are so business-like in their approach to life, they respect people who are professional in their conduct and presentation. Try to be honest, ethical, up-front, and to-the-point when dealing with Golds.

Talk about expectations

What do you expect the Gold person to do as the result of a conversation? What will you do? What effects will this have? What will it change? What are your concerns? What do we have to modify? What can we plan or anticipate? What steps do we need to take? How is it organized? Why do we need to do this? These are the kinds of questions that help Golds focus on specific outcomes.

Focus on Gold interests

Focusing on things that interest the listener is a great technique for learning more about the listener and building a stronger relationship. What topics interest Golds? Politics, education, crime and punishment, family values, work, team sports, and economics, to name a few.

One of my friends is a very Orange salesperson who has discovered that by drawing on family stories he can be more successful with his Gold clients. Of course, it happens that his father and his brother both played professional baseball—which next to apple pie and mom is a direct pathway to the hearts of many Golds. My friend has a ready cache of pro-sports stories about famous athletes and coaches, which he has acquired around the family dinner table. Some are fairly outrageous, but he has a number that are actually inspiring and uplifting. This kind of authoritative insight into a popular topic has created several openings for my friend in an otherwise stuffy industry.

Turn solutions into actions

According to Golds, talk is cheap. They're more concerned about the results of the conversation—who's going to do what and when. They're results-oriented and everything must have its purpose. Thus, try to be practical and pragmatic.

Be authoritative if justified

If you're an authority on an issue, don't hesitate to declare your credentials. Golds respect authority and recognize the wisdom in deferring to it. On the other hand, don't be an impostor and claim to have more expertise than you truly have.

Don't forget the power of "being there" as a path to "authority." Even if you were nothing more than the elevator operator in a hospital, you probably still picked up a few good stories and other items of "medical lore." Also, you probably know personally a half-dozen true experts well enough to call them on their cell phones and have them be glad to catch up with you. You can sometimes gain an inroad by saying something like, "I used to work with a lot of doctors downtown. I talked to them daily. I still keep in touch with a few of them. I seem to recall that they used to say ______ about situations such as this. Would you like me to call around?"

Conversing with Greens

Talk about possibilities

Greens like to spend their energy contemplating the endless possibilities of the future. They're dreamers in the never-ending pursuit of a better process, a better system, a better tool, a better product. Take advantage of the Greens' foresight and creativity. Talk with them about their projections for the future. Ask for their input on product designs or contingency plans. Ask for their suggestions for improving structures or increasing efficiency. Ask questions like, "What would happen if…" or, "What do you think about this… ?"

Stay unemotional

Greens value their ability to remain logical and composed. Like the unshakable, expressionless Mr. Spock in *Star Trek,* they see the value of letting their heads control their hearts, particularly when making decisions that have a long-term impact. This behavior colors all aspects of their lives, including the way they communicate with other people and the way they expect other people to communicate with them. Greens are cool, calm, and collected, and expect others to be likewise. Greens get exasperated when others respond to their levelheaded objectivity with irrational displays of emotion.

Expect skepticism or debate

Greens are naturally skeptical of new ideas from unfamiliar sources. Not only do Greens want to examine and discover things for themselves, they also want to come to their conclusions independently. When an idea is forced on them, Greens will usually reject it unless they can determine its validity for themselves. But once they're committed to a new idea, they can readily become its most ardent defenders, at least until a new piece of significant data appears, forcing them to reevaluate. It's not surprising that most Greens love to debate and discuss the merits of a concept. Debate is an ideal forum for Greens, particularly extroverted Greens, who view it as an intellectual playground where they can sharpen and refine their ideas.

An exciting technology start-up in the Midwest was having some problems boosting itself to the next level, and one of my colleagues was invited to visit a few times and see if he could pick up on the cause of their slump. It became apparent right away that the entire company was built on a culture of Green. They enjoyed discussing their ideas and technology and philosophies, so much that these discussions, rightly viewed as steering the direction of the company, were allowed to consume hours, even days. Passions flared, and often one side would find itself gradually re-considering its position until, after an hour or so, you could witness them arguing with the same fury for the same points they had previously opposed. Funny thing, for all the energy and enthusiasm this seemed to generate, the company never really got off its dime. There were no Golds to continue the execution because the Greens would persecute them. There were no Oranges, because people were too serious and dedicated to tolerate them. A few token Blues were on hand, but they were overwhelmed and ended up looking pretty Green. Eventually about half the staff got so riled up about one idea that they forced the company's hand, and the boss, in order to hang onto what was left, called their bluff. The company split; the renegade team moved to California and became its biggest competitor.

Remain factual and logical

Sergeant Joe Friday from the *Dragnet* television series was famous for saying, "Just the facts, Ma'am." As far as Greens are concerned, this hits the nail squarely on the head. They just want to know the facts—all the facts. Like a good detective, they try to be as observant and objective as possible during the data-collection process. Furthermore, they expect others to be analytical, rational, and reasonable as well.

Avoid small talk

Because Greens make up less than 6 percent of the general population, most of them grew up feeling isolated and peculiar. As children, they probably knew only one or two other Greens—and they were indisputably unusual. It likely wasn't until a Green entered high school or college that he or she finally encountered clusters of people who shared values and interests. But by then, the Greens had already adopted patterns of avoiding social situations. Having never mastered the art of casual small talk, they're understandably distressed at the prospect of having to chitchat. For this reason, they're often mistakenly labeled as unfriendly, sheepish, antisocial, or even self-absorbed. But in truth, most Greens are none of these—they're just painfully aware of their social inadequacies. So to avoid unsettling a Green, stay away from small talk. Take the conversation seriously. Stay focused on one or two intriguing topics. Don't force them to comment on things they don't care about.

Allow for questions

Greens like to examine data from all possible angles. As you talk with them you are, in fact, giving them new pieces of data to examine. Like a good private investigator, Greens have many questions they want answered. Don't let their natural inquisitiveness bother you. Despite their tendency to sound like interrogators, they're just trying to develop a solution, regardless of whether you want one.

For example, a friend of mine is a pain-in-the-backside journalist. I say pain-in-the-backside not because he's a muckraker who stirs up trouble, but because he's Green. He specializes in technical journalism—books and articles written for professionals. When he visits a manufacturer, he usually interrupts their rehearsed spiels and dives right in with some questions. These lead to more questions, and more, and pretty soon the product managers and vice presidents clear their agendas and head down to the conference room to take part. It isn't long before this guy knows the company products and their marketing pitches inside and out, and is busy making suggestions on both. A few days later, when it's time for follow-up questions, he reaches into his Rolodex and talks to the person who can most directly make the decision or give the information. His sphere of influence has become quite extensive. Strangely, he's a pain-in-the-backside because he gets to the truth. Companies that are trying to find the truth themselves love him. The ones who hate to see him coming are those that are trying to pull wool over consumers' eyes.

Talk about Green things

What do Greens like to talk about? Most tend to have a handful of interests that captivate their time and energy. For many, it may be something scientific or technical. For others, it may be something creative or inventive. Whatever it is, ask about it. Then give them opportunities to demonstrate their expertise. As long as you're a sincere listener, most Greens will open up and talk.

Give them time to think

Remember that Greens take longer to process information and reach conclusions than other colors—not because they're mentally slower, but because they usually take more factors into consideration. Regardless of whether they're trying to solve complex problems or simply responding to a casual comment, Greens need "processing" time. Ever the meticulous scientists, Greens test and retest their ideas in order to reveal any fatal flaws. Normally this takes time—lots of time. Their ideas are a reflection of their inner selves, making a flaw in their idea a pernicious flaw in their character. So don't push too hard for a quick answer. Give them enough time to contemplate each matter completely.

Conversing with Oranges

Talk about Orange things

When possible, talk about things that interest the Orange. This could include adventures, experiences, activities, sports, games, and parties. Ask questions and ask for clarification. Oranges like to be the star in the center of the solar system that is surrounded by revolving heavenly bodies. And, like other lovers of limelight, they have plenty to say about themselves.

Be bold and confident

Oranges admire people who are fearless and sure of themselves. If you're timid or insecure, they can easily spot it and might use it to their advantage. Position your body so you're facing them and are able to maintain eye-to-eye contact. If necessary, don't hesitate to be assertive. Keep the conversation moving. Oranges quickly grow weary of long, drawn-out conversations. They aren't fond of redundancy, so don't belabor your point. Keep the dialogue moving as fast as possible.

Talk about past experiences

Most Oranges lead charmed and colorful lives. Because they seem to be always on the go, they've accumulated a wealth of experiences, likely more than most people. With their natural ability to tell elaborate stories, Oranges can talk for long periods about their past activities and accomplishments, especially if these adventures were dangerous or extraordinary. So if you want to get their attention, ask them about their past experiences or talk about experiences that you shared together.

Use ordinary language

Avoid using technical jargon or flowery speech. Most Oranges are down-to-earth and appreciate everyday language. They believe language should be functional and practical. As a rule, pretentious or pompous people turn them off.

When talking to an Orange, less is often more. Use the "two-fifths rule." That is not a rule about variety in liquors, rather an admonition to let the Orange do at least three-fifths of the talking, perhaps more. Even if you feel that you have been given license to waffle on, stop periodically and see if Orange's lights are still on.

Talk in concrete terms

Don't offer intricate explanations or talk about abstract or conceptual ideas unless it's vital to the conversation. Oranges are sensory people. They like to touch, feel, taste, smell, and see things. They live in the present and prefer to stay focused on the realities of the here-and-now.

Focus on action and results

Oranges like to make decisions quickly and move forward. Focus on results. Concentrate on action. Because so many Oranges like to talk "on the go," you may not be able to get your entire point across in a sit down, face-to-face conversation. Be prepared to accompany Oranges as they "move and shake." Oranges appreciate this kind of adaptability.

Be interesting and energetic

If your conversations are dull and boring, Oranges will tune out. To keep their attention you need to keep the conversation lively. Be energetic and animated—use your whole body. Use objects to help draw their attention. Don't be afraid to use jokes and anecdotes to illustrate your points. Consider being theatrical—Oranges are natural actors and appreciate a good, perky performance.

For example, I once heard a story about a woman who was trying to get the members of the family to do a better job in cleaning up after themselves. This is a common stressor when dealing with an Orange spouse or child, because they tend to change horses in mid-stream—saying "What the hay!" regarding picking up or putting in. This particular woman's peeve was the dining room table. The center of activities from Cub Scouts to homework study groups, it tended to sprout piles of non-food–related items. It even developed piles of canned goods now and then, because it was the first and most convenient place to put things down on when returning from errands, and if whomever was assigned to put things away got distracted—which happened a lot—the cycle of clutter-on-clutter ensued, until people had to move things around to eat.

Deciding it wasn't her responsibility to pick up after everybody, the lady of the house one day gave a demonstration her family did not soon forget. She cleaned up the table for what she vowed would be her last time, then let out a scream that could be heard for blocks. As her family tumbled out of bedrooms and up from the basement, they all asked her what was the matter. She just stood pointing to the clean table, and then after everyone had gathered, she gasped, "The kitchen table is made out of wood!"

Be honest and direct

If you have something to say to an Orange, get right to the point. Don't hesitate to say exactly how you feel. They would much rather have you be honest and forthright than waste time "beating around the bush." They say what's on their minds and expect others to do the same. They even look forward to frank and candid discussions.

Understanding Written Communication

What writing style says about personality

Just as you can tell a lot about a person by listening (once you know some of the color codes), you can also learn a lot by observing how someone writes. Written communication has increased in importance since the dawn of the Internet. E-mail has done a lot to make written messages brief and informal, but information-gathering routines often store and classify such messages for years to come. Thus, what we write is likely to be less formal, yet more durable, than ever before. This is a wonderful way of saying that your mistakes will be kept on file even longer than in the past.

Blue writing styles

Blues are made for writing. It's just what they do. They often are journal keepers; hence, expressing things close to the heart in written form is familiar for them. Blues have an amazing ability to pack in messages between the lines. Undertones, metaphors, similes, any verbal device that can increase the depth and meaning of prose, a Blue can write. Of course, much of the language used in business and the Internet is no place for such impassioned prose. Instead, Blues tend to pack their messages with folksy real-speech, keeping the receiver of the message more in mind than the message, and speaking as if the receiver were present.

Below is a sample of a memo written by a Blue employee from the Department of Bovine Effusions, in the randomly chosen state of Wisconsin. (Well, not quite randomly.) See if you can detect the trademark writing styles of the Blue.

> Congratulations! Our agency has reviewed your recent application for our Information Technology Specialist III position, and we would be delighted if you could call us for a further discussion. The position has a fixed, normal schedule, 8:00 - 5:00, and if hired, your starting salary will be somewhere within the range of $37,500 to $42,750. We will make that determination based upon your work experience and salary history.
>
> One thing I should tell you—this position requires that you pass a Medical/Physical Exam, which we'll pay for. We don't require the exam until the job has been offered and accepted, but we wanted you to know it is a requirement.

Gold writing styles

Gold writers tends to be brief and factual, offering no-frills descriptions of what was seen, what needs to be done, and who attended on what day. They underline or use CAPS a lot to emphasize main points. Goal-oriented Golds are always looking for closure, trying to put ideas to bed so they can move to the next item on their to-do lists. This means they form conclusions sooner than other types, and they keep their objective in the forefront as they write. This can be a trap for Golds. In particular, possibility-seeking Green readers, and Orange readers who hate to be constrained or dictated to, may develop alternate meanings as they read along. Although it pains the efficient Gold writer to periodically restate the message's purpose, the reader may not be able to keep the objective in mind unless it's periodically spelled out.

Below is a Gold employee's version of the employment memo from the Department of Bovine Effusions. Notice how different this memo is from the Blue version.

> You have responded to an advertisement for a vacancy in the position of Information Technology Specialist III. The position is for 40 hours per week, 8:00 a.m.–5:00 p.m., at a starting salary range of $37,500 to $42,750 depending on work experience and salary history. This position requires a Medical/Physical Exam, which will be paid for by the State if this job is offered and accepted.

Green writing styles

The Green writer also tends towards narrative, but there is a greater emphasis on precision and facts. This may appear to be cluttering detail to some readers. The Green document will contain everything the reader needs to know and more. It may be a bit of a challenge to read. Greens are not afraid to salt their prose with verbal superfluousness. They may also use a big word now and then just to sound smart.

Below is a Green version of the employment memo.

> Greetings, Job Candidate.
>
> Because you responded to an employment advertisement placed by this State of Wisconsin agency in *The Capitol Courier*, you are aware that a vacancy exists for an Information Technology Specialist III. Further information follows:
>
> — Job Type: Full time, 40 hours/weekly
> — Hours: 8:00 a.m.–5:00 p.m. weekdays
> — Salary: Starting salary* will be between $37,500 and $42,750 per annum
>
> A Medical/Physical Exam is required to make sure you are able to operate the 50 pound spectrograph that analyzes bovine effusions. Attached find a detailed job description and a list of the specific requirements for this position.
>
> *Starting salary will be influenced by experience and salary history.

Orange writing styles

Oranges get down to basics. Who, what, why, where, when, and how. Done. We're out of here. And we might even leave out some of those details. Letter writing can be boring. Informal memo writing is more tolerable, but only once in a while. Oranges may or may not have been the best students in school. As a result, the image-conscious Orange may not be comfortable with his or her appearance in print. Besides, there are more important things to do than pen elaborate works when a short sentence or two would work nicely. Short, sweet, safe—that's the way a lot of Orange writers play it.

Below is an Orange employee's version of the employment memo from the Bovine Effusions Department.

> We may want to hire you for an IT position. Come by our office this week for a follow-up interview. If you get the job, the hours are straight 8 to 5 and it pays between $37,500 and $42,750, based on your experience. If you accept the job you'll need to take a doctor's exam—which we'll pay for—to make sure you can lift 50 pounds.

If you're reading someone's prose and thinking about temperament, then in some way the words are important to you. If you can ferret out the color of the writer, and then consider the prose in that light, it can shed more light on the words. For instance, in the Orange example above, there is a mention of "straight 8 to 5" hours. Is this the writer's way of saying, "Relax, we pay you for every hour you work"? Or is it the author's way of saying, "No overtime available!"? It could be a means of saying, "Warning! Inflexible, time clock–watching overseers in this place!" The correct interpretation has everything to do with the color style of its author.

Of course, anytime you dig between the lines, you can find both extra information and unintended meanings. This may be the principal reason for the old song that goes "Never put it in writing!"

Talking to Groups

Once we've mastered the one-to-one communication process, it's time to advance to figuring out how to work one-to-many. More often than not, this requires us to adjust our message so that we appeal, at some level, to all four colors. The *nexus* concept strikes again.

Some may blanch at this. The temptation is to say, "That's too much work on my part—trying to talk to all four personality styles. Even if I were able to communicate in all four styles, wouldn't that make my speech weak and disjointed?"

You've already got your answer. It's all around you. Every day, speakers are able to masterfully command audiences, even hold them spellbound. And their audiences are the same as yours, typically made up of all four colors. Could it be that these powerhouse speakers are doing naturally the things we are discussing in this chapter? (Or could it even be by design? After all, a lot of them are familiar with these philosophies.)

The attitude you should not take is that the audience, exercising a modicum of common courtesy, should really try to accommodate your unique speaking style. If you have made it all the way to this chapter and still are of the opinion that that's going to happen, you should consider closing this book and reading something else. You're not getting the point.

Or maybe you just don't believe me. If you're Green, then it's no wonder. You need time to think it through and perhaps try it out for yourself. If you're Orange, then you might be itching to get started because it sounds fun to be able to add that much impact to your presentations. If you're Blue, you likely want to know more because it will help you get closer to more people than you would otherwise reach. It will also make you better at standing up for the people you care about. Golds, you may really believe that the audience will give you their full attention whether you use these techniques or not, and that's because you're the kind of person that gives others your full attention when they're speaking or presenting, because that's the right thing to do. In a way, the world would be a better place if more people were as professional and courteous as you are. And if you all learn these techniques, you may just be a step closer to convincing them to try to be that way.

The previous paragraph illustrates the advantage of talking to all the colors at once. If you accommodate the colors, you can focus on the needs of your listeners more than on your own. You certainly will be closer to the mark than if you speak strictly in your own, comfortable personality style. Besides, everyone is actually a blend of all four colors, so even if you don't connect directly to your listener's primary style, you may still hook up via a secondary one.

Hurdles

Here is a brief rundown of what you have working against you when you try to speak to an audience:

- — Blues don't care how much you know unless they know how much you care.
- — Golds will probably listen to anything they believe will help them, but only if it's well organized and well presented.
- — Greens don't care how much you care until they know how much you know.
- — Oranges may or may not sit through any given presentation. You must use your skills to keep them in their seats.

Load-lifters

On the other hand, you also have some advantages speaking to a multi-colored group.

- — The assembly is by nature a communal experience, therefore a Blue is likely having a good time already.

— If your objective is to unify and motivate the organization, and inspire people to work harder, then you're addressing a core Gold value.

— Greens believe that if you were selected to speak to an assembly, it means someone screened you first. You may have something worth saying.

— Jokes are likely to be appreciated by Oranges, and laughter is infectious.

The task is to address the needs of each group, draw on their strengths, if possible, and deliver your message in such a way that your shifting style doesn't result in weak, disjointed speech.

Okay, so now that we know what hurdles and load-lifters will hinder or help your speech, it's time to figure out what to talk about. On the following pages you'll find some suggestions on what kinds of things you should say as you try to slant your pitch towards one or more personality styles.

Blue speaking points

Throw out love vibes. Ask "Isn't this a beautiful day?" "It's great to be here in ______, where _____." Insert something in the blanks that indicates you've soaked up some local culture. Blues want personal stories and examples, such as "My wife and child the other day...." And they appreciate some personal disclosure of feelings or intimate thoughts. They must see the humanness of the speaker—culminating in a sob or a lump in the throat if possible. In fact, for the most profound impact, Blues must have an emotional experience. They must see how this idea or principle can make their life better. They love adjectives and vivid descriptions. They like symbols, poems, and poetic devices. They like to hear changes in the speaker's vocal pitch, volume, and inflection. They love dramatic pauses. These things keep them involved emotionally.

Gold speaking points

Start off by marking the time. You may even choose to comment that you have learned over the years (you just inserted a credential) that highly appreciated speakers bring a message of values, but that really highly appreciated speakers end on time. Looking at your watch, thumping the crystal, even removing it from your wrist and laying it on the podium where everybody can see you seeing it are not overly extreme gestures. Next, make sure that the organization of your materials is evident. Although many colors will feel more comfortable knowing that your materials are well thought-out, Golds will insist on it. They would love to have a copy of your outline so they can see your objectives and your timeframes. Empowering them with the ability to see where you're going and how you're going to get there allows them to feel they're making better use of their time. This keeps their minds from wandering, and allows them to take better notes.

As you might imagine, it was probably a Gold who first said that in order to give a good speech, you must, "tell 'em what you're gonna tell 'em, tell 'em, then tell 'em what you told 'em." Certainly this works well for Gold audiences, who, even after they hear what the topic is, and they know they aren't interested in it at all, will probably appear as though they're paying attention—after all, they don't want to appear rude or disrespectful. The Blues may also appear attentive because they really don't want to hurt your feelings by not assuming the "listening position." But as far as the Greens and Oranges go, you've effectively told them not to bother with listening, so if they stay seated they'll be doodling, day-dreaming, designing their ultimate dream house, or drooling. So if you use this technique, try to use it with your Gold audiences only.

If you sense a need to make apparent the structure beneath your comments, perhaps you can use a point-by-point system. Periodically say, or use special slides to present, a sequential numbered system; i.e., "Number 1… Number 2…." This facilitates organized note taking and shouts, "I'm following a structure!" Don't tell the audience how many points you're making, however, to avoid the distracting "countdown to freedom" effect.

Golds frequently use well-known and legendary quotes. They use authoritative and matter-of-fact tones. They use *shoulds, oughts,* and all the other Gold words mentioned earlier in this chapter. They like a thump on the podium to accentuate a particularly important point. They like lists of things to do and ways to gauge their progress in accomplishing those things. They want to hear about standards, benchmarks, policies, procedures, and values. Keep them involved in the structure, keep it official, and you'll keep your Gold audience in line.

Green speaking points

Greens may be harder to win over. Remember, they critically evaluate nearly every statement. Don't be afraid to call in authorities; better yet, call an authority before you speak, bounce as many of your ideas off of that person as you can before they hang up on you, and then say to your audience, "I was speaking to Ralph Obergnan the other day. Ralph is the Chief Information Officer for the XYZ Corporation, and he says that…." Now you're speaking as someone who knows Ralph. As long as you aren't incoherent, redundant, or rambling, Greens are fairly tolerant of tangential thoughts, especially if they hear some little-known fact or figure they can assimilate and spit out somewhere else. They like puns and witticisms. They admire arcane analogies, amusing anecdotes, astute anachronisms, and artful alliteration. And Greens love those "a-haa!" moments. Keep them thinking, guessing, and intellectually involved, and you can win over this tough segment.

Orange speaking points

If you can be funny, try and connect with your Oranges, who often live from joke to joke. If you can't, you might try to involve an Orange in some way. One good approach is to do something unconventional—something that might make the Golds nervous. One of the finest examples of this principle allegedly took place in a nuclear operators training class offered in the U.S. Navy. Supposedly, the instructor opened a heavy lead container for a moment, allowing some strange glowing, twinkling cloud to rise and permeate the room. Whether the effect was radioactive or pyrotechnic, the result was attention. Every trainee saw the object of their attention for the next several years of their lives. They visualized it, "felt it," and developed an innate appreciation for keeping radioactive materials in their place.

Although almost anyone could think up a lot of good reasons not to attempt to reproduce such a scintillating performance, the point is well taken. Active gestures, passionate theatrics, and melodrama will usually get the point across better than a dozen union enforcers with billy clubs. Oranges also want to move from point to point as quickly as possible. And the points must be unambiguous and memorable.

Oranges also enjoy sensational stories, particularly those that appeal to their values, like heroism and chutzpah. They must be able to see how they can apply the information in real time and in real life. Try to script in visual aids or engaging multimedia. Speak with style, with flair, with charisma, with energy. Keep them entertained.

Oranges in particular need this sizzle because they tend to spring out of their chairs if they aren't held into them either by seatbelts or by absorption with what's being said. If anybody is going to think of a reason to get up before you're finished, it will be an Orange. Just like people coughing in a theatre, one person does it and then another, so if an Orange leaves for some Orange reason, a Gold will leave to make an important phone call. Soon, the people who don't understand the message you're bringing will see folks they know leave, so they'll go, too. Ultimately, you'll end up with a few people who either are true believers that didn't really need to be educated, or folks with sore feet who just needed to perch.

Speaking the "E"asy way

Below is a chart that summarizes how these concepts can help you speak "in the nexus."

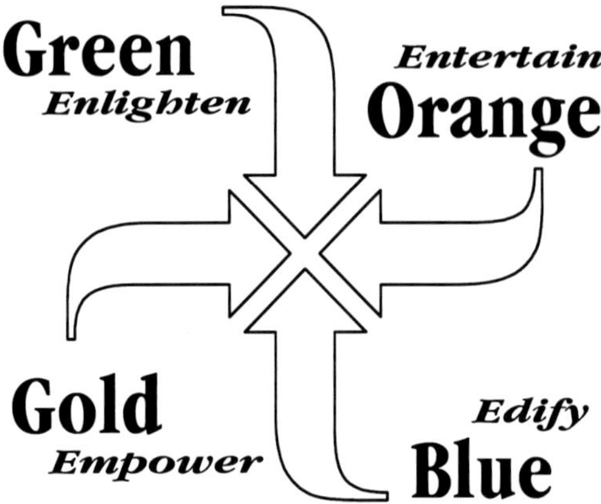

— *Edify*. Blues need to be uplifted—the more emotional their experience, the more they retain and the more they are influenced.

— *Empower*. Golds seek empowerment—their parts of the presentation should leave them better able to control and organize.

— *Enlighten*. Greens need to be enlightened—they must feel they're trading their time for something new that will increase their capabilities.

— *Entertain*. Oranges need to be entertained—let them have a good time. Make 'em laugh and you've made 'em yours.

When speaking one-to-many, be a little bee. Bounce from flower to flower, trying to keep all the colors involved. An Orange joke here, a quote from a Gold authority or outline there, a Green term now and then, and an inspirational story for the Blues. Do well, and your friends will be shocked at how quickly you learned to become such a captivating speaker.

Sample speech

Below is the introduction of a speech I wrote several years ago to introduce groups of people to one of my books on personality styles. Notice how you can talk to each segment of your audience by making sure you rotate through each color's particular style of language.

[Orange] Once upon a time, the very first man met the very first woman. What do you think they noticed first about each other? Do you think the man grunted and said, "Hey, you don't have a, um, um, a dictionary on you do you?"

[Green] Maybe. But chances are the first thing they probably noticed was how different they were from each other. Initially, that probably drew them together. Later, that probably drove them apart.

[Blue] So it continues today. Have you ever had a relationship go bad on you? Have you, or someone you know, suffered from a divorce that was caused by "irreconcilable differences"? How many of your dreams have been shattered because you were misunderstood?

[Green] In fact, if you want to look at the big picture, how many lives have been lost over the years because one group of people couldn't understand or tolerate another group and so they started a war to try to kill each other off?

[Gold] Thankfully, some of the greatest thinkers in the world have been working for centuries trying to explain these differences to us. They've made an awful lot of progress, although much of their work is way too wordy and way too technical for most of us to understand.

[Green] Well, for the last five years, I've been involved in translating some of this work so that it makes a lot more sense to people like you and me. In fact, I've even published some books about it. This little book here summarizes a lot of this information and presents it in truly meaningful ways.

[Blue] So why would you want to know this stuff? Because it can prevent you, and those you love, and those around you, from letting these "differences" destroy your dreams, ruin your relationships, and sabotage your successes.

[Green] Tonight, I'm here to persuade you to read this little booklet so you can learn how to understand people even better than they understand themselves and live happily ever after.

Physical layout

Another important aspect to consider is how your audience is seated. It's surprising how many chairs in hotel ballrooms are set up by people who have never been on a stage to look at them. You've got to control the physical environment as well as the content of your presentation.

Teachers face this situation everyday. Ever wonder why Miss Drake in the fourth grade was forever closing the curtains, opening the window, closing it again, turning the lights on an off when running a filmstrip or video, and occasionally telling people to move their chairs or turn their desks around? She knew that it was important to control what goes on around the audience as well as control what goes into them.

Interestingly, many of the attributes that hold true for individual colors hold true in larger groups as well. In thousands of seminars over the last decade, my colleagues and I have routinely administered the Insight Personality Instrument™ to groups of people. We then ask the participants to group themselves by color for further exercises. We send the Golds to the right rear of whatever room we are in, Green to the left rear, Blues to the front left, Oranges to the front right. It probably doesn't matter which group was assigned to which corner, except we quickly discovered that the Oranges could not be positioned near a door, or near anything with which they could make noise or cause distractions. We found that by corralling them in the front of the room we could better contain their boundless energy and need for action. In other words, we could keep an eye on them.

Once segregated in this position, however, the effects of combining like colors becomes apparent. Almost invariably, the presenter will look down after a few moments and see a pattern similar to the hotel conference room layout below.

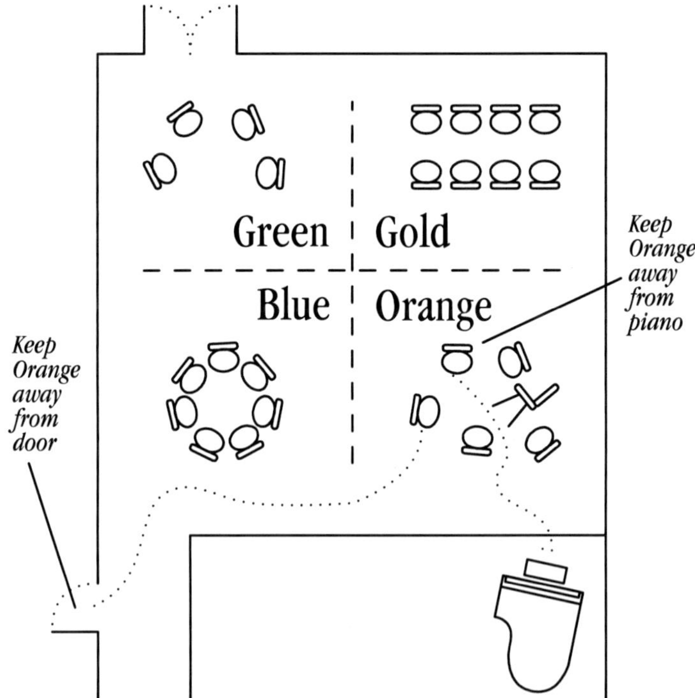

The Greens will have positioned their chairs far enough apart to keep to themselves, but close enough to try and look at everybody's notes. The Golds will have arranged their chairs in neat rows and be sitting quietly awaiting further instructions. The Blues will form a characteristic circle, knees touching knees. Unless we take special care right from the start, the Oranges have likely left the room already.

Speaking one-to-many is an exciting extension of the communications techniques you've learned in talking one-to-one. You're forced to depend a little more on the prototypical color style attributes, because your distance from the audience, or the sheer number of them, often makes it impossible to look for physical clues or audible responses. However, the principles we've discussed apply generally throughout many populations. Set up the environment so as to keep the folks comfortable and contain the Oranges, rotate your presentation so that you constantly appeal to each color, appear organized, end when you're supposed to, and you should be fine.

Chatting in Color

All conversation is not strictly business, even in business. One good friend, who it turns out is a high-powered career consultant, recently proffered this advice: You're on the elevator. Suddenly it stops, and in walks Mr. (or Ms.) Big. You have the incredible opportunity of face time with the person who built this place from the ground up. What do you say or do?

In the first place, you know you won't have much time. Unless the elevator gets stuck, one or the other of you will get off soon, or someone who *is* prepared will get on with you, seize the day, and edge you out of some potentially career-building moments.

The easiest thing would be to say nothing and pretend you have just turned into a potted ficus. Of course, this would also be the nowhere thing to do. You're blowing an opportunity, and at worst you could leave the impression with Mr. Big that you haven't a clue who he is, or else you don't care. And while it may be refreshing for him to share an elevator with someone who doesn't try to polish his apple, you may inadvertently give the impression of being indifferent, standoffish, or even hostile.

Given that you do try to speak, you have to face the issue of what to say and how to say it. Here is where your colors awareness will serve you well. Generally, on short notice, people do or say things that are natural for them. This means that unless you're careful, you may end up saying something that's less than stellar:

If you're Orange: "Say there, old buddy, how's it hangin'?" You slap the VIP on the back so hard it knocks his dental bridge loose. Expect the corporate security folks to be at your desk before you get there. Save time; jump into the dumpster by yourself.

If you're Blue: "Oh, my goodness, Hello! I was so thrilled when I read that our company is participating in those environmental hearings. I just hate those polluters, don't you? Is there anything I can do to help? Here, may I straighten that for you?" (Reach over and adjust his tie.) Nice try for being brief; low marks for trying to start a relationship rather than a conversation.

If you're Gold: "Say, you don't look that much better than me. I've got a portfolio too, you know." Oops—I'm sure we can find a hot dog stand for you to manage.

If you're Green: "Do you think cell phones give you brain cancer?" You're toast already. Your ticket to Graceland never comes via Dreamland. Stay relevant! On the other hand, "Interesting problems up in ______ Department…" won't help either. There are no interesting problems to anyone but a Green. To the rest of the planet, problems are things that need to be fixed. Actually, if you're Green, you might consider just pretending you're the ficus.

Truth is, you're headed for trouble unless you keep in mind the motto TOTOF, an acronym for "Think Of The Other Fellow." This is because, more than likely, the first thing that comes into your mind is something that's either interesting or problematic to someone of your own color spectrum. Your fifteen seconds of fame is probably best spent not using Mr. Big as a sounding board for your own concerns, but as an opportunity to build a communications bridge. To do that, talk about something that's interesting to the other fellow. Colors and chitchat can go hand in hand. The secret is to try and converse about something interesting to the person you're speaking with.

And how will you know what that is, or at least make a good guess? That you're reading this material means you're coming to the right place. You see, the answers are on the following pages.

Comfortable Blue chat

If your VIP has *People, US,* the *National Enquirer,* or knitting needles in some kind of craft bag, ask about holidays, kids, or vacation plans. You might even catch up on some celebrity gossip, or if the executive is a little more high brow, who is performing what at an upcoming symphony or opera.

Blues use conversation as a way to maintain human contact with co-workers and others, and also as a means to remind themselves for whom and why they do their daily labors. Some ideas as well as sources (in parentheses) are listed below:

— Home, hearth, family, either yours or theirs. (Best gained by conversations with others.)

— News and events that will make your community a better or a worse place to raise children. (Local newspapers, letters to the editor, city council meetings or minutes to meetings.)

— General style and fashion topics that tend towards the mainstream rather than the extreme. (Magazines, fashion coverage on *CNN, USA Today,* fashion magazines.)

— Health news, particularly about children or people of the age and station that you're both likely to meet. (Homemaking magazines, medical coverage on TV and National Public Radio.)

— Items relating to the acceptance or disenfranchisement of various groups. (The opinions and ideas section of the Sunday newspaper, PBS.)

— Recipes. (Cooking and homemaking magazines, cooking shows.)

— News affecting pre-school and elementary through high-school aged children. (PTA or PTO newsletters, parenting magazines, talking to teachers or principals, other parents.)

— Small, furry animals you may have seen; animal rescues. (Animal Planet, *National Geographic.*)

— Relationships, who is seeing whom, what is working, what isn't. If the office is too risky a place for such conversations, switch venues to soap operas, situation comedies, or dramatic TV series, such as *ER* or *Alias*. (Soap opera digests, celebrity magazines, *Entertainment Weekly*.)

— Comments about the length of days (more common up north) or weather, and how it affects the family's together time. (Almanacs, personal experience, conversations with friends.)

Safe talk for Golds

If the VIP has a *Wall Street Journal, Fortune,* or *Barron's* under his arm, that's a sign you're talking to a Gold. Comments about the stock market, state of the union, recent reductions in crime, anything that indicates that stable, tried-and-true principles are winning the day, may open the conversational door. You can gather these from the business section of your local paper, from a major national paper such as the *Christian Science Monitor, New York Times,* or *USA Today,* or from one of numerous news services on the Internet. You can scan them quickly. Keep the big picture in focus—the details will follow. Likely your VIP will have something to say as well.

Golds like to focus on business, community, and national issues that revolve around their values:

— News of charitable corporate giving in your area. (Newspaper business pages, regional papers, local and regional business journals.)

— The progress of recent high-profile police investigations—just make sure the topic of investigation is not the VIP's relative! (Local newspapers, occasionally TV, although coverage is likely deeper in the paper.)

— News events involving U.S. armed forces. (National sections of newspapers, on-line sections of national papers, newsmagazines.)

— Society statistics, such as trends regarding the number of births, marriages, etc. Most Golds would likely appreciate hearing good news on these topics. (Local papers, local government sites on the Internet.)

— Stock market trends, particularly old economy blue chips and stocks that have a hold or keep status. (*Wall Street Journal, Forbes, Barron's, USA Today.*)

— News about civic organizations such as Kiwanis, Lions Club, Rotary International, Sertoma. These are business-persons' clubs, usually meeting over a meal, where the atmosphere is cordial but commerce-oriented. Fraternal organizations, such as Eagles, Elks, and Moose often have a more playful agenda that typically involves a bar, although these organizations also do some charitable works. The former is likely always in good taste; the latter can be risky unless you know the VIP is comfortable with such organizations. (Organization newsletters, local papers.)

— Lawncare—not how much you hate it, but how the weather is treating your plants, talking about what kind of results either you or the VIP are getting, what might need to be done about the grounds at various community gathering places, etc. (Local newspapers, radio, and TV programs, reports from state extension services and other government agencies charged with such things.)

— Weather, crops, how good the tomatoes are looking this year, how much produce you dropped off at which charity, and so on. (Most nurseries and some feed stores have an abundance of this information.)

— Nice family vacation spots or recreational opportunities in your area. Say, "You know, the kids (or grandkids) really liked it when we went by Legend City. They have this new display about gun fighting that really makes you think. More kids should see that one, you know?" (Listen to other parents give reviews, also look for newsletters of parents' groups, PTAs, and so on.)

— Good movies and videos with a positive message that will inspire people to be more responsible. Biographies, histories, and rags-to-riches stories are often safe. (Movie reviews on TV, radio, and various Internet sites. Warning:

only talk about movies that you have seen, lest you suggest an oddball flick that works against you.)

Data bursting with Greens

If your VIP is wearing a lab coat, has a pocket protector, or is sporting a technical journal, ask if it's a tremendous pressure to keep up with all the changes. To decipher the answers, take one course in a community college on some technical topic each year just so the world doesn't pass you by. Don't worry if the material sails over your head; it will all be changed in a year anyway. Soak up the ambiance; see what folks are worried about and talking about. Also, many technical magazines are free if you just write on the reader service card that you're a senior design engineer in a department of 250 people and that you have authority over the budget.

Greens are extremely amiable and friendly creatures—in their own minds. To others, they often appear to be supercilious. But these are often just appearances; Greens are genuinely pained by the obvious, the redundant, the inefficient, the foolish. As a mongoose fights snakes, a Green goes after these intellectual plagues on society. Avoid being this way, and you should do fine.

Most Greens have a lot to say that they have suppressed. Once you do break ice with a Green, you might find yourself drowned in pent-up verbiage.

— Anything associated with the words *Pentium* or *gigahertz*. (If that sounds like a foreign language, watch some technical shows on TV, check into some hardware sites on the Internet, read the technology section of the newspaper.)

— Mean average anything that is increasing or decreasing. Greens like their observations pre-processed. (Newspapers, technical programs, such as *NOVA*, or something from the Discovery Channel.)

— The odds and how they're calculated on just about anything. (Articles, newspapers, Slashdot.org on the Internet.)

— The anticipation of new or experimental technologies. (Magazines, Internet.)

— Parallels between any *Star Trek* episode and a current situation at work. (*Star Trek* reruns, fan magazines, and web sites.)

— New electronic gadgets you have purchased or have heard about. (*PC Magazine* new-product reviews, TV.)

— The relationship of Wall Street stock price swings to the technologies that are held by companies, and why the market is or is not in step. (*Wall Street Journal, Wired* magazine, the Internet.)

— The weather and why it seems hotter or colder on top of a tall building. (Almanacs, Weather Channel.)

— Science fiction movies you have seen or want to see. (Movie reviews on TV or in the local paper.)

— Science news, International Space Station news, astronomical or meteorological observations. (Astronomy magazines, science section of newspaper or magazines.)

Fun talk for Oranges

If the VIP has *Sports Illustrated* folded into his overcoat pocket, you can always say, "So what about those ________," where you insert a local team name. Even if you hate sports, try to go to one game each season, just so you know the layout of the stadium and can mutter with authority about the parking. Also, try to know the rookies, the older players who may be near the end of their careers, and who the big upsets were in the current season. TV news is a good source for this.

Orange chitchat tends to be short and extreme. Conversations are a break, a reminder that there's life outside of the four walls of the office:

— Any controversial sports topics—which team member has a complaint, who has been arrested, etc. Also dramatic, close games, or solid trouncings. (Sports pages of local papers and "Sports Central"–type programs, usually found on weekends.)

— Dramatic police chases, rescues, fires, and other emergencies. (Local papers, TV.)

— Extreme anything—hang gliding, snowboarding, skateboarding, BMX bicycles, motocross racing, accidents at Indianapolis or other major races, scuba diving, skydiving, etc. (Television, some magazines.)

— Comments about outrageous fashions and apparel, spoken in a celebratory vein. (Overhearing co-workers, keeping one's ear to the ground, some celebrity magazines.)

— Upcoming holidays, breaks, and three-day weekends, dramatic vacation plans. (Available from a calendar near you.)

— Dramatic news items involving scandal, particularly of individuals who set themselves out as role models. Also that sketch you saw on the *Tonight Show* last night. (Nightly TV news, op-ed pages in newspapers.)

— Counter-cultural items, such as concerts, rallies, benefits for controversial causes. (Alternative newspapers.)

— Trendy and emerging night spots/activities. (Alternative newspapers, discussions with Orange friends.)

— Intense, high-energy activities, such as conventions, trade shows, sales retreats at exotic locales. (Friends in the industry.)

I don't know someone's color

Of course, your VIP may be wearing the standard nondescript overcoat, revealing next to nothing about his or her personality. Take that to mean Gold. Either they're Gold, or they're another color trying to "do" Gold. They will feel successful, maybe even flattered, if they think they've got the part down to the point that it fooled you.

Remember, elevators are not offices. They are for getting up in the world, not holding meetings. Don't try to have conversations in elevators, but shoot for conversation starters. You'll have a better chance of getting your chance if your VIP remembers you, at least subconsciously, as a positive contact. Today's encounter may set the stage for further exchanges.

Other topics for meaningful chitchat (and sources to find out more about them) include:

— *The recent actions of the government.* This includes the legislative, judicial, and executive branches of your federal, state, and city or county governments. Remember that if you're located near a state or national border, the affairs of neighboring governments may be even more interesting than your own. This information is carried, sometimes almost palatably, by newspapers and news and public affairs programming on National Public Radio and PBS. Better yet, go meet your elected leaders at any of several public venues, including their offices. Talking to a non-crackpot without a hidden agenda may be a genuine treat for them. And you will have some stories that begin, "Well, I was talking to (Sen.) Bobby Lovelady the other day, and he said. . . ."

— *The weather.* Knowing historic highs and lows, what may be coming soon, and how hot (or cool) it is in some other city today, all make good tidbits. ("They say it broke the 120-degree mark a day earlier than average in Phoenix this year" or "They have this Rainfair up in Washington, and they hit over a hundred inches this year.")

— *Interesting languages.* For example, know how to say the Klingon names of fifteen kinds of office furniture—OR DIE! (That's a Klingon thing.)

— *Facts on the competition.* You might also know a few facts and issues surrounding a number of your area's biggest companies. On-line services and area business journals are full of this sort of thing.

One other note: If you have been recently involved in an intense training program, such as medical school, you may find that you're absolutely out of touch with the world around you. This is normal. I tease young doctors about it all the time. There are two great things you can do about this. First, realize that you're now your own form of Mr. Big. All but a few people are interested in matters of health. Second, you can catch up on years of recent history in an afternoon by reading "This Year at a Glance" articles in December issues of popular magazines, in the periodicals section of the library, as well as recent almanacs. Also, if you have to come up to speed quickly on some subject you know little about, go to a book store and head for the study guides for advanced placement, SAT and ACT tests, and public service exams. Usually these guides are inexpensive, comprehensive, and easy to read.

Bonus chitchat tips

— If you get the other person talking, keep it that way. Never do more than two-fifths of the speaking.

— Offering different points of view is fine if it's your nature, but do so in an "Isn't that amazing, what do you think about that" tone, rather than a confrontational one. Greens need to watch themselves on this one.

— If you do manage to put your foot in your mouth, or believe that you might have, don't fret about it. It was just a conversation in an elevator.

Talking the Talk

Becoming one with the listener

I've made some hefty promises about how knowledge of temperament can revolutionize your communications with others. Now it's time to take a test drive. Armed with a little knowledge of what a given color will typically act like and aware of your own color spectrum, you are ready to step out and practice controlled empathy.

You've heard of empathy: the ability to see the world from the point of view of the person you are speaking to. On *Star Trek,* empaths can take upon themselves the suffering and illness of another, and then pass it to the environment. John Coffey, the hero of *The Green Mile,* could be said to be an empath.

Those are the exceptions, the stuff of fantasy. Practical empathy, however, is attainable and highly useful. Now that you've mastered the knowledge mentioned above, you are halfway home. Colors make it easy.

We can't possibly communicate effectively unless we first know the audience. Obviously, understanding someone's personality style is the easiest way to make some general conclusions about that person. It speeds up the process of "knowing the audience." Then, once we know the person's color, we can safely make some assumptions and employ the stratagem that can guide us closer to our target.

The wise owl

To visualize this using a metaphor from nature, imagine yourself to be a kindly owl. You're perched in a tall tree, on a high branch that overlooks the broad valley below. You see movement in the distance and recognize it to be human. Because you've befriended the humans in your area, and because you're wise, they often seek you out for advice. The path to your tree is long and difficult for a man. He must stumble and climb and slip and climb some more. Because you're an owl and can fly, you frequently reach out to these men who seek you by spanning the distance for them.

You step into space and unfurl your great wings. You catch the rush of wind and stop your fall, and then the mountain updrafts lift you to the height from which you started. You let the breeze flip through your back wing feathers as you effortless glide towards your visitor. "Whoo-oo is this?" you wonder. "Whoo-oo is coming to see me?"

Because you're wise, you know yourself. You understand your personal color spectrum and how it shapes your view of the world. This allows you to moderate your approach to the visiting human in such a way that you appear less threatening. Now your task is to understand the person you will be speaking with.

Because your eyes are powerful, you can already tell many things about your visitor. The style of clothes and the way they are worn suggest to you a person of great substance. Further, his walk and his posture when he rests imply a sense of mission and purpose. You begin to see frown lines on his forehead, which suggest he is deeply concerned about something. "How unlike a Gold to come seek advice of an owl in the forest!" you exclaim. "Whoo-oo is he?"

You grow closer now and begin to exercise some reasonable caution. The man is alone and doesn't seem to be carrying a bow or a sling. You glide onward, and your mind races ahead.

Because you're meeting a Gold, the way you conduct yourself and the way you appear will speak much to this man. Thank heaven you preened your feathers early this morning. And also, no fancy landings. Golds appreciate quality, not ostentation, in word and deed.

You extend you talons, flay your feathers far apart, and catch a nearby branch with perfect steadiness. You rock a bit from the exertion, but you try and keep it to yourself. After a respectable interval in which the man looks at you, you say again, "Whoo-oo?" The dialogue begins.

Operating on your initial observation that this was a Gold, you have formulated a few questions to help you verify your guess. After pleasantries, you slip one in. "Bingo!" you say to yourself, "Gold!" Now you are ready to try to guess the second color, which you suspect to be Blue. Wrong! It's Green!

Now that your have a firm idea of your visitor's primary and secondary colors, you still have no idea of what he wants from this visit. But that will be easier now, because you know where to start and you have a good ear for colors. As the man speaks, you from time to time voice back to him items about the issue he's facing. You're able to do this accurately, because knowledge of his personality has already given you an idea about how he feels about each item of his story, what it means to him. This creates in the man a feeling of reassurance that you understand and that perhaps, you are a kindred spirit.

At length, the man finishes: "... and when I saw that I just did not know what to do, nor did I see how I could learn what to do, my friends saw my sadness, and they told me I should talk to you."

Gently you counsel the man. It's what wise owls do. Your ideas are obvious to you, probably would be to anybody, but you're helping this man over his own unique hurdle. If he could see it, it probably wouldn't be his problem.

Because you're empathic and understand colors, when you finally speak your words hit their mark easily. The man listens, then cries, then dries his eyes and thanks you. "You have been such a help, Wise Owl," he says, and then turns to leave, but he pauses.

"You know, I don't often talk to folks about things like this," he said. "But I feel that you understand. How do you do it, Wise Owl?" It was exactly the question you'd expect from a Green, and one too forward for a Gold.

"I've been an owl for some time," you answer. "And after a while, one comes to understand that people aren't so very different." It was the most owlish thing you've said this whole day. In truth, people are very much alike, but all are not the same color. This simple understanding, that an infinite variety of four basic hues paints the entire human family and lets them tell their stories, is one of wisdom's great secrets. "And yet, it is so easy to learn," you muse.

But your job is not done yet. Your visitor is Gold, and he will expect a Gold departure. Although you are jubilant—you always are at times like this—there must be no high-fives, at least not where this man can see them. No chest-thumping grouse moves for you, just now. Instead, you step off your branch, let the wind catch you, and then beat majestically home.

A few final words on words

The empathy concept, that of trying to act and think like the other person in order to communicate more effectively, has two dimensions, an external and internal representation. External empathy is to speak and listen the way they do, reflecting their communication style much like a mirror, putting them at ease and thereby tearing down some perceived barriers, reflecting the form, style, and substance of their message. Internal empathy is trying to identify with their perspective and interpret the message the way they would interpret it.

Both of these forms require a fair amount of insight and practice to be successful. As I've stated, we must first learn what the person's communication styles are, and then, because we've read the chapters on Values and Motivation and understand their thought processes, we can move to the third stage and work out, through trial and error, how to gain enough self-control to keep our own personality style from overly coloring and warping our perspectives. In short, we must shift our communication paradigms and become one with our listener.

And of course, we must know ourselves. It's work, to be sure. The results, however, can be astounding. It's a power tool for communication truly fit for kind owls and other wise birds.

CHAPTER 4

Work: Getting What You Want From the Workplace

This chapter will begin by explaining how to choose a career that reflects your natural work preferences. Then it will tell you how to use your strengths to be successful in any job, regardless of whether or not you truly enjoy it.

Choosing the Perfect Career

> "Choose a job you love, and you will never have to work a day in your life."
>
> — CONFUCIUS

As children we were regularly asked the question, "So what do you want to be when you grow up?" Throughout most of the twentieth century, nearly everyone had one stable career where they could work for twenty-five to forty years before retiring. Unfortunately, those days seem to have disappeared from modern life, much like the humble vinyl phonograph record. Even the venerable professions that require extensive post-graduate education aren't as secure as they once were.

If you are employed, or perhaps retired, chances are good that you may one day be compelled to find a new job. Therefore, this chapter is for you. Of course, if you're not currently earning an income, but desperately want to, then this chapter is unquestionably for you.

First, we'll begin by looking at job preferences. People of each temperament choose these occupations over other jobs. Then we'll look at your natural strengths as a worker to see what intrinsic assets you bring to the workplace. Finally, we'll examine how to enjoy any job, regardless of whether or not you really want to do it.

Picking the right job

Imagine a world populated by one temperament. Let's say it was inhabited by Greens—who are so few in numbers on this planet that they really ought to have one of their own. What would our Greenland look like?

Perhaps it would be a technologically advanced civilization, where people spent most of their waking hours learning, researching, inventing, improving, postulating, and conceiving (not to be confused with a procreative activity). In this world, natives develop faster ways to travel, quicker ways to learn, more efficient ways to eat, better ways to produce offspring. Perhaps they live in a self-contained domed city, where self-sustaining citizens don't live in traditional family units since they spend every hour perfecting their skills and don't have the time or desire to interact unnecessarily. Instead, they live in a laboratory-like room filled with all the resources they need to perform their labors. When they're too tired to work, they unfold a futon and sleep until they're rested. There's no need to leave the workspace unless they want to. There's no hoarding of stuff and things. There's no need for money. There's no jockeying for position or jumping through bureaucratic hoops. Everyone freely shares resources, knowledge, and skills with others. It's a Utopia—for Greens.

Other temperaments wouldn't feel comfortable at all visiting such a place. It would be an exceedingly bizarre world, filled with weird Green aliens with seemingly enormous brains who spend their entire lives conducting experiments. Where's the romance and passion? Where are the athletic competitions and sporting events? How about conferences, conventions, and caucuses? Are there concerts, movies, and monster truck rallies? Are there amusement parks, casinos, and resorts? Where are the elections, the power lunches, the planning meetings, the family reunions? "Eeek!" the extraterrestrial visitors shriek. "Get me off this wacky planet!"

Now, let's leave this reverie and return to our Earth and our humdrum discussion of employment. Why did I take you on this apparent tangent? What's the moral to the story? And what does it have to do with the world of work?

If you were an Orange, Blue, or Gold and had to toil for the rest of your life in the environment I described, wouldn't you feel as out of place as a snowflake in the Sahara? Wouldn't you be a tad peeved that your values and strengths weren't appreciated, let alone accommodated? Wouldn't you do everything within your power to leave and find people who were more like you? Can you imagine how someone feels when they're forced to work in a place where their unique traits and talents are disregarded time and again?

On the other hand, most of us would be thrilled to work in an environment that catered to our specific values and needs. In fact, if we knew that the values and needs of others would be met in other places, so everyone had what they required to be happy and content, we'd be overjoyed. What more could we want for ourselves and others?

Can such a place exist in reality? Absolutely. It has existed in ancient times, it exists at the present, and it will exist in the future. Where, you say? If I could take you on a field trip throughout the world, we'd see this environment in tens of thousands of workplaces, including assembly plants, warehouses, showrooms, boardrooms, office buildings—the list goes on. In fact, if you take a look at some of the most successful businesses and organizations in the world, you'll see that they, as a rule, accommodate the preferences of their employees—whether they know they're doing it or not!

Fantasyland

Let's take a division of the Walt Disney Company as an example—the Disneyland park in California. Since 1955 it has been one of the most successful theme parks in the world, attracting millions of visitors each year. Even though you might not have worked there, chances are you've probably visited the park or one of its clones at least once in your life. Let's imagine what kinds of jobs you'd find in the park, and which temperaments would probably enjoy performing those jobs.

What would Blues enjoy? Talking and interacting with visitors. Donning the character costumes and frolicking with the kiddies. Serving food, selling souvenirs, singing and dancing in the parades and events. Guiding tours, seating guests, reuniting lost children with their parents. They would use their creative talents behind the scenes in creating fanciful costumes, applying make-up, and designing floats. Perhaps they'd be in charge of taking care of the horses that draw the streetcars. All of these activities appeal to Blue sensitivities.

What would Golds enjoy doing? Managing the work schedules of the thousands of "cast members" who make the park operate. Setting the timetables for the opening hours, the parades, and the special events. Planning for and executing the nightly cleaning and maintenance rituals and the ongoing refurbishments. Ringing up purchases, taking tickets, controlling ride access, performing inventories of merchandise, balancing the books, keeping the park free of debris, setting up and taking down the temporary gates and chains that keep the lines moving and the crowds contained.

Our future-thinking Greens prefer the design and development work, often staying "backstage" or in the underground labyrinth. They are the *imagineers*, and have a massive job in creating new rides and attractions and in developing new technologies and innovations. They are often found around the computers that control and monitor the rides and attractions. They also staff information booths, where they can sit back and wait for people to approach them with questions. They like working in shops or exhibits where they can demonstrate their skills without having to say much to the clients—like blowing or etching glass, making candy, drawing caricatures, or sewing names on Mickey Mouse hats.

Oranges enjoy making things happen. If there are buttons to push, levers to pull, bushes to trim, eggs to break, taffy to pull, fireworks to ignite, canoes to paddle, roller coasters to test, vehicles to drive, attractions to build—then they're as happy as, well, Happy the dwarf. Oranges also enjoy being in the limelight, so along with the Blues, they participate in the parades, productions, and roving entertainment groups—although they quickly get bored with doing the same act repeatedly, preferring to adjust their performance on the fly to make their jobs more improvisational and unpredictable.

But imagine the pain and suffering an employee would experience if he or she were placed in a job that didn't suit the appropriate personality style. Imagine putting an introverted Green in charge of greeting and chitchatting with guests. Or placing an extroverted Orange in a small windowless office compiling attendance reports. Or having a Gold improvise a comedy routine in a stage show. Or having a Blue stare at computer screens to make sure the audio-animatronic Abe Lincoln doesn't start break dancing. I'm sure each of these employees would—given enough coaching—be able to do the job adequately; they just wouldn't enjoy doing it. And before long, you'd have an extra Grumpy on your hands, one who doesn't enjoy the work and certainly won't whistle while doing it.

Realityland

You may say that this philosophy works fine for a huge organization like Disneyland, which is really a self-contained city with every occupation represented, from firefighters to street cleaners to engineers. But what about a small business that builds model-sized Stirling cycle engines? The principle holds true.

Let's pretend you're the sole proprietor of this burgeoning business, and it's time to hire three part-time employees. You need someone to answer the phones, take orders, and talk to the customers. A Blue person would probably enjoy doing that people-centered job. You need a technical person to assemble and tweak the engines. Many Greens would enjoy this job. And finally, you need someone to inventory, package, ship, bill, and manage the bookkeeping. A Gold may enjoy doing this job more than the other colors. Would you want to hire an Orange to do these non-Orange activities? Maybe you would; maybe you wouldn't. An Orange may be highly skilled in one of these areas and would do a superb job. Hire that person immediately. But these activities don't normally attract Oranges. Since these jobs don't appeal to Orange values, they don't produce joy. An individual who doesn't enjoy doing his or her job usually won't do it for long. Therefore, it would be a waste of your time to hire an Orange. Given the choice, it's always best—for the employer and the employee—to accommodate personality preferences.

In workshops I've conducted over the years, I've asked people of each color to identify the jobs they would enjoy doing. Time after time I've seen that certain colors prefer certain jobs. Surprise, surprise! Below is a list of the jobs that people of each temperament prefer to do. This isn't an exhaustive list by any means, but it will give you a push in the right direction.

> "To find out what one is fitted to do, and to secure an opportunity to do it, is the key to happiness."
>
> — JOHN DEWEY

Blue Occupations

Blues enjoy jobs that allow them to concentrate on people and relationships. They're drawn towards occupations that focus on service and the health and welfare of other people. They work best in warm, supportive, harmonious environments where workers are free to cooperate and communicate with each other. Blues are imaginative, enthusiastic, and concerned about the personal welfare of those around them. They dislike competition, conflict, bureaucracy, and domineering authority figures. They promote creativity, flexibility, individuality, and personal expression.

Business

- ☐ Advertising specialist
- ☐ Communications director
- ☐ Consultant
- ☐ Counter sales
- ☐ Fund-raiser
- ☐ Human resources manager
- ☐ Job analyst
- ☐ Marketing consultant
- ☐ Nonprofit organization director
- ☐ Receptionist
- ☐ Sales manager
- ☐ Small business executive

Communication

- ☐ Columnist
- ☐ Copy writer
- ☐ Creative writer
- ☐ Editor
- ☐ Journalist
- ☐ Newscaster
- ☐ Novelist
- ☐ Playwright
- ☐ Poet
- ☐ Public relations specialist
- ☐ Publicist
- ☐ Reporter
- ☐ Screenwriter
- ☐ Speech writer
- ☐ TV producer
- ☐ Writer

Counseling

- ☐ Career counselor
- ☐ Conflict resolution specialist
- ☐ Employee assistance counselor
- ☐ Job placement counselor

- ☐ Mediator
- ☐ Mental health counselor
- ☐ Moderator
- ☐ Natural/holistic health advisor
- ☐ Personal counselor
- ☐ Personnel director
- ☐ Psychologist

Creative arts

- ☐ Actor
- ☐ Architect
- ☐ Artist
- ☐ Cartoonist
- ☐ Decorator
- ☐ Designer
- ☐ Entertainer
- ☐ Illustrator
- ☐ Inventor
- ☐ Music composer
- ☐ Musician

Education

- ☐ Art teacher
- ☐ Dean of students
- ☐ Educational consultant
- ☐ English teacher
- ☐ Facilitator
- ☐ Guidance counselor
- ☐ Health teacher
- ☐ Humanities teacher
- ☐ Librarian
- ☐ Music teacher
- ☐ Pastoral counselor
- ☐ Preschool teacher
- ☐ Researcher
- ☐ Social science teacher
- ☐ Special education teacher
- ☐ Staff development trainer

Religion

- ☐ Choir leader
- ☐ Church leader (minister/rabbi/priest)
- ☐ Church worker (monk/nun/volunteer)
- ☐ Charitable functions director
- ☐ Missionary
- ☐ Religious educator

Service

- ☐ Conference planner
- ☐ Flight attendant

- ☐ Health care administrator
- ☐ Hotel services worker
- ☐ Leasing agent
- ☐ Recreational director
- ☐ Recruiter
- ☐ Rehabilitation worker
- ☐ Restaurateur
- ☐ Social scientist
- ☐ Social services worker
- ☐ Tour guide
- ☐ Travel agent

Gold Occupations

Golds prefer jobs that allow them to be thorough, accurate, and systematic. They prefer to work in situations where they can see a job through to the end, and then touch and feel the results. They're practical, efficient, and cooperative workers that respect authority, discipline, and punctuality. They want to work in environments that are traditional, structured, orderly, and filled with other hard-working people. They have a compelling need to follow established procedures and routines, and do things the "right" way. They're stable, honest, and dependable workers who generally put the needs of the company above their own.

Business

- ☐ Administrator
- ☐ Clerical supervisor
- ☐ Computer operator
- ☐ Customer service representative
- ☐ Efficiency analyst
- ☐ Factory supervisor
- ☐ Office manager
- ☐ Personnel administrator
- ☐ Project manager
- ☐ Receptionist
- ☐ Retail business owner/operator
- ☐ Sales representative
- ☐ Secretary
- ☐ Supervisor
- ☐ Telemarketer
- ☐ Typist

Education

- ☐ Athletic coach
- ☐ Child care worker
- ☐ Economics teacher
- ☐ Elementary school teacher

- ☐ Government teacher
- ☐ Guidance counselor
- ☐ History teacher
- ☐ Home economics teacher
- ☐ Industrial arts teacher
- ☐ Librarian
- ☐ Mathematics teacher
- ☐ Personal counselor
- ☐ Physical education teacher
- ☐ School administrator
- ☐ School principal
- ☐ Special education teacher

Finance

- ☐ Accountant
- ☐ Auditor
- ☐ Bank examiner
- ☐ Bank teller
- ☐ Bookkeeper
- ☐ Cashier
- ☐ Credit analyst
- ☐ Estate planner
- ☐ Insurance agent
- ☐ Insurance underwriter
- ☐ Investment securities officer
- ☐ Loan officer
- ☐ Payroll clerk
- ☐ Personal banker
- ☐ Purchasing agent
- ☐ Real estate broker
- ☐ Stockbroker
- ☐ Tax examiner

Government/civil service

- ☐ Air traffic controller
- ☐ Community welfare worker
- ☐ Corrections officer
- ☐ Government employee
- ☐ IRS agent
- ☐ Judge
- ☐ Law enforcement officer
- ☐ Legislator
- ☐ Military officer
- ☐ Politician
- ☐ Post office worker
- ☐ Probation officer
- ☐ Public administrator
- ☐ Social worker
- ☐ Telephone operator

Health care

- ☐ Dental hygienist
- ☐ Dentist
- ☐ Dietitian
- ☐ Exercise physiologist
- ☐ Family physician
- ☐ General surgeon
- ☐ Health care administrator
- ☐ Hospital administrator
- ☐ Lab technologist
- ☐ Medical equipment salesperson
- ☐ Medical secretary
- ☐ Medical assistant
- ☐ Nurse
- ☐ Nursing administrator
- ☐ Optometrist
- ☐ Pharmacist
- ☐ Physical therapist
- ☐ Radiology technician
- ☐ Veterinarian

Human services

- ☐ Caterer
- ☐ Cook
- ☐ Cosmetologist
- ☐ Counselor
- ☐ Customer service representative
- ☐ Detective
- ☐ Flight attendant
- ☐ Fund-raiser
- ☐ Funeral director
- ☐ Host/hostess
- ☐ Innkeeper
- ☐ Museum curator
- ☐ Professional volunteer
- ☐ Religious educator
- ☐ Religious leader (minister/priest/rabbi)
- ☐ Salesperson
- ☐ Security guard

Technical

- ☐ Attorney
- ☐ Clinical technician
- ☐ Computer analyst
- ☐ Computer programmer
- ☐ Construction worker
- ☐ Court reporter
- ☐ Database manager
- ☐ Electrician

- ☐ Engineer
- ☐ Farmer
- ☐ General contractor
- ☐ Law researcher
- ☐ Legal secretary
- ☐ Mechanic
- ☐ Mechanical engineer
- ☐ Technical writer

Green Occupations

Greens are driven towards work that involves an analytical and creative focus. They're visionary and independent workers who can tune out the world as they work on things that capture their interest. They're most productive when they can perfect an idea, then move on and leave the project to be maintained and supported by others. They work well with complex strategies, abstract concepts, and theoretical models. They prefer a work environment with minimal structure and little bureaucracy. They don't mind taking risks in order to test their innovative ideas. Their biggest asset is their drive to be competent, logical, and accurate.

Business

- ☐ Administrator
- ☐ Entrepreneur
- ☐ Executive
- ☐ Marketing manager
- ☐ Office manager
- ☐ Personnel manager
- ☐ Sales manager
- ☐ Senior manager

Consulting/planning

- ☐ Business consultant
- ☐ Educational consultant
- ☐ Employment development specialist
- ☐ Labor relations specialist
- ☐ Management consultant
- ☐ Management trainer
- ☐ News analyst
- ☐ Program designer
- ☐ Strategic planner
- ☐ Urban planner

Creative Arts

- ☐ Actor
- ☐ Architect
- ☐ Artist

- ☐ Creative writer
- ☐ Critic
- ☐ Designer
- ☐ Editor
- ☐ Editorial writer
- ☐ Entertainer
- ☐ Graphic designer
- ☐ Inventor
- ☐ Journalist
- ☐ Literary agent
- ☐ Musician
- ☐ Photographer
- ☐ Writer

Finance

- ☐ Business analyst
- ☐ Credit investigator
- ☐ Economic analyst
- ☐ Economist
- ☐ Investment analyst
- ☐ Mortgage broker
- ☐ Personal financial planner
- ☐ Stockbroker
- ☐ Venture capitalist

Education

- ☐ Academic curriculum designer
- ☐ Administrator
- ☐ Mathematics teacher
- ☐ Science teacher
- ☐ Social science teacher
- ☐ University professor/researcher

Technical

- ☐ Anthropologist
- ☐ Archaeologist
- ☐ Astronomer
- ☐ Biologist
- ☐ Botanist
- ☐ Chemical engineer
- ☐ Chemist
- ☐ Computer programmer
- ☐ Computer software designer
- ☐ Computer systems analyst
- ☐ Database manager
- ☐ Design engineer
- ☐ Ecologist
- ☐ Electrical technician
- ☐ Electronic technician
- ☐ Engineer

- ☐ Environmental planner
- ☐ Geophysicist
- ☐ Industrial design manager
- ☐ Marine biologist
- ☐ Mathematician
- ☐ Nuclear engineer
- ☐ Physicist
- ☐ Research and development specialist
- ☐ Scientific researcher
- ☐ Scientist
- ☐ Statistician
- ☐ Surveyor

Medicine

- ☐ Biomedical engineer
- ☐ Cardiologist
- ☐ Embalmer
- ☐ Medical examiner
- ☐ Neurologist
- ☐ Pharmacist
- ☐ Pharmacologist
- ☐ Physician
- ☐ Physician assistant
- ☐ Plastic surgeon
- ☐ Podiatrist
- ☐ Psychiatrist
- ☐ Psychoanalyst
- ☐ Psychologist
- ☐ Veterinarian

Social sciences

- ☐ Attorney
- ☐ Criminologist
- ☐ FBI agent
- ☐ Historian
- ☐ Judge
- ☐ Philosopher
- ☐ Political analyst
- ☐ Political manager
- ☐ Politician
- ☐ Social scientist

Orange Occupations

Oranges tackle their work with enthusiasm so they can quickly move on to other pursuits. They're great at working under pressure and prefer to work on jobs that are lively, risky, and unpredictable. They grow restless with jobs that tie them down and limit their personal freedom. They're straightforward, realistic, and practical workers who bring flair, energy, and excitement to the workplace. They're talented, resourceful, skillful, and adaptable. Because of their upbeat and sociable natures, they usually present a positive image of themselves and their company. They're action-oriented workers who know how to get the results they desire.

Business

- ☐ Advertising specialist
- ☐ Entrepreneur
- ☐ Fund-raiser
- ☐ Labor relations
- ☐ Marketing specialist
- ☐ Office manager
- ☐ Public relations specialist
- ☐ Purchasing agent
- ☐ Real estate agent
- ☐ Salesperson
- ☐ Wholesaler

Civil service

- ☐ Astronaut
- ☐ Detective
- ☐ Fighter pilot
- ☐ Fire fighter
- ☐ Intelligence agent
- ☐ Law enforcement officer
- ☐ Mediator
- ☐ Paramedic
- ☐ Politician
- ☐ Religious leader
- ☐ Social worker
- ☐ Soldier
- ☐ Test pilot
- ☐ Weapons operator

Creative arts

- ☐ Commercial artist
- ☐ Craftsperson
- ☐ Designer
- ☐ Fashion designer
- ☐ Illustrator
- ☐ Jeweler
- ☐ Painter
- ☐ Potter
- ☐ Sculptor

Education

- ☐ Art teacher
- ☐ Athletic coach

- ☐ Drama teacher
- ☐ Elementary school teacher
- ☐ Industrial arts teacher
- ☐ Music teacher
- ☐ Physical education teacher
- ☐ Trainer

Entertainment

- ☐ Actor
- ☐ Bartender
- ☐ Broadcast technician
- ☐ Comedian
- ☐ Dancer
- ☐ Disc jockey
- ☐ Film producer
- ☐ Musician
- ☐ News reporter
- ☐ Photographer
- ☐ Professional athlete
- ☐ Professional coach
- ☐ Promoter
- ☐ Public speaker
- ☐ Race car driver
- ☐ Sportscaster
- ☐ Tour agent
- ☐ Tour operator
- ☐ Travel agent

Finance

- ☐ Banker
- ☐ Insurance sales
- ☐ Investor
- ☐ Personal financial planner
- ☐ Securities analyst
- ☐ Stockbroker

Health care

- ☐ Chiropractor
- ☐ Dental assistant
- ☐ Fitness trainer
- ☐ Massage therapist
- ☐ Medical assistant
- ☐ Physical therapist
- ☐ Radiology technologist
- ☐ Sports nutritionist
- ☐ Veterinarian
- ☐ Visiting nurse

Service

- ☐ Beautician

- ☐ Crisis hot-line operator
- ☐ Flight attendant
- ☐ Floral designer
- ☐ Host/hostess
- ☐ Legal secretary
- ☐ Receptionist
- ☐ Secretary
- ☐ Waiter

Technical

- ☐ Botanist
- ☐ Computer operator
- ☐ Computer programmer
- ☐ Computer repair person
- ☐ Electrical technician
- ☐ Forester
- ☐ Geologist
- ☐ Surveyor

Trades

- ☐ Auctioneer
- ☐ Carpenter
- ☐ Chef
- ☐ Construction worker
- ☐ Cook
- ☐ Dog trainer
- ☐ Farmer
- ☐ Gardener
- ☐ General contractor
- ☐ Hunter
- ☐ Mechanic
- ☐ Pilot
- ☐ Store keeper
- ☐ Tapestry worker
- ☐ Truck driver

Worker Strengths

As a worker, you possess a set of inborn characteristics and strengths that, when properly used, will serve you and your employer exceptionally well. This section explores some of the work-related attributes that appear in each temperament.

What are your strengths as a worker? Furthermore, do you know the strong points of your manager or other coworkers? Knowing this information—and applying it—will help you work better on team projects, reduce personal stress, and resolve interpersonal conflicts. As a result, your job might transform itself from work into play.

Blue Worker Strengths

> People first, that's me. Wherever I am—at home, at work, at church, in my neighborhood—I think, "How can I make people matter here?" I can't always choose where I'll be asked to go or what I'll have to do, but I can always keep people first as I do it. Most people thrive when you do this.
>
> So many people just go gray and disappear behind their jobs, papers, and obligations. I couldn't bear that. Even when I have to act or dress a certain way, I still try to be unique, even if it is just the way I comb my hair or smile.
>
> It really bothers me when people quarrel. Why can't everybody just get along? In most cases people listen to me, so I often am the peacemaker. Most people really calm down if you just listen to them. Some people say I do that well. Another thing that gets to me is when people are two-faced. I'm sincere and open. If you hide behind a mask, that's okay. But if you act like we've connected and then later I find you were just leading me on, that really hurts me.
>
> The way I see it, work is just another thing that people do together, so we might as well all remain people while we do it. That's why I like people jobs. Hey, I can help people and get paid for it!
>
> — HENRI BAKKER, BLUE

Blue workers are authentic and caring. They see the good in people and organizations, and visualize the possibilities. They prefer to communicate in uplifting and enthusiastic ways. They add value by keeping you (and others) close to them. They create highly individualized workspaces, size up situations by what has gone before, adjust to accommodate individual differences and needs, and make decisions using empathy and personal values. They're sensitive and idealistic workers that occasionally need a pat on the back.

Are authentic and caring

Blues prefer to care for people, even in their work, so they gravitate towards service-oriented jobs, and seek out activities within those jobs that allow them to make the most difference in the lives of others. This permits the Blue to stay true to his or her internal charter. Even if a Blue's work includes chores that aren't pleasant—say conducting annual reviews or dismissing workers the corporation has determined to be unessential—a Blue can be counted on to do these tasks with decency and with the concerns of the workers clearly in mind.

See the good and visualize the possibilities

Given their need to nurture, the Blue worker sees the positive in coworkers, departments, and organizations. This means they always see the possibilities in the institutions they serve in and the people they serve with. When times are tough or friction enters the ranks, this provides them with a source of inspiration. They're likely to promote the organization and cheer coworkers onward when things look bleak. After all, even if the organization seems to have lost its way, there are still first-rate people within that organization.

Use uplifting, enthusiastic communications

If at all possible, Blues will accentuate the positive. This leads to infectious enthusiasm in their communications, with the good news switching between company results, new sales, exciting new prospects, or the company bowling team as required—essentially reporting on wherever the bad news isn't. Blues motivate by love and gentle persuasion, certainly not by fear or force, so they will build up and promote whatever positives they can find in the hope that they can weather difficulties more easily. This often puts Blues in the position of being patron saints of sinking ships. It does, however, keep them out of a lot of trouble, so when things do turn around, Blues are often among those left standing.

Add value by keeping you (and others) close

Blues sense innately that people are the ultimate resource. They keep them close, maintaining connections in many departments and companies. Interestingly, this significantly increases the Blue's value. When a Green boss has need to contact a modular human—a role rather than a soul—it's likely the Blue assistants who will track that person down. Even more surprising, the person that can get the boss's request done may not be the obvious choice based on the organization chart. Blues also keep links active by following up now and then, even if people move to a different department. Knowing people at this level allows Blues to form and nourish relationships that extend, perhaps even defy, traditional organizational boundaries.

Create highly individualized workspaces

A Blue simply won't get lost in a crowd, and this extends to the workspace. Look for Blues to bring in personal photos of their children, spouse, significant other, or pets. I have even seen strong Blues bring in a small houseplant, and take it home with them at shift's end, just to have a bit of themselves near them as they labor. The first cubicle or office to sprout macramé, plants, photos, needlework, or a kid's crayon drawings is likely a Blue's.

Need a pat on the back

Blues require constant reassurance that they're doing a good job at a significant task. They need their work to matter, and if it matters, then people are likely to comment about it. In order to stimulate the flow of comments and compliments, Blues are willing to give out the same freely. Blues thus pass out and receive strokes at the slightest provocation.

Size up situations by what has gone before

A Blue remembers. Their lives are the sum of their interactions, and although they're infinitely forgiving, they also know when they're being walked on, sort of like a doormat with a flight recorder. This means that when a Blue enters a new situation, the yardstick by which he or she assesses it is likely to be buried deep within. In a completely foreign situation, Blues are likely to judge matters by the people they're with—"John is here; he'll figure things out"—or by environmental considerations—"Oh look! A windowsill where I can put some plants."

Adjust to accommodate individual needs

Blues are the very definition of "reasonable accommodation." They're often the first to see that the group can easily accommodate the needs of individuals if certain simple changes are put into place. As a result, much stress is alleviated, and increasingly, anti-discrimination laws continue to be obeyed.

Make decisions using empathy and personal values

A Blue must live with his or herself, and they can only assure that by being true to the highest values they have within them. In a perfect world, no one would be laid-off or fired, but when these choices are dictated, Blue is likely to be able to go forward only by finding some way to reconcile the situation with an internal value, such as "the good of the many comes before the good of the one." When the decision could have a devastating effect on others, Blues are likely to consider ways in which it could be made better by sacrificing themselves. This can lead the Blue into forming strange entanglements with problematic individuals, which relationships they will then defend by seeking out the best in and believing in those individuals.

Are sensitive and idealistic

Dealing with a Blue can be frustrating, because they sometimes engage in a clear communication with you and then fail to take action. Even though they can tell you exactly what was expected and why, it's as if there is a hidden set of chocks sometimes firmly holding the Blue's tires. What is the nature of this mysterious force? Likely it's the Blue's sensitivity and idealism getting in the way of his or her capacity. Like a physician whose hands are tied by an oath to "First do no harm," the Blue may balk if an assignment may hurt another. In an ideal world, most people would live closer to Blue's native ideals, and no one would ever have to hurt someone else or make anyone afraid. A Blue may be loath to leave this idealistic mind-set, because to do so would set the stage for further perceived abuses of power.

One way to work around this is to ask the Blue up front if he or she can see how proposed changes would be harmful to the affected parties in the long run. Chances are, once a Blue thinks it through, there may be a way to execute your changes without undue negative influence on others.

Blue Workers

Are authentic and caring
See the good and visualize the possibilities
Use uplifting, enthusiastic communications
Add value by keeping you (and others) close
Create highly individualized workspaces
Need a pat on the back
Size up situations by what has gone before
Adjust to accommodate individual needs
Make decisions using empathy and personal values
Are sensitive and idealistic

Gold Worker Strengths

By maintaining discipline and organization, I get more work done in a day than others can in two. If people are sensible and practical, they generally see that my way is right, not because I am special, but because my life is organized, and that leads to organized work. I always put things away so I can find them when I need them. If people borrow or use something without asking, it rattles me because in my mind it was there, but when I reach for it, it's gone.

Once I start a project, I see it through. "Work not finished is worse than a botch," Grandfather used to say. I keep at tasks until they are complete to the smallest detail, then I move on. My acquaintances say this makes me unimaginative, even dull, but when they need something, I am usually the first one they come to. Of course, I'm not all work and no play; I just concentrate my play into my hobby time. I'm as organized about my play as about my work.

Generally, people misjudge me as being stern and condemning. That's unfair. I think instead I'm practical, concerned, and worried that things are unraveling around us. Largely, people can depend on me. This burden sometimes seems overwhelming, but if I just keep after it, we just might get by.

— KELLY KINCAID, GOLD

Gold workers work to serve and serve to work. They're fastidious, protective, and dependable. They seek to stabilize, reinforce, and improve by increments. They honor performance and service in team-building ways. They find it easier to criticize than reward. They organize contagiously, have as their credo: "In plans we trust," and need timelines, deadlines, and measurements. They hate last-minute hurries. They give attention to the little stuff.

Work to serve; serve to work

The Gold wants to earn his or her position through performance. A step up the ladder, even a short one, such as being named employee of the month, is reassurance that the job is well done, and carries the seeds of future promotion. This twin drive, to belong and to contribute, is the source of much of the Gold's work ethic. Much of the rest of Gold's attributes on the job center around preserving resources by preventing waste, and enforcing fairness, by making sure everybody puts in a day's work for their day's pay. Golds thus at the same time set up and sustain organization, as well as draw shelter from it.

Are fastidious, protective, dependable

A place for everything, and everything in its place. To the Gold, work is a joy if it's productive and on schedule. Few things can more easily mar productivity than clutter, or unreliability of equipment, tools, or vendors. A Gold likes to recognize at a glance if something is out of place. As this applies to co-workers, it often means a Gold notices who is at his or her desk and who is not. Recognizing this tendency in others, Golds will often prominently place a note saying "Out inspecting the yard" or "In a conference" when they leave their own workspace. At the very least, expect a note saying "back at 2:00." It's all part of Gold's way of appearing dependable, even if what called him or her away was entirely legitimate business.

Stabilize, reinforce, improve by increments

Sometimes doing things the same way every time has value. Once you get it right, why waste time re-inventing the wheel? The little pieces can always be improved, but the grander picture is usually best enjoyed just the way the authors framed it. In this way, effectiveness can be monitored, and efficiency increased.

Honor performance and service in team-building ways

The Gold personality approves of tradition, and will depend upon "the tradition tradition" as a means of increasing organizational stability. In fact, Golds will often create some traditions, rather than let anniversaries and milestones pass un-recognized. By so doing, Golds not only add uniformity and continuity in the organization, they also increase the value of the organization by making it tangible on different levels. Because they expect a job well done, however, Golds rarely equate performance with tangible or monetary rewards (such as sales bonuses, which are motivational to Oranges).

Instead, Gold rewards are likely to be institutional and team building in nature, offering the accolades of the group in forms such as letters of appreciation, certificates of accomplishment, and trophies in a case. A statuette on one's desk, or one's name on a plaque, is of value to Golds because they help to cement one's position in the pack and bespeak the honoree's usefulness to the group.

Find it easier to criticize than reward

Giving a pat on the back may have to be a learned behavior for strong Golds, who are likely to be so naturally duty-bound that the idea of rewarding normal and appropriate behavior may seem a bit wasteful. Extravagant approbation and sugary praise for a job well done may motivate others, but is likely to embarrass a conservative Gold. After all, what was the other choice? Perform less than her best?—unheard of! Golds tend to do what they do exceedingly well, and expect others to be as diligent as they are. Incorrect actions, however, are a waste of resources and may even threaten the performance of the group. A Gold may come down hard on these. Good thing for the worker that most of this apparent anger is likely aimed at the waste, not the person, and most of it can be erased from memory merely by not repeating the mistake.

Organize contagiously

Golds are the masters of logistics and organization. They need to know where things belong, where they fit, and how they are arranged. Consequently, not only do Golds organize themselves, but they also organize the world around them, including those closest to them. More than one teammate of a strong Gold has learned to just "do it [Gold's] way." The result is domestic tranquility, and as an added bonus, things run better. In fact, wise partnerships usually work out who is best at what and leave each to his or her strong suit. Gold's bright spot includes planning, using checklists and day planners to make sure the group gets where it needs to be and has what it needs when it gets there.

Have as their credo: "In plans we trust"

Things go wrong, so Golds plan hard so they don't get derailed. A Gold's plan is like a multi-dimensional blueprint—clearly stated objectives and timetables to ensure that needed materials and personnel are where they need to be, when they need to be there. Gold also includes milestones in the plan, which state what portion of the job should be accomplished by a certain time in order to complete the entire project on schedule. Golds shine in determining these milestones, because they associate plans to manageable chunks of time—something that can be ethereal to Greens and Blues, and immaterial to Oranges. Knowing where things should be at several points along the project allows Golds to know whether it's time to call in extra resources. Golds may know that things may fall apart once the action starts, but they also know what they have in place and what they have in reserve.

This creates, however, a two-edged sword. Golds' desire to be dependable leads them to take tremendous pride in doing the job well, not just in results, but also in execution. Thus, having to depend on back-ups and stand-ins is in itself a cause for Gold concern. "Any landing you can walk away from was a good one" is not a true saying for Golds.

Need timelines, deadlines, measurements

Because Golds are skillful at manipulating plans over their occurrence, or projected occurrence, in time, one thing that Golds require is a knowledge of "when."

— When is it due?
— When do you need this?
— What part do you think you need to have ready first?

Providing answers to questions like these help Golds to forecast, which in turn leads to successful execution of the all phases of the project. Besides, Golds hate to be late. Turning in something after the appointed hour can mar an otherwise brilliant project for a Gold.

Hate last-minute hurries

"On time and under budget" is a Golden mantra. They take pride not only in the results, but also in the quality of the execution. One way to assure they hold true to this ideal is to keep track of interim deadlines and meet them. If there's a problem, fix it fast. That way problems don't compound. Nothing could be more vexing for a Gold than to have a project go long, especially if people are sitting around waiting on some key element that's dragging. A Gold would greatly prefer to work long hours a few times during the project's formative stages than have to push during the final steps. It takes a special kind of planner to set up and hold to all the interim mini-deadlines, and then to use that information to advance or delay the pieces of the project that depend on it. This extra dimension of visualizing through time is what separates the Golds from "the boys."

Give attention to the little stuff

Golds are attentive to details. You should probably never let an order ship without having a Gold look it over first. Gold's capacity to get it right is unflagging. Any task that has multiple parts, where any one dropped ball is going to endanger the whole, is a job for Gold. To accomplish this, they call in whole armadas of planning equipment, charts, checklists, calendars—all to help them get jobs done in an orderly, predictable, established way. Part of the Gold drive for detail is a desire to preserve health and sanity—a Gold can get terribly flustered when details aren't right. They have a desire to achieve closure, to accomplish something, to finish off this task and move on to the next. Not only is this proof of productivity, which is important to Golds, it also represents a release of responsibility for the assigned task.

Gold Workers

Work to serve; serve to work
Are fastidious, protective, dependable
Stabilize, reinforce, improve by increments
Honor performance and service in team-building ways
Find it easier to criticize than reward
Organize contagiously
Have as their credo: "In plans we trust"
Need timelines, deadlines, measurements
Hate last-minute hurries
Give attention to the little stuff

Green Worker Strengths

I like to learn about things and study them in an orderly way. When a problem is interesting, I have boundless energy, but when the turf is too familiar I get restless and need to move on. Life is about collections, organizations, and possibilities. I see the underlying structure in things all around me. I want to discover the rest of it and improve it if I can.

One of my biggest thrills is taking the rules and orders from one field or science and seeing how they fit in another. It's like getting to understand two worlds at once.

I suppose I spend a lot of time lost in my thoughts. My work tends to be cerebral. I may seem distracted sometimes, but that usually means I am watching an experiment unfold in my mind, or worrying about what is going on in my test tubes. It's not that I don't care about people or things, it's just that I need to be able to turn them off so I can get back to my work. People claim this makes me cold; I prefer to think of it as an enhanced ability to focus.

One thing that people misunderstand about me is that I am so busy mentally that I often pay less attention than I should to what I wear or what I eat. I may look disheveled, sometimes even deranged, but it's because I have a fire in my mind that drives me forward.

— ISAAC JACOBS, GREEN

Green workers crave competency and have a thirst for knowledge. They're "idea people" who have a constant lust for mental challenges and things to learn. They seek mental stimulation in their work. When given projects, they start starting, but may finish weakly, or not at all. They're often unaware of others' feelings although they're responsive to new ideas. They're objective to a fault, ask a million questions, and need others to be precise.

Crave competency; thirst for knowledge

To be unprepared for an intellectual task is an unacceptable exposure for a Green. Their image of themselves depends in large measure on being skilled and competent. If there are instruction manuals, help systems, technical assistance desks, or willing mentors, a Green will try to absorb as much information as possible. Failing this, he or she will at least scan the available materials by title to know where to locate the information when it's needed.

Are "idea people"

Greens enjoy working with clean sheets of paper. Where others may desire, even insist on firmly established methods to follow, Greens would just as soon make their own procedures, or where possible, not have procedures at all, and be left free to develop methods that fit the program. This naturally implies a certain amount of conceptual work, but that's fine by Greens, who quickly tire of the physical world because it's so obvious.

Lust for mental challenges and things to learn

Greens are intrigued by challenges and riddles, and most puzzles that seem easy but end up hard. Life is a system to be decoded, redesigned, and improved; a great puzzle, one with a special plus—you can enter the puzzle yourself and interact with its pieces. This makes the world a great laboratory for Greens. Most workers may be content to work at their jobs, perhaps never seeing the bigger picture or the global effects. Greens do not miss these opportunities, however, and often cannot wait to jot down lists of individuals in each department, their functions, and their triggers. Once mapped, the organization can be tweaked, and the results noted and incorporated into the next round of adjustments. That people with feelings, fears, and desires fill the positions on the organization chart may be lost on Greens.

The term "Modular Man" may have been invented to describe the work world as seen by Green. It's not that Greens intend to be impersonal, or to offend or harm, it's just that to a Green, most organizations exist now in just one of several possible combinations and permutations. Some other arrangement may work better. How will we know unless we try?

Seek mental stimulation in their work

A lot of what goes on in the world is boring, and Greens don't handle boredom well. Given the chance either to see a long-term project to conclusion or to start something new that needs some extra thought is a no-brainer decision for a Green. Anyone can undertake the obvious thing. The risky, new deal is a challenge as irresistible to a Green as is writing in wet cement to others. Both are ways to make a mark on the world.

Start starting, but may finish weakly, or not at all

As a project progresses and the results become clear, a Green may grow restless for the next challenge. In fact, for most Greens the ideal job involves consulting on the scope and structure of a project and then leaving details of the actual execution to other, more trivial beings. This seldom happens in practice, however. The world is designed for finishing what you start. The pervading attitude is "Work not finished is worse than a botch." Pity the poor Greens. Not only are they hopelessly process-centered, finding their reward is in the doing (especially if it was cleverly done), but they absolutely hate boredom. No wonder most Greens secretly salivate when TV surgeons get the sweat wiped from their foreheads by awe-struck attendants, then throw their scalpels into a pan with a triumphant clunk and leave the busy work to others, saying "Close this! I'll begin the heart transplant now!"

Are often unaware of others' feelings

Sensitivity in interpersonal relations may not be the Green's strong suit. Greens carry a library's worth of information in situations where a 3x5 card would suffice. With so much knowledge on hand, they're not inclined to look for more, especially if it's presented subtly, as happens in office politics and relationships. As a result, Greens often end up buffaloed by subtle hints others around them can pick up on, such as body language or nuances of language. Greens can miss these clues entirely. If a message remains unvoiced, count on the Green to tromp all over it in complete naiveté.

Attracted and responsive to new ideas

Ideas are the Greens' stock in trade, and they recognize the advantage of rotating their inventory. Almost too much, in fact. The urge to follow the state of the art as a lifestyle rather than as a business choice can lead to constant re-engineering. Constant tweaking on a project may prevent finishing and moving on. The cure is for individuals of other colors to step in, pulling projects from the lab onto the factory floor as required.

Are objective to a fault

When it's time to change, Greens have a strong advantage. They're not compelled to cling to existing ideas and methods. If something clearly better is at hand, they switch. The facts of the situation, not the traditions of the organization, compel a Green. For a Green, there's little virtue in not switching horses in mid-stream. Oddly, this can work to their disadvantage. If a Green senses that his or her own department is a weak link or redundant, the resulting recommendation may be against them.

Ask a million questions

There is no such thing as a statement of fact to a Green. A "fact" is merely a starting place for inquiry. With a fact comes a need to know the source of that fact, the reliability of that source, a rundown of similar facts, their sources and the reliability of those sources. To obtain all of this information requires questions, lots of them, and Greens are the inquiring minds that need to know. Be prepared for a question bombardment when you present data to a Green. Then watch as the facts are arranged, classified, validated, and rearranged logically to pull all possible information out of them. The answer, if available, often will be accompanied by its underlying logic, much like a mathematical proof. But getting to that point may require—you guessed it—more questions.

Need you to be precise

Greens want to appear competent above all else. They require a high level of precision from themselves. This can be greatly confusing in many social contexts, where such precision is unwarranted or even unwelcome. Conversation with a strong Green can be particularly challenging, because where the Green sees a need to include adequate details to reduce ambiguity, others are likely to see this as a need to insert unnecessary details and a failure to keep things simple. Remember that for a Green, nothing is simple, because he or she tends to track not just what is happening, but also likely alternative scenarios, along with those potential results. Thus what would be a thin file folder to most others can, to a Green, end up being a whole file cabinet. On the other hand, when this level of analysis is warranted, it's indispensable. For this reason most employers and co-workers of Greens adapt and accept long answers and analysis.

Green Workers

Crave competency; thirst for knowledge
Are "idea people"
Lust for mental challenges and things to learn
Seek mental stimulation in their work
Start starting, but may finish weakly, or not at all
Are often unaware of others' feelings
Attracted and responsive to new ideas
Are objective to a fault
Ask a million questions
Need you to be precise

Orange Worker Strengths

> I suppose that to me work is like a fast basketball game. I like it better when there is action. I love to hear the crowd roar. That's how it feels when I get that sale, pull off something when the odds are long, put out fires, and turn around logjams. I suppose that nothing seems too hard for me because I don't play by the same rules as others. I just look for what works and DO IT! More than anything else, that's probably why I am halfway done while other people are still walking around and talking about how to get started.
>
> Strangely, once I get something built or fixed, or put the fire out, I don't really do so well at maintaining the situation. I get bored. My managers and I know that once things are moving again, it's time for me to go find the next challenge.
>
> Work is play if you hit it hard enough. But you have to know when to kick back, too. I play to win. I work to win. I work to play. I also enjoy travel. Anywhere that survival isn't guaranteed, or people talk a foreign language—you know "No one from your country has ever been here before."
>
> My biggest kick is probably tools. I love to drive things that amplify my powers. Larger-than-life shovels, bulldozers, even jackhammers are fun for me. I am the reason why sports cars, hot aircraft, and really big trucks were invented.
>
> — MARIA LEBARON, ORANGE

Orange workers need speed, action, and freedom. They never "borrow trouble" because they seem to find it on their own. They can switch between options easily and find that nothing is too strange if it works. They're risk seeking by nature, and enjoy calling plays from the field. They don't like long, sit-down meetings, preferring to meet in the hall between crises. They jump in and do whatever is required, allowing the structure to emerge from the process. They make difficult jobs look easy and are always setting things up for the big finish.

Need speed, action, freedom

If employment doesn't directly satisfy the urge for physical action and risk, the Orange will be happiest with the next best thing—a highly autonomous environment in which he or she can chose mostly what to do. It's of great importance that supervisors understand this, and keep their urge to micro-manage to themselves. If there is a need to focus on one activity because its results must dovetail with another, it might be best to emphasize the difficulty or danger of the task rather than its importance to the team or the terrible things that will happen if work is not completed in a certain order. The idea is to introduce freedom, perhaps risk, into the equation. All is lost unless a superhuman springs into action and saves the day. And then the supervisor should go away.

Never borrow trouble

Neat! The dam could break, flood the valley, wash silt into the sewage treatment plant and back up wastewater, overflow a toilet somewhere, make someone get a stomach cramp so they miss work, cause a check not to get cut, cause a bill not to get paid, cause an order not to get made, preventing a delivery, meaning a part could not be obtained, so the truck wouldn't start, so the papers will be late. All that could be enough to make a Gold grab a flashlight and check the levee, but don't expect it to motivate an Orange. Oranges like their problems tangible, such as "Oh my heck! It's a bomb!" or "If something isn't done, that culvert's gonna wash out—how are we going to get down there to patch it?" Oranges don't borrow trouble, they seek it out, or maybe even cause it themselves.

Can switch between options easily

George Orwell's *1984* portrayed a society besieged by its own government. Periodically, when their valiant troops had piled up enough victories to make it hard to sustain both the fervor and the ruse, the need arose to switch enemies. A days-long melee ensued, in which everybody frantically tore down the posters mocking the old enemy, and pasted up new posters deriding the new one. All the efforts involved in learning the ways of and fighting the previous foe had to be discarded, and in a tremendous burst of energy, attention, and public artifacts shifted to the new enemy. Strangely, Orange has not much problem with that. As long as things keep moving. Boredom, or sitting around waiting for someone to figure things out, are much more painful to an Orange than frantic activity for its own sake.

Find nothing is too strange if it works

Oranges are not tied to the conventional, but rather to the practical. Show an Orange that a given course of action produces the desired result, and they're off and at it. This is one reason they shine in high-tension environments. If they discover that some misstep or unplanned event makes things happen, they will repeat it as required, no matter how unorthodox. This is a great thing when it speeds projects along, or gets things done when resources don't appear to be available. It may result in extra risk, but that's a small price to pay as long as things go well.

Are risk seeking

If Oranges' risk-seeking natures were not combined with an uncanny ability to land on their feet, they would be among the most tragic of cases. In truth, they seem to be like the ceiling lizards in the tropics. True, they may fall from the sky and splat onto your head or the dinner table, but then they wriggle away. This very risk-tolerance, which makes them so valuable in a clinch, doesn't make them immortal, however, and it's usually necessary to think things over for them, at least a little. Truth is, they're not immune to pain and injury, they just don't dwell on them, and so choose their possible course out of a broader panel of possibilities than most. Most laws regarding occupational safety and health and worker's compensation were instituted because a few unscrupulous employers recognized that some employees (probably Oranges, if they'd known) need the stimulation of risk, so they provided it to them without covering the responsibility for that risk when things went wrong.

Call plays from the field

Oranges tend to be tactical operators rather than strategic ones. They call the plays from the field, where they can see the action—"10-Right-Six, You cover the big guy! Let's go!" This means that short-term obstacles present them few challenges, as long as the goal is in site. Greens on the other hand, are the voices in the headset viewing the game from up high and calling down to suggest options. Golds call in to quote the rulebook, keeping things fair and avoiding penalties.

Have verbal meetings

Oranges would be happiest if meetings were held informally, preferably standing, maybe in the hallway. The huddle may be an acceptable planning format for this color style. If you really have to get the words to the troops fast, send an Orange. Blessed as they are with the ability to read people, they can adjust the message to the recipient and make sure that what you sent was what was received. Don't burden the Orange with charts, graphs, and white papers. They probably won't be used. Better, make all of these available, but require none of them to be used. Emphasize the message over the medium, and Orange can be your carrier.

There's an old story about a group of telegram delivery boys, one of each color style. One holiday season, they each had to take turns trying to deliver an extremely sad message to a businessman regarding the untimely passing of his mother. For some reason, the businessman, who didn't get many telegrams, was enamored of the idea of getting a singing telegram. He requested each of the delivery boys to sing whatever it was the message was about. The first delivery boy was a Blue. He considered how he could possibly break the news to the poor guy, and at length just excused himself and returned to his office. The second boy assigned was a Gold. "I cannot give this message its proper tone if I sing it," he said, then he excused himself and returned to his office. The third boy assigned was a Green. He told the man, "Your firm insistence that I sing this message suggests to me that you are not in a state of mind to receive it," and left without further comment. Finally the Orange got his turn. Realizing he probably was not going to get a good tip, and suspecting that the customer was a bit barmy anyway, he quickly and cheerfully took voice: "Fa-la-la-la-laa, your mother's dead!"

Do the work, allow the structure to emerge from the process

The maxims about beginning with the end in mind, looking before leaping, measuring twice then cutting once, and so on, were probably coined by others to help Oranges. Oranges can profit from such words of wisdom, but are more likely to view planning as a chance to count resources and generate options. The actual execution will be heavily influenced by situations on the field anyway, so an Orange is not likely to be disturbed if things don't align with the blueprints. Those who assign Oranges would do well to remember that Oranges are best measured by results, not by conformance to plans. Michelangelo is credited with the idea that the best sculptors let their wood or stone present itself to them. The artist merely carves away what is not needed, revealing the structure within. So it is with some business problems.

More than most, Oranges are likely to want to size things up by working organically with the situation, literally diving in and trying things to get a feel for things as they are, as opposed to how they appear to be based on the org charts or the books.

Make it look easy

Oranges have a distinctive and stylish elegance. They love to do things and love to be seen doing things well. Entertainment is part of the effort for Orange, and a victory can best be savored if it was won with style. This requires a sense of inner timing, a grace in terms of what to do when, that makes Oranges at once charming and cunning. In matters of finesse, those ticklish situations where anything going wrong can lose the bid, blow the contract, or start the battle, Oranges will pull it off. They have cat-like can-do, although it's certainly true they sometimes end up stuck in a tree. By and large, however, they thrive where angels fear to tread.

Set things up for the big finish

Oranges like a big finish, and aren't averse to getting there by relying on a last-minute push, whether or not others can see it all coming together. They tend to work in such a way that closure comes in the last few moments, not by increments along the project timeline. This requires special patience on the part of supervisors who like to tick things off checklists. In a perfect world, an Orange's project would appear to be a horrible mess, with fragmented bits of work occurring at seemingly odd intervals, and then one evening they would sweep the sawdust away to reveal the finished project. In most endeavors, the discrepancy between that finished state and the apparent chaos that leads up to it is enough to break employee relationships, especially if deadlines have been stretched. If the project can't fail, or if the company psyche requires the ticking off of periodic milestones, consider not putting an Orange in charge. Better to let them run isolated sub-projects, and then bring together all the disparate pieces at the end.

Orange Workers

Need speed, action, freedom
Never borrow trouble
Can switch between options easily
Find nothing is too strange if it works
Are risk seeking
Call plays from the field
Have verbal meetings
Do the work, allow the structure to emerge from the process
Make it look easy
Set things up for the big finish

How to Enjoy Your Job

Although research indicates that certain colors favor certain professions, the truth is that every profession usually includes representatives of every color. How can this be? The answers are varied, but one enduring theme is that the participants have found something in the jobs, the way they perform them, or the organizations for which they work, that meets their needs or appeal to their internal values. For instance:

— They have found a way to bring their own natural talents and skills to the jobs, making them satisfying

— The jobs may be inherently interesting to them

— They have found out that the jobs are easy for them

— They feel that, by doing their jobs, they're advancing a cause they believe in

— They feel that, by doing their jobs, they're contributing to the good of those they care about (taking a spot in the family business)

Interestingly, even though they do the same thing, each color is likely to view different aspects of the job as being "the main event."

On the job scene

We can look at come examples to get a better idea of how this works. Here are some statements I've gathered from some clients. First, we will examine a fairly common profession, that of teaching in an elementary school.

> My little faces all seem to need me so much when I see them in the morning. They say I shouldn't touch them, but I usually get twenty little hugs before 10 in the morning. You just know that most of these little ones will turn out okay, will figure out who they are, and go on to mean something to someone. But for some of them, mine might be the only hug they get all day. That's what makes it important to me, I think. I get to provide a little love to someone who may not make it without it.
>
> — JENNY BAER, BLUE

> To start out right is to be half done, that's my watchword. These little people will go on to fill all the important roles in society. What is our other choice? If we don't turn this rising generation into the doctors and lawyers and dentists of tomorrow, who will take care of us when we need it? Each day I get to put a little bit more tradition, culture, and values into young minds. If I do it in a way that's sensible and pleasurable, they don't mind a bit. In fact, most of them appreciate a chance to live up to some clear-cut set of standards. The hours can be long—thank heaven for photocopiers—but I think the rewards are there, and if I didn't do this, who would?
>
> — DENNIS KARLSON, GOLD

> Al Gore didn't invent the Internet all by himself. If there is going to be any scientific advancement in the future—and I hope we don't export all the good science to Asia—we need teachers, and technicians, and lab managers, and support staff, and we'll need them at every level. And they don't grow by themselves. You have to find that potential, and awaken it. When Sputnik went up, that's when we got serious about science education in this country. Have you seen the studies? Do you know what became of that generation? Extraordinary. The man on the moon, advances in medicine, even your gains in civil rights—all of it sourced right back here at the schools. Someone has got to get the administration focused on science, wake these kids up, and get schools back doing what they are supposed to be doing.
>
> — SANDY KOWALSKI, GREEN

> I used to wonder, man, how will I ever get out of this place? The rules, the lines, doing all this stuff that doesn't matter. All I ever cared about was doing sports—hoops, football, even tried soccer. But then I had my big chance and I blew it—I mean there is a lot more to the story, but we're going to save that for later, you know? But basically my body won't support me at professional or maybe even collegiate levels. So I'm looking around, what can I do? Then it hits me—I can be the coach! I got game in my heart. And these young ones—they got to not make some of the choices I made if they want to go on and earn their dreams when their chance comes. Who's going to tell them? I know what they got to hear. Besides, what other job gives you the summer off?
>
> — STEPH CLINGER, ORANGE

Obviously, the Green emphasis on learning for its own sake suggests an emphasis on education, and Greens do find a spot as teachers, although usually on the university level. Blues feel a need to nurture, and that dovetails nicely with this age group's need for security as they step beyond their parents' shadows. Many grade school teachers are Blue. Golds find the opportunity to mold youth before they're distracted by the evils of the world almost irresistible, so they number high in elementary education as well. Oranges appreciate the flexibility of the grade school and the ease with which the kids can be entertained, as opposed to the more rigorous accounting that will be required of them in later grades.

On the medical front

Let's look at this from another angle. This time, we'll examine a more technical job from the health care industry—working as a nurse in the trauma department at a hospital. Here is what some respondents said about their career choice.

> I like being a trauma nurse—at first I didn't think I would because of all the blood and hurting. But then I found that "Hey, I'm really trying to help these people." And sometimes they are pretty badly injured and may not make it, so you do a good job and hope that they make it and that their recoveries go okay. Sometimes they are alert, and you can talk to them, and they know that you tried to help them, and I think that makes them feel better. I suppose the best is when their parents come up and they see us and they see their child. And you just want to yell at some of them, "Hey, this your little person. How could you have let this happen to them?" But then other times, they are just so grateful when they look at you. I mean, who could feel bad after a day like that?
>
> — PAULA MCANDREWS, BLUE

I think I wanted to be a trauma nurse ever since my mother had to go into the hospital once because someone ran into the back of our car and she hurt her neck. It was like, all confusing. I wanted to stand up on a table and tell them all, "Hey you people—this is my momma! Why are you running around like chickens? She's hurt and you can help her, and you all look like you don't really know what you're doing!" I guess I've always been that way. You've got a job, you do it right, all the pieces fit together, you move on. I'm the training nurse here now and run a tight ship. The new ones, they hate me. But you know, I have had some of them—not too many—come back and thank me for being hard on them, because when they left here and went to a place where there wasn't enough staff or there weren't enough gloves, well they knew what to do so that doesn't happen.

— JAIME CURTIZ, GOLD

The ER is like the ultimate meeting place of theory and practicality. It can look all well and good in the textbooks, but until you actually try it, you actually have to reach into someone with your finger to do something and then you can say, hey it really does hold when you do it that way, then you know you have a technique you can keep. I'm never going to be a doctor. I probably would go that way if I could start all over. But there is plenty to learn here. New problems every night. New equipment. New things you have to work around, because of the stuff someone never thought of that before they installed something right here. I sit back sometimes, or maybe I have a minute to catch up on my paperwork before the shift is over or while I am still on lunch, and I think, where else would I rather be? I can come up with a few ideas, but after the first few times someone looks at you and says, "How did you know to do that?"—and these are MDs talking—well, the place kind of grows on you.

— KIM TANADEU, GREEN

I think I picked the ER because it was so good looking on TV. I mean, it's the place where the action is. The patients come in all shot or killed up or something, and it's you man, you're the one's gotta keep 'em together 'till the doctor gets up here, and sometimes that's gonna take a while cause this is a big place and it's a bad little city out there some nights. Never the same, heck sometimes we don't even sit down between patients, just make the scoot between tables, put my hand here, hold that arm there. Always moving, always something happening. That's why I like it.

— JAMAL MASON, ORANGE

As expected, Green emergency room nurses may enjoy the challenges and the chance to demonstrate technical competence. Oranges crave the fast pace and high stakes. Golds align with the sense of responsibility involved in making the best decisions on behalf of people who need their help immediately. Blues are likely to warm to the opportunity to be compassionate, although the suffering may pain them.

Is everybody happy?

Obviously, not every worker is happy every moment of each day. In addition to the normal stresses of work (orders or the lack thereof, weather, economic conditions), there are color-specific irritants (tension, boredom, details, confinement). The point to remember is that as long as his or her values are accommodated, anyone can enjoy doing any occupation.

Further, whatever the hook or path by which jobs attract workers of all colors, it's a good thing. Just as the interplay of the colors both preserves society and stimulates its advancement, each trade, profession, skill, or craft is benefited by the presence of a full spectrum of workers within it.

CHAPTER 5

Supervision: Leading and Managing Others

This chapter explains how each color responds to placement in leadership roles, then presents information to help a person function within these roles. The chapter gives specific attention to showing appreciation, team building, and overcoming procrastination.

What is Leadership?

People have peculiar notions about leadership. There's an aura to it. Some people are said to just "have that magic quality" that makes people follow them. Although it's fun, perhaps even human nature, to romanticize those in charge, there is a simple and down to earth way to measure leadership. Leaders get people to do things. Dynamic personalities aside, leadership is about getting things done according to the times and places dictated by a plan. It's about mushing the huskies, organizing the oxen, ordering the troops, coercing, enticing, motivating, loving—whatever it takes—so that one's crew, company, congregation, cohort, or country are where its leadership has determined it should be at the time they should be there.

I know that there are thousands of Scoutmasters and drill instructors who will protest that leadership is about developing inner character in the followers and inspiring intrinsic change and improvement. Wrong! That's the goal of the organization. Leadership obtains those objectives by getting the kids or troops to go where they must and do what they must in order to develop and strengthen those admittedly desirable attributes. The menu of leadership activities may include some training and development exercises, but through most of life, in business and family, it will consist of helping followers through sales experiences, huddling to make management decisions, and marshalling the manufacturing maneuvers.

In other words, many people have their goals (the organization's mission) and their means (training, inspiring, tasking, and measuring the progress of followers) hopelessly intertwined. That's one reason there's so much muddling material floating around about leadership.

The purpose of this chapter is to explain how each of the four temperaments approach leadership and describe their respective managerial strengths. I hope you will then see how anyone, in spite of his or her natural disposition, can become a successful leader, especially if the person applies what you and I now know about personality styles.

As you ponder your personal leadership style and how you lead your people, you may want to refer to the chapter on motivation (chapter 2). There you will find some important keys that will enhance your ability to persuade people to do what you need them to do. After all, a breakdown in leadership occurs whenever followers do not do what they're supposed to. A manager is effective only if the results conform to plan. If you are leading but your followers are not following, then sorry to say it, but you aren't really providing leadership.

Leadership Characteristics

Even if you're not the parent of a teenager, an executive officer in a multimillion-dollar company, a high-school algebra teacher, or the pilot of a jumbo jet, you're probably the designated leader of someone in the world—even if it's only the scary-looking bloke staring at you in the bathroom mirror every morning. Leaders motivate, discipline, nurture, educate, and even baby-sit on occasion. And each color does it in a different way. The following pages describe the qualities and attributes of leaders from each of the four temperaments.

Blue leaders

Blue leaders don't care much for the trappings of leadership. They aren't nearly as concerned with power and authority as other types. In fact, as a rule, most Blues shun leadership positions like the plague. They're reluctant to play the games that leadership often requires, such as politicking for position, an activity they perceive as phony and pretentious, requiring attributes they absolutely abhor. Furthermore, they dislike having to make the really tough decisions—the ones where people are hurt with either conclusion. As a result, only a few Blues will seek out chances to lead, normally doing so only if they think they can use this opportunity to champion a cherished cause or move forward a forgotten agenda.

With a leadership style reflecting more democracy than dictatorship, just about everyone loves a Blue leader. There's something about their kindness, sensitivity, and genuine concern that makes you feel like you're an important part of the organization. Even if your responsibilities are as insignificant as a blade of grass amidst acres of giant redwoods, you're treated like an indispensable member of the team. Because of their inclusionary disposition, Blues will go to great lengths to make sure no one feels neglected or mistreated.

Wonderfully intuitive, Blue leaders seem to sense untapped strengths in others, which is why they frequently provide a host of opportunities for these individuals to discover their latent talents and abilities. Blues will gently prod and poke until a person willingly starts down this path of self-discovery. "It's for your own good," they explain, ever so benevolently. Then, when the talent begins to blossom, the individual is encouraged to share it again and again, until it becomes a natural part of his or her character. If that new skill results in a promotion or an increase in salary, so much the better.

While most leaders claim to care about their personnel, the Blues truly do, often to the point where they worry more about the success of their people than the success of the organization. More than one Blue manager has quietly whispered to an employee that he might be better compensated at a competitor's organization. Fortunately a suggestion like this is rarely taken advantage of, since such an honest disclosure is a rare and wonderful thing—the result of a genuine friendship—and most people value true friendship more than a modest raise in pay. So the worker stays on, proud to be working for such a caring supervisor.

Most Blue leaders, if given the leeway by their own supervisors, will allow their charges the freedom to "personalize" the workspace. In a Blue office, you'll probably see a plant or two, and perhaps some artwork from Monet or Matt, age 7. You'll see photographs of loved ones and perhaps a couple of objects that reflect personal hobbies or interests. Many Blue supervisors secretly dream of tearing down room partitions and completely opening up the space. They'd let in as much natural light as possible, perhaps adding live plants, fish, or even a waterfall in the foyer to add a sense of tranquility to the environment. It's all about creating a place where people can be comfortable, because, "Happy workers are productive workers." Blues believe the workplace is, in actuality, an extension of the home; a place where people ought to be free to express their individual talents and skills, a place where they should be free to do what they do best.

Habitually more open-minded and accommodating than other personality types, Blue leaders will, however, draw a line in the sand when it comes to tolerating offensive behaviors. It's unwise for employees to take part in water-cooler discussions that are disrespectful, prejudiced, or hateful. Blues definitely frown on recurring rudeness, vulgarity, and indecency. Hostile and violent behaviors are completely unacceptable. While normally champions of free speech and the freedom of expression, Blue leaders quickly seek to limit these liberties if they're used deliberately to wound others.

Fortunately for their subordinates, Blues have a difficult time firing employees. If you're failing in a particular task, they reason that perhaps it's their own fault, not yours, for placing you in the wrong job. So rather than giving you a pink slip, they'll try to relocate you within the organization. Or perhaps they'll try to retrain you so that you may perform an entirely different job. But if that doesn't work, and they've exhausted every other alternative, you'll be let go, reluctantly and with much ado. In fact, if you've been there long enough, perhaps they'll throw you a "moving-on" party. Take comfort in knowing that your termination has probably hurt your supervisor more than it's hurt you.

Because they're more casual and communicative with those they lead, Blue leaders have an advantage when it comes to effective motivation. These enthusiastic, amiable smooth-talkers spend a great deal of energy getting to know the people they work with, visiting with them, sharing concerns, trying to figure them out. All of this information is delicately filed away, ready to be retrieved and used just in case someone needs extra prodding. By the way, lest you're afraid of disclosing too much information for fear of being turned in or blackmailed, rest assured that nearly all emotionally healthy Blues have an extremely high degree of integrity. They won't rat on you, unless, of course, you're a rat.

As leaders, Blues are normally upbeat and optimistic, cheering on the troops with boundless energy. They look for the good in people, refusing to dwell for long on the negatives. They're convinced that the best is yet to come, that the sun will invariably come out tomorrow. Of course, Blues have their bad days just like everyone else. But all they need is chance to express their frustrations and then they can move forward. With their natural ability to manage personnel in personal ways, Blue leaders are unrivaled in their ability to build loyal subordinates who will work to please their supervisors as much as they work for a paycheck. And that's saying something!

Blue Leaders

Are people-oriented
Lead democratically
Invite contributions
Build consensus
Encourage personal growth
Allow personalization
Accommodate individuality
Encourage cooperation
Promote creativity
Champion causes

Gold leaders

Gold leaders are the stable, steady mariners on the supervisory sea. Regardless of what wind is blowing through the workplace at any given moment, Golds can be counted on to keep their eyes riveted on the destination, properly setting the sails and never deviating from the planned course. Then, before you know it, they'll arrive at their objective, where they'll stay just long enough to restock and regroup before sailing out on another assignment.

More than the other colors, Gold supervisors tend to document their decisions in writing and circulate them via memoranda, newsletters, and bulletin boards. Of course, their followers are expected to sign off that they have read and understand the communiqué. Failure to do so is a serious infraction that indicates a lack of respect for authority—a warning sign of future rebellion and mutiny.

This is not to infer that Golds are paranoid, dictatorial, or unreasonable. They simply believe that for an organizational machine to work properly, each component must perform its designated function in order, on time, and without fail. Otherwise, it needs to be fixed. The squeaky wheel might initially get the grease, but if it continues to make noise or rub the wrong way, it gets replaced. It's an effective, common sense policy.

Golds don't often make unreasonable requests of their subordinates. In fact, they're quick to set the example and do whatever they ask others to do. Whether it's writing a daily journal, setting weekly goals, using a daily organizer, being prepared for presentations—expect Golds to lead the way. Obviously these are inherently Gold behaviors, but even if they weren't, Gold leaders would still blaze the trail. If a Gold asks a group of people to jump off a cliff, the Gold will jump first, assuming, of course, that the others can't back out of the deal.

Golds hate loose ends. When dealing with matters they try, in a reasonable amount of time, to eliminate the loopholes, close up discussions, and set down in writing as much as possible via ironclad resolutions, contracts, and agreements. In the good old days, they reason, you were able to settle things on a promise or a handshake. But nowadays, it has to be written down, just in case the other party decides to renege on its pledge and the matter must be handed over to the lawyers.

Planning and goal setting are important parts of the Gold management style. If any personality type is driven to set and achieve goals, it is the Gold. As part of the planning process they first clearly define the expectations. Then they identify the specific steps that will take them to the goal. They also plan for unforeseen events that might throw them off course. Then, with a meticulously plotted course in hand, and an emergency backup plan, they persevere until they reach their destination. Yes, this process takes time and effort, but it's a golden formula that consistently yields bankable results.

Order and organization are also Gold trademarks. If chaos is present in any form, Gold leaders will immediate seek to bring it into order. Everything has a place and a set of boundaries. If it's out of place, it must be returned expeditiously. Most Gold supervisors document these expectations in their employee handbooks. For instance, extra office supplies belong in a storage cabinet, not in someone's cubicle. Desks should be cleared off before employees leave for the night. Debris should be placed in wastebaskets. People should wear appropriate attire at all times. You may not send or receive personal email on company computers. And so on. If a subordinate disagrees with these policies, then he or she is normally given the option to conform or leave quietly. Order must be maintained, even if it costs a rabble-rouser his or her job.

Regularly scheduled meetings serve an important function for most Gold supervisors. Meetings give them the opportunity to measure performance, make course corrections, and offer advice. Whenever possible, the meetings are always held at the same time, on the same day, with the same group of people. Normally the ranking supervisor presides and conducts the meeting, although the supervisor may, from time to time, delegate the conducting duties to an assistant. The agenda is clearly defined. Perhaps the meeting begins with a roll call to make sure everyone is present or accounted for. Then the minutes from the previous meeting are read and approved. If assignments were made, then the responsible parties report on them. New items, having been previously submitted for addition to the agenda, are then discussed. Action items are assigned and the meeting is adjourned on time. The sheer predictability of this routine, while perhaps sterile and stifling to other personality types, actually brings a great deal of comfort and peace of mind to Golds. It's like a tattered old blanket—it may not be much to look at, but it keeps you warm at night and therefore does what it's supposed to do. What more can you ask for?

While most Gold supervisors are fairly firm in their leadership style, not many become tyrannical overlords. Only a stray Gold who is feeling out of sorts with the world will unconsciously take what would otherwise be a positive trait and maximize it to the point where it becomes a liability. Perhaps that is why we have boot camps—where people like this can go and exercise ubiquitous dominion.

Golds take established rules, guidelines, policies, and procedures seriously. Someone up the chain of command obviously decided that these should be followed and, if nothing more than out of respect for that person's authority, these guidelines must be obeyed. Consequently a Gold manager will doggedly enforce the rules whenever possible. Discount or defy these and you will serve time in the doghouse. It's not your place to reason why; you should simply do or die.

Gold leaders place their trust in the principle of stewardship. *Stewardship* is basically responsibility coupled with accountability. After making a commitment to do something, you implicitly agree to return regularly to your supervisor and report on your progress. When a Gold manager gives out an assignment, he or she is asking for not only a commitment to do it, but a recurring update of your progress along the way. For this reason, many Gold leaders either schedule periodic face-to-face interviews with their subordinates or require frequent written progress reports. Of course, even if they don't ask for it overtly, it's always a good practice to regularly return and give an accounting of your stewardship.

Gold supervisors are a stabilizing influence in any organization. They can be counted on to make and keep commitments with relentless regularity. They understand the responsibilities and the drawbacks of leadership and accept them unreservedly. They're loyal and faithful to the organization and its leaders and will place their own needs behind the needs of the group. Golds are truly the tenacious workhorses of society who consistently do what is required.

Gold Leaders

Are process-oriented
Lead with authority
Meet deadlines
Remain steadfast
Expect follow-through
Solicit progress reports
Discourage freethinking
Promote company values
Reward commitment
Work the plan

Green leaders

Greens are known for their visionary leadership. Like bald eagles soaring over a vast valley, they survey their stewardship from afar and make decisions from a perspective others can't fully appreciate until they ascend to the same lofty heights. When they return to the ground, they try to explain their vision to others, but more often than not it is ignored. Nevertheless, they have a vision clearly in mind, so rather than trying to articulate it repeatedly, they simply lead off, hoping others decide to follow.

For this reason alone, Green leaders deserve followers. Chances are they've spent far more time thinking through a problem than most people. So even though you may not be able to see the end result, if you put your trust in their visionary and analytical abilities, they probably won't lead you astray. Oh, you may have some interesting side-trips now and then, and maybe a few bumps and bruises, but chances are you'll end your journey in a delightfully surprising place.

If Green leaders seem more aloof and distant than other types, it's because they *are* more aloof and distant than other types. You are seeing exactly what they want you to see. Most Greens have their own rationale for this behavior. Sometimes it may be purposeful—they simply can't afford to spend any more energy on interpersonal relationships and prefer to keep you at arm's length. Or perhaps they're lacking the skills to be warm and friendly and don't want to expose this "flaw" in their characters. Or perhaps they think it's unprofessional to be casual with subordinates. Who knows? The secret isn't about to be disclosed. Therefore, if you feel compelled to strike up an informal relationship with your Green supervisor, just remember that it will happen if, and only if, he or she lets it. If you try to force it, you'll just make the barriers bigger.

Green supervisors typically aren't fast decision makers, especially on matters they haven't considered before. Before they render a verdict, they must have sufficient time. Time to collect data from a variety of sources. Time to make sure the data is a representative sampling and not just an anomaly. Time to juxtapose pros and cons. Time to formulate a trial opinion. Time to test the opinion against the case at hand. Time to analyze the repercussions of the decision. And finally, time to write up the decision so no one misinterprets it. This may seem extreme, but for many Green supervisors this is right on target. Decision-making is a painstaking process if done correctly. It certainly doesn't involve illogical sentimentality, gut instincts, or historical precedents. Greens consider each decision on its own merits and reach conclusions accordingly.

Green leaders love efficiency and innovation. If they can figure out a way to streamline an operation and eliminate an unnecessary expense of resources, then they will consider their time well spent. In fact, a good portion of their time is spent looking for ways to improve a system, process, or product. Furthermore, they regularly encourage their subordinates to do the same. The company known as 3M is a good example of this leadership style. They encourage every employee, regardless of specific job, to try to improve upon or create a new product. Anyone who does is given a piece of the pie. So far, this has led to the development of more than fifty thousand innovative products, including Post-it® notes.

No one appreciates well-thought-out suggestions more than a Green leader. The key concept here is "well-thought-out." If there are holes in your argument or a lack of evidence to support your claim, then it will probably be dismissed out of hand and your competence level in the eyes of the Green will drop down a notch. Furthermore, if you're just complaining and not really supplying a solution to the problem, then all you've really done is heap grief on the Green. And no manager, regardless of his or her color, enjoys heaped grief.

You see, Green supervisors despise mental mediocrity. They believe that most people voluntarily place themselves in intellectual bondage, refusing to think outside of the box—only doing what thinking is necessary to get by. Therefore, Green leaders often demand that their employees push their cognitive skills to the max. For example, when giving an assignment, they will give only brief instructions, leaving the worker to think it through and fill in the details on his or her own. They invite workers to come back if they need further clarification; otherwise, the burden has been shifted and the workers are left alone to complete their assignments. Occasionally this leads to misunderstandings and expectation problems, but Green leaders simply aren't hand-holders in any sense of the word. They expect you to be competent enough to do the job you were hired to do. If they need to walk you through to the solution, then they might as well have done the job themselves.

Genius is a rare thing, and Green leaders respect it. If you demonstrate extraordinary talent in a work-related area or express remarkable knowledge or skill, you will quickly become the fair-haired child and be pulled out from among the rank and file to join the inner circle. Brilliance is not just to be admired; like maple tree sap, it's to be tapped and refined into something tasty and desirable. Green leaders will take you under their wings and help you develop this ability until it becomes a wonderful thing. Call it exploitation if you will, but Greens know a good thing when they see it, and they will put it to good use as long as possible.

You see, Green leaders like to surround themselves with competent people. Personally, most Green leaders already glow with competence. Their current leadership assignment probably had little to do with office politics, their charming personalities, or good fortune. More likely, they were chosen because they were better qualified than others. Their expertise propelled them to leadership. Of course, their fellow leaders may be alienated and green with envy, but Greens are used to being ahead of the class.

Part of the reason Greens surround themselves with competent people is that they need helpers to handle some messy administrative duties. Keenly cognizant of their own Achilles' heel, Greens know that their people skills probably aren't stellar, so they delegate personnel issues to a Blue assistant. Perhaps they aren't good at keeping up with day-to-day details, so they delegate these duties to a Gold assistant. Perhaps they aren't good at rallying the troops and making motivational speeches, so they delegate to an Orange aide. That leaves them free to handle the jobs they do best—researching, strategizing, analyzing, projecting, and developing products, to name a few.

In their personal quest to improve the world, Green administrators repeatedly act as agents of change. This is particularly distressing to their Gold and Blue workers, who are naturally opposed to such frequent change. So Green leaders need to be particularly careful not to make too many changes in a given time period. However, if the Golds and Blues become involved in the early stages of these changes, their concerns may be alleviated, if not eliminated altogether.

Often ahead of their time, Green supervisors aren't content with the status quo. They strive to improve and innovate, advancing the organization to new heights. They thirst for knowledge and competence and encourage others to excel as well. They prefer to develop foolproof plans, then turn them over to others to implement and maintain. They live in the world of possibilities and potential, believing that anything is achievable if you can just figure it out.

Green Leaders

Are product-oriented
Focus on the future
Expect self-motivation
Loathe incompetence
Appear distant, aloof
Identify problems
Explore possibilities
Stay calm in crises
Multitask effectively
Reward expertise

Orange leaders

Orange leaders are the proverbial go-getters. As the old adage goes, "They make things happen while others just sit back and wonder what happened." To a self-respecting Orange, sitting, studying, waiting, wishing, pondering, and planning are all time-wasting activities that simply suck the fun out of life. They'd much rather do something and fail than do nothing at all.

Because Oranges prefer to experience things first hand, they're more likely than other supervisors to be out "mingling with the troops." It's there, on the battlefield, where most Oranges deal with urgent problems. They seldom bark out orders from a distance, preferring instead to hop into the trenches and lead out, inspiring others to follow their example.

On the other hand, while down in the trenches, Orange managers aren't likely to hover over their subordinates, looking for opportunities to give direction or correction. They despise micro-management, preferring instead to give people enough rope to either pull themselves out of a jam or hang themselves with certainty. After all, they reason, if a person doesn't have enough skill to meet the demands of the situation, then they shouldn't have been there in the first place.

In the unlikely event that an Orange has a nine-to-five desk job, chances are you won't find him or her in one location for long. After a quick glance at the daily schedule, the Orange would immediately leave the office, preferring to be out and about solving problems face-to-face. One of the reasons Oranges hate desk-work so much is the tedium of paperwork. Creating or reviewing memos, reports, performance reviews, statistical analyses—all of these cause an Orange's eyes to roll up in his or her head, quickly followed by a call to a subordinate to take over this particular task while the Orange has an urgent need to take care of something else. Consequently, most Orange leaders learn how to be effective delegators early in their careers.

However, when a crisis emerges, Oranges don't delegate. They arrive on the scene as fast as ducks flock to bread floating on water. Here is a chance for them to demonstrate some of their most prized attributes: courage, skill, and grace under pressure. They take charge quickly, assessing the scene with amazing perception, often pinpointing the exact source of the trouble immediately. Then, without a blink of an eye, they set about doing what they can to put out the fire, even if it means dispensing with established protocol and procedures. Of course, if it isn't a life or death crisis, they'll take a little time to hear various aspects of the problem, but then they'll move swiftly and decisively, not often looking back.

Orange supervisors are deft negotiators. They're able to put on their poker faces, then wheel and deal until they emerge triumphant. They will do what they must in order to win the game. If that means that sacrifices must be made, then sacrifices will be made. Unnecessary policies, plans, procedures, people—these are expendable pawns in the struggle for success. The Orange isn't cruel, unwise, or subversive—but he or she will do what is necessary to complete the job.

When it comes time to holding meetings, Orange managers firmly believe that shorter is better. Meetings are far more likely to take place over a cell phone, in the hallway, at the gym, in a restaurant, at the beach, on the golf course—anywhere but in a stuffy conference room. Meetings are convened to solve problems and deliver essential instructions; they aren't held just for the sake of having a meeting. Oranges may have an agenda—perhaps created by someone else—but they certainly don't feel compelled to follow it. If it fits in with the discussion, fine, but if it gets in the way of progress, then it's hastily dispatched. Orange meetings may feel like a whirlwind to the uninitiated, with decisions being made quickly and topics being changed frequently. They're frank and honest, not prone to beating around a bush. They tend to be friendly, captivating, and light-hearted, easily charming their audience into a state of awed acquiescence. Consequently, most people emerge from a meeting with a sense of exhilaration mingled with astonishment. Only later do they begin to wonder what actually took place.

The naturally upbeat Orange supervisor often uses jokes, jabs, and jocularity to lighten the mood. When discussions become too dark and depressing, they'll try to change the subject to something less gloomy. Ever the optimists, Oranges can be counted on to lead out with courage, conviction, and charisma, regardless of the seriousness of their cause or the enormity of their task.

Orange Leaders

Are action-oriented
Focus on results
Decide quickly
Bend rules
Thrive on stress
Detest long meetings
Energize followers
Negotiate skillfully
Delegate paperwork
Reward liberally

Showing Appreciation

By now you should have a pretty clear picture of what each personality looks like in a leadership role. Now we'll shift the focus a bit and provide some information that will help the leader deal with subordinates of differing colors.

It probably goes without saying, but I'll say it anyway: all employees need to feel appreciated for the good things they do. A wise leader knows that nothing boosts morale and productivity as much as sincere appreciation for a job well done. Of course the trick is knowing when a person needs acknowledgement and how to express it in a meaningful way.

Fortunately, the first issue—knowing when a person needs acknowledgement—has a simple solution. All colors want to be appreciated when they do something in harmony with their values. So what do they value? Think back to what you learned in chapter 1. Each color has a specific set of actions they value. These are the things they prize above all others. So when they do something they prize, it brings them joy. Then, when a supervisor comes along and immediately offers praise and thanks for this action, it not only validates their own set of values and builds up their feelings of self-worth, but it brings them even more joy. Once again, the key is to recognize them immediately when you catch them doing something they value.

At this point, someone might say, "But what happens if what the person values is not what I or my organization values? By giving praise, am I not reinforcing behavior I don't agree with?" This would be true only if you're trying to compel people to act outside or against their personal values. And if that's what you're trying to do, perhaps you ought to change your strategy. Imagine the mental anguish, emotional conflict, and moral turmoil you're creating within that person. Do you honestly believe that forcing people to act contrary to their values will make them easier to manage and more productive? It's far better to help people see how behaviors you desire will help them achieve the things they value. And if you can't reframe the actions in those terms, or help people do other things—actions they intrinsically value—then you ought to just give up and find someone else to do the deed—someone who values doing it in the first place.

The second issue—knowing how to express appreciation—is only slightly more difficult to solve. In this case, you need to reach into your bag of tricks and pull out the things you learned from the previous chapters. In order to make the praise significant and deliver it in a meaningful way, you must appeal to the values and attitudes your subordinates admire, use the motivation techniques that they prefer, and communicate in ways that are meaningful to them. Again, the keyword is *their* preferences, not yours. Only then will appreciation be meaningful.

Below are some guidelines you can use to prime the appreciation pump.

Appreciating Blues

People who supervise Blues must remember a couple of things. First, Blues tend not to value expressions of appreciation just because someone wealthy, powerful, or important utters them. Rather, Blues value compliments and appreciation that come from the heart and are personal in nature. Blues typically want to be recognized for their individuality, not their competence, skillfulness, or dedication.

Second, the other three colors seem to handle criticism with greater ease than Blues, who tend to take things more personally. Lead Blues with praise; don't push them with verbal shock prods. Under a verbal cutting, a Blue can lock up, become discouraged, or even go on the offensive. This is all because Blues listen to their feelings.

A third thing that supervisors must realize is that Blues know feelings can be a spinning compass. They likely are constantly stepping outside themselves to see if they're making any sense. The practical impact of this to the praise giver is that not only must one slip compliments and appreciation to a Blue on Blue topics, but also fertilize them with validation and feedback, so the Blue knows to take them seriously and not think, as Blues often do, "Awww, you're just saying that!"

Below are a few actions that Blues value. As they behave in these ways, that would be a prime time for a supervisor to offer a sincere compliment, a thoughtful note, a small token of appreciation, or even just a really big smile.

— Accommodating requests gracefully
— Contributing to morale and well-being
— Being compassionate to the oppressed
— Making peace between opponents

— Creating a comfortable environment
— Joining in worthwhile causes

Appreciating Golds

Golds are inclined to value output more than process. Quality matters, as does seriousness, attention to detail, thoroughness, and accuracy of work. Golds, however, expect these traits to be present in the workers, so they don't often give or expect praise for them. Instead, a Gold likes to hear good things about the item produced, its quality, and the quantity. It gets even better for a Gold if you throw in something about how closely the product aligns to the standards, because accuracy of output translates to excellence in production, and more important, speaks to the reliability and industriousness of the worker.

Here is a key to praising a Gold: focus on something a Gold made or did. Golds need loads of praise, because they wear so much responsibility, but Golds are also duty bound, so they aren't emotionally equipped to process pats on the back. But do a minor rave about what a wonderful and precise thing was crafted by this Gold person—that's Gold soul food.

Things that should trigger praise for a Gold include:

— Fulfilling commitments and obligations
— Protecting and preserving resources
— Keeping things neat and orderly
— Adhering to rules and requirements
— Showing respect and loyalty to leaders
— Being punctual and prepared
— Attending to details

Appreciating Greens

Greens are idea people. Greens will fight for an intelligent listener who will take the trouble to follow their arguments. It's not surprising, then, that the strongest praise one can give a Green is to acknowledge his or her ideas.

Greens are so strongly true to their internal musings that they tend to downgrade the importance of things that others might consider rather basic. A Green's eyeglasses exist to facilitate reading and not walking into things. If they're cracked, tape on the bridge is a viable option until the Green can arrange for replacements. Time at work may preclude the trip to the optician; hence, to a Green, there is no shame in the tape. Other things that may fall by the wayside for the intellectual Green include hygiene, stylishness in dress, brushing teeth, and in extreme cases, even trimming their nails and the condition and orderliness of their house, room, and car. I mention this here because it helps to drive home the point that compliments of a personal nature may lack meaning for a Green. Similarly, approbation for common tasks done well or on time may be empty praise for Greens.

Greens will value appreciation that's aimed at their capabilities. However, Greens also have the annoying trait of rating the value of praise according to credentials of the praise giver. If that person has an important title, that may be important to some people, but to a Green, it's the competence of the person that most matters, not their stature in life.

When you notice one of the following in a Green, it's probably a good topic for a praise tidbit.

— Developing expertise in a subject
— Working overtime without request
— Formulating logical arguments
— Troubleshooting problem areas
— Thinking outside the box
— Correcting errors without prodding
— Caring about accuracy and precision

Appreciating Oranges

Oranges are natural performers. As workers, they like to hear about the graceful, smooth ways in which they accomplish tasks. Praise them for their style and flair, which flow from their urge to do things so stylishly that they look easy.

Oranges are likely to be much more attuned to the work process than the work product. Smooth execution means more to them than high productivity. In particular, give notice to Orange's high-risk activities (if your nerves can handle it). Taking chances is Orange's long suit. If it works, pats on the back and adulation all around. If it bombs, pick them up, dust them off, and let them lick their wounds. Tell them you expect them to have better luck next time. Specific triggers upon which you should express appreciation to Oranges are listed below. Mention these qualities when you see them in action, and Oranges are likely to feel appreciated, and hence will try to do even more and better.

— Demonstrating courage in a crisis
— Being bold and candid when necessary
— Building camaraderie among teammates
— Being able to adapt quickly to changes
— Doing a job with confidence
— Looking good under pressure
— Tackling challenges head-on

Team Building

Go Team!

Teamwork is one of today's more popular buzzwords. It seems as if everyone is on the teamwork bandwagon—after all, two heads must be better than one! Hundreds, if not thousands, of hours are spent on team-building activities and retreats. Whether you are working in a classroom, boardroom, or family room, at some point, you are likely to find it necessary to work as a team.

If we agree that success and efficiency are best met by a group effort, then why is it so difficult for groups of people to operate as cohesive units? Teamwork consultants will tell you that some of the stresses plaguing any team come from lack of trust, lack of direction, lack of a definitive goal, or all three. These are vital components and they must be considered in the planning of any team project or task. There is at least one other component of team planning that is often overlooked—the perception each team member has about teamwork itself.

Blue

Blues love working in groups. Teamwork is right up their alley. They enjoy the social aspect, the collaboration, and the camaraderie of solving a problem or completing a task with others. However, as much as they're enthused by teamwork and group process, they have trouble if the group has not jelled and conflict comes to the table.

Blues require clear goals and expectations. From a Blue perspective, these components allow the team to start as free of conflict and competition as possible. In addition, Blues like to spend a chunk of time getting to know the members of their team, both personally and provisionally. If given their druthers, Blues would work on a project or goal as a whole group, from start to finish.

Gold

Many Golds dislike working in groups or as a team because they often have to do all of the work; at least, they perceive this is the case. In some cases, this perception may be true, as a Gold's need for organization, order, and completion drives him or her to move forward at a faster rate than group members of other temperament types. In addition, Golds tend to complete and check off every detail of the project or task. A Gold checklist may contain tasks that other temperaments think are unnecessary. If this is the case, it's up to the Gold to push for completion or simply do it themselves.

Golds are likely to prefer teaming situations where a goal is given, expectations are explained in writing, tasks are evenly divided among team members, and each member completes his or her assigned task independently. In addition, where credit is given, Golds prefer that each team member be judged on individual merit rather than assessing the team as a whole.

Green

For Greens, teamwork can be akin to a root canal. Although brainstorming sessions to discover possible solutions can be enjoyable, when it comes down to completing a task or project, Greens would simply rather do it themselves and be done. A source of stress for Greens in the teamwork world is that they often find themselves still in the brainstorming phase while other team members are ready to move into production or completion.

Greens are likely to enjoy teams that are designed to capitalize on the skill set of each member. Like other temperaments, they need clear expectations and a defined end goal. It's highly appreciated if they have the freedom to define processes as needed. The ideal Green team may tend to look a bit like the parallel play of toddlers.

Orange

Oranges often have a love-hate feeling toward teamwork. A distinct advantage for an Orange in teaming is they're typically surrounded with team members of other temperaments. This allows them to allow others to do what they do best: organize and deal with the details. In removing the perceived "drudgery" from a task, teaming allows Oranges to be creative, solve problems, and use their flair. However, Oranges may feel as if other members of the team are getting trapped in minor details instead of actively moving forward.

Oranges prefer teams that require active participation, especially when the goal can be met in the short term. They're the presenters and deal closers. They enjoy those team situations where tasks can be completed with as much fun and humor as possible. They want to keep it moving and keep it light!

Implications

The pros of teamwork have been well documented. It's work strategy that works. However, the level of success depends upon many facets. Taking into account the pros and cons of teamwork as perceived by each temperament represented on the team is a necessary step in planning the goals and expectations of the team. In order to operate in the nexus, it's necessary to plan for and build teams on a case-by-case basis. In doing so, the needs of each member are met, skill sets can be matched, and effective work practices can be practiced.

Dealing with Procrastination

Nothing raises a supervisor's blood pressure quite like procrastination within the ranks. Whether you're leading a sports team, a growing family, or a colossal conglomerate, it may be time to take a hard look at this exasperating problem.

According to the *American Heritage Dictionary*, to procrastinate means "to put off something, especially out of habitual carelessness or laziness" or "to postpone or delay needlessly."

Like most things in life, your feelings about procrastination are highly dependent upon your perception and preferences. *Carelessness, laziness,* and *needlessly* are all modifiers that leave a lot to individual interpretation. Therein lies the rub. In order to clarify, let's look closely at the preferences and perceptions of each temperament with regard to procrastination.

Our perceptions are rooted in our personality styles. We tend to think that others should behave and think the way we do. The reality is that what you perceive as procrastination may not be procrastination in the eyes of someone else.

Getting off our "buts"

I remember a few years ago my friends and I used to hand small wooden tokens to each other. They usually were homemade and frequently had the cryptic "TU-IT" on the surface. If you made some that were shaped like a poker chip, you could hand one to a friend who had been forgetful about some chore and say something smart, such as "I see you haven't gotten that Smith project done yet. You must be having trouble getting started. Here you go…" and then you'd flip him one of your little tokens like it was the coin that decided which team kicks off at the Superbowl. Your friend would pick it up, examine the lettering, and then the look of recognition would come upon his face. He hadn't started the project for what ever reason, usually lots of reasons, and what you had just offered him was what he needed most, a round tu-it. Thus equipped, he could begin the project, because he had finally "gotten around to it." (Say it aloud).

The more creative among us would pass out little flat sticks, roughly the size of a big tongue depressor, also labeled with the tu-it logo. This was the cure all for someone who was stuck in a long project that never seemed to end. It was, of course, a "stick to it."

If only we could get projects rolling and keep them that way by such trivial tokens! In truth, there is much more to putting things off than there appears at first glance. It's one thing to figure out what needs to be done and another to do it. Once I gained an awareness of temperaments, I saw that each of the four colors approaches projects differently and each faces different challenges in getting things moving. The danger in viewing procrastination as a one-size-fits-all problem is that what would be a logical solution to one color can induce sheer terror, or boredom, in another. The result is more procrastination.

Reframing the problem and paying attention to the colors involved can often break the logjam and get things rolling. In the first place, each color stays put for different reasons. And of the many things that face each of us, not all activities are equally delayed.

Most people procrastinate doing things they don't do particularly well or find uncomfortable. Below are just a couple of examples of how each of the four temperaments does this. I could write pages and pages on how each color procrastinates—maybe I'll do that someday in another book.

Blue excuses

Blue procrastinators are likely to get sidetracked by personal issues. They may put off doing impersonal tasks in favor of dealing with interpersonal tasks first. However, a Blue procrastinator may not see this as procrastination. Instead, he or she may see this as a priority issue. The Blue priority is people, so that's what gets accomplished first.

Blues drag their feet when it comes to facing negative issues directly, especially when it comes to reviewing someone's performance or criticizing someone else's efforts. Blues also hate having to deliver bad news. Blues would rather do team building or work to comfort the disenfranchised. They would more likely enjoy seeing that all hands have everything they need to proceed with the job, or else doing something to socially enhance the workplace, than they would having to critique or confront someone.

For most Blues, procrastination causes stress because it affects the morale of the team or department. When someone causes delays on a project, it causes conflict as well as the possibility of decreased social interaction with both coworkers and family. Procrastination, unless done as a group, also doesn't lend itself to the cooperative atmosphere that Blues prefer.

Gold excuses

Golds can't get around to not getting around to things. If it detracts from getting the job done they'll put off relaxing, recreating, building up espirit de corps, or just about any other discretionary activity. Better for a Gold to stay on schedule, even if the project is on hold. If there is nothing immediately pressing, a Gold will tidy up, wash the windows, purge the files, or do anything that will allow him or her to have a feeling of accomplishment when the day is over. This often leads Golds to believe they're the ones that do all of the work.

Golds often can't figure out why procrastination is even a word. Once given a task, they're typically tenacious about getting it done. When a team member procrastinates, Golds' stress levels begin to rise. This happens both because Golds can't complete their assigned tasks and because they believe procrastinators are acting irresponsibly. To put it bluntly, procrastination is simply unacceptable.

Green excuses

Greens may tell you that they never procrastinate. In their minds, they are right. You see, few Greens will tell you that a delay on their part is needless. If there's a delay, it must be warranted by the need to check facts, redesign, or improve. However, Greens are also likely to bypass tasks that are highly repetitive in favor of those requiring problem solving and the gathering of new ideas. Again, this isn't lazy, it's a matter of priorities—from a Green perspective.

Greens are tardy when it comes to things involving others. This includes the unpredictable, entangling, "touchy-feely" side of things, such as dealing with tension between workers or team members, or listening to someone's personal problems. It's less of a problem by far to work on the computer, have brainstorm about a new marketing program, or do some other analytical activity. In fact, Greens would likely prefer to spend most of the day thinking things through and developing a unique and novel approach, and then leaving the details and actual execution to more trivial beings.

Procrastination by others doesn't bother Greens all that much, unless it directly causes a slowdown in their work. What often happens in these cases is that the Green simply picks up any ball that was dropped and completes the task so that he or she can get on with the work at hand. This can cause animosity because the Green may then think they're the only ones who can complete the task on time with efficiency and accuracy.

Orange excuses

Oranges procrastinate getting organized, but rarely procrastinate doing. They would rather be actively doing something—calling, selling, telling, building—anything but wasting time with preliminaries. This preference for activity over planning, preparation, and clean-up leads other colors to view Orange with suspicion. If tools are dropped where they were last used, that's a small price to pay for getting in a few extra innings at work, or reacting quickly to a change. Oranges also put off cleaning up because it's stifling. Oranges are happiest when they're frantic. Exploring alternative ways to get something done, or doing something that brings freshness to a routine, is much more rewarding to an Orange than cleaning off a workspace or sorting out files.

Oranges typically aren't disturbed all that much by procrastinators around them. There is a confidence that, no matter what happens, it will all work out in the end. The challenge of making things work—with backs against the wall—is exciting and plays on their strengths.

Overcoming procrastination in yourself

The important thing to remember is that there are more reasons to procrastinate than just being lazy. Putting things off has more to do with avoiding those things that don't come easily to one's temperament. Understanding this can make us less critical of those who seem unable to get started.

Remember the little "tu-it" tokens mentioned earlier? They're a powerful tool towards overcoming procrastination—but not in the folks you give them to, only in yourself. Perhaps this is why we used to think the tokens worked. Creating them and giving them away forced us to think of ways to get through whatever project was in front of us. When we finally worked up a plan that was acceptable to our native temperaments, we were off and running. Obviously it was not the token, but the reframing that got us moving. Therefore, here are some quick re-framing tools:

— If you're a humane Blue, avoid thinking of how long the project will keep you occupied and out of touch with your friends. Think instead of how your project will help others. Is there some aspect of the project that may be difficult or uncomfortable? Do that, and spare your co-laborers or teammates.

— If you happen to be a dedicated Gold, avoid thinking of any project as a waste of time. Consider instead how your efforts will directly contribute to the good of the overall organization. Seeing your good work, others may be inspired to work harder themselves. Don't forget to add that extra touch, such as sweeping, mopping, or applying touch-up paint.

— If you're an inquisitive Green, avoid thinking of how trivial or redundant the project may appear to be. Concentrate instead on solutions. Look for a way to solve the problem with elegance, something that no one besides a Green could come up with. It's best if your plan will then allow you to execute the project either so quickly or with such seemingly little effort that people are mystified as to how you did it.

— And if you're a vibrant Orange, just keep in mind the following: The task ahead is not boring. It's not tedious. It's an obstacle waiting to test you. Let it try and stop you! Once you dive in, you're poetry in motion. If it's hard or dangerous, while others are still thinking about it, you're already half done. You may or may not take a quick bow when it's all finished, because you'll be off to your next big adventure.

Helping others overcome procrastination

Helping others do what they're required to do is often a bit trickier. Remember that each color has its own sticking points: Greens avoid sticky human issues; Blues evade criticism, evaluations, and discipline; Golds prefer to stay away from things out of the norm that may precipitate change; and Oranges pass up anything except the main event.

You can generate considerable enthusiasm if you apply similar reframing techniques to the task at hand, keeping in mind the nature of the task and the nature of the person you're tasking.

— For Blues, emphasize how much the completed task will pull people together and create unity. If there are extremely technical bits that seem uninteresting to the Blue, find a Green to assist.

— Golds can be attracted with promise of participation in a job well done, and pointing out how the task will help accomplish the larger goals of the organization, as well as provide an opportunity to demonstrate their organizational and leadership skills.

— With Greens, you can offer to handle some of the personal interaction for them, so that they can focus on the difficult, ingenious aspects of the task.

— Oranges will respond if you focus on the task itself, and provide some way to make it kinetic and challenging. Perhaps you can help Orange by providing an audience, maybe even making teams and providing a scorecard for all to see.

So, what's the plan

Regardless of the perceptions, the reality is that most tasks need to be done within specific timeframes. In that reality, perceptions are only helpful in structuring the work environment so that stress is reduced and work is efficient. Here are a few things to consider:

— *Set clear expectations.* When team members know exactly what is expected from each member, the feeling of "all for one" is created. In addition, each team member knows how his or her piece (task) fits into the whole project. This often increases the buy-in level of team members. Incidentally, this same concept is important within any work grouping—cooperative team or individual contributions.

— *Define time related goals clearly and stick to them.* When each team member or employee knows that there is a deadline and that said deadline is not flexible, there is a clear and complete understanding of when tasks need to be completed. Allowing floating deadlines (deadlines that are set, but never enforced) is often tantamount to having no deadline at all.

— *Set quality standards and stick to them.* Getting a task finished is not the same as getting a job finished well. Where deadlines are concerned, it's important to clarify the level of quality expected. If this is not done, some group members may feel as if some are being held to different standards. This could cause the very stress that you're trying to avoid.

— *Where possible, provide flexibility for individual work styles.* As mentioned above, each member of your team has different ways of perceiving how work should get done. When possible, allow for those differences. For example, when a three-week deadline is set, allow Greens to use the ENTIRE three weeks to complete the task, avoid questioning their methods and procedures, and don't secretly hope or expect that they will be done sooner.

— *Assign tasks based on strengths.* This sounds like common sense. However, office politics have a way of insinuating themselves into task division. In the long run, your team/department will be better served by assigning tasks by strength rather than by some other measure.

— *Meet regularly (and quickly) for status checks.* Regular status checks are important for all members, especially those who tend to procrastinate. If a member knows they will have to report progress toward a goal, they're more likely actually to make progress toward a goal. These meetings can be invaluable in keeping tabs on what's happening; however, they need to be kept short and on task.

— *Provide incentives for meeting deadlines.* Many people find working toward an incentive highly motivating. These incentives don't have to be monetary. Consider the temperament make up of the team or department and design incentives tailored to their values and needs.

— *Be willing to adjust the plan if warranted.* For many, there is nothing worse than continuing a plan that's doomed to failure. Up-front planning is a must, however, and if the situation changes and adjustments are warranted, call the team together and regroup!

As much as procrastination and the personal reactions it invokes are rooted in perception, it's a real phenomenon. Habitual procrastinators can be a destructive force on a team or department. The good news is: they don't have to be. Initial planning and a concerted effort to create a work environment that's creative, effective, and communication-friendly go a long way toward avoiding procrastination pitfalls.

CHAPTER 6

Recreation: Using Fun and Frolic to Reduce Stress and Conflict

Finding balance between work and play is difficult in our modern world. This chapter will explore how each color prefers to spend leisure time, how they look under pressure, and what we can do to reduce conflict and the negative effects of stress.

The Need for Leisure

If you take a close look at any professional athlete during a game or contest, you will notice that they rarely push themselves to the point of physical exhaustion and breakdown. The highest achievers will regularly take themselves out of the competition, if only for a moment or two, to catch their breath or quench their thirst. Even experienced marathon runners, known for the way they gruelingly push their bodies to the max, will take off at least a week between races to rest and recuperate. Of course, you don't have to be an Olympian to know that you have to rest your body at regular intervals. Try staying awake for 48 hours, starting a new exercise routine at the gym, or climbing up a massive pine tree. Chances are you'll soon be fatigued enough to take a time out.

How much of your waking time do you spend working? People who regularly work more than ten hours per day—excluding breaks—may be pushing themselves a bit too hard. After that, problems begin to sprout forth like weeds in a garden. I hope that you have good health insurance, because you'll be spending a lot more time visiting doctors and getting your arm stuck with needles. You may have a weakened immune system, increasing your chances of catching the common cold or developing other viral illnesses. Your heartbeat and breathing rates may become elevated to unhealthy levels. Your liver may start to malfunction as it works overtime to deliver extra sugar to your bloodstream. You may experience memory loss, a lack of energy, pain in the muscles and joints, headache, mental confusion, depression, burnout, anxiety, and irritability. Eventually overwork may lead to cardiovascular diseases, diabetes, asthma, migraines, gastrointestinal problems, substance abuse, hypertension, and mental disorders. Furthermore, the problems don't just affect you. Your family is affected by long work hours, since you're not able to give adequate time and attention to your loved ones. Your employer is affected because you're not as alert, productive, and healthy, so will have to hire someone else to help get the work done. And on it goes. Even if you were being paid overtime for all your extra work, which most people aren't these days, it simply isn't worth the wear and tear.

So why do some of us feel so guilty and selfish when we want to stop laboring and goof around for a while? Aren't our emotional, mental, social, and spiritual health worth at least as much energy as we spend on our physical health? Do you give enough attention to these other elements of your character? If you do, then great—skip this chapter and move on. But if you don't, then you might just need to learn how to find more leisure time in your schedule.

> "Work consists of whatever a body is obliged to do. Play consists of whatever a body is *not* obliged to do."
>
> — MARK TWAIN

What exactly is leisure? For this book, *leisure* is defined as freedom from time-consuming duties, responsibilities, or activities. Leisure time is your free time—the time you spend refreshing your mind or body. Leisure activities are normally enjoyable, if not pleasurable, and include exercise, relaxation, socializing, entertainment, and hobbies. These activities re-create harmony between the roles you play, such as worker, parent, spouse, friend, sibling, child, leader, teacher, student, and so on. This re-creation, or recreation, becomes a vital part of your long-term health and well-being.

I'm certainly not advocating hedonism. Spending a disproportionate amount of energy pursuing pleasure in any of its forms can't be wise. Work has its place in life as does play. Without the one, you can't fully understand or appreciate the other. Some people believe that for every hour you spend laboring, you should spend an hour in leisure. I'm not necessarily saying that—I believe each of us must strike a healthy balance between work and play, just as we do between so many other things. This highly individualized task varies widely from person to person and from color to color. What's enjoyable for one is not enjoyable for another, as we'll discover next.

Recreational Activities

If you were to ask 100 people to list their favorite leisure activities, you would find, not surprisingly, that those who share the same personality type generally share the same recreational preferences.

Occasionally there may seem to be exceptions to this rule. What if you know a Gold who goes bungee jumping or a Blue who attends a monster truck rally? On the surface, these activities seem inconsistent with their preferences. The question you must ask is "why?" Why does the Gold bungee jump? Perhaps it's a tradition she doesn't want to break. Why would the Blue go to the truck rally? Maybe it was his only opportunity to spend time with a loved one. These individuals are participating in atypical activities to get what they need—what they value—from the event. But if they could get their needs fulfilled from activities that reflect their natural inclinations, they would much rather do those things. Given a choice, most people would still prefer activities that reflect their own value systems.

As you prepare to take go out with friends or family, perhaps you may want to consider activities that reflect their primary color—not yours. Below is a list of thirty leisure activities that appeal to each color to get you headed in the right direction. Again, this isn't an exhaustive list by any means.

Blue

Blues thoroughly enjoy the finer things in life: sitting in front of a fire with a good novel, soaking in a luxurious bath, listening to excellent music, savoring a box of decadent chocolates, vacationing in an opulent resort, dining in a premier restaurant, strolling through a beautiful and fragrant garden, snuggling with a down-filled comforter, watching a celebrated theatrical production, visiting the museums and monuments of Paris, and so on. Of course, what makes these activities—and those listed below—particularly meaningful and especially delightful is doing them with a loved one.

- ☐ Acting in a play
- ☐ Attending a poetry reading
- ☐ Beachcombing
- ☐ Candlelit dinners
- ☐ Going on a double date
- ☐ Going on a train ride
- ☐ Going to a pet show
- ☐ Going to the petting zoo
- ☐ Horseback riding
- ☐ Listening to music
- ☐ Look at slides and photo albums
- ☐ Making dessert together
- ☐ Making pottery together
- ☐ Participating in a protest march
- ☐ Playing relationship games
- ☐ Reciting poetry
- ☐ Riding in a carriage
- ☐ Romantic dancing
- ☐ Romantic picnic
- ☐ Scenic driving
- ☐ Singing a song
- ☐ Staying at a bed and breakfast
- ☐ Taking a dinner cruise
- ☐ Tandem bicycling
- ☐ Visiting in a coffee shop
- ☐ Volunteering
- ☐ Watching a play
- ☐ Watching romantic videos
- ☐ Working on crafts
- ☐ Writing love letters

Gold

Golds won't indulge in recreational activities until they've fulfilled all their obligations. Otherwise, they'll suffer so much from feelings of guilt that they become quite miserable to be around. Even when they take time off to rest and recuperate, they don't "cut loose" like their Blue and Orange cousins. Their activities still reflect all of their values. They'll do the right thing, in the right way, at the right time, in the right place. Their activities are normally conservative, traditional, and formal. More often than not, they're ordered towards a specific goal, such as improving family relationships, maintaining health, or entertaining others. Golds usually organize playtime well so that everyone involved understands the expectations, rules, and timeframes. Even though they may appear to be stiff, proper, and constrained, they're experiencing fun in their own way.

- ☐ Bicycling
- ☐ Camping
- ☐ Cleaning the house
- ☐ Exercising together
- ☐ Going to a convention
- ☐ Going to a formal dance
- ☐ Going to a religious service
- ☐ Going to a symphony
- ☐ Going to an athletic event
- ☐ Going to the local park
- ☐ Lawn bowling
- ☐ Making something useful
- ☐ Marching in a parade
- ☐ Playing bingo
- ☐ Playing board games
- ☐ Playing card games
- ☐ Playing miniature golf
- ☐ Playing shuffle board
- ☐ Playing tennis or golf
- ☐ Renting a limo
- ☐ Researching family history
- ☐ Shopping at a farmer's market
- ☐ Shopping at outlet stores
- ☐ Swimming
- ☐ Visiting formal gardens
- ☐ Walking the dog
- ☐ Washing a car
- ☐ Watching a ballet
- ☐ Watching historical videos
- ☐ Working in the garden

Green

Most Greens appreciate activities that engage the brain in new and intriguing ways. After all, they reason, the greatest adventures in life aren't physical; they're mental. Of course, Greens aren't limited to sedentary cerebral activities; they have their favorite sports and athletic activities as well. In these activities, just like any other Green undertaking, they don't do it just for fun—they do it to acquire competence. So whether it's pursuing new levels of competence in a familiar field of study, or considering something completely different, Greens are up to the challenge. Just give them enough time and space and they'll amuse themselves forever.

- ☐ Attending an intriguing lecture
- ☐ Bird watching
- ☐ Building and flying a kite
- ☐ Debating
- ☐ Driving around
- ☐ Eating something new
- ☐ Going to a book club
- ☐ Going to the library
- ☐ Hiking someplace new
- ☐ Learning magic tricks
- ☐ Meeting on-line
- ☐ Playing billiards
- ☐ Playing trivia games
- ☐ Playing video games at home
- ☐ Reading books
- ☐ Seeing something new
- ☐ Shooting a homemade video
- ☐ Solving crossword puzzles
- ☐ Solving a mystery
- ☐ Star gazing
- ☐ Surfing the World Wide Web
- ☐ Taking a class together
- ☐ Taking a factory tour
- ☐ Visiting a museum
- ☐ Visiting the zoo
- ☐ Watching *Jeopardy!*
- ☐ Watching educational videos
- ☐ Watching how-to videos
- ☐ Watching science-fiction videos
- ☐ Working on hobbies

Orange

The perfect Orange activity is anything that requires at least three Hail Marys before one attempts it for the first time and uses at least two-thirds of the body's available adrenaline. Even though some of the activities below don't quite match that definition, they would if at the end of each item you simply tacked on the word *naked*.

- ☐ Auto, motorcycle, or mountain bike racing
- ☐ Bungee jumping
- ☐ Canoeing, kayaking, rafting
- ☐ Crashing a wedding
- ☐ Demolition derby or monster truck rally
- ☐ Driving bumper cars
- ☐ Gambling
- ☐ Going to a carnival/fair
- ☐ Going to a wild rock concert
- ☐ Going to an auction/flea market
- ☐ Hang gliding
- ☐ Hot air ballooning
- ☐ Hot-tub hopping
- ☐ Inline skating
- ☐ Paint balling
- ☐ Playing videogames at arcade
- ☐ Pub crawling
- ☐ Riding in a helicopter or fighter jet
- ☐ Riding roller coasters
- ☐ Rock climbing or spelunking
- ☐ Scavenger hunting
- ☐ Scuba diving or snorkeling
- ☐ Skinny-dipping
- ☐ Skydiving
- ☐ Snow skiing and snowboarding
- ☐ Surfing, windsurfing, water skiing, wakeboarding
- ☐ Taking a spontaneous weekend trip
- ☐ Tattooing or body piercing
- ☐ Visiting a comedy club
- ☐ Watching action movies

Understanding Self-Image

Defining the terms

Throughout the last few decades, a lot has been said about self-image and self-esteem. Some people believe they're the cure-all for society's problems while others think it's only touchy-feely rigmarole. However, like most things, the truth lies somewhere between the two extremes.

In this book, *self-image* is defined as the perception you have of yourself at any given moment. It's the way you feel or think about your values, attitudes, and actions. It includes an assessment of your qualities and your sense of personal worth. When you have a healthy opinion of yourself, you're said to possess high amounts of "self-worth" or "self-esteem." When you have a poor opinion of yourself, you're "out-of-esteem" or "disesteemed."

The effects of self-image on behavior

There's a continuum linking our feelings about ourselves with our attitudes and actions. Casual observation reveals that as self-worth increases, so does positive behavior. People who have a positive self-image have feelings of satisfaction, confidence, and self-respect. These feelings, when supported by a positive value system, foster positive behaviors.

Abraham H. Maslow was one of the first twentieth-century psychologists to explore the effects of self-image thoroughly. He concluded that people who have a positive self-image are more likely to succeed. They're prone to accept themselves for who they are and treat others with the same unconditional regard. They absolutely enjoy life and look forward to new challenges.

People who have high levels of self-esteem take more control of their lives. If they have a personal or psychological need that isn't being met, they do something constructive to remedy it. When under stress, they usually act in *proactive* rather than *reactive* ways—they understand the importance of not allowing a provocative situation manipulate their responses.

People with a positive self-image know how to put their strengths to good use. They know which of their personality characteristics are good and which are not. They accentuate positive attributes and try to eliminate the negative.

A quick trip to the dark side

So far, in this book, as we've examined the attributes and behaviors of each temperament, we've only seen descriptions of people who have a healthy self-image. Rather than drawing attention to negative attributes, I've focused almost exclusively on the positives.

Why? Well, to be honest, I didn't want to encourage "color bashing." Most people, when they know what someone's weaknesses are, tend to look for them. They use this information as ammunition to attack a behavior they don't like. They'll say something hurtful like, "Oh you're an Orange. No wonder you don't take anything seriously. You're naturally irresponsible." Since an important objective of this book is to help readers become more understanding and tolerant of others, dwelling on the negative seems counterproductive. Of course, you would never do this, but someone else might.

Furthermore, it's not really necessary to point out the negatives. They're fairly obvious. Simply take any characteristic that is normally an asset and maximize or minimize it until it mutates into a liability. Any "good" attribute can morph into a "bad" attribute in the blink of an eye.

For example, many Golds prefer their homes to be clean and orderly. However, they could take this perfectly natural preference and minimize it to the point where their homes become virtual pigpens, filled with debris, clutter, dirty dishes, rumpled clothes, stacks of old newspapers, and so on. On the other hand, they could also maximize this preference. Before long they act like Felix Unger in Neil Simon's play, *The Odd Couple,* and become so obsessed with cleanliness that they make their house as sterile as a microchip-manufacturer's clean room, driving away family and friends in the process.

Why people act out

But why would someone do this? Why would a person choose to act in unusual or uncharacteristic ways? Why would someone do something he or she doesn't value? These are good questions that have kept the science of psychology alive for decades. Fortunately, I think there's a simple answer: most people just want to be happy as they journey through life. If they do something that doesn't bring them happiness, then they'll do something else. It's that simple. People engage in activities they hope will bring them joy. If they feel joy, then they're "in esteem." If they can't find joy, then they're "out-of-esteem."

In chapter 1, we discussed in detail the things that bring each color joy—the set of characteristics and actions that are preferred over all others. Therefore, if you understand someone's color spectrum, you'll know in what order he or she prefers to do things. Your primary color dictates which things you'll do first, your secondary color indicates what you'll do second, your tertiary color determines what you'll do third, and the inferior color explains what you'll do last. Since you spend most of your time acting out of your primary color, this is where you have the most skill and competence. This is how you derive the most joy.

Downshifting

Let me illustrate this process with a metaphor. Pretend you're driving a car through a beautiful valley. The scenery is great and you're really enjoying the trip. You're cruising along in fourth gear, your highest gear. All is well. By and by, you come to the end of the valley where the road starts to work its way up a fairly steep hill. You get concerned as your car begins to slow down as it tries to make it up the hill, so you downshift into third gear. That seems to work for a while, but soon it slows back down and you decide to downshift into second gear. In spite of all your efforts, your car still won't make it over this particular hill, and it's about to stall out, so you anxiously shift into your lowest gear. Finally, you creep up and over the hill. Before you know it, the road levels out and you're able to return to high gear and cruise along, enjoying your journey once again.

Let's say your color spectrum is composed of, in descending order, Green, Gold, Orange, and Blue. When you're doing Green things—activities that reflect your primary color—you're cruising along, enjoying life. You're "in esteem." All of a sudden, something happens and you're forced to change your approach. For some reason Green things aren't bringing you enough happiness. So you downshift into your second color, Gold. You do some Gold things for a while, like straightening up your room, organizing your underwear drawer, paying a few bills. You find you're not as good at doing these things as you were with Green things. But you're still not really happy, so you downshift into your third gear—your tertiary color. Now you begin to do some Orange behaviors. You'll throw a party, go skinny-dipping, take a trip to Las Vegas—but you still aren't truly happy. So finally, desperately, you shift into your fourth color, Blue, and try some of those behaviors for a time, hoping that Blue activities will bring you joy. Perhaps cuddling a few babies and saving a spotted owl or two will make the difference.

You can tell how well people are coping with life's challenges by looking at their attitudes and behaviors. If they're acting in harmony with their primary color values, they're doing wonderfully well. If they're doing things that reflect their secondary color, then they're merely doing okay. If they're acting out of their third color, then they're starting to struggle a bit. And if they're acting out of their fourth color, they're in a world of hurt.

Shapeshifting

Here's an important principle to remember: the further you get from your primary color, the unhappier you become, the more stress you encounter, and the harder it becomes to maintain a positive self-image. When your self-image starts to sink and downshifting doesn't seem to work for you, then you'll probably start shapeshifting.

Shapeshifting begins when you consciously or unconsciously maximize or minimize behaviors to try to find something—anything—that will make you happier. A bevy of negative attitudes and behaviors begin to pop up. Calm people become more easily agitated. Peppy people become more morose and lethargic. Sweethearts bite, songbirds bark, responsible folks let important matters drop. It's as if we are shouting by our attitudes and actions, "Right now I don't deserve to be me!"

Below you'll find several paragraphs that explain how each of the colors might behave when their esteem levels are flushed down the drain. Please understand that these aren't ironclad rules that indicate what will definitely happen—they simply warn what might happen. Because every individual represents a unique blend of all four temperaments, it's virtually impossible to predict human behavior with 100 percent precision.

Blue warning signs

> Out-of-esteem Blues may appear to be demonstrative, depressed, emotional, hysterical, mystical, overindulgent, overly sensitive, scatterbrained, self-absorbed, submissive, unrealistic, unresponsive, unstable, untruthful, or withdrawn.

The Blue characteristic of emotional sensitivity can make them prone to becoming too emotional and too sensitive, often making them feel victimized or oppressed without just cause. On the other hand, naturally gentle Blues seldom stand up for their personal rights or exhibit assertive or aggressive behavior—making them easy targets for cheating or abuse. Since Blues invest so much of their personal energy in other people, especially in other people's problems, a continual stream of negative stimuli can cause a Blue to experience "break-down" and suffer from a variety of emotional problems.

Some out-of-esteem Blues prefer to avoid social events. Fearful of being embarrassed, rejected, or looked down upon, they will withdraw entirely into isolation. While they still desire love and acceptance, they're even more uncomfortable at the thought of being open to criticism and disapproval.

Disesteemed Blues may become distrustful of their close friends and loved ones. They question someone's loyalty and fidelity and look for hidden messages between the lines. Even innocent remarks and events are misinterpreted or treated with suspicion. This emerging paranoia makes them feel like they're being persecuted or exploited. As a result, they become resentful and carry grudges for long periods of time.

There's a tendency for down-and-out Blues to become dependent on others for approval. If they don't get the reassurance and praise they need, they start to act out, trying to get the attention they crave. They'll exaggerate their feelings, even appearing hysterical at times. They'll focus on themselves, worrying about their weight, appearance, and attractiveness. On the other hand, they also don't want to delay gratification, demanding that their appetites and passions be satisfied immediately. This can lead to overindulgence, gluttony, and substance abuse.

Some dependent Blues, convinced that if they displease their loved one they'll be kicked out of the home, willingly submit to whatever is asked of them, even if it's distasteful and debasing. They're afraid to make significant decisions without first seeking advice or approval. If they're left alone for any length of time they feel utterly helpless; if the relationship ends, they're devastated.

Gold warning signs

> Out-of-esteem Golds may appear to be abusive, anxious, compulsive, demanding, disorganized, fussy, guilty, judgmental, obsessive, overly protective, preachy, reactionary, or self-righteous.

Some Golds suffer from a passive-aggressive personality disorder, which means that they appear to be passively resisting your call for them do something, when in fact they're really trying to stick it to you. They figure that if they procrastinate, dig their heels in, work slowly, or purposely do a bad job, then you'll eventually give in and let them off the hook.

Out-of-esteem Golds also tend to be critical of their leaders, quick to point out character flaws and errors in judgment. Of course, they don't do it in the leader's presence, preferring to backbite and gossip in darkened hallways. They often feel persecuted, believing that their leaders are making unreasonable demands of them. They think they aren't being rewarded enough, judging that the performance they give is far superior to that of their peers. They resent suggestions for improvement and blame flaws in their work on others. If they really get upset with management, they'll create some obstacles or obstructions that delay production and make the leader look bad.

If they happen to overdose on criticizing and condemning, down-and-out Golds will eventually switch to carping and complaining. Grousing over their miserable lot in life is a pastime they're addicted to. If you happen to be passing by, you might become entangled in their web of wretchedness, for the only thing better then self-pity is a pity-party. Since misery loves company, hour after hour is spent looking at the half-empty glass, finding everything that is presently wrong or that possibly could go wrong in the future.

While some Golds shift their frustrations to other people, others take them out on themselves. If for some reason they haven't done everything they planned to do, have fallen short of their expectations, or have inadvertently dropped the ball, then they'll feel worthless, inadequate, and agonizingly guilty. They'll engage is some brutal self-punishment. As part of their penance, they'll deny themselves of pleasurable experiences or become involved in situations that cause them to feel pain or suffering. They'll get angry at those who attempt to console them. They might even pick a fight with the hopes of getting someone mad at them. This self-sacrificing, masochistic behavior is completely self-defeating—which is, of course, the desired effect.

A few disesteemed Golds turn their normally positive features into negatives. They may become perfectionists, becoming unhappy with anything that isn't perfect or doesn't meet extremely high standards. They may become bossy, self-righteous, and inflexible, demanding that their desires be executed with exactness. Often they become workaholics, organizing and ordering everything they see. Or they may go the opposite direction and let the world fall apart around them, with chaos and clutter accumulating around every corner.

Green warning signs

> Out-of-esteem Greens may appear to be aloof, apathetic, arrogant, critical, cynical, distant, eccentric, finicky, mocking, non-compliant, reclusive, sarcastic, schizophrenic, self-deprecating, or skeptical.

Greens normally take a reasonable amount of time to make important decisions. But when feeling out-of-esteem, they may become completely indecisive, or at the other extreme, stubborn and inflexible. If they feel pressured to make a decision that might make them look incompetent, then they tend to clam up and withdraw to a place where they can sulk in private. Failures resulting from personal error or incompetence affect Greens more than any other temperament; consequently, they have become the masters of denial and justification. Leave it to the Greens to find the legal loopholes and logical arguments that will get them out of situations that made them look bad.

Normally quite rational and ordered, the out-of-esteem Green's thinking process becomes quite irrational and convoluted. When this happens, they may express some odd beliefs or talk about some unusual experiences. They often subscribe to conspiracy theories, suspicious that others are plotting against them. They may dress abnormally, often wearing inappropriate, eclectic, or bizarre clothing. They exhibit eccentric and unusual behaviors that alienate people, which is just as well, because they also tend to make nonsensical statements or ramble incoherently.

Since they perceive the world revolves around them, some disesteemed Greens constantly strive for acknowledgment and prestige. If they can't earn it the old-fashioned way, they'll try to usurp it through treachery and deceit. If they can't mastermind a plot to take over the world, like Lex Luthor, Superman's nemesis, then they'll try to spread misery as far as possible. Many of the world's most infamous dictators, despots, and terrorists are whacked-out Greens.

In a conceited attempt to establish their mental superiority, a few out-of-esteem Greens will try to manipulate the people and events in their world. Using every trick up their Machiavellian sleeves, they'll devise scams and confidence games to trap and deceive both strangers and loved ones. As a result, their relationships begin to crumble around them, and they feel lonely and empty. Many Greens try to deaden the pain with external stimulants: drugs, alcohol, exhibitionism, voyeurism, etc.

Greens are prone to hypochondriasis, a mental disorder in which they're tormented by glum and gloomy views, especially concerning their health and welfare. Even though experts assert otherwise, they're convinced something is wrong with them and that they're going to die prematurely. They may become preoccupied with death, the occult, or the afterlife, preferring to die now than live in misery. Some melancholy Greens become obsessed with darkness and dress in black from head to toe. They become pale "creatures of the night" staying up extremely late and sleeping throughout most of the day.

Believing they are social flops, some Greens become indifferent to human contact. Given the choice, they'll avoid close interpersonal relationships altogether, choosing instead to stay by themselves or with, in some cases, their imaginary friends. Since sexual experiences typically involve other people, they'll avoid them, preferring autoeroticism. They become completely emotionally impaired, choosing neither to experience nor to express a range of feelings. They become extremely passive, being unmoved by praise or criticism. They look and act like bumps on a log.

Some disturbed Greens can become quite cruel and demeaning. In fact, they're almost sadistic in the way they go about demeaning and humiliating people—in private or in public. They'll try to intimidate others into submission, threatening harsh punishments if they refuse. In some extreme cases, Greens will become fascinated with violence, weapons, martial arts, injury, or torture—things that harm others or inflict pain.

Orange warning signs

> Out-of-esteem Oranges may appear to be aggressive, angry, belligerent, deceptive, defiant, disobedient, impatient, insensitive, intimidating, loud, manic, rude, self-destructive, shortsighted, or violent.

Oranges that are under a great deal of stress tend to find the easiest and the quickest way out of a troublesome situation. This may not be altogether constructive, especially if they're in a leadership position. They may opt for the "band-aid" approach to problem solving, when what's really needed is reconstructive surgery. Rather than solving the problem, they may actually make it worse.

Out-of-esteem Oranges sometimes take their sense of playfulness and light-heartedness to the extreme, becoming rude or coarse in inappropriate situations and offending others with their boisterousness. Or their naturally positive approach to life may make them too unrealistic or naive, often causing acquaintances not to take them seriously, passing the Orange off as a clown or a goof-off.

Sometimes Oranges have so much self-esteem that it becomes a bad thing. Psychologists call this narcissism. These people have a bloated sense of how important they are, demanding to be recognized, admired, and praised. As self-anointed VIPs, they arrogantly expect others to give them special treatment and privileges, believing that they don't have to obey the rules that govern others. They have a difficult time appreciating others' perspectives, believing that no one's needs should interfere with their own. They often fantasize about possessing a never-ending supply of success, power, brilliance, beauty, or love.

Out-of-esteem Oranges regularly discount or infringe upon the rights of others. Their behaviors may be aggressive, reckless, promiscuous, or destructive, and may involve breaking laws or rules, deceit, or theft. Lying and cheating are perfectly fine, especially if you have been treated unfairly and you're just trying to get your due. Believing in the "survival of the fittest," they'll use whatever force or cunning they need to ensure they'll wind up on top. If something becomes too difficult, then they summarily drop it. As a result, they have a difficult time planning ahead, finishing important projects, maintaining jobs, keeping promises, repaying debts, being loyal to friends and loved ones, and so on.

When some Oranges get out-of-sorts, in one breath they claim to be completely independent, and in another they say they're downright needy. This fluctuation carries over into their attitudes, thinking, sleep patterns, energy levels, and personal relationships. They may be happy, peppy, and bursting with love, then a few minutes later they're ranting, raving, and tearing out their hair. They're either extremely talkative and are laughing, joking, and punning, or they're somber and silent, perhaps moping or crying. On impulse they shift from one extreme to another, leading them to gamble, shoplift, flirt, impulse buy, drive recklessly, try drugs, binge eat, drink excessively, start fights, drop water balloon bombs off rooftops, etc.

Unable to keep their tempers in check, disesteemed Oranges can become violent and brutal. Sometimes they get so rowdy, angry, and explosive that they alienate their loved ones. Frantic that they might be abandoned, they'll resort to physical, emotional, sexual, and verbal abuse in a misguided attempt to keep their families together. More likely than not, the relationship will quickly fall apart and the Orange will find someone else. It's no wonder they have so many short-lived relationships.

Not only do they move from relationship to relationship, Oranges tend to move from job to job and from place to place, feeling trapped if they're forced to root in any one location. This wanderlust, while providing a host of interesting and exotic experiences, also makes life tenuous and empty for an Orange. To try to fill this emptiness, they're constantly raising the stakes, exhibiting behaviors that are increasingly risky or dangerous. They must get a higher high to make up for their spirit-breaking lows.

This cycle continues indefinitely, unless someone or something intervenes to break it up.

Tips for building esteem in other people

As has been shown, with each temperament, there are certain characteristics or tendencies that often surface when that individual's self-esteem declines. These characteristics are easily labeled as negative and can become a focus of ridicule and derision by others. However, if we see these traits as symptoms of a low self-image, we can use our knowledge of personality styles to help build self-esteem back up so that they can again display normal, acceptable behaviors.

A word of practical advice—it's usually wise to tolerate out-of-esteem behavior for a while until the person has vented his or her feelings and regained self-control. Becoming combative to out-of-esteem behavior often exacerbates the problem and prolongs its resolution. It's also wise to refrain from offering solutions to the person's problem. Most of the time, an out-of-esteem individual already knows how to solve the problem. What they want—and need—is empathy.

To help rebuild the self-image of others, it's critical that we give them opportunities to feel good about themselves. If we know their color spectrum, we instantaneously know their innate strengths. By encouraging them to concentrate on those strengths and guiding them towards meaningful successes, their self-esteem will undoubtedly climb. The following chart summarizes some ways to build self-image.

Building Self-Image	
Green	**Orange**
Listen to their ideas Permit independent work Provide mental challenges Provide access to resources Recognize their competence Provide sufficient time	Recognize talents Promote optimism Provide chances to shine Appreciate their humor Give leadership positions Reward immediately
Gold	**Blue**
Recognize leadership skills Provide attainable goals Provide structure Give responsibilities Recognize achievements Value their work ethic	Show caring and concern Give creative opportunities Recognize individuality Accept feelings Express appreciation Assist to build relationships

Stress Management

You can feel your heart beating faster and faster. The muscles in your neck and back are starting to tighten up. You feel irritable, anxious, or a tad depressed. What's going on? More likely than not, you're feeling the negative effects of stress—a mentally or emotionally disruptive condition that is caused by any number of undesirable influences. Perhaps you've recently experienced some significant changes in your life or have been forced to deal with some monstrous problems. Perhaps you've had to shoulder some heavy emotional burdens or have had to deal with some intensive mental pressure or strain. Regardless of the cause, your body is unconsciously trying to cope with this trauma. But it can only do so much. If you leave the stress unchecked, it can be quite disruptive, even devastating, to your health and happiness.

Since our modern world seems filled to the brim with pressure, noise, chaos, and hubbub, trying to figure out how to cope with and manage stress has been the subject of countless self-help books, seminars, and retreats. Individuals and organizations trying to reduce the negative effects of stress regularly spend tremendous fortunes on this problem. Fortunately, you may not have to spend another dime searching for solutions; below are the main keys for understanding and dealing with stress.

Things That Cause Stress

All of us get stressed-out now and then. Sometimes, we're bothered by the same things—like getting married, having a baby, accidents, illnesses, death, divorce, the loss of a job, terrorism, war, etc. These are the big events that actually change our lives forever. However, as you've probably noticed, a particular stressor often affects people in different ways. What may seem catastrophic to one may only be a slight annoyance to another.

Why? Because an individual's personality style determines which things cause them to feel stress. For example, since a Gold values a clean, orderly room more than the other types, he or she will probably be stressed-out by a messy room. Therefore, the key to deciding if something is stressful or not is to see if it goes against that person's values. Usually, if it discounts, ignores, or runs contrary to a person's values, it's stressful. The deeper the value, the greater the stress.

On the following pages, I've compiled a list of actions that add stress to the lives of each personality type. It isn't complete by any means, but it certainly indicates the type of things you should avoid.

Blue

- ☐ Insincerity and hypocrisy
- ☐ Backbiting and slander
- ☐ Lying and cheating
- ☐ Personal rejection
- ☐ Violence, conflict, aggression
- ☐ Intimidation and coercion
- ☐ Contention and disharmony
- ☐ Persecution, discrimination, oppression
- ☐ Stereotyping
- ☐ Limits on communication
- ☐ Failure to talk things out
- ☐ Lack of close friends
- ☐ Inability to socialize
- ☐ Broken promises and commitments
- ☐ Infidelity and unfaithfulness
- ☐ Insensitivity
- ☐ Disregarding feelings or impressions
- ☐ Lack of charity and compassion
- ☐ Self-centeredness
- ☐ Lack of affection and romance
- ☐ Mistreatment, harshness, cruelty
- ☐ Waste of natural resources
- ☐ Destruction of any kind of life
- ☐ Isolation and confinement
- ☐ Ridicule and sarcasm
- ☐ Revenge and vindictiveness

Gold

- ☐ Disobedience and noncompliance
- ☐ Insubordination and rebellion
- ☐ Chaos and anarchy
- ☐ Squandered resources
- ☐ Gambling, risk-taking, speculation
- ☐ Irresponsibility
- ☐ Loose ethics or standards, indecency, obscenity
- ☐ Freeloading and begging
- ☐ Nonconformity and unorthodox behavior
- ☐ Ambiguity and vagueness
- ☐ Inadequate planning or preparation
- ☐ Incomplete directions
- ☐ No chain-of-command
- ☐ Disorder, disorganization, filth, clutter
- ☐ Criminal and illegal behavior
- ☐ Unfulfilled expectations
- ☐ Impromptu or unrehearsed speeches
- ☐ Lack of discipline, structure, routine
- ☐ Laziness and idleness

- ☐ Apathy and indifference
- ☐ Carelessness
- ☐ Lack of follow-through
- ☐ Inability to make or keep commitments
- ☐ Disrespect and insolence
- ☐ Bad manners and rudeness
- ☐ Ingratitude

Green

- ☐ Incompetence, stupidity, feeble-mindedness
- ☐ Blind obedience
- ☐ Lack of independence
- ☐ Forced compliance
- ☐ Routine and monotony
- ☐ Subjective or prejudicial decisions
- ☐ Emotional reactions, ranting, raving
- ☐ Lack of self-control
- ☐ Small talk
- ☐ Irrelevancy
- ☐ Body language
- ☐ Disregarding facts
- ☐ Intellectual idleness
- ☐ Plagiarism
- ☐ The "crowd" mentality, fads, fashions, bandwagons
- ☐ Irrational behavior
- ☐ Illogical arguments
- ☐ Poor performance
- ☐ Inaccuracy
- ☐ Groundless criticism
- ☐ Vanity and narcissism
- ☐ Goals set by others
- ☐ Physical aggression
- ☐ Jocks, prima-donnas, apple polishers
- ☐ Social functions
- ☐ Not enough time

Orange

- ☐ Rules and regulations
- ☐ Restrictions and conditions
- ☐ Physical confinement or limitations
- ☐ Being backed into a corner and forced to comply
- ☐ Too many responsibilities
- ☐ Repetition and routine
- ☐ Indecision and inactivity
- ☐ Deadlines and time frames
- ☐ Non-negotiable arrangements
- ☐ Impractical or abstract ideas
- ☐ Too much structure or bureaucracy
- ☐ Oppressive control and domination

- ☐ Unfair judgments
- ☐ Reading instruction manuals
- ☐ Being ignored
- ☐ Being dismissed as immature
- ☐ Excessive planning and preparation
- ☐ A lack of humor, money, sex
- ☐ Paperwork
- ☐ Record keeping
- ☐ Permanent commitments
- ☐ Ignoring their performance
- ☐ Lack of activity and adventure
- ☐ Sickness, disease, infirmity, weakness
- ☐ People who find fault or have a negative disposition
- ☐ Couch potatoes, nerds, apple-polishers, basket-cases

Things People Do That Stress-Out Others

Now it's time to put the shoe on the other foot. Just as each color is stressed-out by different things, so too is each color prone to do specific things that irritate the other types. Therefore, a person who really wants to win friends and influence people will avoid doing these things as often as possible.

Read through the list that reflects your primary color and see if you're doing any of those things. If so, don't worry about it, unless of course you're NOT alone in a cabin in the woods writing your memoirs. Otherwise, see what you can do to eliminate some of these negative attitudes or actions. Chances are, they're just some of your natural strengths maximized or minimized to the point where they're becoming liabilities. Figure out how to fix them and move on.

Blue

- ☐ Being overly sentimental
- ☐ Wearing their feelings on their sleeves
- ☐ Talking too much
- ☐ Being too idealistic—not being realistic
- ☐ Not planning ahead and thinking about the future
- ☐ Reading too much into things
- ☐ Obsessing over minor hurtful comments
- ☐ Blowing things out of proportion
- ☐ Being too passive—not being assertive
- ☐ Spending too much time with friends
- ☐ Being sugary sweet
- ☐ Being too generous or charitable
- ☐ Being too trusting, gullible, naive
- ☐ Letting others make difficult decisions

- ☐ Suppressing unpleasant emotions until they explode
- ☐ Failing to see others' point-of-view
- ☐ Avoiding conflict and confrontation
- ☐ Sweeping problems under the rug
- ☐ Being absorbed in the lives of other people
- ☐ Attempting to please everyone
- ☐ Lashing out at others when strained
- ☐ Having difficulty in setting priorities and goals
- ☐ Squandering energy on ill-chosen tasks
- ☐ Overextending themselves
- ☐ Overindulging or spoiling other people
- ☐ Taking in stray or hurt animals
- ☐ Accepting abuse from other people
- ☐ Frequently talking about personal issues
- ☐ Being blindly loyal to undeserving people or causes
- ☐ Idolizing other people

Gold

- ☐ Working too hard
- ☐ Being inflexible or unchangeable
- ☐ Becoming obsessed with unimportant details
- ☐ Trying to control too much
- ☐ Taking on too many responsibilities—can't say "no"
- ☐ Being bossy and domineering
- ☐ Being too strict or stern
- ☐ Demanding or expecting too much from others
- ☐ Being pessimistic, gloomy, apocalyptic
- ☐ Being judgmental or preachy
- ☐ Imposing values on others
- ☐ Being ultra-conservative or reactionary
- ☐ Keeping their "heads in the sand"
- ☐ Being prudish or strait-laced
- ☐ Being high-strung, anxious, up-tight
- ☐ Worrying, fretting, and agonizing over little things
- ☐ Following the letter of the law with exactness
- ☐ Concentrating on production, quotas, statistics
- ☐ Being a bureaucrat, do-gooder, apple-polisher
- ☐ Convening too many meetings
- ☐ Planning and preparing in excess
- ☐ Rigidly following agendas and schedules
- ☐ Being obsessive or compulsive
- ☐ Focusing on wealth, status, security
- ☐ Not being able to stop themselves from giving advice
- ☐ Inability to relax and take what comes
- ☐ Getting lost in the details and missing the big picture
- ☐ Getting stuck in a rut
- ☐ Being too formal, boring, stuffy

Green

- ☐ Taking too much time to make decisions
- ☐ Getting too involved with work or hobbies
- ☐ Asking too many questions
- ☐ Not being sensitive to feelings
- ☐ Sounding arrogant or overly confident
- ☐ Not expressing feelings
- ☐ Being too independent
- ☐ Not being sociable
- ☐ Spending too much time alone
- ☐ Questioning authority
- ☐ Not going with the flow
- ☐ Living in the future
- ☐ Being too focused and absent-minded
- ☐ Spending too much time with books and computers
- ☐ Doing several things at the same time
- ☐ Over-extending themselves
- ☐ Being overly critical, perfectionistic, cynical
- ☐ Never finishing a project because of constant improvements
- ☐ Using technical terms or jargon
- ☐ Being wordy or redundant
- ☐ Being condescending, flippant, sarcastic
- ☐ Being too abstract or complicated
- ☐ Being impersonal and indifferent
- ☐ Trying to solve the problems of others
- ☐ Focusing on minor inconsistencies or flaws
- ☐ Being competitive when intellectually challenged
- ☐ Inability to set realistic priorities and time frames
- ☐ Not letting go of impractical ideas
- ☐ Not caring about what others think

Orange

- ☐ Ignoring rules, policies, procedures
- ☐ Shooting from the hip and getting away with it
- ☐ Preparing in haste and excluding important details
- ☐ Failing to follow through with commitments
- ☐ Neglecting to report failures
- ☐ Appearing to be immature or playful
- ☐ Making decisions too quickly
- ☐ Appearing to be self-absorbed
- ☐ Abandoning responsibilities
- ☐ Being undisciplined
- ☐ Having too much fun
- ☐ Not planning ahead
- ☐ Being careless about details
- ☐ Being late or forgetting important events
- ☐ Making commitments for people without consulting them
- ☐ Being quick-tempered
- ☐ Going overboard with unjustified praise

- ☐ Being loud, aggressive, intimidating
- ☐ Refusing to accept blame or running away from problems
- ☐ Having a “flexible” conscience and bending the truth
- ☐ Acting restless and fidgety
- ☐ Doing too many unexpected things
- ☐ Being manipulative
- ☐ Undervaluing the contributions of others
- ☐ Not being serious enough
- ☐ Thinking out loud
- ☐ Being too honest, bold, truthful
- ☐ Being too generous, extravagant, or debt-prone
- ☐ Impulse buying

Conflict Resolution

Now that you’ve read the section on stress, you may feel guilty for inadvertently doing some things that really annoy the people around you. And, being the marvelously considerate person that you are, you’ve made up your mind to eliminate as many of those irritating actions as possible. But in spite of your best efforts, some people seem to be perpetually chapped-off with you.

On the other hand, perhaps you’re being aggravated so much by the behaviors of others that you’re contemplating doing something drastic—something that might send you to the big house. Before you do something you’ll later regret, let me put forward some simple suggestions for averting messy confrontations. In fact, by following these guidelines, you may find yourself surrounded by a lot more friends than enemies. And who wouldn’t want that?

Understanding the source of the conflict

Building effective conflict management skills starts with identifying the different temperaments that are involved. To illustrate, suppose you have one friend who dislikes small talk and another who wants to talk everything out to its end. Or you have a family member who is always in motion, moving from one unfinished task to another, while another needs to finish one task before moving on to the next on the list. Unless people with these opposite temperaments understand and respect each other, coming to a solution may be just as much of a conflict as the issue itself.

The key lies in listening to each person from his or her own point-of-view. Each person brings to the table both a position on the issue at hand and a personal perception of the communication process. Understanding that these are sometimes mutually exclusive will help you break them into two distinct pieces in order to deal with them effectively.

Before tackling the issues, it may be helpful to do a reality check on your own point-of-view, as well as the points-of-view of the other people. Are you behaving in a manner inconsistent with your temperament? Are the others? In times of conflict, incongruous behaviors are commonplace. Recognizing this will help identify the "people issues" involved in the larger problem at hand.

Resolving conflicts with Blues

When Blues confront you with a concern, please understand that it took an awful lot of irritation to get them to this point. Blues are able to endure a Herculean amount of personal discomfort for long periods, but it has finally reached the point where they can't take it any more. So they'll do one of the things they normally dodge—getting in your face. They can't bear to do this because they're afraid they'll say something that will permanently damage the relationship. Consequently, confrontation invariably adds more stress to their burden, which increases their suffering, which increases their internal turmoil. No wonder you get an emotional eruption!

When you're confronted in this manner, before you're tempted to make an unfortunate knee-jerk reaction, it's important that you first wholeheartedly listen to the Blues' concerns, regardless of his or her state of mind. If they're upset or emotional, quietly encourage them to continue expressing their feelings, even if it leads to bouts of weeping, wailing, whimpering, or whining. This may take a degree of patience, gentleness, and compassion that would make Mohandas Gandhi proud of you. But if you do it sincerely, without judgment, the storm will blow itself out.

Then, and only then, if you feel compelled to express your concerns, do so quickly, kindly, and softly, with as much genuine pleasantness as you can deliver. If you appear to be the slightest bit indifferent, peeved, patronizing, judgmental, or argumentative, you will have burned the pot of beans.

Resolving conflicts with Golds

Golds, who prefer to think of things as right or wrong and black or white, establish distinct opinions on most matters. Even if they don't have a definitive opinion, they'll sure act like they do. They project a matter-of-fact tone that shouts, "That's the way it is. Period." If you find it necessary to talk them out of it, you've got a mighty difficult task ahead of you, since most Golds doggedly adhere to their judgments like lobbyists cling to legislators. Thus they become formidable opponents in the battle of wills who won't back away quietly.

When a Gold confronts you, you've obviously done something wrong—otherwise the Gold wouldn't need to be there. They normally come clothed in the robes of authority, which they declare immediately: "I'm Deputy Sheriff Fife." Then they ask for your identity and credentials, "And who might you be?" If you can't cite a higher or equivalent authority, the interrogation resumes: "Why are you here? What in the world are you up to? Who said you could do that?" And so it continues until the Gold confirms that he or she was right and you were wrong.

The best way to respond to confrontation with Golds is to be as courteous and polite as possible. Show respect, even if it doesn't seem justified. Be appreciative of their concern for you. Try to identify some common ground or set some rules that you can both abide by. Don't try to shift blame to someone else or sidetrack the issue at hand. Ask and answer questions firmly and clearly, without resentment or guile. If they become overbearing or obnoxious, it's because they're really irritated—so do what you can to reduce their frustration.

Resolving conflicts with Greens

Unlike the other three temperaments, it's hard to tell when a Green is being deliberately confrontational. Green emotional outbursts are about as rare as a snowstorm in the Sahara. Therefore, unless Greens are undergoing some serious stress, you'll probably see them cool, calm, and collected even when they're burning up with indignation. Furthermore, to some folks, especially the Blues, Greens appear confrontational nearly all of the time. They're always questioning things, trying to prove their points, arguing over minutiae, trying to find faults in reasoning, saying that feelings aren't logical, and so on. So if you can't rely on outside appearances to determine if Greens are upset, you'll just have to listen to what they say, not how they say it.

As you can probably infer, Greens don't think that confrontation is a bad thing, unless it becomes an emotion-laden, irrational expression from a frustrated mind. Otherwise, a confrontation is merely another opportunity to figure out where people stand and why they stand there. It's simply a meeting of the minds—nothing more, nothing less.

Therefore, when a Green approaches you with an opposing viewpoint, don't interpret it as a personal attack. View the exchange as a game. Detach yourself from the situation. If possible, set aside your predilections and adopt, at least for a moment, the Green's perspective. Try to articulate clear, logical arguments that support your conclusions. Focus on the facts and sift away the fiction. If you show a smidgen of passion about your position, it's okay, as long as it doesn't shut down your objectivity. Then, when all has been said and done, smile and say, "Thanks for that intriguing discussion. You've left me much to think about." Then revert to your original opinion and go merrily on your way; the Green probably will.

Resolving conflicts with Oranges

Oranges are built for combat. Having spent most of their life battling with conservative authority figures and a few obnoxious peers and family members, they're almost always ready to engage the enemy on a moment's notice. Because they're expert fighters, it's best not to get them riled up in the first place. Actually, that's not too hard to do since most Oranges are tolerant, open-minded individuals. Unless they get thoroughly bored, they don't go looking for conflicts. However, if you do rub them the wrong way, you will be warned immediately. If you do it again, you'll probably receive a verbal lashing. But if you repeatedly do it, be prepared for a thorough thrashing.

The first weapon in the Orange arsenal is intimidation. They'll come at you with as much ferocity as they can muster, hoping their bluster will cow you into submission. If that doesn't work and they see the fire of defiance in your eyes, then they'll try other weapons: insults, ridicule, contempt, profanity, hostility, violence. However, if you respond with quiet dignity, without malice or condescension, staying cool and calm, you stand a good chance of disarming them completely. You don't have to surrender; in fact, giving up your ground may actually exacerbate the issue in the future. Just don't counterattack, responding tit for tat, throwing out castigatory arguments and retaliatory barbs. Simply try to reduce the emotional intensity of the confrontation. Perhaps you can lighten the mood with some jokes or humor. Getting up and moving around the room is also good since it helps discharge physical tension. Only turn your back and retreat if tempers are lost completely and the situation becomes uncontrollable or unhealthy.

Building bridges

When it comes right down to it, making a decision or finding the wisest solution to a conflict involves balancing the interests of all parties as objectively as possible. If we take steps to understand both the people involved in the process and their interests, strive to develop a clear understanding of the issues from the opposite point of view, and if we realize that there are often multiple solutions to any given problem, we can begin to manage conflicts creatively and effectively. We can build bridges of understanding. We can more easily maintain the lines of communication, now that they are open. We can agree to compromises and contracts without nearly as much difficulty. Life returns to normal—or maybe even just a bit better than normal.

CHAPTER 7

Childhood: Rearing Vibrant Children

In this chapter, you will learn how personality is apparent in young children, how to cultivate and nurture a child's natural talents and strengths, and how to effectively discipline misbehavior.

Characteristics of Children

> "Children today are tyrants. They contradict their parents, gobble their food, and tyrannize their teachers."
>
> — SOCRATES

Ah, the joys of childhood. Remember being treated like a prince or princess? Back then you were waited on hand and foot. Every need was anticipated and fulfilled. If the service was slow, all you had to do was cry out a little, and a servant came running. You had a roof over your head and a comfy blanket to keep you warm. Every day, someone would provide clothes for you to wear and help you get dressed. There was someone around to clean up your messes, wipe your nose, dry your tears, and powder your posterior. There was someone willing to chauffeur you from place to place, pay your doctor bills, buy you an occasional toy, and play with you at the park. You could eat Twinkies and Ding Dongs without regret and drink as much whole milk as you desired. You could nap whenever you felt like it and got to take lengthy bubble baths with a rubber ducky. You were allowed to play hour after hour without a care in the world, daydreaming, watching cartoons, coloring, playing in the backyard with friends, making forts, playing school—no one seemed to mind how you frittered away your time. Then, at the end of the day, you were either rocked to sleep or tucked into bed after hearing a story where everyone lived happily ever after.

Of course, most of us didn't have such a rosy childhood, even if we were reared in a bona fide palace. In fact, for some, childhood wasn't all that great at all; merely remembering it can be a painful experience. For some reason, our parents didn't quite get it, and we suffered because of it. But those were the old days—before anyone knew about Blues, Golds, Greens, and Oranges. Now, empowered with this information, you are better equipped to take on the role of parent, grandparent, guardian, aunt, or uncle. Now it's your turn to perform the adult duties of babysitting, nurturing, disciplining, teaching, potty-training, grocery shopping, cooking, chauffeuring, dusting, vacuuming, sweeping, gardening, repairing, bookkeeping, laundering, window-washing, trash-disposing, etc.

Fortunately, the transition from childhood to adulthood doesn't take place overnight. In fact, it takes eighteen to twenty years for most people, although for some it takes much, much longer. This chapter will focus on the first 12 years of that period. Chapter 8 will focus on the second half, a mind-numbing, bone-jarring, white-knuckled era known as adolescence.

We will begin by exploring what each temperament looks like in childhood. We will examine their characteristics in the following categories: family, toys and games, family activities, relationships, behavior, needs, and growing up.

Blue Children

Blues are imaginative children who spend a lot of time coloring, writing, playacting, and daydreaming. They love it when older people take the time to tell them stories, nursery rhymes, and fairy tales. They like playing with toys that have personality, like dolls or animals. Because they're naturally gentle and sensitive, they're easily upset when other people become overly competitive, aggressive, or violent.

Family

The idea of a family as a place of mutual love, caring, and support is more important to Blues than the idea of the family as an institution. A Blue child wants a family where good feelings and harmony are present on all sides. Blues are sensitive emotionally and react badly to household conflict. If raised amidst a lot of peripheral contention, a Blue child may become inhibited and refuse to participate in family activities. Blue children may have a difficult time handling anger or other negative emotions in themselves or others. They are by nature gentle, kind, and compassionate. They don't make waves and tend to go along with the majority. Though they will probably appreciate the addition of brothers or sisters in a family, it may cause initial stress to Blues, who need to feel they're special and unique.

Toys and games

Blues enjoy toys to which they can attach personalities, and these toys can become quite real to them. As such, the loss of a special doll or toy can be devastating to a Blue child. Both Greens and Blues use their toys as fantasy objects, but the Blue is more likely to involve them in stories and attach personality. Blues are the children most likely to have an imaginary friend with whom to share things.

Blues enjoy games that are interactive but non-competitive. Blues identify with the feelings of other children. Because they're so sensitive, they don't find great appeal in competition. Even if Blues win a contest, they will feel sorry for the loser. Meanness or cruelty in other children or adults that might not phase the other colors can deeply hurt the Blue. Even seeing other children experience rejection may cause the Blue distress, causing them to cry when someone else cries.

Favorite activities

Blue children like to do things that involve other people. The activity is not as important as the act of sharing an experience with friends or family. Blues enjoy family picnics or other outings as long as everyone is getting along. Blues love to read and be read to because it engages their imagination. They also enjoy activities that require imagination and creativity, like the visual and performing arts. Consequently, Blue children can be avid painters, sculptors, actors, and musicians.

Relationships

Relationships and interaction with others are especially important to Blue children. Because they have a tendency to be trusting, agreeable, sociable, and harmonious, they're usually well liked and enjoy their friendships. It's important for the Blue to do things with friends regardless of what's being done. Sometimes this connection to their friends may lead them to do things they otherwise wouldn't do.

Blues love to have secrets and share them only with close friends. Commitments and promises are important to Blues on a personal level, not on the level of right and wrong. If a promise is not kept, the Blue will take it personally and will probably become deeply offended.

Behavior

Blues often display a gift for language early in life. They seem to relate to others naturally and enjoy communicating. Extroverted Blues tend to be talkative and always have something to say; some exasperated parents claim they never stop talking. They are often skilled writers and will probably enjoy keeping a journal, writing poetry, or creating short stories.

Blue children are imaginative and may be gifted storytellers. They're sometimes accused of lying because of stories they make up. Blues also tend to daydream, especially if they're introverted. They can get lost in their thoughts and sometimes others wonder if they're in touch with reality.

Even as children, Blues seek a sense of identity. They may empathize strongly with characters in stories. Characters—creations of imagination—are more real to Blues than to other colors.

They may be especially drawn to mythical, fanciful, romanticized stories with happily-ever-after endings. However, if Blue children are exposed to graphic illustrations of violence or horror, they may carry these images in their minds for a long time and become emotionally involved with the characters. This negative identification may lead to nightmares and psychological problems.

Needs

Blues need a peaceful environment and close companionship. They need to feel valued by those around them. They need constant reassurance and recognition. They want to feel included and accepted as a significant member. Blues tend to do what adults expect of them if they feel that the adults like them. The Blues want and need those personal touches that make them feel important.

Growing up

If they're introverted, Blues may feel somewhat apart from other children, even though they desperately want to fit in. They may be shy and extremely sensitive to rejection. But normally Blues, raised in a good environment, grow up as warm, happy, helpful children.

Gold Children

Golds have a reasonably easy time growing up. They're well-mannered children who can be counted on to do their chores and follow the rules. They look to their parents and teachers for direction and approval. They're down-to-earth and become upset over change. They like to play with toys that make them appear to be more grown-up and important. They like to work on crafts that are useful or practical.

Family

The structure of the family is extremely important to Gold children. They need family stability and consistency. A Gold child will do well in a large family and will appreciate having brothers and sisters. They generally like family gatherings and relate enthusiastically to extended family members—grandparents, cousins, aunts and uncles, etc.

Golds appreciate the traditions of the family. They will do the appropriate thing at the appropriate time. If the family has always gone to Aunt Mabel's house to celebrate a particular holiday, the Gold child will be upset if that tradition is broken. As Gold children grow up and leave their families, they try to maintain familiar traditions.

Toys and games

Golds can be possessive about their toys. They're also clear about the right and wrong way to use a toy. They'll enjoy playing house or pretending to be adults in other ways. Board games or team sports may appeal to Gold children, but they'll be disturbed if other children don't abide by the rules.

Favorite activities

Gold children also like to make things, but their interest is focused on the product rather than the activity (which would be the focus of Oranges). They want to do things that will please adults. Prominently displayed objects created by Golds will add to their self-esteem. The parent of a Gold child is likely to have a refrigerator covered with magnets holding up treasured "works of art."

Older Gold children often form clubs and join cliques to meet their need for belonging. They're the backbone of these groups, and enjoy establishing the structure, rules, and policies. Golds are often involved in some type of sporting or organized group, such as Scouting, and will spend large amounts of time and energy proving their worth to the organization.

Relationships

Gold children tend to be more authoritative than other children. They will often jockey for positions of power over their brothers and sisters and crave opportunities to be "in charge" of other siblings while parents are away from the home. Because they like to make rules for others to follow, they're frequently viewed as bossy. This often leads to feelings of resentment by the subjects of their control, especially if they use physical aggression to enforce their rules. A domineering Gold child, who must maintain control of the environment, may intimidate adults and children alike.

Behavior

Gold children usually respond well to being assigned specific chores or responsibilities around the house, as long as these are items they can do well. In fact, Gold children may even request to do additional chores that will help the family. They tend to become "mother's little helpers" because of their desire to be of service. Regular maintenance tasks that might seem tedious to other colors may even be enjoyed by the Gold. They will dutifully and quietly follow through with their assignments.

Gold children enjoy having schedules and routines. If they're told to make their bed every morning before leaving their rooms, they will usually obey. If they're supposed to finish their homework before they play, they will finish their homework—after all, work comes before play. Schedules and routines give Gold children the opportunity to demonstrate their ability to be responsible, reliable, and punctual. They also give them a sense of security and control, because the children know what's expected of them and when they need to do it.

Gold children want to do what's right. In their childhood, at least, *right* is defined as what pleases adults. They may be viewed as the "perfect child" because they're constantly looking for the right thing to do and then doing it. They will often try to get other children to follow rules and do what's right as well.

Gold children value order. They will try to have an orderly room with things in specific places, though this ideal won't always be achieved. They're likely to return their toys to the toy box, make their beds, and hang up their clothes, because this is what they're supposed to do. At school, they have orderly desks and lockers, with everything in its proper place. They may spend time getting their things "just right" and be angered by anyone who messes them up.

Needs

Golds need consistency and security in the family. This also extends to a neighborhood. Moving residences frequently will disturb and unsettle the Gold child. Golds like to know what the rules are. They will be more comfortable growing up in the same neighborhood, going through the same school system, and staying with the same friends.

Golds need to know where they stand. They respond well to instructions that are clear and step-by-step. They will probably not react well if asked to improvise or come up with new ways of doing things. Golds don't want to be innovative; they want to do what's expected. The expectations of parents don't necessarily have to be logical, but they have to be clear.

Growing up

Gold children generally don't run into too many difficulties growing up. Since Golds represent a large part of the adult population, children are likely to have at least one Gold parent. Gold children will probably get along well with any combination of parents except two Orange parents, whose unpredictable nature would be a source of great stress. Schools are Gold by nature and society values Gold attributes, so Gold children generally receive the support they look for while growing up.

Green Children

Greens are independent children who appear to be older than their years. They're normally early talkers and learn to read long before they start school. They ask a lot of questions are never quite satisfied with an answer unless they can experience it for themselves. They like to play with chemistry sets, plastic models, magnets, magnifying glasses, puzzles, and construction sets.

Family

Greens appreciate a supportive, open family that allows personal space and intellectual freedom. The family, like all other institutions, should be subject to examination by logic. Family gatherings or traditions won't mean much to the Greens, since they want logical reasons for everything. The fact that something has always been done a certain way will not hold much weight. Since Green children can often be stubborn, it's easiest to clearly explain the justification for traditions. If they understand and accept the justification, they will more than likely agree to participate. However, Green personalities are usually uncomfortable in social gatherings and may still try to generate rational excuses to avoid them.

Toys and games

Greens can become deeply involved with toys, playing with them, examining them, and then abandoning them when they're understood. They may take apart their toys just to see how they work. Don't confuse this with Oranges, who will also take things apart, but for the joy of disassembling rather than desire for understanding. Greens may enjoy building models, designing forts, experimenting with chemistry sets or microscopes, and solving puzzles and logic problems. Games that involve thinking, such as chess or strategy games, appeal to Greens.

Favorite activities

Greens tend to maintain extensive collections of things that can be documented and classified. They may also develop a passion for computers. Greens are natural engineers and inventors. Give a Green child a piece of graph paper and a pencil, and he or she will stay busy for hours.

Greens enjoy reading books and being read to because of the ideas contained in the books. If a book is too lacking in content, they may become impatient quickly. Anything that no longer holds a challenge loses its ability to interest the Green. Because of the thirst for constant challenge, Greens tend to read above their grade levels and enjoy adding new words to their vocabularies. Besides encyclopedias and technical manuals, Greens also enjoy reading mysteries, science fiction, and intellectually stimulating novels.

Relationships

Greens may find their greatest challenges to be social. While often intellectually gifted, Green children may find social interaction awkward and even somewhat mystifying. The Green may be oblivious to manners and the feelings of others. Displays of affection are uncommon for Green children, who sometimes seem to distance themselves from others. This distancing is the result of self-doubt. They can often benefit from social coaching by adults. Greens should also be encouraged to see the value of other colors and develop tolerance, since they may have a tendency to look down on others because of their perceived intellectual inferiority.

Behavior

Green children may be puzzling to their parents. They're usually bright and learn early, but may seem somewhat serious and withdrawn. Parents, especially those of other colors, may sometimes feel that Green children are not enjoying their childhood enough.

Green children, even more than other children, are naturally curious. They want to see how things work and find out what will happen in different situations. The desire, manifested early, of Green children to learn about their world can result in a great number of questions. "Why is the sky blue? How does a plane stay in the air? Why do balloons float?" This tendency can drive some parents and teachers crazy. The Greens' quest to understand things may be annoying to those around them. This is totally unintentional and Greens will be somewhat aloof if reprimanded.

Greens are independent. They're also concerned with their dignity, and may be seen as prideful. Others may be annoyed by this perceived pride and feel they have to bring Greens down a peg. Because of the independence of Greens, they react best to a hands-off parenting style. They need the opportunity to experiment, follow their curiosity, and find answers. If Greens are not allowed this opportunity, they may react with disobedience or undesirable behaviors.

Greens also tend to be somewhat non-conformist and may question rules and restrictions. "Why do I have to make my bed if I'm just going to sleep in it again at night? Why do we have to eat dessert last? Why do I have to go to bed when I don't feel tired?" A Green child will never be satisfied with a "because I said so" or "that's just the way it is" reason. They don't have any objection to obeying rules, as long as they can see the reasons for them. Greens dislike repetition and will become impatient when instructions are given several times.

Greens may be inconsistent in maintaining an orderly room or closet. At one time they might be neatly organized and at another absolutely chaotic. In most cases, the room may appear disordered, but the Green knows where everything is located.

Needs

A Green needs things to explore, but parents should be careful not to supply too much at once. Greens need toys appropriate for their age and maturity. Because of the Greens' brightness, parents may be tempted to push them too quickly. If they're pushed too quickly and experience failure, Greens may retreat from reality and become withdrawn.

Once involved in school and academic pursuits, Greens sometimes need encouragement to spend time in recreational and social activities, which they may see as less worthwhile. They may need help with setting priorities. Greens, whether children or adults, must eventually come to the conclusion that they cannot learn everything, and so must determine what's most important for them.

Growing up

Green children, because they represent a small portion of the population, probably won't have a Green parent or sibling. This can cause them to feel that they're somewhat isolated from the rest of the world. They may believe that no one else in the world thinks like they do. Unless they develop a relationship with a

Green playmate, most Green children don't overcome this feeling until they enter school and associate with other Greens.

Orange Children

Orange children are noisy, energetic, and freedom-loving. Because they want life to be action-packed and fun, they do what they want to do when they want to do it. So it seems like they're always getting into trouble. They like physical contests and games, especially if they can be played outside. Their bedrooms are usually messy and cluttered with toys, clothes, and sports equipment.

Family

Orange children appreciate families as a source of companions or playmates. They will generally be happiest in a family with several brothers or sisters, although they may be competitive with these siblings. Oranges can be loyal, but in their desire to be free and spontaneous, they won't feel strongly the pull of tradition or duty.

Toys and games

Orange children enjoy active toys. They like things they can manipulate or take apart. They should be given sturdy toys, clothes, and pets, as they can be hard on them. Oranges usually like almost all types of sports. They like games that are competitive and can be ruthless in their desire to win.

Favorite activities

Outdoor activities or activities that involve risk or performance appeal to Oranges. Swimming, riding all-terrain vehicles, water skiing, or climbing mountains may be favorite activities. They can be drawn to drama or music. They often enjoy working with tools and making things, though the activity is more important to Oranges than the product. They're activity-oriented rather than task-oriented.

Relationships

The idea of equality is important to Oranges. They relate to others in a fraternal manner, which makes them excellent team players. However, they do like to shine above others, and they don't want others to have control over them. Oranges can be exciting, entertaining friends. They're almost always involved in doing something and like to bring others along for the ride.

Behavior

Orange children are usually more active than other children. They're always on the go, pushing the limits. As a result, they may sometimes be classified as hyperactive and rambunctious, or may be misdiagnosed with attention deficit disorder. Oranges are simply difficult to keep up with. They don't like to sit still and are often involved in energy-intensive contests and competitions with their friends. They will stir things up when they find life too boring.

If Oranges have the urge, they can spend hours and hours in a specific area, practicing an instrument, playing with a specific toy, or drawing pictures. This impulsive interest may fade quickly and be shifted to something else without apparent reason.

The Orange may not want to do anything to "get ready" for tomorrow. Today is what matters. Orange children won't be motivated by statements like, "You'll need this when you're older." The future is too far away to be of any concern. Whatever will happen, will happen.

Of all the colors, the Orange children are the least likely to have clean rooms or neat and orderly closets. They won't even understand the reason that parents make such demands. Oranges are too busy doing things to take time out just to arrange things. Such activities will seem like a waste of time when the Orange could be off doing something fun.

Needs

The Orange wants movement at all times and greatly values excitement and physical freedom. Orange children won't be happy when confined. They like to be free to roam around. They never react well to parents who try to make them fit into a specific role. They need to be allowed to be themselves, but they also need to be taught to get along in society. Though they don't respect rules by nature, Oranges need to be taught enough respect for them to keep out of trouble in the future.

Growing up

Since almost all children share some Orange traits, some adults feel that these traits are "childish" and try to help their children "grow out" of them. But for true Oranges these traits are an inherent part of their personalities; attempting to change an Orange will only result in maladjustment. Oranges should be taught those Gold behaviors that they will need to get along in society, but this process involves teaching, not changing.

> "I love children, especially when they cry, for then someone takes them away."
>
> — NANCY MITFORD

Childhood Characteristic Checklist

I've compiled the following checklist to help you determine if your youngster is exhibiting Blue, Gold, Green, or Orange attitudes and characteristics. As you work through the items, don't consider what the child is acting like today or yesterday, but what he or she normally acts like over a substantial period of time. Only a long-term view will provide the accuracy you need and help you look at the whole child, and not the parts.

Blue children

- ☐ Are gentle, kind, and compassionate by nature
- ☐ Are happy, warm, and helpful children
- ☐ Are easily disciplined and adapt well
- ☐ Do not respond well to physical punishment
- ☐ Like to please others
- ☐ Will do what an adult expects them to do
- ☐ Are sensitive individuals
- ☐ Are sensitive to rejection
- ☐ Like personalized attention to feel important
- ☐ Talk early
- ☐ Are shy if introverted
- ☐ May have imaginary friends
- ☐ Attach personalities to their toys
- ☐ May be devastated by the loss of a favorite toy
- ☐ Enjoy creative activities
- ☐ Are good storytellers
- ☐ Have to have friends
- ☐ Have feelings for other children
- ☐ Like to share with their family and friends
- ☐ Want everyone to get along
- ☐ Are daydreamers
- ☐ Are usually well liked
- ☐ Consider promises important
- ☐ Like games that are noncompetitive
- ☐ When playing a game, will feel sorry for the loser
- ☐ Like to use their imaginations
- ☐ Like to read and empathize strongly with the characters
- ☐ Like the performing arts
- ☐ May be good at art, music, or have literary skills
- ☐ Like to feel special and unique
- ☐ Like having secrets
- ☐ Tend to "go with the flow"

Gold children

- ☐ Are helpful and responsible
- ☐ Are generally obedient to authority figures

- ☐ Try to do the right thing
- ☐ Need a secure home environment
- ☐ Like crystal-clear instructions
- ☐ Need to know what is expected of them
- ☐ Usually do well in school
- ☐ Like to help their teachers
- ☐ Will take charge when playing with other children
- ☐ Like order and organization
- ☐ Thrive on routine
- ☐ Need distinct boundaries and specific rules
- ☐ Like to make rules for others
- ☐ Consider rules important when playing games
- ☐ Are possessive with their toys
- ☐ Take care of their toys
- ☐ Know the right and wrong way to play with toys
- ☐ Like having brothers and sisters
- ☐ Like being in charge of siblings and can be too bossy
- ☐ Like family gatherings
- ☐ Like family traditions
- ☐ Want approval from adults
- ☐ Need feedback and public recognition
- ☐ Like being members of teams, clubs, and cliques
- ☐ Don't mind doing chores around the house
- ☐ Prefer their rooms to be neat and orderly
- ☐ Are unsettled by changes in routine or environment
- ☐ Like structured activities
- ☐ Need positive role models to emulate
- ☐ Need consistent, predictable discipline
- ☐ Like to earn and save money
- ☐ Like to win trophies, certificates, and awards

Green children

- ☐ Are curious children
- ☐ Ask many questions and like learning new things
- ☐ Are usually bright and learn early
- ☐ Don't care to be cuddled
- ☐ Aren't affectionate with others
- ☐ Like playing alone
- ☐ Don't like social gatherings
- ☐ Are independent
- ☐ Can be stubborn
- ☐ May seem to be self-centered
- ☐ Take apart their toys to understand how they work
- ☐ Like building things
- ☐ Like toys that require thinking
- ☐ Like collecting things
- ☐ Like reading mysteries, science fiction, and encyclopedias
- ☐ Are innovative and creative
- ☐ May be oblivious to manners and the feelings of others

- ☐ Don't interact very well socially
- ☐ May be serious and withdrawn
- ☐ Can be neat and orderly and at other times messy
- ☐ Listen to adults who use reason and logic
- ☐ React poorly to physical punishment
- ☐ Are critical of themselves
- ☐ May look down on others who seem to be inferior
- ☐ Can be puzzling children
- ☐ May be non-conformists
- ☐ Will obey rules if they see the logic
- ☐ Love to learn new things
- ☐ Love to experiment and investigate
- ☐ Like to invent new things
- ☐ Like to play with gadgets and scientific gear
- ☐ Tend to "do their own thing"

Orange children

- ☐ Seem to be more active than other children
- ☐ Are rowdy and rambunctious
- ☐ Are generally happy children
- ☐ Are hard on their clothes
- ☐ Like action toys they can manipulate
- ☐ Will take apart their toys to see if it is possible
- ☐ Like working with tools and machinery
- ☐ Like risky and exciting activities
- ☐ View family members as companions and playmates
- ☐ Are competitive with siblings
- ☐ Have to win when playing games
- ☐ Can be loyal
- ☐ Will do things with the promise of an immediate reward
- ☐ Don't care if they get in trouble
- ☐ Don't think of the future
- ☐ Have messy rooms and think cleaning up is a waste of time
- ☐ Believe that having fun is important
- ☐ Like sports and outdoor activities
- ☐ Like to perform in front of others
- ☐ Are fun and entertaining to other children
- ☐ Need to have readily accessible playmates
- ☐ Can be devoted to something they enjoy doing
- ☐ Want freedom and independence
- ☐ Do not respect rules
- ☐ Like to dare others and accept dares
- ☐ Don't like to sit still for long
- ☐ Are easily distracted
- ☐ Need heroes and mentors
- ☐ Can be aggressive when out-of-esteem
- ☐ Like to test their limits and push the boundaries
- ☐ Want to be the center of attention
- ☐ Seem to have Attention Deficit Hyperactivity Disorder

Parenting Principles

Now that we know what each color looks like in childhood, it's time to figure out how to get them safely into the next stage of life. Most of this burden falls squarely on the shoulders of parents. Of course, you don't have to be the biological parent to qualify as a parent; for many children, this duty has been delegated to an extended family member, guardian, teacher, coach, or religious advisor. Nevertheless, the job that has to be done is called parenting, and the information in the rest of this chapter will add color to your parenting skills.

The ethics of cloning

Any kindergartner can tell you that a baby duck doesn't grow up to be an eagle. It doesn't matter how hard the duck's parents try to make it become an eagle, it doesn't matter how much the duckling wants to become an eagle, it simply won't happen. It can't happen. All you'll end up with is a baby duck with eagle envy—who'll never quite be satisfied with being an ordinary member of the local raft.

> "If it looks like a duck, waddles like a duck, and quacks like a duck—I bet it tastes like a duck."
>
> — W. C. FIELDS

It's a titanic temptation for most parents to try to turn their child into a mirror image of themselves, into someone who will share their ideals, viewpoints, mannerisms, and behaviors. It seems like an instinctive thing to do—after all, doesn't a duckling need to learn how to act like an adult duck? And who better to teach it duckish behavior than its own parents?

That's a fair philosophy for ducks, but for humans it's fowl play. You might pull off this Pygmalion project if your child happens to share your personality spectrum, since you both have an instinctive, preexisting regard for the same things. On the other hand, if your child doesn't share your spectrum, you're attempting to put a square peg into a round hole. Trying to shape and mold and chisel and carve a youngster into something he or she wasn't ordained to be isn't just futile, it's unethical—even immoral. To do so categorically negates the in-born values of the child and bellows to him or her, "I don't care what you want. I'm the parent. I'll decide what's best for you. When you're 18 you can do as you will, but until then you will do as I say."

In case this notion hasn't yet sunk in to every fiber of your being, I'll say it one more time. It's impossible to change one temperament into another. A quiet, sensitive, considerate Blue boy will never grow up to be an adrenaline-pumping, alpha Orange. It just won't happen. It can't happen. Caterpillars transform into butterflies and maggots turn into flies, but as a rule, humans are non-metamorphic; unless, of course, you're a shapeshifting werewolf or vampire.

So how can we effectively parent our offspring without overtly forcing our values upon them? First, we need to be aware that we may inadvertently be doing it. Second, if you're doing it, stop at once. Third, make a conscious effort to recognize and validate the values of your youngster, no matter how foreign these values seem to be. Finally, introduce your child, in a palatable way, to the positive values and characteristics of other temperaments. If he or she finds some attitudes and behaviors to admire, your child will figure out a way to adopt them and make them fit within his or her own value system. As a result, your child will probably turn out to be a normal, healthy, well-adjusted individual—in spite of your parenting efforts.

Parenting Styles

Below are some phrases that describe the parenting styles of each temperament. You'll immediately find something on each list that applies to you because, when it comes to parenting, we often find ourselves doing things that may not necessarily reflect our natural preferences. You see, not many of us have had formal training on how to be a parent, so most of our behaviors and attitudes are borrowed from our own parents, friends, religious leaders, therapists, neighbors, and anyone else who has ever given advice—solicited or not—on how to bring up babies.

In other words, as your read through the following lists and find that you raise your children in a Blue way, for instance, it doesn't necessarily mean you're a Blue parent. You might just be parenting in a way that's meaningful for your Blue children. If you're doing that, hooray! Close up this book and treat yourself to a massive hot fudge sundae. You're doing exactly what needs to be done. On the other hand, if all of your children aren't Blue, then you're not accommodating the needs of those children. Shame on you. Put down the sundae and continue reading; you still have more to learn.

Blue parents

- ☐ Are benevolent and compassionate parents
- ☐ Desire a supportive, nurturing home environment
- ☐ Run the household democratically
- ☐ Value the contributions of each family member
- ☐ Encourage children to express their feelings and dreams
- ☐ Give their hearts and souls to their children
- ☐ Seek to bond family members together
- ☐ Support expressions of individuality and creativity

- ☐ Try to fulfill their children's desires
- ☐ Want to be at home as much as possible
- ☐ Dislike arguments and fighting between children
- ☐ Take their children to artistic, cultural events
- ☐ Keep the peace in the household
- ☐ Attend their children's games, concerts, performances
- ☐ Empathically listen to their children's concerns
- ☐ Help their children feel good about themselves
- ☐ Mirror the emotions of their children
- ☐ Place kids' needs before housework, spouse, self
- ☐ Provide comfort when kids are sad or upset
- ☐ Try to anticipate their kids' emotional needs
- ☐ Want to be intimately involved in their children's lives
- ☐ Use lots of physical touch to show affection
- ☐ Encourage children to participate in social activities
- ☐ Enjoy talking with family around the kitchen table
- ☐ Enjoy watching shows, even cartoons, with kids
- ☐ Look to popular, public experts for advice
- ☐ Make big deal of holidays, birthdays, anniversaries
- ☐ Want to see the family do things together
- ☐ Pride self on "caring" more than other parents
- ☐ Chat with children about friends and activities

Gold parents

- ☐ Encourage children to earn and save money
- ☐ Have their children routinely perform household chores
- ☐ Propel children to succeed; drive them towards it
- ☐ Urge children to go the extra mile
- ☐ Help children set and achieve goals
- ☐ Ensure chores and homework are done before play
- ☐ Seek advice of established authorities or professionals
- ☐ Are self-reliant; don't see need for outside interference
- ☐ Encourage children to volunteer at school
- ☐ Expect children to be polite and respectful of elders
- ☐ Insist children use proper manners and etiquette
- ☐ Teach children the correct, appropriate thing to do
- ☐ Provide a safe, secure home environment
- ☐ Strictly observe and enforce rules and laws
- ☐ Keep a close eye on their children
- ☐ Exhort children to endure to the end
- ☐ Must pre-approve friends and activities
- ☐ Control household budgets and finances
- ☐ Methodically plan out family activities
- ☐ Need things to be done in the proper way, order, time
- ☐ Prefer bedrooms to be orderly, well-organized
- ☐ Require children to take good care of their things
- ☐ Set up family schedules, assignments, and deadlines
- ☐ Expect children to be on time for meals, activities
- ☐ Administer discipline firmly, consistently

- ☐ Establish family mission statements and goals
- ☐ Focus on household tasks and won't get side-tracked
- ☐ Keep their homes "ship-shape" and run a "tight ship"
- ☐ Take pride in their family name, heritage, traditions
- ☐ Treat their children's failures as their own

Green parents

- ☐ Give children room to experiment and discover
- ☐ Encourage learning, not necessarily school
- ☐ Aren't easily angered or upset by children's actions
- ☐ Have an overall parenting game plan
- ☐ May read parenting books and magazines clandestinely
- ☐ Won't be easily conned or hoodwinked
- ☐ Become irritated at incompetence, foolishness
- ☐ Believe raising children is like a lab experiment
- ☐ Don't appear personally involved with children
- ☐ Won't hover, smother, and prod
- ☐ Don't impose lots of unreasonable rules, limits
- ☐ Promote self-directed decision-making
- ☐ Teach principles that govern behavior, not detailed rules
- ☐ Allow children to experience natural consequences
- ☐ Tend to question, cross-examine their children
- ☐ Think through decisions before implementing them
- ☐ Enjoy exploring new ways to parent, discipline
- ☐ Avoid small talk with their children
- ☐ Can embarrass their children with their peculiarities
- ☐ Have to be thinking; can't sit around and do nothing
- ☐ Encourage children to think outside the box
- ☐ Tend to give instructions only once
- ☐ Won't state obvious facts and insignificant details
- ☐ Get caught up in their own projects
- ☐ Enjoy intriguing, thought-provoking discussions
- ☐ Administer discipline objectively, without prejudice
- ☐ Easily separate behaviors from the person
- ☐ Encourage children to improve and progress
- ☐ Often baffle kids with their puns, witticisms
- ☐ Remain neutral while gathering facts

Orange parents

- ☐ Aren't bothered by being non-traditional parents
- ☐ Promote being active, athletic, in good shape
- ☐ Like turning dull things into entertaining games
- ☐ Expect disobedience, but aren't dismayed by it
- ☐ Encourage freedom and self-determination
- ☐ Are good-natured, playful, kids at heart
- ☐ Allow children to have fun and enjoy what life offers
- ☐ Wrestle and play physically hard with children
- ☐ Treat kids as pals and playmates, someone to do things with
- ☐ Urge children to "reach for the stars"

- ☐ Share the limelight with children; aren't behind the scenes
- ☐ Need help in providing structure, routines, schedules
- ☐ Believe when it's time to play, play with gusto
- ☐ Aren't strict disciplinarians, allow children off hook
- ☐ Will drop everything to do something fun with the family
- ☐ Are unpredictable, impulsive parents
- ☐ Aren't necessarily more responsible than their children
- ☐ Don't like doing the same things repeatedly
- ☐ Enjoy watching kids try to con them
- ☐ Get frustrated when children don't "seize the day"
- ☐ Have a hard time sticking to schedules, timeframes
- ☐ Tend to be overly generous and overindulge their children
- ☐ Discourage shyness, apprehension, fear
- ☐ Are liberal, tolerant, flexible parents
- ☐ Aren't opposed to arguing with their kids
- ☐ Bring children with them on their adventures
- ☐ Complete household chores swiftly, resentfully
- ☐ Don't like to sit around the house and do nothing
- ☐ Prefer a casual, laid-back environment at home
- ☐ Like to joke, tease, and play around with their children

Effective Discipline

Even though it may seem far-fetched, from time to time children (not to mention teenagers and older adults) behave badly. At which point someone needs to step in and rectify such naughtiness. As a parent of one of these culprits, it behooves you to know how to remedy the problem and dole out effective discipline. This section will help you do that.

What is discipline?

The word *discipline* has a variety of dictionary definitions, such as "control obtained by enforcing compliance or order" or "punishment intended to correct or train." My favorite meaning, however, is "training expected to produce a specific character or pattern of behavior, especially training that produces moral or mental improvement." In short, discipline is simply education.

For discipline to deliver long-term results, it can't be forced down people's throats. To some degree, people have to accept discipline willingly in order for it to produce meaningful changes. It must be served in appetizing ways so that the recipient actually desires it—or at least doesn't gag at the sight of it. Otherwise, what you'll get, if you're lucky, is superficial behavior change that only lasts while you're in the room. But as soon as your back is turned, old behaviors reappear.

Why do people misbehave?

People misbehave because the misbehavior pays off. It's that simple. When they do something wrong they get some sort of satisfaction out of it. Hence, we have a child who throws a tantrum until her mother gives her a cookie, a student who cheats on a test to get a better grade than he deserves, and a teenager who pierces her tongue to impress her friends.

Calling upon our colors lingo, we might see a Green misbehaving so she can be sent to her room and get away from her obnoxious family, an Orange clowning around at school to get attention from his peers, a Blue joining a gang because his friends did and he wants to stay with them, and a Gold who tattles on her brother to appear obedient. They're all misbehaving to get something they want—something they value.

In these examples, the penalty for misbehavior is more attractive than the reward for good behavior. Consequently, if you are able to substitute the desirable penalty with something less desirable, do it. Stick to your guns, even if it takes a dozen or so showdowns before you see a change in behavior. Bad behaviors weren't developed overnight; consequently, they won't be overturned quickly; it takes persistence and consistency on your part.

Change the scenery

It's a sultry summer evening. You're sitting on the front porch, sipping a frosty glass of limeade, listening to the kids play on the tire swing, and trying to recuperate from a hard day's work. As you watch the sunset, a mass of dark clouds rapidly moves in and obscures your view. A breeze kicks up and begins to rustle the leaves on your old oak tree. In the darkened sky, you see a few flashes of light and hear a distant rumbling. It appears as though a monsoon thunderstorm is approaching swiftly. It's time to gather the kids, go inside, close up the windows, and light some candles.

Some misbehaviors are as easy to anticipate as a summertime storm. As soon as you see the telltale signs, you need to get prepared for a disturbance. However, there is a way you can divert the storm, or at least weaken its effects. Simply change the scenery. Get the person to focus on something else. Remove him or her from the environment. Change the stimulus. Eliminate the means. Give the person something else to do—preferably, something that's desirable and touches core values. In fact, if there's a positive alternative that has a greater payoff, most people will choose that option every time.

With younger children, it's quite easy to redirect their attention. As soon as they start to misbehave, try saying, "Look over there, Kevin! Is that a hummingbird at the window?" Or, "Tamilyn, would you like to go to the grocery store with me?" Try to engage them in some sort of dialogue that's meaningful to their temperament. For example, ask Blues about their friends and teachers, Golds to repeat something they memorized recently, Greens about one of their hobbies, and Oranges what they want to do for fun this weekend. If you have the time and energy, redirect the wrongdoer into a different room where you can get him or her engaged in an enjoyable project. The trick is to get the offenders thinking about or doing something else—something that has positive returns.

In a similar vein, sometimes there are misbehaviors you can't see but that you know take place. In these cases, you might be able to get rid of the means. If a teenager is drag racing, hide the car keys. If a child is watching too much television, unplug the TV. If a preteen is downloading pornography onto his bedroom computer, relocate the computer into the kitchen. If misbehavior can't happen, it won't happen.

> "Never raise your hands to your kids. It leaves your groin unprotected."
>
> — RED BUTTONS

The techniques just mentioned work great for all colors. However, there are certain techniques that will work for one color that won't work for another. Again, it's the "different strokes for different folks" thing. These colorized strategies are found below.

Disciplining Blues

Blues don't like to be reprimanded in public because of the wallop it delivers to their sense of self-worth. Drawing attention to their misbehavior in public, especially in front of their family or peers, is embarrassing, if not crushing. They've worked hard to build up reputations and get included in their social groups, and public punishment might sully their image and cause them to be rejected. Instead, lure Blues aside and take care of the discipline deed in private.

How the disciplinary message is delivered is extremely important to a Blue. Just like Goldilocks, you need to settle on something in between too hot and too cold, something that's "just right." If you become loud, obnoxious, or abusive in the slightest way, or conversely, become cold and callous, showing no emotion at all, then you've just created a communication chasm that won't be crossed anytime soon. Carefully and cautiously figure out how to deliver your message with the correct amount of emotion. Perhaps you can role-play with a different Blue until you get it just right.

Blues are sensitive to insensitivity. They tend to disregard information given to them by people whom they feel haven't treated them considerately in the past. They need to know that you care about them as people—and this needs to be an overt expression of concern that they judge to be honest and sincere. Only then will they attend to your disciplinary message.

Before assigning blame or jumping to conclusions, always ask to hear what the Blues have to say. Intently listen to it all and don't ever cut them off. This will be a pleasant change for them since most people immediately rush in with solutions. Blues need to get their feelings off their chests before they can begin to consider what someone else has to say.

Concentrate on the Blue's errant behaviors, not the Blue's character. Blues are never bad people—they are nice, decent, amazing, insightful individuals who unfortunately did something wrong. Consequently, if you attack them, rather than their behavior, you've just made a serious mistake. To help make sure this doesn't happen, you regularly need to notice and comment on the good character traits and the good behaviors of Blues. Then, when you need to discipline them, they know that you've noticed the good stuff before and aren't just focusing on their misbehavior.

Blues are extremely sensitive to rejection and respond best to personalized attention. They're often motivated by a desire to make everyone happy. Therefore, you're more likely to elicit cooperation by explaining calmly to a Blue how a particular misbehavior made you feel. Questions like, "How do you think this behavior affects other people?" will get them thinking. And if they don't want to offend others, they may be motivated to change.

Disciplining Blues

Reprimand in private
Be kind and gentle
Don't use derogatory words
Show loving concern
Listen to their feelings
Appreciate good intentions
Focus on behavior
Discuss effect on others

Disciplining Golds

Of all the color types, Golds are often the easiest to discipline. Perhaps it's because they have a clear picture of what's right and wrong and who's in charge. When you're the boss, and you have the responsibility to correct misbehavior, then all you have to do is assert your authority and you'll receive their undivided attention. Besides, Golds have this little voice in their heads that has already told them they did something wrong, and it has been gnawing at them for some time now. They already feel guilty and ashamed and are just looking for a way out of their misery. The opportunity to confess and correct their misbehavior usually is welcomed with open arms.

You normally don't have to treat Gold children with kid gloves. In fact, they appreciate a let's-get-down-to-business approach. It makes them feel more grown-up. Treat them with respect and professionalism, without any condescension—almost as if they were royalty—and they'll respond well to your message.

Golds need consistency with their discipline. If they do something wrong, they expect to be punished. Don't let them off the hook. Likewise, they're bothered if parents aren't consistent with their punishments. If Mother advocates one thing and Father another, they'd rather the two get their act together and present a unified front. Unpredictable behavior in parents shakes the foundation that Golds have built their lives upon. It needs to be shored up and stabilized immediately.

With Golds, it's important to state a problem in clear terms. Furthermore, it's preferable if they state the problem. You could say, "We're here to talk about your unacceptable behavior today during lunch. Tell me exactly what you did." Then, after they state the behavior, you could say, "What is appropriate or acceptable behavior in this situation? How should you have behaved?" Keeping things black and white and matter-of-fact is helpful.

After stating the problem and determining appropriate behavior, the next step is to form a plan for the person to stop the inappropriate behavior and do something more acceptable. Of course, if the plan is already established, so much the better. All they have to do is work the plan. Moreover, since Golds tend to be faithful to their word, if they commit to something there's a high probability they'll follow through with it without further intervention.

When Golds step out of line they tend to be more concerned than other colors about what they missed. When you allow them to make up what they missed, by disobedience or absence, they are appreciative and it seems fairer to them. Let them earn their way back into your good graces.

Since Golds are the people with whom you have the fewest problems, it's appropriate to point out that any problem is likely a rare occurrence. Because of all their Gold strengths, which you could name, it will probably never happen again. After all, they receive an emotional boost by receiving approval from their parents. A task has no appeal in itself if it's not reinforced with positive feedback from an authority figure.

Disciplining Golds

Assert your authority
Be professional and consistent
State problem clearly
Ask for expected behavior
Formulate a plan
Ask for commitment
Allow make-up
Reinforce Gold attributes

Disciplining Greens

When disciplining Greens, it's helpful to show respect, not so much for them as people, as the Blues want, but respect for them as fellow human beings who have good ideas. When you don't do this, Greens react poorly to negative criticism. Because they value competence and innovative ideas, they can be deeply hurt if their abilities and ideas are ridiculed. They hate to have their weaknesses exposed, even in private. It's humiliating to have someone come along with a critique, even if it's justified. Besides, that's redundant information—they're probably painfully aware of their shortcomings. The last thing they want is someone confirming their suppositions, turning them into indisputable facts.

Rational Greens react best to someone who calmly reasons with them when discipline is necessary. In fact, it's imperative that you don't get emotional. Greens often judge people by how cool they can remain under pressure. Because Greens usually aren't persuaded by emotion anyway, you're much more likely to resolve a problem and earn their respect if you act cool and calm. Otherwise, your opinions might be discarded as quickly as a smelly diaper.

Even a Green^2 (a green Green; a Green who's young and immature) believes that unimpassioned, objective people are uniquely qualified to provide criticism. With emotions out of the way, logical thought reigns, and what could have been a personal attack quickly turns into a meaningful educational experience. Your job, as the resident expert, is to help Greens discover what went wrong and how they can fix it so it won't happen again.

The best way to administer the discipline—the education—is to ask a few questions. Pretend you're a wise chemistry professor who's guiding students through a laboratory experiment. Your role is ask a few well-thought-out questions—to which you have answers, but you won't readily reveal them unless asked—and get the students thinking about their experiment. In this case, the experiment is the misbehavior. Your questions might sound like, "Did biting your sister produce the result you wanted? What did you want to happen? If you had to do it all over again, what would you do differently? How can you help your sister feel better?"

After they've worked through the diagnosis themselves, and have come up with some solutions to prevent the behavior in the future, you may need to reinforce the lesson by asking them to either punish themselves or accept your punishment. Many Greens will choose the self-discipline path, which will likely end up being far more punitive than what you had in mind. Just make sure the penalty is fair and appropriate, and the Green will usually do what needs to be done. All you have to do is monitor their progress from a distance.

Despite the outcome of any disciplinary measure, help Greens know you still recognize their strengths and talents, and how you're convinced that "once they think about what has happened today there will be no need for this to happen again." Green children need a great deal of success to maintain their sense of competence. You can help them most by patient answers to questions, appropriate intellectual stimulation, encouragement, and room to develop and find answers.

Disciplining Greens

Show respect for ideas
Remain cool and calm
Use logical reasoning
Involve them in analysis
Be an independent expert
Ask guided questions
Accommodate self-discipline
Monitor from a distance

Disciplining Oranges

Discipline, for the Orange, must be hands-on, and I'm not talking about placing your hands on their backsides or around their necks. Verbal reprimands delivered by parents to passive Oranges won't do them any good. Their bodies may be sitting in front of you, but their minds are far away, thinking about other things to do. To tell the truth, if you insist on delivering a lecture, they just might be thinking about how to get back at you. This is a bad thing.

To effectively discipline an Orange, the first thing to do is eradicate your burning desire to pontificate, moralize, rebuke, and scold. Because they regularly seem to get into trouble, Oranges are reprimanded so often and from such an early time in their lives that they become indifferent to these reproofs.

Next, you have to get their attention. This isn't as easy as it sounds. Sometimes this might take a raised voice, a gentle nudge, turning down the radio, pulling off headphones, making their friends go home. More often, it takes an air horn, a cattle prod, pepper spray, and handcuffs. By removing distractions, you can help them focus on what you have to say.

After getting their attention, you need to get right to the point. There's no need to beat around the bush with Oranges, just go after the problem and tackle it as fast as a linebacker attacks the quarterback. They can handle it and they'll appreciate it.

Don't give in to the temptation to compete with an Orange. It's always counterproductive. It's akin to throwing down a gauntlet and challenging them to a duel. They'll take up the challenge with pleasure and will try to beat you in the battle of wills. If you fight, argue, and try to dominate—even if you're completely justified in doing so—these actions will only increase the tension between the two of you, exacerbate the problem, and create a wider gulf.

Oranges love to play around and they appreciate humor in others. If, in the disciplinary process, you can incorporate jokes, humor, and laughter, an Orange will receive the discipline much easier. Remember the main objective of discipline is to teach—and you can't teach Oranges unless you have their attention and their interest. You can gain this by not being a grumpy stick-in-the-mud. Instead, paste on a big smile, force a hearty laugh, lean back in your chair, and try to have a good time. No one said discipline has to be onerous.

That doesn't mean you should take the matter lightly—in fact, it's imperative that you give the impression that misbehavior is serious business and you won't tolerate it for long. Even then, you don't have to keep the atmosphere heavy for long. Once the discipline is done, lighten up the mood and move on.

Oranges love to negotiate the terms of their punishment, even if it's simply choosing between two penalties. If the exact punishment doesn't matter to you, and the child will learn something in the process, then let them strike a bargain. They will appreciate your flexibility and will be far more likely to complete the punishment without forcing you to bring out the heavy artillery.

Orange can invent extremely creative non-traditional punishments, such as "I know I shouldn't have snuck that scoop of ice cream after school. Punish me by making me eat an entire gallon of chocolate ice cream." When you stop to think about it, that punishment might actually work—she'll get so sick of ice cream that she won't think about it for a long time. When you provide an Orange with disciplinary alternatives, especially inventive variations, it will always be more effective than taking yet another trip to the woodshed.

Disciplining Oranges

Remove distractions
Don't lecture and scold
Be frank and direct
Don't try to compete
Keep the atmosphere light
Use humor and jokes
Accept negotiation
Allow unusual punishments

A practical example

One spring evening, while my wife was putting our four boys to bed and I was cleaning up the dinner dishes, I heard a knock on our door and opened it to find one of our Gold neighbors standing there. She seemed distraught, for her eyes were red, her hair was tousled, and her face was flustered. She just stood there and started to shake her head slowly. Instantly I sensed what the problem was—it had to have something to do with her 4-year-old daughter, Olivia.

If you've ever read Beverly Cleary's book, *Ramona the Pest,* you've been introduced to a slightly older version of Olivia. Throughout the neighborhood, this girl is well known for her exasperating antics and unusual personality. She's an extroverted Green with Blue undertones. That's an onerous combination for a full-grown adult to endure, let alone a preschooler.

I invited my neighbor in and had her take a seat in our living room while I went downstairs to bring up my wife. This was going to require both of us. My sweetheart is the Yin to my Yang and, as an extraordinary empath with soft shoulders to cry on, is able to counterbalance my tendency to rush through the examination, diagnose the problem, prescribe a remedy, and move on.

"So," I asked my neighbor. "What's Olivia done now?"

I was sort of disappointed that she didn't seem impressed with my ability to read her mind. Rather, she just looked over at us and started to divulge her story. Indeed, Olivia was rapidly driving her family to the loony bin. This little girl walks to the beat of a different drummer and often refuses to do what the rest of the family is doing or eating or playing or singing or praying. She gets so pigheaded at times that she can't be persuaded to do something she doesn't want to do. She'll throw a tantrum for hours on end until her parents eventually give in. When forced to go to bed, she'll start to bother her older sister for a couple of hours, until the sister falls asleep our of sheer exhaustion. Even then, Olivia will continue to talk to herself, keeping the loud conversation up until the wee hours of the morning.

"I've given birth to an alien, Nate." My neighbor wasn't smiling. "It's as though Olivia was sent here to probe and prod and discover everything that makes us upset. We can't take it anymore. What can I do?"

My wife moved over to hold our neighbor's hand. They were close friends, and she wanted to show her support. The two of them talked a bit more, airing out their feelings, while I mulled over the problem. When the conversation came to a lull, I chimed in with my two-cents worth.

I asked, "You're husband's a Blue, isn't he?"

"Yes."

"I bet he's at his wit's end too, isn't he?"

"Yes. He has a lot more patience that I have, and that helps. But even he'll get fed up with her, and when that happens someone has to take care of her. And that person's me. And I can't do it any more."

My wife gave my neighbor a knowing nod and a gentle squeeze.

I continued with my questions. "And your other two kids, your oldest daughter is Gold and your youngest, he's Blue. Right?"

"I think so."

"Well, there you have it. No wonder everyone's so exasperated. No one shares Olivia's temperament. She really is an alien in your household, and she knows it. Everyone else is either Gold or Blue. She's the only Green. She probably feels like she doesn't fit in at all."

My neighbor nodded her head in agreement. "That's true. Olivia often says that nobody loves her; that nobody understands what she wants. We try to tell her otherwise, but it doesn't seem to matter."

"You know, only 2 to 3 percent of the people in the world are female Greens, and only 1 percent of those are extroverted—that's the smallest group in the whole spectrum. These children always have a difficult time growing up, especially if they're in a family where no one shares their colors. They don't have any role models to follow, so they have to figure things out on their own."

I paused to catch my breath, then resumed the monologue. "So obviously, as a natural-born scientist, Olivia's experimenting with a bunch of behaviors to discover what makes people tick—and what ticks them off. She's probably not trying to be mischievous; she's just trying to get her arms around her world. Until she figures out where she fits she'll continue to be a little hellion."

"Oh great," my neighbor muttered mordantly. "That's exactly what I wanted to hear."

I proceeded as if I hadn't heard her remark. "Of course, as a Gold parent, for your sanity and for the protection of your child, you need to control the laboratory and set the rules by which her experiments take place. Greens need a few operating parameters or else they'll blow up themselves and their loved ones. You can't let your daughter run amuck and continue to disrupt your family life. Correct?"

"That's absolutely correct," my neighbor said. She was starting to gain hope. "So what did you have in mind?"

"Sometime tomorrow, you and your husband need to gather your children together and have a formal family meeting. With everyone's input—especially Olivia's—you need to agree on some simple behavioral rules and guidelines that everyone must follow. You also need to set some clear consequences for disobedience. Make sure you write these rules and penalties down, and have everyone sign it—like a contract. Will you do that?" I asked.

"Sure. That's not too tough."

"Well that's not the hard part. Now you need to stick to the plan like a bug on a windshield. You and your husband can share the disciplinarian duties, but neither one of you may deviate from the plan."

"We'll try. But my husband is Blue, you know." She rolled her eyes. "And Olivia has a history of carrying on and on. Sometimes he caves in and tries to rescues his princess from her misery."

"You can't let him do it—that will simply reinforce the negative behavior. If she can get relief from her misery by behaving badly, then she doesn't have any motive to behave properly."

"That makes sense, Nate. What else you got?"

"When Olivia disobeys, don't discipline her in front of other family members, including your husband. Quietly take her out of her environment, speak with as much civility, clarity, and conciseness as you can muster, and calmly explain that she violated a rule and must now pay the price. Ask her to explain the penalty to you, or if she can't remember it, remind her. Ask if this penalty is adequate or if it needs to be altered. Keep asking questions like this until she seems engaged and committed to paying the penalty. Then let her execute the punishment without further ado. Don't be harsh or condescending, nor casual or light-hearted; just show focused concern with lots of comfortable eye contact. And if the punishment can be levied in private—so other family members can't see her errors—she'll save face and won't be as rebellious or aloof."

My neighbor seemed to be accepting my message. She did have a question, though, and asked it. "What kinds of punishments will work for Olivia? Sending her to her room doesn't seem to work. Nor does spanking her, or yelling at her, or trying to make her feel guilty."

My wife got up and found a piece of paper for our neighbor to write down some notes. That's so like my wife, sensing our Gold friend's unvoiced need to record the information I was sharing.

"A good penalty is one that takes the values of the individual into consideration; as a result, Green penalties will be quite different than Gold, Orange, and Blue penalties."

"That makes perfect sense to me," she said. "What I did to punish my older daughter seemed to work well for her, but it sure didn't work for Olivia. The exact same punishment produced very different reactions."

"Precisely. Punishments are supposed to unpleasant. Bad behavior simply cannot pay off. What's undesirable to a Green is often desirable to another color. So what we have to do now is identify the things that your daughter finds undesirable—things she finds disagreeable, unpleasant, distasteful, even revolting."

"But isn't that just being cruel and abusive? Won't inflicting pain scar her emotionally?" This was a common reaction. And I had an answer.

"Have you ever broken an arm or leg?" I asked.

"Yes," she replied.

"Did it hurt?"

"Yes."

"Are you emotionally unbalanced because of your pain?"

"Of course not."

"Then why would you think your child will be scarred because she experiences a little pain now and then?"

"I see your point," she conceded.

"As long as you don't get carried away and lose your temper, or become vicious and violent, then children can learn from short-term pain. When children touch a hot stove, the pain teaches them not to do it again, right? Pain is nature's way of telling us to stop doing something that's not good for us."

"Okay," she said. "Which punishments are appropriate?"

"Psychologists like to say that punishments can be either positive or negative. That doesn't mean good or bad, by the way. A positive punishment simply means you're applying something undesirable. A negative punishment means you're removing something desirable. So whether it's positive or negative, the penalty always has to be undesirable to the child."

Our neighbor was too busy writing to comment, so I paused to wait for her to finish before continuing. "Now, let us think of some positive punishments for a Green. What does your daughter hate doing? Being lectured to? Having to do something repetitive and boring? Participating in a group hug? Doing something she isn't skilled at in public? Being forced to play with a group of children or participate on a sports team? Having to sit still and chit-chat? Ask her. She'll probably go on and on about what she hates."

"Next, what are some negative punishments? What does she want that you can temporarily take away? Staying up late? Choosing her own clothes? Prized toys or objects? Time alone to think? Objects to investigate? Access to favorite books, movies, music, video games, or television shows? Answers to questions? Acknowledgement of special talents and skills?"

We talked for a few minutes about specific positive and negative punishments. She came up with a rather lengthy list. I was starting to see her frazzlement dissipate.

"Since punishment only tells the child what not to do, it always needs to be followed up with a lovingly delivered lesson on what to do. For a Green, this lesson doesn't need to be explicitly delivered. In other words, you don't have to say, 'And thus we see that....' Greens prefer to connect the dots and draw their own conclusions. The only thing you can try to do is make sure those conclusions are reasonable and accurate. They need clear-thinking guides and mentors—not emotion-filled parents that criticize and harangue."

"Ah, so you've been to our house." She smirked. "I need to remember to close the windows before haranguing."

We laughed good-naturedly. Then I added, "One last thing. Keep in mind you're not Green. As a result, you'll probably find these tips to be counter-intuitive at best and wrong at worst. However, the key to parenting success is to parent the way your child needs to be parented, not the way you prefer to do it. That'll make all the difference in the world."

We talked for a few more minutes, resolved a few tangential concerns, and then parted company. I think we charged her batteries enough to get her through another day.

After she left, my wife came up to me and gave me a big hug. She whispered in my ear, "You're so smart, honey. Thanks for helping tonight."

My ears flushed, like they always do when I get embarrassed. "Thanks for being there with me." I said, trying to conceal my discomfiture. "Sometimes people really need someone who'll listen to them. And you did that wonderfully well. Besides, I'm not smart at all. I'm just lucky to have stumbled across this information."

"Well I think you're smart," she said. "After all, you married me."

I couldn't argue with that.

CHAPTER 8

Youth: Terrific Techniques for Tolerating Teenagers

In many families, the teenage years can be difficult and trying—not only for the teenagers but also for their parents, siblings, and peers. This chapter will clarify teenage temperament and then suggest some techniques for dealing with the teenagers in your life.

The Teen Years

Perplexing pubescent personalities

If you're bewildered, baffled, and bamboozled by your teenager, then join the masses. This age group is by far the most difficult for parents, leaders, and teachers to understand. In fact, most adults don't bother anymore with trying to comprehend a teenager's behavior, much less predict it. Rather, they're simply trying to survive this stage, hoping it lasts less than a decade. Fortunately, with an understanding of temperament, those who do the parenting, leading, and teaching of teenagers don't have to be so perplexed. This chapter will help demystify teenage attitudes and actions, as well as offer a few pertinent suggestions for dealing with their more confounding characteristics.

> "Adolescence is a period of rapid changes. Between the ages of 12 and 17, for example, a parent ages as much as 20 years."
>
> — ANONYMOUS

Setting the stage

In the mid 1800s, some of my ancestors were among the pioneers who left their homes in western Europe and the eastern United States to journey westward across the Great Plains of America, headed for the Rocky Mountains. Some rode horseback; some pulled homemade handcarts, but most walked next to ox-drawn wagons as they slowly made their way across barren valleys, over rugged mountains, and through brush-filled canyons. Some of these ancestors helped settle many areas of Utah, Idaho, and Arizona. Where there was nothing but sagebrush and rattlesnakes, these early settlers built homes, planted trees, plowed fields, dug canals, constructed roads, built sawmills, erected schoolhouses, stores, and churches, organized towns and cities, and so on. Some became well known, like Ebenezer Bryce, my grandfather's grandfather, who built a ranch at the mouth of a beautiful canyon in southern Utah—now known as Bryce Canyon National Park. Famous or unknown, all of these ancestors, each in his or her way, were rugged individualists who left a legacy of commitment, true grit, and faith to their descendents.

They also left a number of tall tales to tell their children, who told them to their children, and so on. After a long day of driving cattle, picking cotton, splitting rails, weeding the garden, or removing scorpions from the house, the family would get together for a relaxing hour or two of storytelling. While some of these homespun yarns were told just for fun, others were recounted to teach, directly or indirectly, a lesson to one of the listeners.

When I was a little boy, I recall sitting in the backyard with my cow-punching grandfather and listening to his colorful version of these stories. One of them had to do with the characteristics of young horses. I've taken the liberty of expanding on this theme a bit to create the following tale about teenagers.

The colt and the cowboy

Once upon a time, a young horse (or ass, depending on your mood), whose name was Zeke, made his way out of his mother's womb into the world. Like most children, Zeke was full of vim and vigor. Almost immediately, the foal was up on his wobbly legs, trying to stand. Before long, he was walking about the stable, investigating every crook and cranny, sticking his nose in places it didn't belong. Soon he wasn't content just to walk around the barn, he yearned to trot, lope, and gallop, which he couldn't do within the confines of the walled shelter.

One day Zeke was finally allowed to leave the barn and go into the corral, where he was introduced to a new world filled with stimulating sights, sounds, and sensations—and unprecedented liberties. He immediately ran amuck, dashing here and darting there, enjoying the pure joy of physical freedom. After awhile, he started to explore his new enclosure, checking out the water and feeding troughs, sampling the different grasses, feeling the mud squish into his hooves, finding the perfect place under the sycamore tree to escape the midday sun. He eventually bumped into the barbed-wire corral fence, which he traced around and around, getting a sense of the borders it created. He found a couple of other young horses, and before long, they were hanging out together, chewing on straw, making fun of the older horses.

After awhile, Zeke got bored with his surroundings and began to look longingly at the world on the other side of the fence. He saw green pastures that appeared to be filled with acres of blue-violet alfalfa and mouth-watering wild oats. He noticed a dirt road near the corral that wound its way through the pastures and over a nearby hill. He hankered to leave the paddock and experience this other world. So he started to take a closer look at the corral's gate and fences, hoping to find a weakness that he could exploit to his advantage.

Worse than the boredom, however, was the fact that a cowboy kept coming around trying to subdue every horse in the enclosure. Just who did this man think he was? The older horses readily complied, allowing the cowboy to stick a cold metal bit into their mouths and place a leather bridle around their heads so he could lead them around the corral. But whenever the cowboy came near Zeke, tempting him with a tasty apple, Zeke would just turn around and mosey away. He would have nothing to do with this manipulative man.

Nevertheless, Zeke had to admit that the cowboy took good care of them. If the wind, rain, or thunder got bad, he'd let the horses back into the barn. He always gave them plenty of food to eat and water to drink. He'd even take a currycomb and brush them down, which felt incredibly good, especially after a long day of playing around the corral. In fact, the talk around the barnyard was that each year the man bought every horse a new pair of exceedingly durable, custom-made shoes. So maybe the cowboy wasn't as bad as he could be, although Zeke still felt like a prisoner.

Then one day, the cowboy did something the young horses had never seen before. He approached one of the older mares, put a bridle around her head, threw a leather saddle on her back, cinched it down tight, then climbed up into the saddle!

Zeke felt incredibly sorry for the old gray mare. It was obvious she wasn't what she used to be. Her independent spirit had been broken, and now she was forced into submission. Imagine having to do things you didn't want to do. How demoralizing! How infuriating! Zeke's nose flared with indignation.

The cowboy made a clicking sound and his steed walked around the corral for a moment or two to warm up and ensure that the saddle was positioned properly. Then the cowboy gave the reins a tug and the mare walked over to the gate, where the cowboy's wife was waiting. She opened the gate wide enough for the horse to walk through, and then closed it behind her. The man gave his mount a gentle kick in her flanks, and the mare broke into a trot down the road that led to greener pastures.

Zeke looked on with an anguishing mix of envy and horror. The mare had escaped the prison, sure enough, but at what cost? Was it worth having a metal bit in your mouth and a saddle on your back? If he wanted to leave the corral, would he need to submit to the will of the cowboy too? Wasn't there any other way?

And so, as the cowboy and the mare disappeared over the horizon, Zeke turned around and went back to the shade of the sycamore tree. He had some mighty hard cogitating to do. Fortunately, he had no place to go and nothing else to do.

Interpreting the story

There are many different ways to interpret this story, but we'll focus on the most obvious explanation: Zeke is a teenager, the barn represents his home and family, the corral represents his teenage years, the area beyond the corral is the adult world, and the cowboy represents the laws, folkways, and mores that define Zeke's culture.

During childhood, horses and people are purposefully penned up. Their parents or caretakers do this to protect them from the harmful elements and conditions that would endanger their lives. But their home also doubles as a safe place where they can observe and practice the basic life skills they need to survive in the real world. For horses, who don't have a lot of complicated skills to learn, this happens rather quickly. But for human beings, this stage typically terminates during the teen years, or at a point where they're able to eat an ice cream cone without completely coating their clothing.

When the proverbial barn doors open up to young teens, their temperament dictates how fast they leave the barn. Oranges will leave with haste, anxious to explore their new digs. Blues might be a bit hesitant, preferring to linger and leave with a close friend or two. Golds will see the open door, but will somberly wait for further instructions. Greens will avoid the initial hubbub, then eventually meander over to the door and begin examining the mechanics of its hinges.

With their entrance into a dramatically expanded world, most young teenagers experience a form of culture shock. Regardless of their personality style, not quite sure of what to do or how to do it, they invariably spend their energy running around in a frenzied, confused state. Fortunately, this only lasts for a year or two, during a stage known as the ninth grade.

The identity crisis

One of the more useful things to know about young teenagers is that they're in the process of discovering their own unique identities. Not what their parents expect them to be, not what teachers taught them to be, not what leaders say they must be, not what their peers pressure them to be—but who they are when they're able to figuratively stand naked in the shower, out of the presence of authority figures and peers.

Even though it's been said in an earlier chapter, it bears repeating: people prefer to do things that bring them joy. Nothing brings as much joy and satisfaction as the attitudes and activities that reflect a person's values. Adolescents, struggling to find their true identities, are essentially struggling to find the set of values that brings them joy. Of course, they had it figured out once before, when they were younger and supposedly naive, but now, after exposure to so many different value systems and lifestyles, they start to question their own identities. Consequently, they embark on a whirlwind journey of self-discovery.

Even though they don't know it, many adolescents start by abandoning their primary color and shifting to their secondary, tertiary, or inferior colors. In chapter 6 we called this process *downshifting,* although teens aren't doing it as a coping mechanism as much as they're doing it for the sake of exploration. For some reason they're questioning whether the preferences of their primary color truly cut the mustard. Therefore, they experiment with other colors in their spectrum, seeing if there isn't something worthwhile they've been inadvertently missing.

This is why it's often difficult to identify a youngster's color spectrum. They're in a constant state of flux, and if asked to self-disclose, they'll probably describe who they want to be at the moment, not who they are deep down inside. For this reason, it takes a dedicated observer, someone who can look objectively at the collective behaviors of the young person over a significant span of time, to identify his or her spectrum with more accuracy.

By the way, regardless of your age, exploring the different colors in your spectrum isn't a bad thing to do. In fact, it can be quite healthy, especially if you identify other attitudes and actions that also bring you joy. Nevertheless, if you completely neglect or abandon your primary color, as teens are apt to do, you leave a huge hole in your personality. If this hole is big enough, it can be quite discouraging, since most people can't find an adequate joy-producing replacement. So they get depressed, despondent, and even suicidal. If this is happening to you or a loved one, do what you can to help them return to the things that bring them the most joy—the attitudes and actions that are valued by their primary color.

In time, after several years of experimentation, most teenagers will return to their primary color, although it's now surrounded by the hues of their spectrum, which, once dim, are now easier to see. Throughout the remainder of their lives, if they choose to adopt the behaviors valued by their secondary, tertiary, and inferior colors, these hues will become even more vibrant, even though they will seldom reach the intensity of the original primary color.

Watching this process as a concerned adult is a bit disconcerting. You see teenagers take off on their journeys, knowing that they'll be spending most of their time in foreign lands, and perhaps even under the enemy's tent. But rest assured that the vast majority of teens eventually return to their roots. Not only have they been on a remarkable journey, but they've circumnavigated the globe!

The feeding trough

While predicting youthful behavior is fraught with uncertainty, there's one characteristic you can count on: nearly all teenagers seek to satisfy their escalating appetites and cravings. I'm not just talking about their incessant intake of cheeseburgers and milkshakes. I'm also referring to their social, intellectual, emotional, financial, spiritual, and sexual hungers.

Many teenagers view the world as a huge all-you-can-eat buffet, and they want to sample as many different flavors and varieties as possible. Sometimes they systematically do this in order to identify what they like or don't like. But more often than not, they just heap their plate with as much food as possible because it's there and they can. Of course, they can't finish it all and waste a lot, and sometimes they break out into hives because they've eaten something they're allergic to, but what the heck! Some parents encourage this behavior, believing that if their teenager is overfed, they won't want dessert and will leave the highly desirable forbidden fruit alone. Then again, have you ever met a teenager who didn't save room for dessert?

Once again, I'm not simply talking about food in this analogy, I'm talking about behaviors, academic subjects, after-school activities, friends, religious beliefs, books, television shows, hobbies, lifestyles, and so on. As teenagers seek out that which fulfills their needs and brings them joy, they sample many different and often unusual things. By the time they finish adolescence, they've identified most of the preferences they'll keep throughout adulthood.

Resistance to authority

Of course, as teenagers are introduced to the world, they see many things that capture their imaginations. More often than not, they seem to notice the forbidden things. Therefore, as they seek to turn their dreams into reality, they rebel against those who stand in their way, perceiving barriers to be undeserved limitations even though the barriers are meant to protect them from harm they cannot comprehend. For instance, Zeke didn't realize that the barbed-wire corral fence, which he saw as something that limited his freedom, was also designed to keep him safe from coyotes and cougars. Or that the bit and bridle were there to teach young horses to obey their master's touch, which might keep them from running off a cliff just as much as it could lead them to a creek of cool, clear water.

One of the great lessons teenagers need to learn is that restrictions and rules might seem constraining, but without them, life would be filled with unnecessary perils and pitfalls. Only those that bridle their passions and willingly obey the rules that govern freedom are granted freedom. Of course, some people, regardless of their age, never learn that principle. Our jails and prisons are filled with these folks.

Just like Zeke, teenagers are often filled with emotional angst. They can't really see the big picture yet and aren't quite sure how they fit into the puzzle. As a consequence, they often become perplexed and bewildered. But soon they'll be off to comfortable old stomping grounds or racing forward to a new adventure—leaving their parents perplexed and bewildered!

Teenage Characteristic Checklist

You've already seen some in-depth explanations of the characteristics of each color as they appear in various roles and stages of life. Here's one you can use when trying to identify a teenager's colors. While this list was created specifically for youth, it works for children and adults as well.

Please keep in mind that any attitude or behavior can be emulated by any color at any given time. For example, an Orange adolescent girl may spend hours at the school library studying a calculus textbook. This appears to be a Green or Gold behavior. If that's the only picture we have of this person, we might assume she is a Green or Gold. The real question to answer is why is she doing it? Is it because she enjoys sitting quietly, studying complicated mathematics? Probably not. In her particular case, she's there because if she doesn't do it she'll flunk a test and will be kicked off the rugby team. She's only doing Green and Gold behaviors because they fulfill an Orange need to play on the team.

So as you look at the characteristics listed below, keep in mind that you're only seeing a snapshot in time. Before you can identify a teenager's colors, you need to observe him or her over a significant period—the longer the better. Over time, you'll see the person doing certain things repeatedly. If the teenager enjoys doing these things, you're probably observing actions that are motivated by his or her primary color. On the other hand, if the teen is miserable, outside forces may be coercing the behavior. Given the choice, he or she would prefer to do something else. Discover what that something else is, and you'll discover the teenager's true hue.

Blue

- ☐ Appreciates creativity and self-expression
- ☐ Avoids interpersonal confrontation
- ☐ Champions the underdog
- ☐ Compromises and conciliates
- ☐ Desires internal peace
- ☐ Discusses feelings easily
- ☐ Doesn't stick to routines
- ☐ Encourages closeness, intimacy
- ☐ Expresses amplified emotions
- ☐ Hates aggressive competitions
- ☐ Likes the personal touch
- ☐ Needs personal time and attention
- ☐ Provides enthusiasm and encouragement
- ☐ Seeks and provides comfort
- ☐ Serves as the peacemaker
- ☐ Strives for personal best
- ☐ Surrounds self with supportive people
- ☐ Thrives on personal conversations
- ☐ Wants romantic affection
- ☐ Works well with people, plants, animals

Gold

- ☐ Approaches life with seriousness
- ☐ Arrives on time and prepared
- ☐ Completes tasks on the agenda
- ☐ Creates order out of chaos
- ☐ Dislikes spontaneity and impulsiveness
- ☐ Does the right thing in the right way
- ☐ Finishes work before play
- ☐ Follows directions from authority figures
- ☐ Likes to earn recognition, status, success
- ☐ Needs specific details before proceeding
- ☐ Obeys the established rules
- ☐ Prefers schedules and routines
- ☐ Respects hard work, dedication, perseverance
- ☐ Saves up for a rainy day
- ☐ Seeks increased responsibilities
- ☐ Sets and achieves goals
- ☐ Stabilizes the structure
- ☐ Uses resources wisely according to budget
- ☐ Wants expectations clearly defined
- ☐ Works the plan persistently

Green

- ☐ Acts in unconventional, peculiar ways
- ☐ Advances science and technology
- ☐ Advocates efficiency and improvement
- ☐ Avoids popular hangouts, fads, and trends
- ☐ Demands excellence from self
- ☐ Develops models and systems
- ☐ Enjoys demonstrating abilities
- ☐ Explores tangents and esoteric facts
- ☐ Fears incompetence and failure
- ☐ Likes ingenious, innovative ideas
- ☐ Needs access to resources
- ☐ Questions everything
- ☐ Requires evidence and proof
- ☐ Respects capability and brilliance
- ☐ Seeks autonomy and self-rule
- ☐ Seems driven to learn new information
- ☐ Sees flaws in arguments, systems
- ☐ Solves complicated problems
- ☐ Thrives on intellectual stimulation, mental challenges
- ☐ Wants time to think things through

Orange

- ☐ Accepts risky, physical challenges
- ☐ Acquires practical, useful skills
- ☐ Acts boldly, fearlessly, impulsively
- ☐ Avoids work done at a desk
- ☐ Deals swiftly with concrete problems
- ☐ Enjoys action-packed activities
- ☐ Fights against authority figures
- ☐ Finishes work quickly so he or she can play
- ☐ Hates delay, red tape, bureaucracy
- ☐ Ignores unnecessary details
- ☐ Knows an opportunity when it surfaces
- ☐ Likes choices, changes and variety
- ☐ Lives in the moment, for the moment
- ☐ Negotiates the best deal
- ☐ Prefers flexibility, no fixed structure
- ☐ Seeks adventure and thrills
- ☐ Tends to be playful, mischievous
- ☐ Tests own physical limitations
- ☐ Thrives on high-pressure situations
- ☐ Works around barriers and obstructions

Reputation

The importance of reputation

Each year, corporations shell out billions of dollars to public relations firms in an attempt to build up or maintain a positive reputation. Since a company's name and goodwill have everything to do with how well their products or services sell, bad reputations are usually devastating.

To illustrate, suppose you were driving your little red convertible downtown and noticed that you were nearly out of gas. As you come to the next intersection, you notice that there are two nationally known gas stations across the street from each other. The price and quality of the gas is the same. Both stations look clean and well maintained. They both have mini-marts that sell your favorite brand of chocolate donuts. However, you remember hearing on the news a year ago that an oil tanker, belonging to the parent company of one of the gas stations, had an oil spill off the coast of Nigeria. The oil spoiled the coastline and irreparably harmed the marine life. It turns out the pilot of the tanker was drunk while on duty and his inability to think clearly made the accident worse. Which gas station would you go to? If you're like most people, you'll go to the other one—the one that didn't have the accident. So they lost one customer, big deal. But when thousands of people across the country are also making the same decision at the same time, it won't be long before that company declares bankruptcy and turns off its pumps for good.

> "A good reputation is more valuable than money."
>
> — PUBLILIUS SYRUS

Teenagers are keenly aware of the importance of reputation. They spend far more energy worrying about and trying to create an attractive reputation than most adults. If they could hire a PR firm, they would, even if it meant going without pizza, potato chips, and French fries for an entire year.

You see, a rather large part of the teenage self-image is composed of what others perceive them to be. At a time when they're struggling to discover what makes them unique, external feedback becomes extremely important. If the feedback is positive, then the teen knows he or she is on the right track. But if it's bad, then they have to change their attitudes and actions to find something better. Since behavior change is difficult under the best circumstances, even for mature adults, imagine how much more difficult it is for teens—especially if they don't have someone around to give them the intensive support and direction they need.

Of course, what makes a reputation good or bad is a value judgment—a colorized value judgment. Being known as a "risk-taker" is a good thing for Oranges, but bad for Golds. Being "sensitive" is good for Blues, bad for Greens. Below is a short list of some of the positive reputations that each temperament values. This is merely a jumping-off point. If you want more specifics, turn back to chapter 1 where we looked at the characteristics people desire—the attributes they admire and seek to be known by—in much more detail.

Blue reputations

Blue teenagers want to be known as true friends—someone who cares enough to be there for you through the good times as well as the bad. When the scene at school or home becomes overwhelming, you can go to a Blue friend for empathy, reassurance, and support. Not only do they provide a shoulder to cry on, but they do it in a non-judgmental way, sensing that it's far more important to listen and validate your feelings than to try to solve your problems with reasoned arguments. Blue friends are trusted confidants who treasure these communications and thrive on the trust and intimacy they involve. With all the angst that most teenagers experience, no wonder Blues seem to spend so much time with their friends—they're providing much-needed counseling.

This compassionate service extends beyond friendships. A true Blue is usually engaged in supporting anyone or anything that needs support. Whether it's taking in an abandoned mutt who's been roaming the neighborhood or befriending a neglected classmate who's always picked last to play on a sports team or starting a neighborhood newspaper recycling campaign to help preserve old-growth forests—Blues have the reputation of putting aside their own comforts and conveniences in order to take care of others. Their motivation to do this doesn't come out of a sense of duty or responsibility, but out of genuine concern and affection. Deservedly, this is one of their most admirable characteristics.

Most Blue teenagers, however, don't become so passionate or extreme that they turn into outcast fanatics. They're social creatures, and need to know where and how they fit in with their cliques and groups. While they may secretly yearn to be part of the "cool" group, if that group becomes too exclusive or condescending, they'll form their own look-alike group that is far more tolerant of diversity. Since they want to be included, they'll include others. Therefore, Blues have the reputation of tolerating and accepting others, especially the underdogs.

Gold reputations

Gold teenagers seek the reputation of being a dependable, hard-working contributor to their organizations. In their teenage years, this is often manifest by being a significant part of student government, a well-known club, or a sports team. Notice the keyword is *significant*. That means that if they aren't providing direct leadership in that organization, they are providing something of meaningful value that shows they're committed constituents. Membership is something to be earned, not granted willy-nilly to any ne'er-do-well. Therefore, Golds will do all they can to prove their worth to the organization, and trust that someday they will be recognized for their seen and unseen contributions.

Sometimes this extra-mile effort leads other people to label the Gold as an obsequious, brown-nosing goody-two-shoes. Nothing could be further from the truth. A self-respecting Gold wouldn't even consider trying to circumvent the process in order to gain favor with the higher-ups. That would be wrong—perhaps evil. To do otherwise would weaken the system and make it unstable. Golds want nothing more than to stabilize the structure in which they've invested so much effort, which makes them known as honest people who play by the rules and color within the lines.

As teenagers, Golds are known as being more responsible than most of their peers. They take their obligations seriously and can be counted on to finish what they say they'll do. Besides doing their homework, they'll help around the house, doing chores that trigger moans and groans in other people. Strange as it may sound, Gold teenagers will much rather earn an allowance than beg for a handout. Let them earn that money by capitalizing on their responsible nature as they baby-sit, walk the dog, water the plants, weed the garden, wash the car, and so on. They do remarkably well in part-time after-school jobs and actually save most of the money they earn. Imagine that!

Green reputations

Nothing is quite so flattering to a Green teenager as being called a big brain, poindexter, egghead, or know-it-all, even though it might have been intended as a put-down. Greens are constantly in the pursuit of knowledge, and it's quite satisfying to be recognized as having more than most. They want to be known as the resident expert, even if the expertise lies in something arcane or trivial, like how to say in Klingon, "Where do you keep the chocolate?" (nuqDaq yuch Dapol)

Green teenagers also want to be recognized for their original ideas. Thinking outside the box is their modus operandi—it's something they try to do all the time. Whether they're inventing or innovating, Greens take a great deal of pride in creating something that hasn't existed before. Quick to take on a mental challenge or point out the flaws in someone's argument, Greens also enjoy mental contests and competitions where they can outreason or outwit an opponent. This pattern of thinking in nonconventional ways often bleeds into other areas of their life, such as the way they dress, talk, and behave, making the Green a rather odd duck.

Because of their peculiar attitudes and actions, Greens often have the reputation of being unusual, unsociable, or awkward. Of course, this is only in the minds of Blues, Golds and Oranges—to a fellow Green, they're perfectly normal, more normal than 94 percent of the general population in fact. While Greens don't seek isolation and exclusion, they soon learn to live with it, accurately perceiving that they don't fit into most popular social groupings.

Orange reputations

In contemporary teenage vernacular, an Orange strives to be awesome, bangin', bomb-diggity, boss, coolarific, gnarly, jiggy, killer, phat, rad, savvy, schwank, shagadellic, spankin', sweet, and wicked bad. In other words, they want to be known as someone who is charismatic, full of energy, very cool, and fun to be around. Consequently, most extroverted Oranges are remarkably popular, especially at social events. As a flame attracts moths, Oranges attract attention wherever they go. People hang around waiting for the Orange to tell a joke, relate recent exploits, or do something completely outrageous.

Oranges like to be known as gutsy trendsetters. Never content with what the mundane masses do, they prefer to lead off and do something that hasn't been done before—at least by their peer group. Therefore, they'll be the first to acquire a love interest and the first to have a make-out session. They'll be the first to wear make-up, dye their hair, shave their heads, get a tattoo or brand, or pierce something besides their ears. They'll be the first to participate in an extreme sport, enter a drag race, go cliff diving, bungee-jump off a bridge, go skinny-dipping, and crash a motorcycle. Of course, if this desire isn't channeled in a positive direction, they might also be the first to get expelled from high school, be arrested, try illegal drugs, and so on.

Orange teenagers sometimes get a bad reputation. Because of their risk-taking, sensation-seeking nature, most people assume that they're hellions out wreaking havoc on the community. Fortunately, this is hardly the case. Most Oranges, especially those that are being reared by patient and loving caregivers, channel their seemingly boundless energy in relatively healthy, productive pursuits. Oh sure, there are a few bad apples (rotten Oranges) roaming around, but there are dysfunctional Blues, Golds and Greens doing the exact same things.

Clothing

Our choices in fashion and style make an obvious statement about our personal temperaments that becomes increasingly evident in our teenage years. Since "clothes make the man," it would also seem that "clothes identify the man." To a large degree, clothing is volitional; that is, we make individual choices each day regarding what we will put on when we get dressed. This makes clothing and other appearance choices a valuable tool for self-disclosure, literally an open book that others might read to learn more about us, if they only understood the language.

Wearing your colors

It appears that, given the freedom and opportunity, different teenaged (and adult) temperaments not only prefer to wear different styles of clothes, but also adorn themselves with different hairstyles, jewelry, accessories, makeup, tattoos, and piercings. Blues, Golds, Greens, and Oranges each seem to have different tastes in fashion and style. Certainly, an individual's unique personality spectrum is revealed in his or her outward appearance as well; i.e., a Green-Gold will look much different from a Green-Blue or a Green-Orange. If we know how to read these signs, observing the appearance of others can help us understand much about them.

However, please keep in mind that this is a gross generalization that may or may not apply specifically to your teenager or to you. There are other factors in play here besides personality, such as how natural preferences are tempered by economics, cultural customs, religious traditions, ethnic identities, parental decrees, employment requirements, sibling or peer pressures, and so on.

For instance, some schools have strict dress codes that limit many of the appearance choices your teenagers might make. In addition to requiring students to wear specific clothing, they might even standardize hairstyles and jewelry choices.

When teenagers and adults go to work, they are often required to wear a uniform, such as the lab coat worn by many technicians and health care providers. In this case, clues can still be obtained by looking at the cleanliness of the garment, whether or not it is starched or ironed, even the arrangement of common tools. Are pens and pencils just dropped into a pocket or are they aligned in a row and clipped into place?

This means that as you begin to look around and see what other people are wearing, the most important thing to discover is not what they're wearing, but why and how they're wearing it. More likely than not, if they're able to choose what they wear and how they wear it, they will pick out things that reflect their unique personality styles.

Appearance basics

A general guide to the styles of clothing used by each color type is presented in the figure below. Notice how their appearance can be mapped on a graph of Fashion vs. Function and Causal vs. Formal.

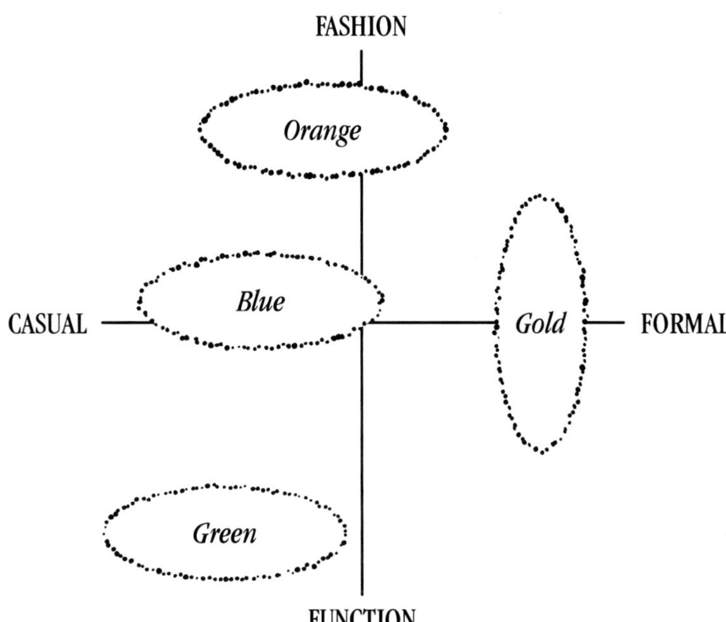

As we see, Blues will opt toward stylish clothes rather than functional ones and definitely prefer a comfortable, casual look to a distancing, formal one. This aligns with the Blue desire to grow closer to others.

Golds tend to select a formal appearance. It may be stylish or functional based on the activities they perform, such as the demands of their jobs. Golds who are physicians will wear physicians' garb in a Gold way; Golds who are businesspersons will opt towards suits.

Greens seem to be oblivious to fashion. They often choose their clothing for convenience or comfort, regardless of the statement it sends. In a way, this is simply logical—casual and comfortable clothing costs less and bangles get caught in equipment.

Oranges tend to select clothing and accessories that are trendy, even avant-garde. They can vary between casual or formal as required by the occasion. Sometimes, they take advantage of the norm in a given environment to make a statement of their individuality, such as wearing racy clothes in a conservative office, and sporting piercings and tattoos.

While you can rely on the chart for sweeping generalities, other dynamics are also important. Below is a rundown of how teenagers and adults of each color make choices about their appearance.

Blue appearance highlights

Blues tend towards stylish and casual because one must appear safe, comfortable, classy, and approachable, while at the same time able to provide a hankie or a hug, whichever may be required, at a moment's notice.

Blues create their look by combining materials on hand to create unique combinations of styles, textures, and colors. They do this with some flair, calling on the hidden artistic muse that inspires some of them. Because the art of presenting oneself can also be an act of personal disclosure, Blues enjoy creating a "unique" look in their choice of garments. They're capable of being trendsetters. This may be rooted in their perpetual drive towards self-expression and self-discovery, and clothing is a terrific means of self-expression.

Blues tend to wear art. Both male and female Blues are seen with silk-screened clothes featuring people, flowers, wildlife, landscapes, and an occasional fantasy figure. Tie-dyed clothing is delightfully whimsical. Homemade jewelry is popular, as are hand-painted or embroidered clothes. Whether they made it themselves or it was a well-meaning gift from a young family member, they'll proudly wear it regardless of how folksy it may seem to others.

In a strange twist in life's fabric, Blues often are so careful about what they wear that they become defensive about their clothing, since a part of their identity comes from their clothing. One Gold daughter, who was caught in a sudden downpour, decided to borrow a few items from her Blue mother's wardrobe. She ran into another tempest when her mother saw her. Another man in the neighborhood, renowned for being friendly and community minded, took real offense when he was asked to lend an extra t-shirt to a visitor. In both cases, these actions seem strikingly out of character for a Blue, when in fact they express their character remarkably well.

We see this manifested further when the time comes to part with old clothing. Some Blues simply cannot part with their garments. To throw one away is to discard a carefully crafted statement about oneself. Perhaps this is one of the reasons various cell phones and digital music players now have changeable shells or skins. To a Green, say, such customization would be trivial at best. To Blues it might really serve to make the appliance theirs, and thus something to be replaced when lost, stolen, or worn out.

If you want to make a statement, whisper. This advice fits for Blues, who like to be outstanding in a quiet sort of way. Oranges may want to dazzle you, but Blues want to get to know you. Instead of flash and sizzle, look for soft, clean lines, and muted colors. Just remember that still waters run deep.

Gold appearance highlights

Gold clothing is functional, formal, and conservatively fashionable. Because they strive always to wear appropriate attire regardless of the occasion, Golds have a rather broad wardrobe. It isn't unnecessarily large, because even wealthy Golds are known for their fiscal frugality and will only have as many clothes as they need.

In the workplace, the Golds can be counted on to follow the dress code to the letter, understanding the important image they ought to project to both outsiders and insiders. In white-collar professions, where you'll find many Golds in upper- and middle-management positions, Golds are usually found wearing white shirts, dark suits, and tactful ties. Most Gold guys can get away with brown and black shoes, two suits, and two belts—one if it is reversible. But Gold women have it much worse. Not only are their clothes equally or more expensive, they need many more of them. Many female Gold professionals have a complex wardrobe of pantsuits, gowns, blouses, skirts, blazers, skirted suits, jacketed dresses, wraps, scarves, gloves, and hats, each with matching shoes, handbags, and jewelry.

When shopping for clothes, Golds know value when they see it, just as they do when they shop for cars, trips, and summer homes. They will usually purchase the best they can afford and then take care of it assiduously. Materials that are unduly frilly, difficult-to-clean, or less-than-top-drawer end up costing more in the long run, and Golds know this.

Golds knows that not only will their clothing need to last a long time, it will also make a statement about the wearer in whatever circumstance they finds themselves. A classic look is timeless; hence, it is the better value. In addition, if one is not sure how he or she will be received at some meeting in the future, understatement is usually the safer course.

Most Golds wear neat, clean, and well-tailored clothing. If they can afford it, they'll choose drycleaners, launderers, and tailors with the same care others choose their dentists. Over the life of a garment, it will be regularly cleaned and de-spotted, shaved for pills, and altered as the need arises. This takes a special kind of service provider, likely one that will recognize the Gold's personal laundry bag.

Golds use clothing to denote stable social position. This dictates few pieces, but fine ones. More than one Gold uses the year-end bonus check for a pair of black shoes, and then gets a pair of brown ones the year following, at which time the oldest pair is given to charity. In fact, the knowledge that clothes going to charities may help others get or keep jobs by looking stylish and conservative is likely one of the only reasons Golds ever discard serviceable clothes. Sometimes Golds keep their clothes so long, they come back into style.

Having a few well-chosen clothes makes it difficult to shop. Any new item must either blend in with what's already on hand, or will have to be accessorized to the point it can stand alone. Golds likely will not stand for the latter—too impractical and extravagant. Thus they find themselves carrying fabric swatches to make sure what they buy will fit in with what's already in the closet.

At home, Golds are a bit more informal, although many refuse to walk around the house barefoot. They wear conservative pajamas to bed, never considering sleeping in their underwear or, heaven forbid, in the buff. When they get up from bed, they immediately reach for their slippers and robes. Modesty is their watchword; propriety is their creed.

Green appearance highlights

Many people believe Greens dress like the stereotypical nerd—the kind with pocket protectors and tape on the bridge of horn-rimmed glasses. In reality, however, most Greens do not intend to dress this way. As a rule, they're more concerned with function and utility than style. For example, if you need to carry around different pens, pencils, and sharp scientific instruments in your shirt pocket, then perhaps a pocket protector is warranted to protect you, or your shirt, from a mortal wound or a nasty stain. In this case, the pocket protector is purely functional. If other trendy or stylish people happen to believe it's a geeky accessory, then so be it—we'll see who has the last laugh when you trip and fall with sharp objects in your pocket. Remember, most Greens have probably taken the time to analyze the pros and cons of wearing the pocket protector. Since current fads and fashions aren't nearly as important to them as they are to others, naturally the benefits outweigh the disadvantages.

Greens tend to dress functionally and comfortably. If they're doctors, they live in lab coats; if they're engineers, they live in a shirt and tie, no jacket (think Dilbert). They prefer to hang out in fatigues, flight suits, dungarees, farmer's overalls, mechanics' coveralls, Mao pajamas, and smocks. There's even something to be said for the classic one-piece tunic—if it was good enough for the ancient Asians, Egyptians, Babylonians, Greeks, and Romans, then it's good enough for them.

To a Green, logical usage supersedes conventional practice. Watch out, fashion police, we have a Green on the loose! A friend spent several years in the South Pacific almost thirty years ago. To this day, he wears a sarong around the house and sometimes outside to get the mail or morning paper. (A sarong, for those brave enough to ask, is worn like a skirt by both sexes, and is rather like a cloth tube that one steps into, then rolls from the top downward to lock it in place.) His reasoning is sound: the garment probably costs less than a dollar, and millions of people wear them without any problem. His wife and children, however, introduce him as the strange man who rents the trailer out back.

There may be a declaration implied in clothing choices, especially in the case of Green-Oranges. If the internal thinking is "We think, so you don't have to," then the implied reward is to dress how one wishes, regardless of tradition. Frankly, dressing down tweaks Golds, and allows Greens to gloat, saying in effect, "I will wear whatever I want, and you won't stop me because you can't get by without me."

Greens think about their clothing once and they will continue in the same pattern until something changes. A good friend was a librarian at the local community college. A strong Green, he fell into the habit of wearing the same general outfit to school each day. One day he found a piece of paper with the following graphic on it.

Mr. Cropper caught in an elevator.

Price and durability come first. As Volvos are to automobiles, Green duds are to clothing. Greens have likely calculated the price-performance ratios for their wearables; consequently, they can argue their way into the most horrible-looking outfits.

Greens keep clothes through their functional life, not through the style cycle. You might say they stick to their clothes through thick and thin. "Who says neckties are getting skinnier? Who put them in charge? It's still fine; why should I throw it out?" When their clothing wears out, they consider it a personal offense. "I treated this bra with care, why has it let me down?"

Greens often wear what's easiest to get to, that which is closest at hand. As the "Firefighters of the Mind," Greens need to be ready to jump and run, in case someone needs them to offer an opinion. This means suits have that lived-in look; sweats often can walk by themselves.

Some Greens are prone to adopt a beard or hairstyle that mirrors the "absent-minded professor" or "crazed prophet roaming the hills" look. They may secretly dye their hair gray little by little to acquire that "distinguished look" years before their time.

Oranges appearance highlights

The stylish and casual definitely point to Oranges, who tend to be action-oriented and free-spirited, yet need to make a statement by their presence. That statement is different from disclosure, however, which would be characteristic of Blues. If your head turns because you see an Orange, it worked.

The experientially driven Orange, when performing activities that are not clothing-optional, gravitates towards dashing, bold, and daring combinations. Either the look will be overtly sexy when decorum is required or bright when somberness would fit the occasion. Whatever the wearable, it will look great on an Orange. They control their images to make strong statements and they aim to present with flamboyance.

Not that many Oranges would ever let themselves go to the point that "relaxed fit" is good enough; still, they appreciate casually moving clothes because of their active lifestyles. One never knows when a basketball may present itself for dribbling, or a perfect prop for a sight gag might come along. Spur-of-the-moment course changes require flexible sails. Perhaps this is why so many Oranges wear sweats, tees, golf shirts, ball caps, shorts, and bikinis.

Given the choice between a formal, starched look and casual-but-stylish ensemble, Oranges will go for casual. It fits their image of being stylish without tying them up with tradition. Greens will wear sneakers with ties and tails because they couldn't find their spats. Oranges will wear jeans with an overcoat because it makes a statement.

If a crocodile logo or Nike swoosh lends to the scene, Orange will be the first to adopt it and the first to let it go once others catch on. If the first glance says "Wow," then an Orange feels dressed. Clothing for an Orange is an expression, not an investment. Thus, if one designer piece can sizzle against a bargain basement background, Orange will opt for it. This leaves precious resources available for partying, cover charges, and perhaps even another outfit.

Sometimes the magic works…

One precaution: forming a guess about another's personality based solely on appearance is fraught with hazards. There's a strong likelihood you'll be wrong since you don't yet have the whole picture. For this reason, we encourage you to use a survey of external appearances as merely the first step in sizing up an individual. If you make a guess about a person's color spectrum based on clothing, however, it's always a good idea to confirm your original guess by asking a probative question or two.

We see that what we wear can say a lot about ourselves, and tell us a lot about our teenagers. And why not? For some, fashion is an attempt to help us perpetuate the image we wish to portray, or a sign of leadership. For others, it's a symbol of acceptance into a group; for a few of us, we wear clothing because it stops the discomfort caused by drafts and provides pockets.

Relating to Teenagers

This section provides an overview of how teenagers of each color relate with parents of each color. The following paragraphs summarize the essential relationship dynamics of the sixteen possible combinations.

Blue teens–Blue parents

Parents and teenagers who are of the same personality style often make a good combination. They listen to each other and understand the meaning of what each communicates. They both possess sensitive feelings and are sympathetic to the others' emotions. The downside to their compatibility is that Blue teens may have such a strong desire to please and take care of their parents that they spend too much time and energy in doing so. Their social development may be impaired as a result of being overly attached, and they may want to spend the better part of their free time at home with the folks. They may become too dependent, develop fears, and fail to develop self-confidence.

Blue teens–Gold parents

Blue teens like to please others. They normally obey their parents and are thought of as being "good" kids. They usually follow the house rules and fit well into the family. Because of their chameleon-like attribute of adapting to others, Blue teens often act differently depending on the people with whom they are associating. Conflict may arise because the Blue teen thinks in idealistic terms while the Gold parent thinks in realistic and practical terms. The Blue teen may spend a lot of time day dreaming or doing imaginative, creative things. Because the Gold parent is more realistic, the Blue teen is regarded as lazy and not doing his or her share. Both the Blue teen and the Gold parent have the same desire to belong and to help others. They both value moral behavior and believe in being honest.

Blue teens–Green parents

Blue teens thrive on love and attention. They need to talk and share what they experience and feel. The Blue teen needs a parent that listens, empathizes, and shows affection. A Green parent often leaves a Blue teen feeling neglected and unloved because a Green parent is not one to display as much affection or spend as much time as the teen desires. A Green parent is also a person of few words and can often seem hard to reach. Blue teens need to please their parents and receive their approval, but if a Green parent is always looking for perfection, a teen may have a hard time measuring up and consequently develop a poor self-image. Blues make decisions based on feelings and Greens expect decisions to be made based on logic. Blue teens take a much more relaxed look at life than does a Green parent and may feel their parent is too demanding.

Blue teens–Orange parents

A Blue teen and an Orange parent get along well with each other most of the time. Both like fun and people and both are well liked. A Blue teen enjoys the Orange's spontaneity, adventurous spirit, and humor. They both have an optimistic, upbeat outlook on life. Blue teens don't like competition because they want everyone to feel good and be a winner whereas Orange parents believe competition is the name of the game. Orange parents may feel Blue teens are too clingy and emotional. Blue teens may feel their Orange parents don't give out enough attention and aren't sensitive to their needs. Orange parents thrive on crisis and confrontation while their teens want peace and harmony. Blue teens feel insecure and frightened if their Orange parents have a hot temper. Promises are important to Blue teens; they will feel hurt and offended if their Orange parents don't keep their word.

Gold teens–Blue parents

Gold and Blue personalities both have a strong need to belong and help others. A Blue parent is idealistic where the Gold teen thinks in practical terms. A Gold teen needs concrete rules and consistency instead of nebulous guidelines and a parent who doesn't carry through. Gold teens like traditional activities and may feel uncertain or feel their Blue parents are peculiar when their parents want them to do an activity that's out of the ordinary.

Gold teens want to be independent and may feel their Blue parents are too attached because they want to hold on longer than needed or do too much for their children. A Gold teen likes organization and may feel stressed over the apparent lack of organization in a Blue parent's home.

Gold teens–Gold parents

Both the Gold teen and the Gold parent share the same traditional, responsible values. They're organized, punctual, hardworking, and seek to follow established rules. They both set goals and plan for the future. They both have a clearly defined sense of right and wrong. They both are conservative so the Gold parent doesn't have to worry about the teen adopting trendy and outlandish dress styles. A Gold teen respects his or her parents as authority figures and regularly follows guidance. Gold parents establish rules to follow and give Gold teens the structured environment they need to thrive. Gold teens are responsible and conform to what's expected of them.

Gold teens–Green parents

A Gold teen isn't extraordinarily imaginative and tends to think in terms of black and white while the Green parent is quite imaginative and tends of think of "limitless possibilities." The Green parent needs to be careful not to make the Gold teen feel inferior or stupid. The Green parent, being an independent person and understanding the need for freedom, needs to give the Gold teen the space he or she needs to be independent too. Because Green parents value perfection, Gold teens may be motivated to do well but may end up feeling they cannot measure up or be as perfect as their parents are. Both personalities like to be appreciated for a job well done.

Gold teens–Orange parents

Gold teens and their Orange parents in many ways are on different planets. Gold teens need structure and stability that they don't get from Orange parents who live with few rules. Orange's impulsive nature and lack of planning cause Gold teens to feel confused and uncertain. Gold teens need rules and a strong moral code that they may not get from Orange parents, who like to live a life of few constraints. Gold teens like neatness and organization and may worry or feel embarrassed about their parents' relatively messy home. Orange parents value their freedom and dislike restrictive commitments and may let family responsibilities slip if they feel too constrained, leaving Gold teens feeling abandoned and thinking their parents are irresponsible and negligent. A Gold teen and an Orange parent are alike in that they both feel a need to see a job completed and touch the final product.

Green teens–Blue parents

A Green teen doesn't like to be interrogated by a Blue parent who likes to be kept informed of the teen's activities. A Green teen feels uncomfortable with displays of emotion and a Blue parent considers it important to share feelings and express affection. A Green teen and a Blue parent are socially poles apart—a Green teen prefers spending time alone while the Blue parent enjoys an active social life. On the other hand, a Green teen likes to be complimented on his or her excellent work and a Blue parent is more than willing to give praise.

Green teens–Gold parents

A Gold parent and a Green teen both look seriously at life and don't like taking physical risks. A Gold parent and a Green teen often don't get along. When being scolded, a Green teen will argue and infuriate the Gold parent. Both can be stubborn. A Gold parent expects rules to be followed and a Green teen questions authority. The Gold parent may say things like, "Because I told you so," and the Green teen won't see the logic in that kind of statement. When a Gold parent dispenses physical punishment, the Green teen feels violated and better responds to logic and reason. They like to have part in deciding their punishment. A Gold parent likes to do traditional things and Green teens may comply if they accept the justification for participating.

Green teens–Green parents

Green parents and Green teenagers get along well because they share the same interests and outlook on life. They both communicate in the same way and understand each other. They're both analytical, like to spend some time alone, think logically and intellectually, and strive for competency. Since they're always striving for perfection, they may find themselves in competition with each other, which may or may not be healthy since the teen may try to be as good as or better than the parent. Neither parents nor teens make a display of their affection or emotions. They both dislike crowds and prefer small groups. Because of the Green teen's questioning nature, he or she may question the parent's authority.

Green teens–Orange parents

An Orange parent and a Green teen both value freedom. Orange parents want freedom to do what they want, when they want in order to enjoy life, and their teens want freedom to explore and experiment with new ideas. Green teens enjoy time alone and don't require a lot of individual attention from their parents. Green teens are logical and slow to make decisions and have difficulty understanding their parent's impulsiveness. Orange parents are gregarious and fun loving where their Green teens are "loners" and don't enjoy a lot of socializing. Their parents think them to be a "stick in the mud" and the teens think their parents are "crazy." The Green teen and the Orange parent understand each other's need to spend time on what they like to do. The Green teen wants to become competent and reach perfection through practice and the Orange parent reaches competency and perfection as a result of doing something repeatedly because it's fun.

Orange teens–Blue parents

The Orange teen and the Blue parent are compatible most of the time. They both like to do fun things, and a Blue parent is able to adapt easily to Orange activities. A Blue parent appreciates uniqueness in others and may excuse the behavior of the Orange teen because "that's the way she is" or "she's just expressing herself." The Orange teen doesn't want to be tied to apron strings and may rebel against a Blue parent that wants to be too involved in his or her life. Since a Blue parent is sensitive to the feelings of others and readily empathizes, the Orange teen may find the parent too easily manipulated—something the Orange teen is good at doing. The Orange teen needs a parent who is direct and spells things out. A Blue parent may hint or be too vague.

Orange teens–Gold parents

The Gold parent and the Orange teen frequently clash. Problems arise when the teen wants to play first and work later and the parent expects the teen to work first and play later. Because Gold parents are cautious and deliberate, they consider their Orange teen's impulsive nature to be hasty and irresponsible. Oranges don't want to wait and be patient, while their Gold parents believe in setting goals and patiently working towards them, however long it takes. An Orange teen lives for the moment and thinks little of the future, whereas a Gold parent plans for the future and thinks of consequences. An Orange teen needs freedom and a Gold parent may exert too much control and restraint. However, a Gold parent and an Orange teen are alike in that the teen needs plain, direct communication and the parent likes to "get straight to the point."

Orange teens–Green parents

Orange teens live for the moment and value freedom. They are casual individuals and seek excitement and fun. Problems arise when their Green parents, who are sometimes described as being "dull," would rather have a teen put his or her time to better use. Because of the Orange teen's whimsical nature, the Green parent has difficulty understanding the teen's carefree attitude and behavior. Because of the Green parent's quest for excellence, the parent tries to motivate the Orange teen to self-improvement—and the teen rebels and feels that he or she is being controlled. Orange teens are the least likely to complete homework assignments with regularity whereas their Green parents expect teens to give their best. The Orange teen and the Green parent are alike in that they're both competitive and like to be competent at what they like to do. Their communication with each other is direct and to the point.

Orange teens–Orange parents

Whenever a teen and a parent share the same values, it makes for a good match. However, Orange parents may not teach their teens enough about responsibility because the parents are somewhat impulsive and are not known for making plans and honoring commitments. Orange teens value freedom and will be able to enjoy it because their parents take a liberal view and will impose only a few rules. Both parents and teens enjoy physical activities and learn best in a "hands-on" style. They often will compete against each other, which can cause problems over who is the best or who can tell a bigger tale. Both enjoy fun adventures. They both have an optimistic outlook on life and enjoy living in a casual atmosphere. They both take risks, are gregarious, and possess good negotiating skills.

Household Chores

> "If you want to recapture your youth, just cut off his allowance."
>
> — AL BERNSTEIN

Weekly chore lists, check sheets, and allowance incentives. These are the trappings of an organized attempt to get household tasks accomplished, teach responsibility, and build a lasting work ethic. However, other items often appear on this list. Headaches, stress, conflicts, and manipulation are sometimes the byproducts of assigning chores.

As a parent, when you have a lot of work to take care of, it's often helpful to remember that different personalities are attracted to different types of jobs. A quick identification of your family's temperament styles will help you identify and assign jobs. Family members will more readily accept and complete jobs if they align with their styles. For example, Blues prefer jobs that make the home a more enjoyable place to live, Golds prefer routine jobs that involve order and upkeep, Greens are great problem-solvers and trouble-shooters, and Oranges prefer action-oriented jobs where they're free to move about and use tools and work-saving devices.

Once you know what household tasks the members of your household prefer, you can sit down with each member, discuss options, and make a plan. If everyone is to adhere to the plan, it's important that each member have some part in the planning. When each member helps to set his or her own goals, there's a better chance for success. A family meeting to present the plan puts the plan in action.

In undertaking the responsibility of assigning chores, it's also important to communicate that there are many times when it's necessary to do things we'd rather not do, like changing the oil in the car, sharpening the blade on the lawnmower, or unclogging a toilet. Nevertheless, this is one of the practical skills every family member ought to learn before he or she graduates to adulthood.

Assigning chores based largely on preferred style will take some of the headache out of getting your family to help around the house. Taking time to set up a family game plan will help ensure that all members are given the chance to contribute their suggestions and, most important, understand their role in making the plan work.

Blue household chores

☐ Cooking meals for family
☐ Taking care of someone who is sick
☐ Shopping for food and clothes
☐ Baby-sitting and caretaking
☐ Beautifying rooms with plants and artwork
☐ Dusting mementos, trinkets, and knickknacks
☐ Watering and feeding plants
☐ Taking care of family pets
☐ Feeding young children
☐ Designing and making clothes
☐ Redecorating rooms
☐ Refurbishing furniture
☐ Washing toys and personal possessions
☐ Helping someone else do his or her chores

Gold household chores

☐ Sorting laundry and ironing clothes
☐ Sweeping or mopping floors
☐ Cleaning up after animals
☐ Cleaning out closets
☐ Organizing drawers and shelves
☐ Picking up trash and clutter
☐ Weeding the garden
☐ Raking, edging, and trimming the lawn
☐ Pruning trees and bushes
☐ Scouring sinks, toilets, and bathtubs
☐ Cleaning out the garage
☐ Cutting out coupons
☐ Paying the bills
☐ Planning family activities

Green household chores

- ☐ Figuring out solutions to family problems
- ☐ Making something more efficient
- ☐ Fixing things that are broken
- ☐ Arranging furniture
- ☐ Organizing bookshelves
- ☐ Designing and planting a garden
- ☐ Optimizing processes and procedures
- ☐ Returning library books
- ☐ Remodeling and improving things
- ☐ Keeping records up-to-date
- ☐ Balancing the checkbook
- ☐ Sharpening knives and tools
- ☐ Gathering information for big purchases
- ☐ Designing a dog house or fish bowl

Orange household chores

- ☐ Mowing lawns
- ☐ Shoveling snow or dirt
- ☐ Hammering nails
- ☐ Drilling holes
- ☐ Taking out garbage
- ☐ Vacuuming carpets
- ☐ Chopping wood for a fireplace
- ☐ Washing and waxing car
- ☐ Painting with a roller or spray can
- ☐ Sweeping sidewalks and driveways
- ☐ Changing the oil and rotating the tires
- ☐ Cutting down or pulling out trees and bushes
- ☐ Constructing fences, decks, and sheds
- ☐ Working with heavy machinery

CHAPTER 9

Education: Teaching in the Nexus

You will discover that students have different learning styles and that teachers have different teaching styles. By understanding these differences and incorporating them into the classroom, teachers can be more effective educators and students can become more excellent students.

Understanding Education

If you're an American, by the time you reach adulthood, you've probably spent at least thirteen thousand hours in a classroom. If you're from other industrialized countries, you've probably spent up to twenty-one thousand hours being educated. That's a significant chunk of time, even if it was distributed over twelve or thirteen years. But how many of those hours you did spend staring out the window, wishing the earth would be invaded by aliens who want nothing more than to carry off your schoolteachers and suck gray matter from their brains?

Education seems to be a painful experience for many students—the majority, in fact. Why is that? If I can be so bold as to make an observation that might offend some readers: perhaps it has something to do with the disparity between the way teachers teach and the way students learn.

I'll chant my old mantra again: each temperament is unlike the others in significant ways. In this book we have so far seen how this is true concerning values, motivation, communication, work, supervision, recreation, childhood, and youth. And it is true for education as well.

Each color has clear preferences on how they'd like to learn information and how they'd like to teach it. When learners and teachers of the same type get together, then magic transpires and everyone's preferences are accommodated. If you think back, you may discover that your favorite teachers were those that accommodated your learning preferences and, if you look closer, probably shared your primary or secondary colors. Unfortunately, that situation doesn't happen so often, and millions of people suffer needlessly in classrooms across the planet.

You may be inclined to rebut, "But it's totally unrealistic to match Green teachers with Green students and Orange teachers with Orange students and so on." Perhaps you're correct, given the current educational system, but that still doesn't mean it's not the most painless way to teach and learn.

How can we make it more realistic? How can we get teachers to accommodate the preferences of their students? If teachers are unwilling to change, is it possible to help students accommodate the preferences of their teachers? How can we do this without adding more work for our already overburdened teachers? Stay tuned for the answers. But first, let's examine the learning preferences of the each temperament. Then, we'll examine teaching preferences. Finally, we'll see how to improve the educational process so that we are able to learn and teach without going bonkers. Here's a hint: it has something to do with the nexus.

Learning Styles

Below is a listing of each temperament's learning preferences as they relate to:

— favorite subjects
— motivation to learn
— ideal classroom environment
— sources of esteem
— individualized learning styles
— preferred ways to do homework
— ways they prefer to be tested
— behaviors in the classroom
— preferred extracurricular activities, and
— roles in the classroom or school

Blue Learners

Blue students learn best in an open, supportive, and interactive environment that's focused on the individual learner. Activities that appeal to them include small group discussions, creative exercises, and noncompetitive academic games or contests. They prefer learning information that will help them make the world a more harmonious, pleasant, and beautiful place. The keyword for this temperament is *feeling*.

Favorite subjects

Blue students are more apt to choose subjects that focus on people, rather than abstract subjects like science, mathematics, or technology. Favorite subjects may include creative writing, literature, drama, social studies, languages, and art. No matter what the subject, it can be made interesting if the Blues can see how it ties in with people.

Motivation

Blue students are motivated by their feelings, the desire to fit in, and the drive to develop fulfilling relationships. They may perform in school to please their parents or teachers. They may also pursue education to better help other people or as part of their quest to "find themselves."

Classroom environment

Blue students need to feel like they're making a difference in the classroom. Therefore, they appreciate an environment that supports democratic principles, where students have input into how the class is governed. This is important, not because of the procedures that are developed, but because it shows that the teacher values the students. Blues need an environment where they can receive and give emotional reinforcement and support, where they can receive personalized instruction, and where all people in the classroom feel comfortable, nourished, and at-ease.

Sources of esteem

Blue students need to know they're important to the teacher and to the other students in the classroom. They seek to be recognized and acknowledged for their uniqueness. They look for personal feedback on their performances. An official computer-generated notice that they're on the honor roll will mean far less than a note of encouragement from a teacher. Anything that conveys the attitude, "you're important to me" will greatly enhance the self-esteem of a Blue. A Blue will appreciate an occasional friendly comment or touch on the shoulder, as they recognize the Blue's importance as an individual apart from the class as a whole. When the teacher is discussing an assignment with a Blue, the Blue will be lifted more by a compliment on the deep feeling of his or her work than on its correct form or procedure.

Learning style

Learning is tied to feelings for Blue students. Blues need to feel that they're important to the teacher before they really listen to what that teacher has to say. Blues thrive on interaction and dialogue. Unlike the Greens, who prefer to work independently, the Blues prefer to work in a group. They enjoy opportunities to communicate freely with other students where they learn and share their feelings and reactions. In fact, the high point of the day may be the time they spend in small study groups. Blues learn best from group discussions, role-plays, experiential learning exercises, dramatic presentations, and academic games. If learning involves interaction, Blues are generally active participants.

Activities that emphasize cooperation rather than competition appeal to Blues. Competition may cause contention—and conflict is stressful to the Blues. A competitive game, if employed, needs to remain "just a game." Teams, if any, should be changed frequently so each team has a chance to win. Whichever side they're on, the Blues will empathize with the losers.

Blue students usually are fantastically creative. Exercises or activities involving their imaginations will appeal to them. Creative writing or twists to regular assignments will help to involve the Blues in the learning process.

Homework

Blues try to complete their assignments regularly to avoid disappointing their teachers. However, if conflict comes up with another activity, Blues will likely follow their heart rather than their duty. They will try to please everyone, but they will give priority to the area that holds the strongest emotional commitment.

Testing

Blue students are likely to prefer essay tests where they can express themselves more completely. Unless they're especially introverted, they will also like oral tests or other tests that rely on communication skills rather than simple fact memorization.

Behavior

The behavior of Blue students may be difficult to distinguish from that of Gold students. Both groups may dutifully complete their assignments. A Blue student may also offer to do things to help the teacher, much like a Gold. The difference is in the focus. Golds are focused on the system; Blues are focused on people. Golds perform out of responsibility, while Blues perform in order to please others.

Blues may be over-sensitive and easily hurt. Ridicule or sarcasm may scar a Blue student. They react poorly to conflict or anger, and may even become physically ill. Sometimes Blue students may become introverted in the classroom, especially if they have experienced some form of rejection. However, with encouragement and attention, the Blue student will generally become more involved and active in classroom discussions.

Extracurricular activities

Blue students are natural communicators. Even from an early age, they're eagerly taking part in activities that rely upon effective communication. Because of this, they may be involved with working on student papers or on the yearbook staff. They may also be involved in drama productions. Their social nature may cause them to be involved in planning dances or be part of social or service clubs.

Role in school

As in other life roles, Blues in schools want everyone to get along. Blues with plenty of self-esteem, especially extroverted Blues, usually find school appealing because it gives them the opportunity to communicate and socialize with a large number of people.

Blue Learning Preferences

Harmonious environments
Cooperative learning
Open discussions
"Feeling" perspectives
Artistic applications
Non-pressured situations
Imaginative activities
Caring teachers

Gold Learners

Gold students learn best when course content is structured, clearly defined, and presented in a concrete, chronological manner with timelines, maps, diagrams, and models. Rules and directions are helpful and let them know when they're on the right track. They're traditional, responsible, dedicated students who learn best from specific examples, involvement, and discussions and tend to have a distaste for generalization and abstraction. The keyword for this temperament is *judging*.

Favorite subjects

Because Gold students have a great deal of respect for custom, they generally prefer traditional school subjects, such as history, English, general mathematics, political science, home economics, business, and foreign languages. However, they will do whatever they can to succeed in classes, regardless of whether they enjoy the subject or not.

Motivation

Gold students place a great deal of value on educational institutions. They're motivated by the desire to fit into the system and earn a place for themselves. Report cards are more important to Golds than to other students. They see them as valid measurements of their accomplishments and contributions to the class. Golds also value diplomas. They believe that the road to success begins with a diploma, degree, or certificate of accomplishment, and without that "piece of paper," their chance for obtaining success is diminished substantially. They keep this goal foremost in their minds and will actively work to obtain it, and cannot understand why other personality types place so little emphasis on it.

Classroom environment

Golds are the most comfortable in traditional classroom environments where student desks are arranged in columns and rows that face the front of the classroom. At the front of the room presides the teacher, who may be sitting or standing behind a desk or podium. Golds appreciate a room that's neat, clean, and orderly. They will feel most comfortable in a room where the rules are clear and enforced.

Sources of esteem

Gold students derive a sense of great satisfaction from being useful and respond well to special class jobs. They place particular meaning on traditional kinds of acknowledgment for their outstanding performances, such as honor roll membership, certificates of merit, badges, ribbons, plaques, stars, and special notes sent home about their good work and contributions to others.

Learning style

Because Gold students have a concrete, sensory approach to life in general, abstract concepts are sometimes difficult for them to grasp. Explanations of subject matter or procedures are easier for them to understand when presented in a chronological and clear manner. They enjoy working with timelines, diagrams, maps, and models. They prefer teacher-led question-and-answer sessions.

Traditional written assignments such as workbooks, chapter study questions, worksheets, drill work, and review pages appeal to Gold students. They enjoy working on them and will learn well from them. Deskwork and optional extra credit assignments are also appealing to many Gold students.

Gold students need to understand what's expected of them. They want specific information on acceptable procedures, approved materials, and the schedule of assignments. They appreciate knowing how they should behave: when it's appropriate to walk about in class, talk to others, ask questions, how to get help, etc. Gold students thrive on regularity, efficient use of time, and predictability. They desire step-by-step instructions that include illustrative examples.

Golds do well in classes where they're required to take notes on a lecture. While other students may find the didactic process to be tedious or pointless, Golds take pride in the quality and quantity of their notes. They prefer to write legibly on ruled paper and will erase all traces of mistakes or smudges. It's frustrating to them if the lecturer doesn't follow an obvious outline or jumps back and forth among subjects. Because of the clarity and comprehension of the Gold student's notes, other students may attempt to copy them for their own use.

Homework

Gold students can be counted on to fulfill their commitments and meet their homework obligations. Because of this, more than any other color group, Golds develop regular study habits and routines. They may designate a particular study place and a regular time to study. If it's time to study, that's what they will do, even if a more entertaining activity is offered. They will probably follow conventional study procedures, such as outlining, highlighting, summarizing, and reviewing. They will do their homework in a neat and orderly way, and often use a typewriter or computer to prepare final versions of their assignments.

Testing

Gold students will probably feel more comfortable with testing activities that require providing "black and white" facts than with activities where they must speculate, invent, guess, or improvise. They may prefer true or false, multiple choice, short answer, and fill-in-the-blank questions. They're usually good at learning to respond by giving the expected answers.

Behavior

The Gold student is usually obedient and agrees to follow the standards of classroom conduct as defined by the teacher. The teacher is the acknowledged leader and the Gold will accept his or her definition of acceptable behavior.

Gold students place a great deal of trust and faith in their teachers, and will usually give them the benefit of the doubt. They believe that people become teachers because they possess a certain amount of expertise in their fields. Golds believe in hierarchy and believe that if teachers did not fully understand the subject matter, they would not have achieved their positions. Because of this faith, Gold students rarely question the authority or judgment of their teachers, even if a deficiency becomes obvious. It's not their responsibility to correct any inadequacy or inaccuracies—that's the responsibility of the teacher's supervisor.

Gold students run the risk of being labeled as the "teacher's pet" by their peers. A variety of factors may contribute to this label. While observing a student-teacher dispute, Golds will tend to side with the teacher rather than the student. The Gold will point out when rules are being broken, not for the purpose of getting the rule-breaker into trouble, but because rules are not supposed to be broken. Gold students regularly volunteer to assist teachers and administrators by running errands or grading papers. They will spend time after school helping the teacher prepare for the next day's activities, often erasing the boards, straightening the desks, and emptying the trash.

Extracurricular activities

Student government and school clubs are usually organized, staffed, and populated by Golds. They will spend large amounts of time working in these organizations. Gold students often want to serve in the presidency of the class or club, where they have the power to develop policy and procedure. Golds can be counted on to pass on the traditions of the school and promote the school motto, mascot, or song. They take the responsibility for organizing assemblies and producing yearbooks. They can serve as capable coordinators, social directors, team captains, or committee chairpersons.

Role in school

The Gold student feels at home in most school environments, especially when teachers are consistent and stable. Of all personalities, the Gold is likely to become the ideal student, showing responsibility, dependability, and respect for authorities.

Gold Learning Preferences

Structured environments
Traditional activities
Clear expectations
Specific goals and objectives
Established routines
Rewards for achievement
Task-oriented groups
Organized teachers

Green Learners

Green learners are driven to understand the world around them. They learn best when they're exposed to the driving force or overall theory behind a subject. They're impatient with drill, review, and routine. They prefer to work independently on abstract and intellectually challenging subjects. They have an analytical and conceptual approach to learning and rely heavily on logical thinking and rational evaluation. The keyword for this temperament is *thinking*.

Favorite subjects

Green students want to obtain competency in whatever subject they choose to explore. However, they most often choose subjects that allow them to understand, predict, and explain the world around them. For this reason, science, technology, mathematics, drafting, engineering, logic, analytical writing, and vocabulary courses appeal to the Green student.

Motivation

Green students value learning. A diploma or degree is only important as far as the education it represents. In the course of their educations, Greens may earn a variety of degrees, but these pieces of paper are not ends in themselves. They're merely steppingstones on a path of self-improvement. The educational process for a Green never stops—it's a life-long pursuit. Greens will be motivated by anything that promises increased understanding or intellectual growth.

Classroom environment

Greens need a classroom atmosphere that fosters rationality, experimentation, creativity, and freedom to think. They enjoy decor that promotes thought, such as maps, globes, charts, diagrams, and illustrations. They require intellectual stimulation and freedom to develop their thoughts. They will be content if, after they finish their class work, they're free to explore with scientific equipment or find an interesting book to read. They need an environment where their ideas are acknowledged for their value and usefulness. At times, Greens may demonstrate eccentric behavior, for which they need an appreciative, easygoing environment.

Sources of esteem

Greens receive esteem from being competent. They won't seek or seem to need approval as much as the other colors, but recognition of their work or competency, especially from a teacher who is respected, will greatly reinforce self-esteem. Asking Green students to give their opinion or take part in solving problems will also add to esteem.

Learning style

Green students dislike repetition and prefer teachers to be as clear and direct as possible. They're independent learners. They seem to possess an unquenchable thirst for learning and will seek to acquire information until they're satiated. They prefer to work by themselves, where they can control the learning pace and intensity. Consequently, they may resent being confined to a learning group with other students and may rebel by withdrawing their energy and minimizing their contributions. They're naturally curious, investigative, and inquisitive. They want to know why things are the way they are, how ideas are conceived, what contradictions may exist, and what questions remain unanswered. They use a scientific approach to knowing and understanding that's based on careful, empirical observations and logic. They'll subscribe to established scientific laws, rules, and principles, but only if they're consistently proven to be valid.

Green students enjoy innovating and experimenting with the ideas of other people. They will often take an idea, manipulate it, change it, and expand upon it, until they finally produce something that may not remotely resemble the original idea. They would rather pursue their inspirations than spend time in other courses of study. They enjoy studying particulars and have a tendency to veer off on tangents. They may neglect to study subjects that they find to be less interesting, although they usually will do enough to receive passing grades.

Green students don't mind logical, didactic presentations as long as they're supplemented with comprehensive transcripts or reading material. A lecture in and of itself may not supply enough data to the Green student—they must have access to other reliable sources of information. They enjoy going to the library, where they have the opportunity to research, study, and gather as much data as they need.

Greens don't appreciate make-work projects or busy work. However, they will fully endorse projects they view to be legitimate learning activities. Activities that appeal to them would include experimentation, discussion, debate, student-written review questions and answers, or graphing a project in a new way. They may enjoy class debates and intricate mysteries that require days to solve. They need back-up material for their intellectual stimulation and opportunities to engage in independent activities once they have completed class requirements.

Homework

Because of the value Green students place on learning, it's important to them to be able to retain the information they're taught. In general, Greens find it easy to grasp abstract concepts and may find it a waste of time to engage in traditional learning activities such as drill, practice, and repetition. Consequently, when they're faced with such homework assignments, they tend to put them off until the last minute, or they may not turn them in at all. But when they're tested on the material, they normally display above-average competency. This can be somewhat aggravating to teachers who place more emphasis on effort or process rather than results. On the other hand, if the homework includes independent work or research on a topic of interest to the Green students, they will invest great amounts of time and effort.

Testing

Green students are usually competent at taking all types of tests, but they don't need a test score to feel competent. Their sense of learning is based on internal rather than external approval. They may even resent having to prove that they're learning to their teachers. Essay tests may appeal to Greens because they give them an opportunity to show the depth of their learning or research.

Behavior

Greens, particularly extroverted Greens, have a tendency to become the classroom experts, whom the teacher and other students trust will always have an answer or an opinion. While they may enjoy this prestige, they can quickly become overwhelmed. Their performance standards are always on the rise and they have a hard time accepting the fact that they cannot know everything.

Green students need to understand the reasons why. "Because I say so" is an inadequate response to a question. This kind of response may lead to a power struggle between strong Green students and their teachers. Greens want the right to question ideas, even those that are well established. Greens have a definite need to explore and receive validation for their own ideas, and if the opportunity is not given, they may cause trouble.

Most classrooms only have two or three Green students. If they fail to find others who are like themselves, they tend to become introverted and somewhat isolated. They're accustomed to having others fail to grasp what they're saying, and may decide to communicate only with people they perceive to be on an equal intellectual plane; sometimes this may only include the teacher.

Many Green students, particularly if they're bright, may succumb to the tendency to become snobbish and arrogant. Sometimes these students need help understanding that other people don't place such a high value on intellectual capabilities. Greens may live in a world of their own and, at times, students in other color categories feel antagonistic to them due to the aloofness or lack of social ease they sometimes display. Their social skills may be underdeveloped, especially in the realm of interpersonal relationships. They may balk at an attempt to be taught these skills, preferring to avoid social relationships entirely and keep to themselves.

Extracurricular activities

To the Green, learning is play. They may even view conventional recreational activities as a waste of time. They would much rather get on with the business of learning. However, if they do engage in extracurricular recreational activities, they may join groups with specialized interests, such as a computer users group or a chess club. Extroverted Greens may join a debate team. The few Greens that participate in athletics tend to concentrate on being technically proficient.

Role in school

Greens represent a small portion of the student population in most primary and secondary schools. Because they value learning, they may feel comfortable in a school environment (as long as the curriculum is not too restricting), but it may not be challenging or exciting enough for bright Greens.

Green Learning Preferences

Quiet environments
Cognitive challenges
Non-linear learning
Hypothetical analyses
Independent learning
Sufficient time
Experimentation
Competent teachers

Orange Learners

Orange students learn by seeing and doing, rather than by listening and reading. They're motivated by their own natural competitive nature and sense of fun. They thrive in an open atmosphere where they're free to move about and get physically involved in the learning process. The active experimenter takes a pragmatic approach to learning and is always asking, "Yes, but it will it work?" The keyword for these learners is *doing*.

Favorite subjects

Orange students enjoy subjects that focus on action or performance. Favorite subjects may include drama, music, physical education, mechanics, art, and vocational arts. Any subject that involves active learning and lots of movement will probably appeal to an Orange.

Motivation

Orange students are motivated by a desire for spontaneous action and freedom. Because they're not motivated by future rewards, education must be applied to the here-and-now to be appreciated by Oranges. In this way, they're incredibly pragmatic. The concept of learning for its own sake is foreign to Oranges.

Classroom environment

Excessive classroom rules and limits will be a source of irritation with Orange students. Rather, they appreciate a flexible, casual, dynamic environment that facilitates a lot of movement and excitement. The more clutter, chaos, and noise, the better. To have the desks and chairs in the same place day after day is expected—thus boring to an Orange who thrives on variety and change. Obviously, they dislike seating charts, preferring to move about on a whim. If they're interested in something, they want to be able to move in and get a closer view; if they're bored, they'll want to move as far away as possible. Allowing this movement will provide an important clue as to their interest in the subject matter. They like to see regular change in bulletin boards, posters, models, exhibits, software, and decorations. If they don't find something to catch their fancies in the room, they'll turn their attention to something less educational, such as peering out windows, doodling their own pictures, or placing thumbtacks on chairs.

Sources of esteem

Oranges esteem themselves on their ability to perform. Giving Oranges the opportunity to make a presentation to the class, demonstrate an unusual ability, show off their newly acquired skills, or be the center of attention in some other positive way will increase their interest in the learning process and bring them joy.

Learning style

The typical classroom doesn't fit the learning style of the Orange students. They don't conform well to the traditional idea of a class filled with quiet, attentive students listening to an instructor and taking notes. Oranges are active learners. They need hands-on activities and experience. They're concrete rather than abstract thinkers.

Oranges love competition. They will become heavily involved in learning activities in the form of games and contests. They can be excellent team members, but they like to work with a society of equals. They may rebel against close supervision. They like to take risks and perform.

Lectures, workbooks, quizzes, and other written work will cause Oranges to lose interest quickly. They learn better from visual and verbal activities. Oranges learn well from videos and other media presentations. Basically, they're happy as long as the learning activity doesn't involve pencils and paper.

Homework

Orange students are the least likely to complete traditional homework assignments with regularity. The idea of sitting down to complete a written assignment is unlikely to pull them away from more active, exciting activities. Instead, if they can do something nontraditional, innovative, or creative, and perhaps something they can do with their friends, they will probably complete the activity wholeheartedly, without the normal grumbling. Furthermore, simply changing the terminology and renaming a *homework assignment* to a *take-home activity* is likely to engender additional cooperation.

Testing

Traditional tests are not well suited to the Orange personality. Most measure memorization or written language skills, neither of which is likely to be a strong point for an Orange student. Oranges will do better with performance tests or oral exams that call for quick thinking on their feet.

Behavior

Oranges bring excitement and fun to classes, though perhaps not at the moment or in the manner desired by the teacher. If their energy is channeled properly, however, Oranges can be a great resource to a class.

Most often Oranges are labeled as the "problem students." This is because of the difficulty they have fitting in with the school environment, which is mostly Gold. Oranges want action. If they're not given the opportunity to take part in hands-on projects or other approved activities, they may find other outlets for their energy that are more disruptive to the classroom.

Extracurricular activities

Oranges are often involved in extracurricular activities such as sports teams, art clubs, or music groups. These activities may even be the only thing that keeps an Orange in school. They are also likely to be involved in drama productions and possibly debate teams.

Role in school

Oranges are generally the most misunderstood of students. They compose a large portion of primary and secondary school students, but most teachers are Gold or Blue and have a difficult time understanding them. When worked with properly, however, Oranges can be an invigorating addition the school community.

Orange Learning Preferences

Noisy environments
Real-life applications
Immediate rewards
Competitive situations
High-energy activities
Variety in lessons
Physical involvement
Entertaining teachers

Teaching Styles

People tend to teach or train in the way they were successfully taught or trained. People often begin teaching or training by trying to imitate their favorite instructor. Your preferred learning style therefore is likely also to be your preferred teaching style.

The following pages describe the teacher temperaments in a variety of categories: representation, purpose, preferred subjects, classroom environment, instructional techniques, lesson plans, comportment, strengths, weaknesses, stressors, and their role in school.

Blue Teachers

Blue teachers prefer to encourage and inspire their students, provide variety and creativity to the learning process, and motivate students to develop their hidden strengths. Their lessons are flexible and tailored to the needs of individual students. Blue teachers are warm and personal, enthusiastic, and insightful.

Representation

Blues represent a sizable portion of the teacher population, second only to Golds. They're drawn to teaching because it gives them the opportunity to work with and serve people. They enjoy teaching because they can share ideas and help young people develop in a positive way.

Purpose

Blues are natural nurturers. They're committed to their students. They're concerned with the whole person—a student's emotional and social development as well as intellectual development. Blue teachers measure their success by the degree to which they can help their students live more meaningful lives.

Preferred subjects

Blue teachers are most likely to be drawn to the arts and humanities. Subjects such as literature, music, drama, and foreign languages may appeal to the Blue. They will shy away from any subjects they feel are cold or impersonal.

Classroom environment

The classroom led by a Blue teacher is open and interactive. It may be conducted in a democratic fashion. The students are often involved in making decisions that affect the whole class. Blues encourage cooperative learning and group discussion. They don't feel the need to be the focus of attention at all times.

Instructional techniques

Blue teachers may use various instructional techniques, such as group projects, class discussion, or games, but they tend to prefer to create their own materials rather than use workbooks or other established material. They generally prefer interaction to lecture. Blues can be unconventional in their approach to teaching. They may mix activities that further social development in with the normal intellectual activities.

Lesson plans

Blue teachers individualize instruction. Lesson plans will be built around a specific class's needs. Blues are generally in touch with their students and will change lessons if they see the need. They try to get to the feeling level of the subject matter they're teaching.

Comportment

Blue teachers are personable. They approach the class in an open, friendly way and often become close to their students. The end of the school year can be a devastating time for Blue teachers who have to give up a class full of people they care about.

Strengths

Blues are excellent at recognizing strengths and bringing attention to them. The attention of the Blues to their students can result in an environment that strengthens self-esteem. This increased self-esteem often translates into improved academic performance. Blues also excel at recognizing body language and subtle indicators of moods, allowing them to stay in touch with the feelings of the class.

Weaknesses

Because they're in touch with their own emotions and those of students, Blue teachers may have difficulty dealing with students they dislike or students who dislike them. They may try to submerge this dislike because they feel it's important to care about all their class members. They may also avoid dealing with unpleasant situations and have difficulty enforcing any kind of discipline on their students.

Stressors

Blue teachers are aware of all their students and like to interact individually with each one. Because they're empathic, they're vulnerable to negative as well as positive input. They may be over-stressed by dealing with so many different individuals and problems. They will be stressed by bad feelings on the part of anyone in the classroom. They seek for harmony at all times. Blue teachers may avoid the administrative parts of their job and put off paperwork as long as possible, until it reaches a crisis point. They may also be frustrated or discouraged by their inability to help certain students.

Role in school

Blues focus on people more than procedures. They're generally enthusiastic teachers who enjoy their jobs and get along well with others on the faculty. They usually devote a lot of personal time to help students reach their potential.

Blue Teaching Preferences

Harmonious environments
Interactive presentations
Nurturing formats
Individualized lesson plans
Democratic discipline
Artistic approaches
Esteem-building activities
Student-based projects

Gold Teachers

Gold teachers emphasize facts, practical information, and concrete skills, just like the Oranges. However, Gold teachers expect quiet and order in the classroom, with clear structure, schedules, and predictable responses to their questions. They're definitely in control of the classroom and aren't tolerant of unexpected student behaviors.

Representation

The majority of teachers are Gold and Golds generally feel comfortable in the school environment. They're drawn to teaching because it's an established institution and it provides the opportunity to pass on traditional values and heritage to successive generations.

Purpose

Gold teachers are interested in helping students become useful members of society. They want to help develop those characteristics that are so valued by all Golds: responsibility, duty, dependability, and respect for rules. They will measure their success by their students' grades and ability to fit into the system.

Preferred subjects

Gold teachers are most likely to be drawn to teaching school subjects such as business, social sciences, history, geography, political science, clerical skills, and so on.

Classroom environment

The classroom of a Gold teacher is likely to be neat and organized. Everything will have a place. Students' desks will be arranged in clear rows and columns. If anything is hanging on the walls, it will be straight. Gold teachers expect their students to follow established rules. They're firm but fair in discipline.

Lesson plans

Gold teachers will have their lesson plans laid out well in advance. Their routines will be well established and the rules of the classroom will be clearly explained. They'll likely follow an established textbook and workbook curriculum. Golds usually have a day-by-day breakdown of what material they'll cover, and they stick to it. They resist changes that would force them to break with established routines.

Instructional techniques

A Gold teacher is likely to use traditional instructional techniques, such as lecturing, drilling, giving tests, providing teacher demonstrations, using workbooks, etc. Repetition doesn't bother Gold teachers and may be seen as a useful means of driving a point home.

Comportment

Gold teachers will always show proper conduct in front of students. They maintain their role as teacher at all times. They're not aloof, but they want some distance between themselves and students. They show great patience and tolerance in working with obedient students, but have little patience for nonconformists.

Strengths

Golds are organized, consistent, and thorough. They go to great lengths to teach their designated curriculum. They prepare students to deal with the structure of society, which is usually Gold. They also show great dedication serving their students and the school, putting duty before personal desire.

Weaknesses

Gold teachers readily point out errors on the part of students and may be less likely to point out their strengths. This can cause problems, especially with Blue students. The Gold may be seen by other colors as rigid or authoritarian. Their desire for responsible students who do what's expected of them may be seen as stifling individuality and creativity.

Stressors

Gold teachers are most stressed by Orange students who want action and adventure and who often pay little attention to a Gold lecture or homework assignment. Green students can also cause Gold teachers stress if they question the Gold's competence or authority and fail to conform. On the other extreme, Blue students may attach themselves to the teacher, constantly seeking approval. They may seek opportunities to "help" the Gold teacher that are not truly helpful and may even become annoying. A Gold teacher is more pleased by students who just do what's expected of them.

Role in school

Gold teachers work well within the structure of the school, which is generally Gold also. While they may criticize, they will also be loyal to the institution. They're supportive of the traditional components of schools, including parent organizations, student government, and athletic programs.

Gold Teaching Preferences

Controlled environments
Organized presentations
Traditional formats
Detailed lesson plans
Firm discipline
Structured approaches
Concrete learning activities
School-based projects

Green Teachers

Depending on the topics they teach and the needs of their students, Green teachers are rather flexible, expecting their students to ask probative questions and take control of their own education. Their role as a teacher is to provoke curiosity and provide guidance as students uncover solutions to their problems. They sometimes work on an impersonal, abstract level, and are often found working on complex problems that challenge their individual expertise.

Representation

Greens represent a small portion of schoolteachers and are most likely to be found at university levels. Those Greens who choose to become teachers usually do so for the opportunity to remain in the realm of ideas in some field that interests them.

Purpose

Green teachers are interested in developing the intellects of their students. They encourage their students to understand the nature of things. They measure their success by their competence in their field and their ability to involve their students in the quest for knowledge.

Preferred subjects

Green teachers are most likely to be drawn to teaching math and sciences. They may also teach philosophy, linguistics, or other subjects that are intellectually challenging.

Classroom environment

The classroom of a Green teacher will probably feature many models, charts, or thought-provoking objects in the room. While it's demanding, the atmosphere of a Green class will probably be somewhat casual and relaxed when compared to that of a Gold class. Greens are generally clear about their expectations in the classroom. They will likely give a student exactly the grade they feel accurately represents the student's work, regardless of any personal or other considerations.

Instructional techniques

Greens usually prefer teaching through lectures, tests, writing assignments, individual projects, and research reports. If their students have shown the capacity, they will be encouraged to take on projects that only require minimal supervision. Greens usually employ a "hands-off" teaching style.

Lesson plans

Their lesson plans will likely be flexible, but the Green will be well prepared in the subject matter. They prefer not to teach the same thing repeatedly because of their dislike for redundancy. Even if covering the same subject matter, they will often look for new ways of teaching it. Material that's completely understood will no longer interest them. For this reason, many Greens are drawn toward the more intellectually challenging environment of higher education.

Comportment

Green teachers may seem aloof or impersonal to students. They like to maintain some distance. A display of emotion in front of the class would be extremely unlikely. Green teachers may also be somewhat eccentric. In teaching, Greens may just assume that students want to learn instead of motivating them to learn.

Strengths

Students who show interest in intellectual growth please Green teachers. At their best, Green teachers can open up new horizons and stimulate the intellectual creativity of students who share similar interests. They will do all they can to help develop the curiosity and discovery of their students.

Weaknesses

Unfortunately, the Green dislike for redundancy may cause Green teachers to move too quickly for many students. They may also be completely unaware of the emotional state of a student or the entire class. Greens often have difficulty communicating approval or appreciation. Because the Green doesn't always realize the need of others for appreciation, even students who are doing well may feel inadequate in a Green class.

Stressors

Greens can be stressed if there are too many administrative rules or procedures that limit their intellectual freedom. Students who show no interest in the subject, who don't live up to their potential, or who are overly emotional can also add stress to the lives of Green teachers.

Role in school

With regard to the school, Greens are generally supportive of the institution and other teachers, but they expect competency from others. They may become impatient with paperwork or meetings that they consider unproductive. Because of their dedication to knowledge, Greens can become proficient and skilled in their fields. They will likely keep up with developments in their subject area and continue learning.

Green Teaching Preferences

Interesting environments
Logical presentations
Lecture/discussion formats
Flexible lesson plans
Student-initiated discipline
Hands-off approaches
Critical thinking activities
Subject-based projects

Orange Teachers

Just like the Golds, Orange teachers emphasize facts, practical information, and concrete skills. However, Orange teachers expect students to be free to express themselves in a variety of ways. They also expect movement and some noise during study time. They focus activity specifically on what students should accomplish, but tend to use untraditional teaching approaches to make learning fun and engaging.

Representation

Oranges have the smallest representation among teachers. Because of their desire for freedom and spontaneity, many Oranges abandon higher education early on. Those who do receive the education necessary to become teachers often go into careers that foster flexibility and performance over process and routine.

Purpose

Oranges may become teachers for a variety of reasons, but chances are those reasons center around action. Oranges love to perform, and teaching gives them the opportunity to do so daily in front of a "captive" audience. They value spontaneity and freedom and try to develop these attributes in their students. Most Oranges aren't really interested in learning for its own sake or for preparing for the future. They want help their students apply learning to the here and now.

Preferred subjects

When Oranges enter the teaching profession, they're most likely to be drawn to teaching music, physical education, art, drama, sports, or vocational arts—areas of action or performance.

Classroom environment

An Orange classroom may be noisy and cluttered with many objects, with a considerable amount of freedom and relatively few rules. The environment may be one of high energy, but almost always it will be informal. Orange teachers generally are not disturbed if homework is late or not turned in. Nor do they feel any great urgency to grade and return assignments quickly.

Instructional techniques

The strength of Orange teachers is in providing a variety of activities. They may view learning as a form of competition and treat it that way in the classroom, setting up games or contests between students. They like to make use of videos and other materials for instruction. Oranges, like Golds, encourage primarily teacher-student interaction. This is because the Orange teacher loves to be in the middle of the action.

Lesson plans

Orange teachers are likely to have sketchy lesson plans. Oranges value spontaneity and can be exceptionally unpredictable. They will avoid regimentation at all costs. If forced to turn in lesson plans, they're not likely to follow them consistently. They want the freedom to follow whatever impulse they receive.

Comportment

Students in a class with an Orange teacher may never know what to expect. The Orange follows no rules for what a teacher "should be." While a Gold teacher most often takes a parental role in relationship with the students, the Orange is more like an older brother or sister.

Strengths

Oranges have a high-energy style of teaching. They thrive on performance and their presentations are usually entertaining to students. The Orange teacher has the ability to hold the interest of a class like no other color. They convey enthusiasm and involve their students in a physical, active way. Their style of teaching can reach students who have not had success with traditional classroom methods.

Weaknesses

While the classroom experience is nearly always enjoyable, the students may or may not learn the established curriculum. Also, the Orange's unpredictable nature may disturb Gold students, who want to know the rules beforehand.

Stressors

Oranges don't like to be held accountable. Pressure from administrators to do things a certain way or to follow the established curriculum closely can cause them stress. Being in the same place and teaching the same material year after year can also stress Oranges, who value freedom and variety. For this reason, many Oranges stay in teaching for a few years and then move on.

Role in school

Orange teachers may have difficulty fitting in with other faculty members, because their impulses may not fit with the school's established rules and regulations. They're usually highly skillful teachers, but have little regard for rules that limit their freedom.

Orange Learning Preferences

Informal environments
Entertaining presentations
Spontaneous formats
Open-ended lesson plans
Unstructured discipline
Dynamic approaches
Kinesthetic activities
Activity-based projects

How to Engage Learners

Assigning blame

Who's to blame if learning doesn't occur? Is it the teacher's fault for not teaching effectively? The student's fault for not wanting to learn? The parent's fault for not spending enough time working with their children? The school's fault for not hiring the best teachers? The educational system's fault for making learning more difficult than it needs to be? The fault of the universities who fail to teach teachers how to teach successfully? The state's fault for not requiring more hours of education for its students and more training for its teachers? The government's fault for not funding its schools adequately? The business owner's fault for not paying employees more so they can be taxed at higher levels? Yes. Everyone is to blame. It takes an entire village to muck up the learning process.

> "I have never let my schooling interfere with my education."
>
> — MARK TWAIN

Consider the following analogy. Let's suppose you love to eat kelp. If you go to a restaurant that specializes in kelp, then you will likely have a satisfactory experience. Your friend, however, who swears he can't live without eating beef or meat at least twice a day, turns up his nose at the kelp quiche and decides to leave the restaurant somewhat unfulfilled. All's fair to this point; each party's preferences were accommodated. But what if suddenly the restaurant's manager charges out to the sidewalk as you are leaving and accuses your friend of being an unworthy customer. Having been served the finest in kelp, and having had the experience wasted on him, your friend is given a tongue-lashing that he won't soon forget. In fact, you're told that a system of grades for diners has been established whereby his gastronomic experience is recorded and distributed to every other chef in every other restaurant prior to his admission.

In the first place, you'd likely think that this restaurant takes itself way too seriously. Then, on second thought, you might begin to suspect that there is a story beneath this story. As long as the restaurateurs work together to condemn anyone who doesn't eat kelp, then they are spared from answering questions regarding how well they have prepared it.

Sad thing is, the experience could be avoided. It isn't reasonable to expect every restaurant to accommodate every cuisine, but we can be thankful that schools aren't restaurants. The experience of learning is individual, to be sure, but there aren't an unlimited number of temperaments. There are four. Any teacher can present the material in more than one way, and more should.

Fortunately, all it takes is one caring teacher to make a significant difference—at least in the lives of his or her students. Just imagine what would happen if every teacher in the school started serving up subjects in appetizing ways—imagine the feeding frenzy! Miracles would occur, including an acceleration in achievement and a decline in delinquency and dropouts. At least that's been my experience as educators around the world have adopted the principles and strategies in this book.

> "Education is what survives when what has been learned has been forgotten."
>
> — B.F. SKINNER

Teaching difficult learners

One day you'll probably find yourself in the role of a teacher, instructor, presenter, facilitator, or trainer—whether or not you've had any formal training in how to teach people. Chances are you'll find yourself working with people who are truly hard to teach. These are your difficult learners. However, a learner who is difficult for you to teach may be easy for someone else.

What make them difficult to teach? You can probably guess my answer: the "difficult" learners don't share your temperament. Most teachers prefer to teach the way they prefer to learn. Thus, a Blue who teaches in Blue ways appeals to Blue students, but not necessarily to other colors who are having a difficult time learning in Blue ways. Therefore, they become difficult learners—for the Blue teacher.

Nearing the nexus

To engage all of your students effectively, difficult or not, you'll want to teach in the nexus—or at least close to it. The nexus is the place in the center that appeals to all four colors. It's the place where you're able to connect to the values of each color, a place where you're able to cater to every temperament. This is where we want to be.

There's no need to abandon your preferences completely as you do this—it would be silly to set aside your strengths and teach out of your weaknesses. Nor am I suggesting that every lesson you present must appeal to all four colors. If you can do that, fine, but it's not necessary. It's far more important that you vary your style from time-to-time so that every learning style gets a chance to learn in ways they prefer. For example, you can choose to vary your teaching style throughout the week. If Blue students know that every Thursday you're going to conduct some Blue learning activities, they'll likely tolerate as many Green, Gold, and Orange activities as you can dish out. They know that if they sit tight, they'll eventually get what they need.

Of course, if you have a classroom full of Greens, then it makes sense to teach exclusively in Green ways. Having a class full of one color seldom happens, though. Most classes comprise a blend of personalities that mirror the general population—the majority will be Gold and Orange, and the minority will be Blue and Green. Thus, you'll need more Gold and Orange activities than Blue and Green.

However, here's a pertinent piece of information to consider: the majority of teaching that goes on in classrooms is conspicuously Gold. Thus, Gold students get the kind of teaching they prefer in just about every class they're in. Let's say you were to go out on a limb and teach your lessons in a completely Orange way—it probably wouldn't throw your Golds off kilter. In fact, they'll most likely adapt just fine. Golds and Greens seem to have an innate ability to take information that comes to them in Orange or Blue ways and translate it or organize it so that it makes sense. It's more difficult the other way around, though. Oranges and Blues have a truly tough time translating Green and Gold messages. (This is why so many Orange and Blue students have trouble succeeding in school.) Therefore, if you have a mixed bag of students from all four temperaments, and you can't vary your teaching style and dwell in the nexus, then the next best thing is to teach in largely Orange and Blue ways.

Below are some strategies that you can use to teach to all four temperaments. Incorporate a few from time-to-time into your lesson plans and your success with students—especially your difficult learners—will shoot up dramatically.

Blue strategies

- ☐ Provide periodic one-on-one instruction
- ☐ Allow group assignments and tests
- ☐ Keep the atmosphere informal, friendly, pleasant
- ☐ Permit democratic decision-making
- ☐ Use open-book learning and testing
- ☐ Send "I care about you" messages

- ☐ Gently guide learners toward solutions
- ☐ Test in creative, nontraditional ways
- ☐ Create flexible assignments and timeframes
- ☐ Rename *assignments* to *projects*
- ☐ Teach principles and concepts rather than facts and figures
- ☐ Spotlight the people behind the facts
- ☐ Draw attention to artistry, creativity, originality
- ☐ Encourage role play and imagination
- ☐ Promote interaction, contact, communication
- ☐ Show personal application of the information
- ☐ Show enthusiasm and optimism
- ☐ Don't tolerate contention or discord
- ☐ Support unrestricted group discussions
- ☐ Promote freedom of speech and expression
- ☐ Allow students to express unique talents
- ☐ Give personalized feedback on assignments
- ☐ Build lessons around student interests
- ☐ Support the underdogs, champion causes
- ☐ Encourage journal keeping and creative writing
- ☐ Maintain a supportive, risk-free environment
- ☐ See the potential in all learners
- ☐ Focus on cooperation rather than competition
- ☐ Teach with emotion, passion, sensitivity
- ☐ Increase the learner's sense of self-worth

Gold strategies

- ☐ Be polite, professional, predictable, punctual
- ☐ Establish class rules, procedures, and policies up-front
- ☐ Provide a syllabus and assignment schedule
- ☐ Give guidelines, parameters, instructions, deadlines
- ☐ Teach in traditional, conventional ways
- ☐ Create a routine; stick to the schedule
- ☐ Post changes to assignments on the bulletin board
- ☐ Let students organize learning teams and study groups
- ☐ Allow students to help manage the classroom
- ☐ Hold students accountable for their assignments
- ☐ Provide opportunities to serve and help others
- ☐ Reward voluntary service with extra credit
- ☐ Grade and return assignments promptly
- ☐ Give clear, specific feedback on assignments and tests
- ☐ Recognize outstanding achievement in public
- ☐ Give time to write down assignments and take notes
- ☐ Provide linear, step-by-step instructions
- ☐ Number your points, outline your presentations
- ☐ Allow make-up work for missed assignments, poor scores
- ☐ Show that there may be more than one correct answer
- ☐ Help students prioritize their work
- ☐ Ensure learning activities have a clear purpose
- ☐ Maintain authoritative control of the class at all times

- ☐ Keep discussions focused on specific topics
- ☐ Bring discussions to closure; summarize lessons
- ☐ Keep the room formal, neat, organized, free of distractions
- ☐ Be fair-minded, honorable, worthy of trust
- ☐ Employ visual aids such as overheads, slides, handouts
- ☐ Use seating charts and attendance rolls
- ☐ Be prepared and organized for every class

Green strategies

- ☐ Establish your credentials and competence early on
- ☐ Approach anything as something to solve
- ☐ Teach theories, models, and concepts—not just facts
- ☐ Answer questions with further questions
- ☐ Don't promote blind acceptance of theories
- ☐ Encourage creative, nonconformist thinking
- ☐ Allow tangential—off-the-beaten path—learning
- ☐ Encourage exploration, research, investigation
- ☐ Permit autonomous, self-directed work
- ☐ Form teams of 2–3 like-minded, compatible learners
- ☐ Encourage sharing of findings with other students
- ☐ Examine the who, what, why, where, when, and how
- ☐ Teach lessons that require examination and analysis
- ☐ Be a knowledgeable resource; an expert mentor
- ☐ Provide access to a wide variety of data sources
- ☐ Use discovery learning—let them tinker and disassemble
- ☐ Encourage theorizing, postulating, hypothesizing
- ☐ Design exams that test understanding, not memory
- ☐ Assess competence in more than one way
- ☐ Play question and answer games; knowledge bowls
- ☐ Let learners design tests and assignments
- ☐ Teach lessons that create curiosity and engage the brain
- ☐ Use brain-teasers, quizzes, trivia, puzzles, clues
- ☐ Develop logical, credible, coherent, presentations
- ☐ Teach and model critical thinking skills
- ☐ Provide time to process; don't proceed too fast
- ☐ Fill room with gear, gadgets, reference charts
- ☐ Maintain a fairly quiet environment to promote thinking
- ☐ Ignore sporadic cynicism, arrogance, aloofness
- ☐ Encourage advanced students to tutor others

Orange strategies

- ☐ Be engaging, entertaining, fun to be around
- ☐ Identify real-life, practical applications of subject matter
- ☐ Show connections to exciting, glamorous, high-profile jobs
- ☐ Allow students to use tools of the trade
- ☐ Use activities that permit physical movement
- ☐ Tolerate free, open, candid communication
- ☐ Use physical activities like relays, contests, competitions
- ☐ Allow choice of learning activities, topics, assignments

- ☐ Show alternative, unexpected ways to do things
- ☐ Reward positive behaviors often, immediately, openly
- ☐ Help students perceive learning as fun, fulfilling, freeing
- ☐ Permit friendly rivalry between students
- ☐ Allow the content to be secondary to the learning process
- ☐ Create inventive activities that use all senses
- ☐ Move activities out of the classroom; take fieldtrips
- ☐ Invite "real world" experts into the classroom
- ☐ Avoid traditional teaching techniques
- ☐ Turn the learning process into a game
- ☐ Make use of humor, absurdity, laughter
- ☐ Provide concrete, hands-on learning activities
- ☐ Don't waste time with unnecessary paperwork or busywork
- ☐ Provide time to practice within the classroom
- ☐ Avoid conventional homework assignments
- ☐ Help learners stay on task and complete assignments
- ☐ Assess competency with physical demonstrations
- ☐ Avoid tests that rely entirely on pen and paper
- ☐ Allow students to test until achievement
- ☐ Encourage trial and error; tolerate failure
- ☐ Permit make-up work, negotiation, second-chances
- ☐ Provide immediate, material rewards for performance

> "The mediocre teacher tells. The good teacher explains. The superior teacher demonstrates. The great teacher inspires."
>
> — WILLIAM ARTHUR WARD

CHAPTER 10

Love: Strategies for Sensational Relationships

In this chapter you will discover the different ways the four temperaments view family and intimate relationships and how this information can be used to resolve conflicts, clarify expectations, increase love and intimacy, and build mutually rewarding relationships.

Forming Friendships

Contrary to the children's rhyme, friendship comes before love, marriage, and the baby carriage. It's rather difficult to fall in love with someone you don't know. For most of us, important, long-term relationships begin with a simple friendship. Through a process of trial and error, we find acquaintances who share some of our interests, are enjoyable to talk with, and are fun to do things with. As the friendship develops, some of our friends become increasingly significant, and we begin to love them. Eventually, we find someone extra special who makes us better than we would have been, someone we want to share our lives with, and before you know it, you're no longer just friends—you're lovers. However, before we get all twitterpated like Bambi's friend Thumper, with fantasies of romance and sex, let's back up and spend a few moments talking about how to find a friend.

> "A friend is one who knows us, but loves us anyway."
>
> — FR. JEROME CUMMINGS

When it comes to forming friendships, comparable colors cling together, just like those flocking birds of a feather. And why is that? By the time you've reached this chapter, you probably already know the answer: people with the same primary color share similar values, attitudes, and behaviors. It's far easier to communicate and interact with those with whom you have so much in common. Besides, your philosophies and beliefs are constantly validated and sustained by a built-in support system.

Then again, making friends with people who are just like you can get somewhat predictable. If that's what you want, then you're satisfied, but if you want your life spiced up a bit, then perhaps making friends with someone who has a different spectrum is a better recipe. Of course, you probably don't want to choose someone who has a completely opposite blend of colors—that could be disastrous since you may never see eye-to-eye. It's best to start by finding someone who might have a different primary color but who has a secondary color that matches one of your dominant colors.

There are six possible ways to pair the four temperaments. Fortunately, each pair has some obvious characteristics in common; these are identified below. In theory, anyone can find something in common with anyone. That doesn't mean that the two will be able to build a long-term relationship, but it gives them a solid place to start.

Blue–Gold

Blues and Golds are both natural caregivers. They share a common belief that it's sometimes necessary to sacrifice personal needs in order to fulfill the needs of others, particularly their friends and family. Of course their motivation is a bit different in that Blues are often motivated by affection while Golds are frequently motivated by a sense of duty—equally noble motives that yield similar results.

Both of these people are sociable joiners who enjoy hanging out with groups of other people, especially like-minded people. While the Gold likes the group to be structured and the Blue likes it to be casual, they both like to be affiliated officially with a particular crowd, clique, or gang. Because they want to converge and unite, they build their relationships on similarities and commonalities. The more you have in common with your friends and the members of your group, the stronger the bond.

Because of their social sensibilities, unless they are unusually introverted, they enjoy group events, such as assemblies, sporting events, concerts, plays, parties, dances, group dates, festivals, conferences, and meetings.

Blues and Golds avoid making changes. While Blues don't like change in established relationships, Golds don't like change in established procedures and structures. Both cause a fair amount of stress and anxiety. Therefore, both advocate maintaining traditions, rituals, anniversaries, and customs—all things that don't change and keep people bound together towards a common goal.

Along a similar vein, Blues and Golds don't like upset apple carts. When people get out-of-order or out-of-control, they get out-of-sorts. Of course, they don't make a big scene about it—both colors are known for their courtesy and civility. Nevertheless, given that they prefer their interactions to be governed by a fair amount of harmony and accord, the rabble-rousers and nonconformists are politely dispatched with haste.

Gold–Green

Golds and Greens seem to have an aura about them that tends to keep other people, even casual acquaintances, at arm's distance. Most of the time, they aren't trying to project that image, but because they aren't as naturally open or carefree as their Blue and Orange cousins, they appear to be separated, serious, sedate, and sometimes snooty. Golds and Greens start their relationships in a polite, calm, calculated manner. After awhile, when they finally see each other as worthwhile friends, they'll remove the barriers and let their hair down.

These two colors think in similar ways, making them great study partners. They process information in a linear manner from part to whole, meaning that before they can draw conclusions, they need to take pieces of information, line them up, and arrange them in some logical order. They also find it easy to interpret and memorize abstract symbols such as letters, words, codes, notations, and formulas. Each color plays off the other's abilities, with the Green advancing new theories and alternative approaches, and the Gold providing the schedule and organization.

Both see the importance of well-thought-out guidelines, rules, and plans. Neither one of them likes to reinvent the wheel, so once directions, policies, and procedures are established, they're written down and referenced as needed. They don't like flaws or failures in their designs, so they painstakingly look for problems that might arise and try to devise solutions. Because of this attention to detail and thoroughness, they work remarkably well together, each egging the other towards perfection. Of course, problems arise if the Green isn't satisfied with what's written down and constantly tries to improve it, thereby annoying the Gold who simply wants to follow what's in place and move forward. One of the reasons this teaming works well is that the Gold helps force the Green to wrap things up and stick to the schedule; otherwise, the Green would troubleshoot ad infinitum.

Green–Orange

These two epitomize the term *free agent*. Their cardinal desires are self-governance and self-determination. Specifically, Oranges want freedom to act while Greens want freedom to think. When commitments, obligations, or laws limit these freedoms, they'll try to find a way around them. Consequently, both of these people prefer to live outside the box—to think and act on their own two feet with as little outside interference as possible. In fact, if you insist on telling them what to do and when, where, and how to do it, you'll probably get into a fight, or at least an intense argument.

With their focus on self-rule, others regularly label these two colors as being self-centered or self-absorbed. However, that isn't necessarily a bad thing. Isn't any color acting selfishly when they choose to pursue the things they personally value? By this definition, even self-sacrificing Blues would be guilty of being self-centered because they are simply trying to fulfill their desire to be altruistic. Therefore, because Greens and Oranges value activities that don't require other people, that doesn't mean they are more self-absorbed than any other colors. They just don't value other people as much as they value themselves. (That still sounds bad, doesn't it? Alas. Perhaps I'll just move on.)

Unlike their Blue and Gold cousins, these two cope better with change. In fact, they often initiate it. Easily bored with ruts and routines, they are always looking for something new to do or master. Both like going to new places, eating new foods, seeing new sights, being exposed to something different and stimulating—although the Green prefers a mental stimulus while the Orange craves a physical stimulus. Hence, when they're doing something new, one does it for pleasure, the other for research.

Opposite to the Blues and Golds who want to know how similar they are to others, the Greens and Oranges seem to focus on what makes them different from others. What makes them stand out from the crowd? Are they faster, smarter, taller, or funnier? Are they more muscular, buxom, hairy, or tattooed than their peers? Do they have a distinctive skill, a rare talent, or a bizarre ability? Have they seen all the *Star Wars* movies more than fifty times? Somehow, they'll find the characteristic that makes them different from the rest, and then try to get the most mileage out of it.

Greens and Oranges aren't choosy about whom they befriend. You don't have to have a lot in common or meet a certain standardized criterion to be their friend. You're invited to tag along as long as you don't get in the way or become an irritant. Friendships for these people are a thing of convenience or usefulness, not an absolute necessity. When you cease to be fun, engaging, relevant, or stimulating, then you're discarded like a used tissue. You've served your purpose, now run along and play someplace else. Don't take it personally—the Orange and Green probably won't.

Orange–Blue

Anyone can be an excellent artist, musician, actor, poet—but many Oranges and Blues do it more naturally, without as much effort, coaching, or practice. Their creations and performances seem less technical and structured and more dramatic, flowing, original, poignant, and provocative. Happily for them, most fine arts and performing arts classes are populated with Blues and Oranges, making it a great place to meet other creative people.

Blues and Oranges are alike in other ways. For example, they are both doodlers, filling their notepads with pictures rather than words. They make decisions largely on their impulses and feelings, not from reasoned arguments. They prefer dialogues rather than lectures. They are more subjective than objective. They find it easier to remember people's faces rather than names. They both use numerous hand gestures as they communicate. Their rooms and desks are normally cluttered with stuff they might need. They prefer to read for main ideas than read for specific details.

Most Oranges and Blues, especially the extroverted varieties, are openly communicative. They don't hold back their feelings or harbor secret agendas, which makes it easy to know where they stand on a particular topic. They're typically friendly, optimistic, animated, and light-hearted. If there's a lull in the communication they'll probably take up the slack, so you can't wait around for a pregnant pause to throw in your two cents' worth—you might need to interrupt to interject.

When it comes time to party, while the Golds are finding something to do to help out and the Greens are sitting in a quiet corner exchanging ideas with a friend, the Blues and Oranges take advantage of the situation and have fun. Of course the Oranges are a bit more wild and crazy than the Blues, but both colors will readily move out to the dance floor or step up to the karaoke machine. It's a party after all, and they're here to have a good time.

Blue–Green

Blues and Greens often pair up as friends. Even though they are opposites in a number of ways, they do have several important qualities in common. Perhaps their largest shared attribute is the ability to gather information intuitively. Meaning that when exposed to a new piece of data, they immediately look for possibilities, meanings, and relationships. They try to picture what it would look like in their mind's eye.

As intuitives, both temperaments like to live in the world of what could be. They're able to envision the ideal relationship, the perfect theorem, the happiest marriage, the best sex. If things in the real world don't pan out the way they hoped they would, they'll be a bit downhearted for a while, but they can always return to their mental fantasy and hope for the day when it finally turns into reality. They never close the doors to their mental theatre, holing up within until the storms pass over and it's safe to come out.

Drawn together by their ability to imagine, these two colors work well on projects that require creativity. Staying completely within their minds and hearts, they'll let their imagination run rampant, shattering the status quo and redefining reality. When it comes time to execute their ideas, they'd rather not be bothered. They're the architects; others do the building. In fact, if the project's never realized, that's okay too. They don't have to bring ideas like this to closure. The vision itself was, and still is, delightfully satiating.

Another reason they pair up is that both are minorities. With less than 20 percent of the world's population being either Blue or Green, these temperaments will never be able to persuade the majority to appreciate, let alone tolerate, their different perspectives. They can't help but feel a bit oppressed, correctly believing that they and their kind have been, generally speaking, undervalued, underrepresented, and undermined. By banding together, they instinctively understand and relate to the other's anguish, even though they seldom talk about their shared minority status. It also gives them the courage to accept their standing and focus on living their lives as they desire, regardless of what the rest of the world does.

Gold–Orange

Golds and Oranges are both sensory types, meaning they take in information with their concrete senses. They prefer activities where they can taste, smell, touch, listen, and see things. To spend time talking about their dreams, fears, or desires is unappealing. They'll always choose to go and do rather than sit and talk.

These two colors receive a great deal of joy from doing things with their hands. They enjoy gardening, house painting, roofing, cooking, tiling, carpentry, mining, mechanics, sculpting, assembling, packaging, delivering, etc. It's deeply satisfying to let your body do something without a lot of mental intervention. Besides, once your body learns how to do it, then you can turn on the autopilot and let it happen.

Golds and Oranges, since they're often at each other's throats, make effective friendly adversaries. Both of them like challenges and contests, both think that their way is the best way, and so they try to prove it to the other. The tension spurs them to compete with each other, which then drives up production and achievement. Thus, it turns out to be a mutually beneficial pairing, each driving the other to success.

These two temperaments like things spelled out clearly and concisely. They need clear expectations so they can decide whether to follow them. They don't want to have to guess and imagine what someone is trying to say. They just want to take the info and start processing it. They don't want an infinite variety of options—two or three will do nicely.

Golds and Oranges are practical, down-to-earth people focused on present realities. Theories and dreams are worthless unless it can be shown how they can be achieved in a reasonable amount of time. Furthermore, the theory or dream has to have an obvious benefit—either for themselves or their organization. There's too much to do in this world to spend time spinning plates on the ends of long poles—unless you're being paid to do it.

Navigating the Sea of Love

> "Love: a deep, tender, ineffable feeling of affection and solicitude toward a person, such as that arising from kinship, recognition of attractive qualities, or a sense of underlying oneness."
>
> — AMERICAN HERITAGE DICTIONARY

Let's suppose you've been friends with a person for a while, and now you want to kick the relationship up a notch. How do you know if you've been bitten by the love bug? Regardless of your temperament, the symptoms of terminal love-sickness are similar:

— You feel joy when you make your partner happy
— You try to be available whenever you're needed
— You aren't interested in other attractive people
— You smile whenever you think about your partner

— You want to care for and trust each other
— You like to be together as much as possible
— You overlook the imperfections in your partner
— You think more of the other person than yourself
— You feel "complete" when you're together
— You realize love has little to do with sex

Still, knowing you're in love doesn't necessarily mean you'll have a long, healthy, breathtaking relationship. If you climb aboard a sailboat and merely hope the wind will take you to a tropical paradise, even though you're not planning on charting a course, setting the sails, and steering the ship, you're not going to arrive anywhere. In the same way, if you don't put some sweat and blood into your relationships, you can fall out of love just as easily as you fell into it. Except rather than feeling wonderful along the way, you'll feel miserable, depressed, and lonely.

To be successful in our relationships, what we need is a way to navigate the high seas of love—a system of markers, buoys, or beacons by which we can make sure of our own position, and from that, detect the position and heading of our intended love interest.

Sailors long ago worked out the finer points of coastal navigation (sailing within sight of land). One technique we can borrow immediately. It's called *triangulation,* and it refers to the act of fixing one's position even though one is moving—a nautical conundrum.

Here's the problem: coastal navigation works by sighting, or taking a fix, on a landmark using a compass. On a chart, the sailor draws a line from the landmark out into the water along the compass course just sighted. But this only tells the sailor that he or she is somewhere along a certain line. To figure out more precisely where requires taking a second sighting on a different landmark and plotting that line as well. The intersection of the lines shows the boat's approximate location. I say approximate, because in the time it took to take and plot the first sighting, then take the second, the boat will have moved! Forward movement of the boat and the actions of wind and current, all create the possibility of error. A common trick to resolve this problem is to take yet a third sighting. When the sailor plots the third line, it will yield a triangle on the chart called "a cocked hat." You are just about guaranteed to be somewhere within the cocked hat. If you know your approximate speed and direction, and can compensate for the winds and currents that tend to pull you off track, you can guess your position well enough until it's time to plot it once again.

Whew, all that work just to tell where you are, and all this when you are close enough to the coast to see land! Why bother? The answer becomes apparent if you know what lies beneath the surface. What kind of sandbars, rocks, wrecks, and reefs wait to strand you or foul your propeller? To avoid being added to the list of wrecked boaters who are forced to accept help, or worse, becoming one of the "lost at sea," you'll need to take your navigation seriously.

So why, in love, where there is equally, perhaps even more, to lose, are we content to charge on "where angels fear to tread"? The question is as deep as time itself, and has occupied the poets for millennia.

Fortunately, knowledge of a prospective partner's color spectrum can go a long way towards being a chart for our relationships. Consider: people are at their best when they are mutually interested. No one wants to rock the boat. Reefs and shoals will stay hidden, only to surface unexpectedly when couples let their guard down. Also, the nature of the pairing and its goals must match or complement the temperaments of the participants. Otherwise, it's like trying to push with your motor against your own sail—not only is your progress hindered, but you may stress and break your mast. Even the doldrums, those long periods of sustained tranquility when there's no breeze to fill the sail and push the journey along, can damage a relationship.

> "Love begins with a smile, grows with a kiss, and ends with a teardrop."
>
> — ANONYMOUS

Knowledge of colors is one of your most powerful tools for increasing the chances of success in loving relationships. Knowing your own temperament will help you a lot, because you will understand not only what kind of things are likely to be important to you, but why this is so. Knowing your partner's color spectrum is also critical. Love is blind, but relationships require constant compromise and forgiving. Knowing that at least part of the motive for some puzzling or apparently hurtful actions (or inactions) by your partner is rooted in his or her color spectrum allows you to regroup before returning fire in a campaign based on the world as folks of your color spectrum see it.

So how can understanding personality styles sweeten the odds in this crazy little game called love? Three powerful things: First, as mentioned, a knowledge of temperament theory provides you with some insight as to what color spouse is likely to be the most natural for you. Notice that I didn't say, "best," because people have an infinite ability to cope and tolerate. If you know going in that you're seeking a Gold or a Blue, it will help you a great deal. Second, I can provide some concrete tips on how to recognize a potential partner's colors without having to submit them to a colorizing quiz, although that's not a bad idea! Finally, and this is probably the most important, knowing about colors as you work in romance gives you the power to avoid much misunderstanding and heartache. "It's not me; he's just Green!"

Again, if a couple understands colors, they can avoid wasting energy trying to correct the basic world view of their partner, and learn to appreciate the partner for the good qualities exhibited by his or her colors. Here, therefore, are some clues in recognizing colors inside your romantic relationships.

Sex and Intimacy

> Sex: the thing that takes up the least amount of time and causes the most amount of trouble.
>
> — JOHN BARRYMORE

Not surprisingly, the four personality styles view sex and intimacy quite differently from each other. Note that I'm NOT talking about gender differences here—I'm talking about disposition differences. A Blue male and a Blue female, for example, sing from the same hymnal. They're definitely not from Mars and Venus. What is sauce for the goose is sauce for the gander.

Therefore, before embarking on a romantic relationship where physical expressions of love are involved, it would probably save an awful lot of angst and disappointment if you and your partner thoroughly understand the information listed below, especially if you have different primary colors. Chances are you do, for in matters of the heart, people are regularly attracted to their opposites. There are far more pairings of Oranges with Golds, and Blues with Greens, than any other combination!

Blue

Blues don't have sex—they make love. The difference is real and meaningful to Blues. Sex is viewed as a biological function—all forms of life do it. Making love, though, is something that's unique to humanity. It's something that enhances a relationship and not something that a relationship requires. It's an integral part of expressing intimacy, devotion, and unity.

Blue lovemaking is a process, not an event. It's more spontaneous than planned and more drawn-out than rushed. It's the epitome of gentle passion, selflessness, and genuine affection. It goes way beyond the physical act of sex, which may or may not be the high point of the evening.

Blues depend on their senses for external stimuli. Romantic music, soft lights, tantalizing clothing, fragrant perfumes, and colognes—these things set the mood.

Sharing a steamy shower or a bubble bath, dancing to a gentle ballad, lying together in front of a fireplace, or giving each other a sensual massage—activities like these are integral parts of making love to a Blue.

Blues have mastered the art of demonstrating love. Whether its verbal or nonverbal, they're able to communicate their affection and devotion to others with sensitivity, sincerity, and tenderness. They add creativity, drama, and intensity to their relationships.

Gold

Golds are traditional in the bedroom as in other areas of their life. They don't do a lot of sexual experimentation, believing "if it ain't broke, don't fix it." They don't play amorous games or express fantasies to their partners. Nothing is surprising or unusual. They wear conservative clothing in the bedroom like flannel pajamas, nightgowns, robes, and slippers. Sex takes place in the bedroom, behind locked doors, with the lights out, under the sheets, and as quietly as possible. Like most things in their lives, sex is something that's reserved for the proper place, the proper time, with the proper person.

Some Golds reserve sex for procreation only. Others use sex to reduce stress, ease fatigue, and remedy other problems. Many Golds see sex as a duty, a responsibility, and a right. Sex is seldom seen as mutually pleasing entertainment. Instead, it's a service that one performs for another. In fact, Golds usually express gratitude to their partner after making love.

Golds like to be in control of their sex life. Traditionally, they adhere to cultural norms. If the rules say males are dominant and women are submissive, then that's what they'll do. However, because Golds are naturally domineering, they prefer their sexual partner to be submissive. When they aren't in control, they often feel demoralized and weakened.

A Gold husband may feel he deserves sex when he fulfills his responsibility, especially if he's the primary income earner. He may view that it's the duty of his homemaker wife to take care of his sexual needs. Likewise, a Gold wife may put the sexual desires of her husband above her own and chalk up the experience as part of her wifely duties.

Golds have a tendency to believe that sex is a commodity—a product that can be purchased if you know how to pay the right price. However, rather than exchanging money, payment comes in the form of honored commitments, duties performed, and fulfilled expectations. To the Gold, sex is serious business.

Green

Greens don't pay a lot of attention to the sexual rules and guidelines of their culture. For the most part, they're self-governed individuals who have carefully set their own standards. If these happen to coincide with those of society, so be it. They aren't looking for approval or acceptance. They're comfortable doing their own thing.

Many Greens quickly get bored with sexual routine. Always the scientist, they investigate as many different ways of having sex as possible, as long as it's tolerated by their partner and within acceptable boundaries. Like other aspects of their life, they're likely to supplement their own findings with those they find in books and technical manuals. As a result, they often become imaginative, creative, and technically proficient lovers.

As with other areas of their personal lives, most Greens don't openly discuss their sex lives with others, even close friends or family members. Don't mistake this as an attempt to be prudish or sanctimonious. Their own search for personal independence demands that they extend those same privileges to others. Consequently, they have no choice but to take a tolerant view of sexual behavior—whatever consenting adults do in the privacy of their homes is no concern of theirs. However, most Greens have a personal sense of decency and view public displays of promiscuous, lewd, and vulgar behavior as irrational, depraved, and crude.

Orange

Because Oranges are sensory people who rely on their feelings of taste, smell, touch, vision, and hearing, they seem to be highly motivated by their sexual drives. Sex is an important part of their lives and they try to have as much of it as possible.

They take pride in their bodies and often go to great lengths to make them attractive and visible to others. They enjoy going to beaches and pools, where they can engage in three of their favorite activities: playing, displaying, and surveying.

Oranges are candid and frank, and apt to talk about their sex lives to any interested party. Both males and females enjoy talking about their experiences and sharing detailed stories with others. Always the performers, Oranges like to portray themselves as some sort of sexual superstars. They enjoy the attention from other people when they talk about their exploits.

As with most things in their lives, Oranges like variety. They enjoy sexual experimentation and exploration. However, they also like change, and this desire may pose a big challenge to long-term relationships. A successful relationship with an Orange will need to include some way to satisfy this desire.

Since Oranges are always in pursuit of excitement and adventure, they may make love in public places or in unusual settings. Some add elements of danger or risk as a change in pace. Sometimes, they turn to external devices like erotic clothing, toys, games, stories, and movies to spice up their sex lives. Unfortunately, they also find that these devices never satisfy their needs and so they become drawn towards progressively lewd and pornographic material. Ironically, what was meant to enhance a relationship ends up damaging it.

Commitment

If you were to ask a Blue, a Gold, a Green, and an Orange person to define the word *commitment* you would probably get four rather dissimilar definitions. Is there any wonder why so many problems creep into our relationships if we can't even agree on the definition of a simple word?

> "All marriages are happy. It's living together afterwards that is difficult."
>
> — ANONYMOUS

The following pages describe how each color views the emotional and intellectual bonds that define their commitment to each other, especially in the early stages of a relationship.

Blue

From the time they were just little Blues, they've learned from stories and fairy tales that it's possible to fall deeply and madly in love—and live happily ever after. They've even learned that they might have to kiss a few toads to find their Prince or Princess Charming. But that doesn't stop them. They have a mental picture of the ideal relationship that permeates their hopes, dreams, and ambitions. Their purpose in life is to love and be loved. As a result, Blues are deeply committed to their relationships. More than any other personality type, they work to ensure their relationships will last forever. "Till death do us part" is not enough for Blues—they marry for eternity.

To woo a Blue, be prepared to invest more time and energy than you normally would with other personality types. Love to a Blue is everything romantic: flowers, candlelight dinners, poetry, chocolate, slow dancing, warm embraces, and tender kisses. Relationships blossom when these elements are present and wither when they are not.

Both the Blue male and female enjoy the traditional courting activities of yesteryear, such as spending a summer's evening on a porch swing, walking hand-in-hand in a park, taking a scenic drive in a car, strolling down the beach, enjoying a picnic lunch on a blanket, sharing a banana split, swimming in the moonlight, and riding a bicycle built for two.

Gold

Golds take a traditional view of love and intimacy. Some Golds may have been sexually active prior to marriage, but after marriage they're strictly monogamous. They're committed to upholding their marriage vows. Their energies become focused on establishing a home and family, serving the community, and conserving for the future. If anyone knows what it means to be committed, particularly to a marriage covenant, it's the faithful and dependable Gold. If they're dissatisfied with the direction the relationship is going, they'll do all they can to put it back on course. Even if there are irreconcilable differences, many Golds stay together, having taken seriously the vow, "for better or for worse." They consider marriage to be the glue that holds society together; without it, chaos and disaster await. On rare occasions, they may go outside the marriage bond to explore other relationships, but for the most part, they're devoted, unwavering, steady, and constant. Their word is, unsurprisingly, as good as gold.

Green

Greens aren't good at making commitments, especially when they involve long-term interpersonal relationships. Before they commit, they feel it's necessary to conduct a thorough examination of the details to ensure that they aren't making an error. They carefully analyze the terms and conditions. They undergo a comprehensive cost-benefit analysis. They interject a complex series of variables in an attempt to uncover potential problems. All of this intricate analysis might distress those who feel decisions of this kind shouldn't be so excruciating. They erroneously infer that if this much cogitation is required, something must be wrong. Unless the Green quickly remedies the situation, the relationship may suffer irreparable damage.

Another barrier to relationships is the Green idea of self-rule. Because they're so independent, they have a difficult time learning to compromise in their interpersonal relationships. They've been doing things their own way for so long that they may not know how to change. Unless potential partners realize this and are willing to invest tremendous amounts of time, energy, and patience, the autonomous Greens are likely to remain independent.

Unsurprisingly, it takes a long time to develop a meaningful intimate relationship with a Green. Chances are they will first be attracted to others by the brain as much as, if not more than, the body. The relationship will begin on an intellectual plane and, if it passes the initial assessment, will eventually expand to include physical and emotional components. Commitment on the Green's part is slow in coming, but when it happens, it's usually the result of an in-depth mental analysis rather than an emotional proclamation from the heart.

Most Greens are monogamous and only have one or two deep relationships during their lives. Because they live in the world of ideas, both Green females and males tend to look for partners who share their same level of intellect. If that's not possible, they may look for someone who isn't quite as smart—even though they crave intellectual challenge, they still want to be more of a winner than a loser.

Orange

Oranges are able to sweep their partners off their feet in a whirlwind romance. They know how to charm and attract those they're interested in. As long as they have a reasonable amount of compatibility for each other and don't try to change each other, they may develop a deeply satisfying relationship.

Oranges sometimes enter into relationships as the result of an impulse. This is an important concept to remember when forming a relationship with an Orange. A relationship that begins on impulse may also end on an impulse. If this occurs, rather than confronting their partner, Oranges tend to abandon the situation and ignore attempts at communication.

Sometimes Oranges enter into relationships without considering whether their partner really has their best interests in mind. Whoever or whatever happens to be there is likely to be accepted. Oranges take people at face value.

Because of their thirst for freedom and independence, Oranges often have a hard time committing to a long-term relationship. They like to be able to express emotions as they occur and the thought of being involved in a long, drawn-out relationship is stifling and confining. If pressured into such a relationship, they'll resist and might even lash out in an attempt to end the tension, disregarding completely the feelings of the other person.

> "Marriage is a great institution, but I'm not ready for an institution."
>
> — MAE WEST

Liabilities

Any characteristic or behavior can be maximized or minimized until it mutates from a normally constructive asset into a destructive liability. So it is in relationships. As a person becomes upset with the circumstances in his or her life, or feels picked upon by others, or becomes disgruntled, annoyed, or irritated, he or she tends to act abnormally. Frequently these actions become handicaps that limit the growth and development of their relationships. Of course, not all liabilities stem from stressful or unpleasant situations. Often they're the results of ignorance—the person simply hasn't yet learned the life skills needed to cope with the situation in a positive way.

> "We come to love not by finding a perfect person, but by learning to see an imperfect person perfectly."
>
> — ANONYMOUS

Regardless of the cause, here are some of the liabilities that regularly pop up as the different personality styles interact with their loved ones.

Blue

Always idealists, Blues often don't see the flaws in their loved ones until later on in their relationships. They have a mental picture of the way things ought to be and are willing to go through all sorts of contortions to make that dream come true. They tend to overlook many of the bad aspects of the relationship and highlight only the good.

Because of their compassionate and merciful nature, Blues can easily forgive those who offend them. They believe that most people are genuinely good and worthy of their forgiveness. In general, they're willing to give others as many "second chances" as they need. While this is normally admirable, it can sometimes work against them, especially when others take advantage of their tolerance.

For example, most battered wives are out-of-esteem Blues who repeatedly overlook the abusive behaviors of their Gold or Orange husbands. In spite of the abuse, most Blues are still deeply in love and patiently await the day when their husbands will "come around" and return to the affectionate relationship they once shared. Others silently endure the abuse in hopes of keeping the relationship together for the sake of their children or other family members. Still others blame themselves for the abuse and believe that they did something wrong or didn't try hard enough to make the relationship succeed.

This same sense of compassion and tolerance does have its limits, however. While Blues can endure a lot of personal mistreatment, when the mistreatment extends to others, particularly innocent members of their families, Blues will speak up and adamantly express their feelings. Their sense of equality and fairness cannot allow them to forgive this kind of offense unless they sense sincere repentance from the offender.

Gold

In relating with loved ones, Golds tend to be possessive, overprotective, dominating, judgmental, and demanding. They're control-oriented, which might make more independent family members feel stifled, fettered, and rebellious. When someone departs from traditional and acceptable behaviors, Golds quickly try to reform the deviant; they do not tolerate misbehavior. Those around them are often alienated by their tendency to be autocratic and dogmatic, and unless Golds learn to loosen up a little and appreciate the qualities of other personality styles, they may end up as the subject of a discussion between an estranged family member and a psychoanalyst.

Golds are worriers that fret and fuss over things that others consider trivial. They worry over the past, the present, and the future. They agonize over things that are beyond their personal control. They fear for their family, friends, and neighbors. They worry over potential natural and unnatural disasters. These worries often dominate conversations with family and friends, making it hard for others to listen for any extended period. This compulsion to worry usually has a negative long-term affect on relationships and on the Golds. It's no wonder that many obsessive Golds suffer from anxiety attacks, ulcers, high blood pressure, hypochondria, depression, psychosomatic disorders, and other stress-related afflictions. Fortunately for their loved ones, most Golds also have extensive life-insurance policies.

Green

Greens are often difficult to get to know and understand. They have been isolated for so long that their communication and relationship skills are usually lacking. Add to this their conscious decision to conceal characteristics that aren't quite ready for public exhibition, and you have a truly perplexing picture of their personality.

Greens tend to be conservative in the amount of praise and recognition they give to their loved ones. Nor do they often verbalize their love and devotion, especially in public. They tend to overlook the little signs of affection that are so important to other types. This seemingly inconsiderate attitude should not be interpreted as a lack of love and concern—just a lack of understanding of the genuine needs of others.

When Greens find employment that's appealing and mentally challenging, they easily become workaholics. When the work is intriguing, they don't mind laboring without breaks in order to keep the momentum going. They don't mind putting in long hours of overtime—paid or unpaid. They frequently have a hard time disengaging from their work when they're away from the job site or on vacation. Unfortunately, this behavior invariably adds stress to personal relationships. Because of the Greens' concentration on their work and their desire to be as competent as possible, loved ones may feel as though they aren't as important as they should be. They complain of being neglected, unloved, and unappreciated. This concern, legitimate or not, if unresolved, often leads to ruined relationships.

Orange

Oranges know how to manipulate people. This is one of their greatest assets and one of their greatest liabilities. In a relationship, they can use this ability in a positive way or a negative way. They can build relationships that are so strong that they stand up against any trial, or they can damage relationships to the point that they annihilate those involved. Therefore, when in a relationship with an Orange, it's vital that you understand this ability and learn to recognize when it's being used.

For example, a common manipulative tactic is to play on the emotions and plead for a "second chance." If mercy isn't granted, the Orange claims to have been victimized. If mercy is granted, the Orange claims to be "reformed" and deserve special treatment and support. Either claim is self-serving. Learning to identify such tactics will help prevent them from being successful.

Finances

> "Love is an ocean of emotions entirely surrounded by expenses."
>
> — LORD DEWAR

If your significant other shares your primary color, then this topic probably isn't a big concern for you. For the rest of us, though, it certainly can be a sore spot. Everyday, an increasing number of families are being ripped apart because of money and how they think it should be earned and spent.

This issue doesn't have to affect you if you're empowered with an understanding of personality styles. You've probably already guessed that each color has a significantly different view of money and how it should be earned and spent. This section will explain those viewpoints in greater detail. Understanding those perspectives—and trying to accommodate them—is the key to not letting financial matters irreparably harm you and your loved ones.

Blue

Money, to Blues, is a necessary part of life that has the ability to be used for good and bad. It should not be earned at the expense of other people, nor should it be used exclusively for selfish desires. In fact, it should be used to benefit the lives of other people and, preferably, as many people as possible.

Because of this philosophy, money is more often spent than saved. Despite their talk about doing the "Gold" thing and maintaining an ever-increasing savings account, most Blues believe the needs of the present always outweigh the projected needs of the future.

Don't misinterpret the Blues' ability to spend their money with a desire to accumulate and acquire. They don't want things just for the sake of having them and they don't buy things just to keep up with the people next door. They spend money to buy things for other people.

For example, most Blues enjoy shopping with their friends and willing family members. Besides being a social event in and of itself, it also gives valuable insight into the wants and needs of their shopping companions—information that can be filed away until they have an opportunity to do something about it. Blues are generous with their resources and love to present gifts to other people, especially those who are close to them.

Gold

In addition to being social and sexual conservatives, Golds are fiscal conservatives as well. Money is something that, once earned, should be saved until it can be put to a better use. Savings accounts were created for Golds, by Golds. They live by the aphorism, "Those who understand interest earn it, those who don't, pay it." As a rule, they stay out of debt, with the notable exceptions of buying a house, a car, or an education. Of course they avoid credit-card spending; if they can't afford something, they scrimp and save until they can.

Only after they take care of essential needs will Golds consider spending money on wants and desires. Even then, they spend money judiciously. They try to find things on sale or use discount coupons. They evaluate objects to determine if they're safe, durable, functional, and made from high-quality materials. They like to buy things that maintain high resale values.

Golds are thrifty and frugal. If they have something that's broken, they'll try to fix it themselves. Clothing should be carefully maintained so that it will last as long as possible. Things are used until they're worn out and then, rather than throwing them away, they're donated to a worthwhile charitable organization.

Checkbooks are in balance even before bank statements arrive. Golds have a strict budget and stick to it. They keep detailed financial records, storing pay stubs, statements, invoices, receipts, and tax returns for years on end. They use safety deposit boxes and fireproof safes to store valuable documents, such as stock certificates, insurance policies, and deeds.

They play it safe with their financial portfolios and understand the intrinsic value of insurance policies, savings accounts, bonds, and other secured investments. They stay away from risky ventures and get-rich-quick schemes, firmly believing that if something is too good to be true, it usually is.

Green

Greens view money as an unfortunate component of modern society without which wants and needs could not be fulfilled. They aren't obsessed with the accumulation of wealth or material possessions and are just looking for enough money to provide a modest amount of security and comfort. They look with disdain on debauchery, hedonism, and chicanery. They aren't impressed with those who greedily amass wealth, hoard resources, seek power, or manipulate others in order to gain a self-serving advantage. For this reason, a loved one that places an elevated emphasis on material things is bound to be dismayed or annoyed by the Green's philosophy.

Don't infer from this that Greens don't enjoy the "finer" things in life. Like most people, they would rather be richer than poorer and they unquestionably enjoy the pleasures that money has to offer. But they look upon luxury as just that—a luxury. It's not an essential ingredient to their personal satisfaction. They're just as happy reading a fascinating book in a rustic cabin as they are in an opulent palace. They don't have to own a masterpiece in order to enjoy its beauty—an inexpensive photo reproduction or a trip to a gallery or museum will be enough. They don't mind the life of the bourgeois middle class and, consequently, don't normally aspire to something greater.

When the mood strikes, some Greens are driven by their sense of independence and autonomy to the point where they catch the entrepreneur bug and launch a business. Unfortunately, the details of day-to-day management often prove too routine, predictable, and painstaking to the Green, who would rather be off pondering, conceiving, or inventing something else. As a result, they don't usually stay around long enough to experience the big payoff. This behavior may also create stress in a loved one who is perplexed by the perceived lack of ambition or follow-through.

Orange

Financial pressures can be a great stumbling block to many relationships, particularly marriages. Oranges are naturally generous and like to give on impulse. Sometimes, they give away more than is prudent, causing added stress to a relationship.

For an Orange, living may be feast or famine. One day they may have more than enough money, the next—nothing. They don't appreciate the need to save resources for a rainy day. Because they live in the present, if they had a choice between saving and spending money, they would probably spend it. They believe that money is to be enjoyed and used to fulfill their desires, like exploring the newest restaurant, the newest gadget, the newest fashion, the newest companion, or the newest automobile.

> "You can't buy love, but you can pay heavily for it."
>
> — HENNY YOUNGMAN

Homelife

Most people like to be surrounded by things they value—things they hold dear to their hearts. These things may be people, animals, or inanimate objects. So, equipped with a bit of insight, it becomes easy to identify someone's primary color by their environment, especially their private living space. An individual's true colors can be poured out of the can and painted on the walls for all to see at home.

At home people are free to abandon some of the roles they're forced to perform outside the home. They're no longer employers or employees, teachers or students, leaders or followers, buyers or sellers. Here they're simply wives or husbands, mothers or fathers, sons or daughters, sisters or brothers. These intimate roles are much harder to imitate, so their true personalities are more easily observed.

The following pages briefly describe the homelife preferences of each of the colors: what they have around them, what kinds of things they like to do, and how they relate with others in the home.

Blue

The Blue home is warm, inviting, and friendly. It's a place where family members and visitors can receive and give emotional reinforcement and support, where they can receive personalized attention, and where everyone feels comfortable, nourished, and at-ease.

> "My home is not a place, it is people."
>
> — LOIS MCMASTER BUJOLD

The Blue home is normally a democratically controlled home where all individuals have a voice in matters that affect them. Everyone is encouraged to express his or her concerns and communicate freely with each other. The rights of the individual are respected, as well as the rights of the family as a whole.

Most Blues are creative and enjoy adding their personal touch to every room in the house. Walls may be covered with original paintings, drawings, and photographs of family members. Shelves display homemade crafts and art projects. Lots of plants, living or semi-living, add life to rooms, as do the variety of pets that freely roam the house.

Gold

Even though Golds believe in equality and fairness, they also believe that there are specific roles that men and women should take. More than any other personality style, you will find Golds supporting the patriarchal model of a family that has been around for millennia. In general, this means the man will be the head of the family, the primary breadwinner, the disciplinarian, and the ultimate decision-maker. The woman will be the second-in-command, the homemaker, the nurturing mother, and the dutiful wife. This situation seems to work well for Golds, as long as the husband is honorable, fair, considerate, and loving and doesn't let the authority go to his head.

The Gold home is one of order, routine, punctuality, civility, discipline, and obedience. Gold parents believe it's their primary duty to teach their children to do what's right, good, and proper.

> "It is best to do things systematically, since we are only human, and disorder is our worst enemy."
>
> — HESIOD

Most of the time, these values are handed down from generation to generation—what was good enough for grandma and grandpa is good enough for them. Regardless of what culture they represent, Golds can be counted on to pass along its values, attitudes, and beliefs to their posterity.

Ideally, the Gold home is the archetype of neatness and cleanliness. Outside, trees and bushes are neatly trimmed, lawns and flower beds look manicured, fences and siding look like they have been freshly painted, hoses are carefully coiled and stored, everything is in ship-shape condition. Inside, bathrooms are spotless, dirty clothes are in hampers, clean clothes are pressed and carefully stored, beds are made, closets and drawers are organized, delicate knickknacks are free from dust, carpets are clean, floors are waxed, silver is polished, windows are sparkling, everything and everyone is in its proper place.

Green

Greens like to surround themselves with intriguing and fascinating things. Most have hobbies and collections that cover the walls and fill the shelves. Among other things, they're fond of puzzles, optical illusions, intricate models, scientific equipment, brainteasers, and computers. But above all, Greens surround themselves with sources of data. Most have an ever-expanding library of books, magazines, charts, videos, DVDs, and CDs that reflect their various interests. Now, with the arrival of high-speed cyberspace technology, massive numbers of euphoric Greens are found surfing the "Net" and gathering data from sources they once only dreamed about tapping.

> "A house is no home unless it contains food and fire for the mind as well as the body."
>
> — MARGARET FULLER

Greens aren't terribly concerned with cleanliness and neatness in their living or work space. When given the choice of order or chaos, they would probably opt for order, but it certainly won't get in the way of progress. When they become immersed in a project, they work it through to completion, often creating a mess in the process. When the mess gets so big that they can't find what they need, only then will they spend time cleaning it up. As a result, Green homes tend to be in a state of disarray more often than not.

Greens are seldom accused of being snappy dressers. Most of the time, they're so caught up in their thoughts that they don't spend much time considering their own appearance. Like their archetype Albert Einstein, true Greens are lucky if they've remembered to wear pants before leaving home. Clothing is chosen for its functional qualities, not for its fashion. Moreover, they usually wear the same style of clothing year after year, unconcerned about current fads. It's no surprise then, that many Greens appear in public wearing disheveled, outdated, and truly tacky clothing. Fortunately, this can change once they find a non-Green to help them make more appropriate clothing decisions.

The Green home is usually free of interpersonal conflict and strife. While they occasionally enjoy a stimulating intellectual argument, most of the time Greens prefer a peaceful and subdued environment—one that's conducive to contemplation. They believe in personal autonomy and try to help others learn to govern themselves. They treat others with deference, respect, and dignity, and wish for the same in return. They coolly respond to emotional outbursts with logic and try to stay clear of hostile confrontations. They enjoy posing intellectual challenges and bouncing ideas off one another. They understand their role in the relationship and try to fulfill their responsibilities as capably as possible.

Orange

What does an Orange home look like? There may be an eclectic collection of homemade arts and crafts decorating the house. The rooms may be painted in strong colors and filled with unusual objects and plant life. There may be piles of clutter, representing an assortment of projects in various stages of completion. In fact, some rooms, particularly the bedrooms, might be in a disastrous state of disarray. In general, the overall atmosphere is relaxed and casual. Their homes are always open to visitors and are usually the place where kids congregate after school and where adults come to watch a sporting event or play games.

Oranges can be so caught up with living in the present and meeting the demands of the moment that they forget which things are important and which are trivial. A small crisis may be given as much attention as a crisis of great magnitude; a claim from a stranger can be given as much attention as a claim from a spouse. To avoid problems, help the Orange set and remember priorities.

> "A person travels the world over in search of what he needs and returns home to find it."
>
> — GEORGE MOORE

Enhancing Relationships

If you're trying to perk up a friendship or reinforce a relationship, it's vital to know the person's colors. That way, using the information in this section, you can say and do those things that will make the relationship stronger, not weaker, which is what happens invariably when we fail to consider the other person's point of view and interact in ways that are meaningful to them. What better way is there to show that you truly care for someone than to provide the things they need to be happy in the relationship—and not just the things that make you happy? In this way, you're caring about the other person more than you care about yourself—and that makes you irresistible.

Relating with Blues

Show caring and concern

Blues have a burning need to feel that they're needed and loved. If you want to improve relationships with Blues, show them that you sincerely care. Attend events that are important to them. Remember important dates and anniversaries. Support them as they pursue their talents and interests. Show them in tender and affectionate ways how you're thinking about them. Prove your devotion and loyalty in meaningful ways.

Spend quality time together

A relationship with a Blue isn't built overnight. Blues take their relationships seriously and will invest lots of energy to make them as permanent as possible. They expect others to do the same. If you want the relationship to succeed, be prepared to spend lots of quality time together. Go out together. Visit art museums. See a play. Go to a concert. Eat an enjoyable meal. Share the pleasures of life together. Talk about things that are important to you. Every moment you spend together is vital to the relationship.

Be supportive and reassuring

Blue people go to their loved ones with their concerns and problems. If they come to you with their concerns, don't turn them away. Feel honored—you're someone they can trust. As they explain their problems, be supportive and sympathetic. Let them get it off their chests. Then, unless they specifically ask you for advice or counsel, simply offer encouragement and reassurance.

Give creative opportunities

Blues are naturally creative people. They like to take something that's rather ordinary and turn it into something special.

Whatever the project, Blues have an incredible ability to give it character and personality. If you need some creativity in your life, invite your Blue friends to help. For example, let them help you design posters, write letters or stories, compose music, develop creative solutions to problems, decorate your home, pick out gifts for mutual acquaintances, arrange special parties, etc. Give them opportunities to express their creative genius.

Recognize individuality

More than any other personality type, Blues need to feel that they're unique and important. Regularly express how you perceive their individuality. Talk about their particular talents and abilities. Recall their important contributions. Paint a picture of what the world would be like with their influence. Be careful, it's easy to go overboard and turn honest recognition into lavish praise or flattery—and that will only make you look insincere.

Accept feelings

Blues have deep feelings and emotions. Most of these are the result of personal experience, and as such, are extremely relevant. Don't disregard or discount a display of emotion—they present an accurate picture of the inner self that cannot be seen in any other way. Acknowledge their feelings and accept them as genuine. Trust their intuition and welcome their perceptions—they're usually correct.

Encourage expression

Sometimes you may need to encourage Blues to express their viewpoints. Because they don't want to make waves or make other people feel uncomfortable, they often stifle their own opinions, even if they know they're right. If this is the case, help them reveal their ideas without creating conflict. Ask them questions, invite them to contribute, solicit their opinions.

Cooperate and compromise

Most people believe that the world would be a much better place if more people would cooperate rather than work against each other. Rather than waiting for it to happen, Blues take an active part to make sure it happens as soon as possible. Whenever possible, they'll lobby for cooperative and collaborative efforts. When unanimous consent isn't possible, they try to find the middle ground and strike up a compromise. They're willing to go to great lengths to appease those involved and expect others to be as accommodating.

Relating with Blues

Show caring and concern
Spend quality time together
Be supportive and reassuring
Give creative opportunities
Recognize individuality
Accept feelings
Encourage expression
Cooperate and compromise

Relating with Golds

Recognize their responsible actions

Perhaps the greatest strength of the Gold personality is their ability to be responsible and accountable. They judge their lives by the number of fulfilled assignments and completed jobs they have accrued. Recognize their reliable nature and praise their responsible actions. Despite their slightly tough exterior, Golds need a kind word or two to keep them motivated to do the right thing.

Praise their achievements

Golds are productive people. They're high-achievers. They're driven to excel and reach their goals. Along the way, they need reassurance that their efforts are not in vain. Give them recognition, in public and in private, for their accomplishments. Take notice of their credentials, background, and qualifications and give credit when it's due.

Appreciate their work ethic

Golds believe in hard work and self-discipline. They know how to focus on a task and do whatever it takes to see it through to the end. They watch the details and make sure that everything is carefully and accurately completed. Don't take these attributes for granted and fail to acknowledge their thorough and consistent performance. Golds need to be appreciated for having such an industrious nature.

Clearly define expectations

Golds need to know what's expected of them so they know the appropriate way to act. When building or improving relationships with Golds, be open and honest about what you expect from the relationship. Make sure the expectations are clear, pertinent, and attainable.

Be dependable and efficient

Since Golds believe it's important to be dependable and efficient, they expect those around them to believe the same thing.

So, regardless of your own personality style, try to show Golds that you're trustworthy and reliable. Don't be wasteful or careless with your resources. Try to be as efficient and proficient as possible.

Plan ahead and be punctual

People who don't plan ahead and are late for appointments frustrate Golds. Their "golden" rule is always to be punctual, prepared, and polite. They're especially annoyed when they're forced to break this rule because of the inconsiderate actions of others. Consequently, do your best to be ready to go when the Gold is ready to leave. Be thoroughly geared up for meetings and other appointments. Let them show you how to be better prepared—they will be thrilled at the prospect.

Be clean and orderly

"Cleanliness is next to Goldness." Golds love to keep themselves and their possessions neat and clean. Given the choice of chaos or order, Golds will always opt for order. When you're around them, remember to look neat and well groomed. If you live together or work together, try to keep your things arranged and uncluttered—even if their own space is not as orderly and spotless as they would like it to be.

Make and keep commitments

One of the quickest ways to delight a Gold is to make (and keep) specific commitments. They think they have the corner on responsibility and are pleasantly surprised when other people volunteer to do things within a defined timetable. It shows Golds that you share their sense of duty and honor and can be relied upon to do the noble thing.

Relating with Golds

Recognize their responsible actions
Praise their achievements
Appreciate their work ethic
Clearly define expectations
Be dependable and efficient
Plan ahead and be punctual
Be clean and orderly
Make and keep commitments

Relating with Greens

Listen to their ideas

Most people who associate regularly with Greens know that they're people who live in the world of ideas. Most of the time however, people don't ask about their ideas for fear of being subject to a complicated, one-sided dissertation. Nevertheless, Greens need to express their ideas in order to validate them and receive essential feedback. To build positive relationships with Greens, take time to listen to their ideas. Don't be overly aggressive and frequently bombard them with requests for input, just be prepared to listen when they're prepared to talk.

Don't invade their space

Greens, more than any other personality type, are apt to have a private place where they go to be by themselves. Most of the time, they don't go to this place to escape from the world, but they go to concentrate on things that are occupying their thoughts. They go to work, to reflect, and to create. Don't invade this space unless you're invited. It's a part of their being and reflects their state of mind.

Provide mental challenges

Alfred Hitchcock, the famous Green movie director, once said, "I love a mental challenge. It's like sex for the brain." When they're in the mood, Greens love brainteasers, challenging puzzles, and cerebral games. They like to find fallacies in logic, solve intricate mysteries, and invent new ways to do things. As a friend or a loved one of a Green, provide these kinds of amusing and gratifying mental challenges and you will undoubtedly stimulate your relationship.

Think ahead to the future

Greens don't make decisions quickly. They need time to explore the possible ramifications of their decisions. Greens are frustrated by people who make decisions based on past or present needs without considering the future. While the Golds also keep their eye on the future in order to be prepared for it, Greens keep their eye on the future so their present decisions won't be proven wrong later—a rather daunting task. So as you work with or live with Greens, remember their need to look ahead to the future and try to do the same thing.

Support their need for competence

A Green's need for competence is extremely real and may be the most powerful influence in his or her life. Don't discount this need. As they're going about trying to find flaws in their abilities so they can eliminate them, try to be supportive. Don't be too quick to point out their flaws or agree with their conclusions; this is their job and they generate more than enough self-criticism to motivate them to improve. Accept their need for competence and perfection and, if necessary, encourage them not to be so hard on themselves.

Respect their independence

Greens seek independence and freedom from mental or emotional oppression. Some Greens are extremely introverted and prefer to keep to themselves while others are more extroverted and apt to enjoy social interaction. However, both types are independent and resist outside pressures. They want to control their own destiny. Respect this need for independence and don't limit their autonomy.

Ask for their opinions

This is a quick way to win over a Green. Even if they don't have an opinion on a subject when you ask for it, they will quickly formulate one. Just remember that an opinion from a Green is something that's subject to revision. With every new piece of data, the opinion is carefully reviewed and examined under the new light. Green opinions are not created out of passion or instinct—they're the result of objective thought and critical analysis.

Help them with everyday details

Sometimes, Greens are so caught up in the world of ideas that they lose touch with some of the more mundane elements of daily life—like eating and sleeping. Greens that are deeply involved in a project are apt to forget meals, appointments, and commitments. They tune out the world and may need people who are willing to make sure they go out with their clothes on.

Relating with Greens

Listen to their ideas
Don't invade their space
Provide mental challenges
Think ahead to the future
Support their need for competence
Respect their independence
Ask for their opinions
Help them with everyday details

Relating with Oranges

Recognize their talents

Oranges as a group tend to be more talented and skillful than other personality types. Perhaps this is because they enjoy doing a particular activity so much that they master it by sheer repetition. Whatever the reason, it's important to recognize their expertise. More so than other colors, Oranges need immediate recognition for their performances. They rely on those around them to validate how they feel. It's one of their primary sources of self-esteem. If they don't receive this external approval, they'll try other ways or other sources to get what they need—which may not be a good thing.

Be optimistic and friendly

This is usually simple to do because it's almost impossible to be pessimistic or depressed around an Orange. Most of them have an effervescent personality that makes you feel exhilarated just by being around them. So don't even try to talk about negative things. Dwell on positive, light-hearted, and encouraging things. Don't be dreary; don't be gloomy. Much can be learned from adopting the Orange's positive perspective on life.

Don't tie them down

Those who have tried to force an Orange into a tightly controlled environment know the futility of such an action. An Orange can't be contained any more than the wind can be bottled-up. However, if you're in a situation where you're leading an Orange or rearing an Orange child, help him set his own limits and teach him the ramifications of exceeding them. Explain how the consequences of breaking the rules will result in the loss of personal freedom. Once he understands, give him the room to make his own choices and govern himself.

Appreciate their humor

Oranges have a remarkable sense of humor. Many of them are natural entertainers and are ready to perform at a moment's notice. Some of the world's greatest comedians are Orange or Orange-Green. Take advantage of the Orange's unique outlook on life. They give many people pleasure and enjoyment. Don't be too quick to dismiss their behaviors as "childish" and "trivial." Enjoy their playful dispositions.

Be competitive and energetic

Many Oranges seem to have a competitive nature. They, like the Golds, often battle other people to become "king of the hill." However, unlike the Golds, they aren't motivated by the need to dominate or reign. They just want to play the game with as much gusto as it takes. If they happen to win because of their performance, that's even better. They play because they enjoy playing. They don't take themselves or the game too seriously. So when you play with an Orange, expect to be seriously challenged, but don't make a big deal out of winning or losing; try to be a good sport.

Value their need for excitement

Oranges are active people. Like most people, they prefer to spend their time doing fun and entertaining things. But for them, fun and entertaining things require lots of action, adventure, thrills, and physical pleasures. So, if you want to spend time with an Orange, be prepared to jump into a lifestyle that's packed with activity and demands lots of energy.

Because of their energetic approach to life, Oranges often get more things accomplished faster than most people. They agree with the saying, "When I work, I work hard. When I play, I play hard." Don't get in their way when they're working. Don't bog them down with a lot of detailed planning or impose a structure that's too confining. Then, as soon as they complete the job, make sure they're immediately rewarded for their performance.

Historically, American culture has been dominated by Gold values, attitudes, and behaviors. So it's easy to criticize Oranges for their carefree and fly-by-the-seat-of-their-pants lifestyle—the exact opposite of the Gold lifestyle. But they're not strangers to that kind of criticism. They've heard it most of their lives, and it hasn't been helpful; in fact, it has probably driven a deeper wedge between the Orange and Gold temperaments. So rather than condemning Orange lifestyles, learn to appreciate their strengths and tolerate their differences. Of course, the same can be said of all personality types.

Expect the unexpected

If you're going to form a relationship with an Orange, be prepared for the unexpected. Oranges are not predictable except in their unpredictability. As long as you don't feel too uncomfortable with the situation, consider going along with what the Orange wants to do. They like doing things without forethought or planning. They live on their impulses.

Oranges are naturally generous and lavish givers, regardless of whether or not they have something to give. If they have the resources, they will host the most extravagant dinners, throw the wildest parties, and give the largest presents. If they don't have the resources, they will still give you half of what they have, even if they're down to their last loaf of bread. Compliment their generous natures. Admire their desire to share what they have. But don't take advantage of it or rely on it—Oranges are also whimsical, and can change their minds in a flash.

Get involved and take risks

Because Oranges seek variety and want to experience what the world has to offer, they constantly seek new adventures and new thrills. They crave adventure. They live for danger. They don't mind putting their lives on the line. They want to test their skills and prove their abilities.

These attitudes can be extremely distressing to Gold, Blue, and Green individuals. If you talk about rules and regulations or harp on consequences, the Orange will usually ignore you. The last thing Oranges want is a wet blanket dampening their fun. Besides, more likely than not, they already know the consequences.

However, if you're in a supervisory role, and the Oranges want to go off and do something legal but dangerous, you can do several things.

First, help them practice their skills in a safe setting until they can demonstrate competence. Second, try to accompany them as an active participant. Third, quietly make safety precautions and design emergency plans to satisfy your own needs. Nevertheless, be aware that if an emergency actually occurs, chances are the Oranges will end up rescuing you.

Relating with Oranges

Recognize their talents
Be optimistic and friendly
Don't tie them down
Appreciate their humor
Be competitive and energetic
Value their need for excitement
Expect the unexpected
Get involved and take risks

CHAPTER 11:

Personality Theory History

The four temperaments discussed in this book have been described for millennia. This chapter correlates the major quaternary theories of history with the four colors of the Insight Personality Instrument.

Personality Theories

Since the dawn of civilization, people who have studied human behavior have developed many different and often conflicting theories to explain why people do the things they do. Educated scholars base some of these on scientific analysis. Others are simply pragmatic observations by independent thinkers. Regardless of who discovered them, these theories are meant to help us understand what makes people tick and how to understand their feelings, thoughts, attitudes, and behaviors so we can get along better with each other.

Over the years, as I have researched and studied these theories, I believe many of them promote true principles that, if followed, will unquestionably enhance our relationships. Therefore, rather than trying to advocate one theory over another, I've tried to identify in each of them the principles and philosophies that are reasonable, accurate, tested in the real world, and found to be consistently beneficial. These ideas, along with some of my own original observations, form the basis of the Insight Personality Instrument™ and the concepts in this book.

On the following pages are just a few of the theories that I have found useful. In fact, they're quite complementary to each other and describe essentially the same personality types. All of us owe a huge debt to the people who developed these theories, many of whom have dedicated their entire lives to the study of human behavior. Their contributions to our present understanding are invaluable. If you're interested, I encourage you to look further into their work and examine for yourself the vast treasures of information they have discovered.

> "When thou hast made the quadrangle round, then is all the secret found."
>
> — GEORGE RIPLEY

Theory	Year	Blue	Gold	Green	Orange
Elements	15000 BC	Water	Earth	Air	Fire
Egyptian gods	3000 BC	Nun	Geb	Shu	Ra
Empedocles	440 BC	Nestis	Hera	Zeus	Aidoneus
Hippocrates	400 BC	Yellow Bile	Black Bile	Phlegm	Blood
Plato	340 BC	Idealist	Guardian	Rational	Artisan
Aristotle	325 BC	Ethical	Proprietary	Dialectical	Hedonic
Astrology	AD 135	Cancer, Scorpio, Pisces	Capricorn, Taurus, Virgo	Libra, Aquarius, Gemini	Aries, Leo, Sagittarius
Irenaeus	AD 185	John	Matthew	Luke	Mark
Galen	AD 190	Choleric	Melancholic	Phlegmatic	Sanguine
Yoga	AD 490	Bhakti	Raja	Jnana	Karma
Toltec	AD 650	West	North	East	South
Paracelsus	AD 1550	Nymph	Gnome	Sylph	Salamander
Ojibway	AD 1600	Fall	Winter	Spring	Summer
Anishinabeg	AD 1750	Adulthood	Old age	Birth	Youth
Sioux	AD 1780	Evening	Night	Morning	Noon
Adickes	AD 1905	Dogmatic	Traditional	Agnostic	Innovative
Spranger	AD 1914	Religious	Economic	Theoretic	Aesthetic
Kretschmer	AD 1920	Hyperesthetic	Depressive	Anesthetic	Hypomanic
Fromm	AD 1947	Receptive	Hoarding	Marketing	Exploitative
Myers	AD 1958	Feeler	Judger	Thinker	Perceiver
Keirsey	AD 1978	Apollo	Demeter	Prometheus	Dionysus

The Elements

When did humanity first begin to believe that people were fundamentally different from each other? When did we first believe that something intangible—something mysterious—influenced how a person thought, felt, and behaved?

The answer must be, almost as soon as we were capable of intelligent thought, which, anthropologists believe, was somewhere in the Middle East about 15,000 B.C. It was here that the earliest agricultural systems evolved and humanity began to realize that the earth, when combined with the sun, water, and the air, could produce crops of an infinite variety. We realized that a plant would not grow without nutrient-rich soil to germinate in, sunlight to give it energy and warmth, water to give it succulence, and air to distribute the seeds and pollen.

It probably took only a few thousand years for these early civilizations to make the leap in thought that people were as different as these four fundamental elements and each brought different gifts to life.

- — Some people were like **water** and provided gifts of relief, enrichment, and refreshment to those who were thirsty and in need of a helping hand.
- — Others were like the **earth** and provided the structure and day-to-day nutritional requirements that support life. They provided practical, down-to-earth gifts.
- — Still others were like the cool **air** and seemed to go from thought to thought like the wind went from plant to plant, distributing new ideas and new life. They brought gifts of insight and introspection.
- — The rest were like the **sun**—full of passion and vibrancy. These people brought gifts of energy and strength, charging up others with their optimism and charm.

Egyptian Theology

About five thousand years ago in the Nile delta, the ancient Egyptians were one of the first cultures to record a version of this theory. They believed that four different gods were responsible for supervising the four elements of life. Each had a set of strengths and characteristics that the other gods didn't possess. And the Egyptians said that each of us is driven by an unconscious force to follow one of these gods.

- — Followers of **Nun**, the peaceful god of the water, are quiet, sweet, meditative, and sensitive to beauty. They like historical, artistic, or philosophical studies. They can be idle and lazy.

— Followers of **Geb**, the crusty god of the earth, are industrious, practical, and good leaders. They're motivated by economics and often involved in financial enterprises. They can be bossy and stubborn.

— Followers of **Shu**, the all-knowing god of the air, are self-disciplined, intellectual, and independent. They like to teach or work with the law. They can become cynical and arrogant.

— Followers of **Ra**, the fiercely bold god of the sun, are dynamic, fiery, daring, and physical. They usually work with their hands and can be skillful artisans. They tend to be reckless and headstrong.

Empedocles

A version of this belief was also evident in the classical period of Greece. Empedocles of Acragas (495–435 B.C.), a Sicilian physician of sorts, assumed that everything in existence, including each person, was composed of four essential "roots" or ingredients. These roots are—surprise, surprise—water, earth, air, and fire. In his *Tetrasomia*, Empedocles described these ingredients not only as physical manifestations or material substances, but also as spiritual essences. He associated them with four gods and goddesses:

> Hear first [of] the four roots of all things: bright Zeus, life-giving Hera, and Aidoneus, and Nestis who moistens the springs of men with her tears. (*Tetrasomia,* fragment 33)

Empedocles was rather unclear as to which components match up with which gods. According to Peter Kinsley, author of *Ancient Philosophy, Mystery and Magic*, the following correlations seem likely: Nestis–water, Hera–earth, Zeus–air, and Aidoneus–fire.

— Since Empedocles was from Sicily, he chose **Nestis**, the local goddess of water. Although scholars aren't exactly sure if she had a counterpart in Greece and Rome, they often link her with Persephone or Proserpina. According to legend, Nestis is the goddess of harmony and peace. That's her natural, adaptive state, preferring to relax or sink into her surroundings, not willing to make waves unless others act upon her.

— Before the Romans renamed her Juno, the goddess of the earth, the Greeks knew her as **Hera**. She was the queen of the gods and ruled over the fruitful and productive earth, from which all life is formed. Consequently, she's often known as the mother of all life. As the supreme mother, she watches with particular interest over all earthbound mothers, and is the advocate of marriage, fidelity, and commitment. Firm and stern, she conserves her resources and only releases them after humanity has worked hard enough to earn them.

— The Greeks called the god of the air **Zeus** and the Romans called him Jupiter or Jove. He's considered to be the king of the gods, or as known in Latin, the *dies pater,* which means, "shining father." He's the luminescent ruler of the sky, of the light, and of all weather. Because of the clarity with which he sees things, he's the advocate of sound legal advice, and supervises such things as property, oaths, and treaties. Like the air, his understanding is constantly escalating and expanding.

— Although Empedocles called him **Aidoneus**, most of the ancient Greeks called him Hades, while the Romans renamed him Pluto. His is recognized for being the god of fire and the god of the underworld, where lakes of molten lava are constantly churning and burning. He has a passionate, fiery temperament and is feared for his occasional wrath and vengeance. In order to keep him at bay, black sheep are offered to him as sacrifices. Hence the beginning of the belief that the "black sheep of the family" are those nonconforming individuals that follow after this god.

Hippocrates

A few years later, another Greek, Hippocrates of Cos (460–377 B.C.), the "Father of Medicine," proposed that four components are intricately related to a person's health and well-being. He elaborated on the theory that our bodies are composed of a combination of the four elements, hypothesizing that those who have more of one element than another will also have an overabundance of a particular bodily fluid. As these fluids build up, they cause particular illnesses and influence our dispositions—that he called temperaments. As a result, he identified four basic temperaments.

— If your liver makes too much **yellow bile**, also known as choler or gall, you have a choleric temperament and are gifted, sensitive, self-sacrificing, moody, faithful, conscientious, and passive.

— If your kidneys or spleen produces too much **black bile** (melan choler—dark blood mixed with other secretions) you have a melancholic temperament and are strong-willed, self-sufficient, practical, productive, decisive, prepared, domineering, and consistent.

— If your lungs (and other respiratory passages) produce too much **phlegm** or mucus, then you have a phlegmatic temperament and are easygoing, objective, capable, timid, uninvolved, and have a dry sense of humor.

— If your heart makes too much **blood**, then you have a sanguine temperament and are lively, happy, enthusiastic, amorous, generous, warm, passionate, outgoing, and loud.

The Hippocratic humoral theory had a widespread and lasting impact on European medical thought, though it doesn't seem to have much value in today's high-tech medical marketplace where we talk about hormones, neurotransmitters, endorphins, and the like. Nevertheless, it wasn't seriously challenged until the fifteenth century because it offered an easy-to-understand explanation for most medical phenomena.

Plato

While Empedocles, Hippocrates, and other medical practitioners were focusing on human anatomy, Plato (427–347 B.C.) established himself as one of the premier philosophers in Greece. Plato wasn't especially interested in physiology; rather, he was more interested in what people could do if they really put their minds to something. He focused on describing a perfect society. In his writings, Plato believed that Utopia would require four types of people to perform four specialized roles. Happily, these four types of people seem to exist naturally.

— The **Idealists** are endowed with intuitive sensibility and play a moral leadership role. They're subject to "intuitive thought"; that is, pure thinking performed free of the rules of logic or the rigor of investigation. Plato felt this mental state entitled one to define the full meaning of life and to discern right from wrong.

— The **Guardians** are endowed with common sense and play a caretaking and protecting role. These trustworthy souls can be counted on to keep watch over the activities and attitudes of the people. As watchers and keepers, they are alert to both the needs and perils of their charges.

— The **Rationals** are endowed with reasoning sensibility and play the role of logical investigators. Plato's word for this type of person was *dianoetic,* meaning "capable of dialectical thought"—those who could coordinate thought and reasoning to make rational the world around them.

- The **Artisans** are naturally endowed with artistic sense and play an art-making role. They tend to shine in music, literature, dance, drawing, painting, and sculpture, as well as theatre, athletics, industrial arts, and medicine—anywhere the activity is free-form and constant.

Aristotle

One of Plato's students, Aristotle (384–322 B.C.) was also interested in figuring out why people do the things they do. He believed there were four sources of happiness and that everyone prefers one source over another. Hence, this is another way to place people into different groups.

- **Ethical** people prefer moral virtue. They study ethics and moral codes in an attempt to understand the path to happiness. They want to make a statement to the world, which is usually one of tolerance, cooperation, and harmony. They focus on the spiritual/emotional world.
- **Proprietary** people prefer acquiring or controlling assets. They're focused on the material/financial world, where one's status is largely determined by the ability to make money and buy things.
- **Dialectical** people prefer logical investigation so they can get the facts straight and scientifically arrive at valid conclusions. They like to discover and prove truths for themselves, expounding on theories as they go. They're focused on the intellectual/theoretical world.
- **Hedonic** people prefer sensual pleasure, or the satisfaction obtained from tasting, smelling, seeing, touching, and listening to things for oneself. They're focused on the physical/sensory world.

Astrology

Astrology is the study of the positions and aspects of the sun, moon, planets, and stars in the belief that they have an influence on our lives. It has been around for at least four thousand years, present in nearly every civilization including those found in ancient Babylonia, Chaldea, Assyria, Egypt, India, China, and America. It wasn't until A.D. 135 when the old idea of four elements was first figured into the astrological scheme by Claudius Ptolemaeus (Ptolemy), the Greco-Egyptian astronomer, mathematician, and geographer. The elements alone help to describe our basic natures. When the elements are combined with an astrological chart, astrologers believe they help define us as whole and complex people.

For example, in looking at an individual's astrological chart, the presence of more fire signs may well indicate a fiery, combustible personality. Along the same lines, the absence of earth signs would indicate someone who isn't grounded or practical. The presence of a mix of all of the elements would be a sign of a well-rounded individual.

— The element of water is associated with the signs of **Pisces**, **Cancer**, and **Scorpio**. People with water signs are intuitive, sensitive, and feel more intensely than others. Emotional and nurturing, they run deep, like still waters in a river. Feelings matter to these folks, and since water is also about compassion and understanding, they listen and perceive remarkably well. They love to translate their impressions of the world into beautiful artistic works that make others happy. Those of the water signs feel most fulfilled when they're helping others, usually doing so in enchanting, even romantic, ways. These people base their actions on intuition rather than on logic or intellect.

— The element of earth is attached to the signs of **Taurus**, **Virgo**, and **Capricorn**. Those whose horoscopes are graced by earth signs tend to be practical, grounded (of course), and dependable. They seek steady progress, not risk. Their observables, the things they've built and done, all tend toward substance. Whether it's building homes of bricks or populating rooms with possessions, those of the earth signs look for things that are dependable, sound, solid, of enduring quality, and preferably, comfortably abundant. From this stable position, they're empowered to follow their inclination towards duty to others in their sphere, and have a place to bask in the rewards of their efforts.

— The element of air is attached to the signs of **Gemini**, **Libra**, and **Aquarius**. Airy people are alert, curious, and perceptive. They love to analyze, synthesize, and probe. They can handle abstract reasoning. From the air, the world is an interesting place, and from on high it's easier to see all sides of a given issue or situation. Air people are communicative, intellectual, clever, inventive, and fair. They can blow cold if they're disturbed; however, they're normally cool, calm, and collected.

— The element of fire is associated with the signs of **Aries**, **Leo**, and **Sagittarius**. Fire in the soul makes one an enthusiastic, spontaneous, zestful, and sometimes larger-than-life being. Those influenced by a fire sign are self-sufficient, courageous, lively spirits. They're strong, self-assured, creative, and fun. Being touched by fire can make one an inspiration to others.

Gospel Writers

Irenaeus (A.D. 130–202), the Bishop of Lyon, was the leading Christian theologian of the second century. His work *Adversus Haereses (Against Heresies)* was centered on trying to get the young church to reject Gnosticism and focus on an authoritative canon of scriptures, a standardized creed, and the authority of church leaders. Apparently, some communities were choosing to follow only one of the four gospel accounts of Matthew, Mark, Luke, and John. This was causing the church to splinter into factions. Trying to put a stop to that, Irenaeus wrote:

> It is not possible that the Gospels can be either more or fewer in number than they are. For, since there are four zones of the world in which we live, and four principal winds, while the Church is scattered throughout all the world, and the "pillar and ground" of the Church is the Gospel and the spirit of life; it is fitting that she should have four pillars, breathing out immortality on every side, and vivifying men afresh. (*Adversus Haereses,* Book III, Chapter 11, Section 8.)

He went on to describe how each gospel writer had a different perspective of the life and teachings of Jesus of Nazareth. Likewise, each point of view has a place since, "the Gospel is quadriform, as is also the course followed by the Lord." Only by looking at all four accounts can we get a clearer picture of the ministry of Jesus in ancient Palestine.

— **John**, the "beloved disciple," was one of the original twelve apostles and leaders of the church. John was deeply loyal to Jesus and seems to have been the only apostle who was with Jesus at his death. The Gospel of John is a simple, yet highly symbolic account, emphasizing the divine nature of Jesus. It's quite different from the other three in vocabulary, phraseology, and presentation of events. It has a tender, spiritual tone to it, and makes gifted use of metaphors and other imagery. It was obviously intended for believers, because rather than dwelling on gospel fundamentals, it presents unique material that's geared towards inspiring people to increase their faith, set aside self-interests, develop better relationships, forgive their enemies, and humbly serve others.

— Before becoming a disciple of Jesus, **Matthew** earned a living by collecting taxes levied by the Roman government on his fellow Jews. Many people thought he was collaborating with the occupation forces and were surprised when he was chosen to be one of the twelve apostles. He was also a trained bilingual scribe, which suggests that he was well versed in Hebrew law and heritage. Perhaps this is why the Gospel of Matthew begins with a thorough genealogical report, then continues with a chronological, step-by-step account of Christ's teachings. Matthew's writings focus on Jesus' fulfillment of the ancient messianic prophesies, his place as the king and judge of mankind, and people's obligation to obey God's laws and keep his commandments. Matthew's audience was primarily the better-educated Jews who already believed in Jesus, but had a tendency to argue over points of the law.

— **Luke** (meaning "bearer of light") was perhaps the most educated of the gospel writers. Born of gentile parents in Syria, he eventually studied Greco-Roman medicine and became a physician before converting to Christianity. We're not sure whether he converted while Jesus was alive, but we do know he became so committed to church principles that he traveled extensively with Paul as a missionary to the gentile nations. He eventually records his knowledge in the Gospel of Luke and in his follow-up book, the Acts of the Apostles. Luke's account is more polished and scholarly than the others, carefully presenting the facts of Jesus' teachings and actions in an orderly manner, trying to help people learn for themselves the truths he understood. As a doctor, he recorded with particular detail the healing of the sick and disabled, the raising of the dead, and the things a resurrected body can do. Scholars believe that this account was written for wealthier gentile Christians in an urban setting, who were becoming complacent and needed to turn their faith into practice.

— **Mark,** who apparently came from a wealthy family in Jerusalem, was believed to have been one of the young disciples who followed Jesus as he traveled about. Tradition holds that when Jesus was arrested, his disciples started to flee. The soldiers caught Mark, but he was able to struggle free, leaving his clothes behind him. This sort of descriptive detail, coupled with action, is typical of the Gospel of Mark. Much like a quickly assembled eyewitness news summary, it features a variety of loosely organized highlights of Jesus' actions and how they affected the bystanders. His writings focus on miraculous events, battles against wickedness, and enduring to the end. They are filled with action, suspense, and spectacle, often using action-oriented words such as *and then, immediately,* or *straightway*. It appears that Mark wrote his account for the recently converted Gentiles who were facing challenges and persecutions of their own and needed to have their spiritual batteries recharged. He later became known as "Mark the Lion," probably because of his own boldness and courage.

Galen

Several hundred years after Hippocrates, one of his admirers revived his theories. Galen of Pergamon (A.D.129–199), a notable Greek physician and philosopher, looked closer at the four temperaments and determined they each displayed some negative characteristics, especially when they were feeling bad. Galen's ideas would form the basis of European medicine until the Renaissance.

— **Cholerics**, normally gifted, sensitive, responsive, unselfish, and faithful, can be overly sensitive, irritable, emotional, and unstable.

— **Melancholics**, normally self-sufficient, practical, productive, and decisive, can be gloomy, dull, pessimistic, bossy, rigid, and judgmental.

— **Phlegmatics**, normally easygoing, objective, capable, and timid, can be critical, cynical, morbid, selfish, stubborn, and apathetic.

— **Sanguines**, normally lively, happy, enthusiastic, and outgoing, can be aggressive, manipulative, defiant, confrontational, and destructive.

Yoga

While all of this was going on near the Mediterranean, the people of India were yawning. You see, these philosophies were old hat to them, because they'd known for millennia that through yoga, there were four different paths people could follow to become "one" with the world.

No one knows exactly when yoga began, but it certainly predates written history. Stone carvings depicting figures in yoga positions have been found in archeological sites in the Indus Valley dating back five thousand years or more.

In ancient times, the desire for greater personal freedom, health, long life, and heightened self-understanding gave birth to this system of physical and mental exercise, which has since spread throughout the world.

There are more than a hundred different schools of yoga. However, most fall into one of four paths that are each suited to a different temperament or approach to life. By the end of the fifth century A.D., all four of these paths had been defined to some extent.

— **Bhakti** yoga is the path of devotion or unconditional love. This path appeals particularly to those of an emotional nature. Your goal is wholeheartedly to love others for love's sake—not for your own selfish interests. Everything you do is motivated by this unqualified, undying love. This state is achieved through meditation, prayer, singing, and chanting.

— **Raja** yoga is the path to self-discipline. This path appeals to those who want more control over their own lives. Your objective is to gain dominance over your body, energy, senses, and mind. You achieve this through a regimen of exercise and breathing practice coupled with consistent meditation and study.

— **Jnana** yoga is the path of knowledge. It seeks to understand the laws of the universe. It's a difficult path, geared toward those who have an intellectual curiosity, who like to reason and analyze. The main objective is to withdraw the mind and emotions from perceiving life and yourself in a deluded way so you may behold and live more attuned with reality.

— **Karma** yoga is the path of action. It's the path chosen primarily by those of an outgoing nature who want to overcome personal cravings and addictions. Activities are undertaken for their own sake, without concern for personal benefit. By detaching yourself from the fruits of your actions, you find personal harmony.

Directions

On the other side of the planet, the native inhabitants of America were realizing that there was something remarkable about the number four. For most American Indian tribes the number four is sacred and has figured prominently in their culture, religion, prophecies, and oral traditions or stories for hundreds, if not thousands, of years. Although there may be some variations from tribe to tribe, one of the more popular beliefs is that there are four types of people on earth, and that each follows a certain path in life. The paths are named after one of the four cardinal compass points: West, North, East, and South.

According to artifacts discovered in Mexico, the now-extinct Toltec tribe of seventh-century Mexico believed the following:

— To the **West** is the path of reflection and spiritual insight. It's here where you find your loved ones, where you discover your true self, where your dreams turn into reality.

— To the **North** is the path of accomplishment and perseverance. On this path, you will find people who are stalwart and dependable, prepared and organized, ready to do whatever needs to be done.

— To the **East** is the path of wisdom and knowledge. Here you will find those who seek to understand the world, who invent new devices, who question the status quo.

— To the **South** is the path of excitement and adventure. People on this path seek to push the limits of their potential. They're always on the go, preferring thrilling adventures and substantial challenges.

Paracelsus

Many years later, Europe finally began to emerge from the Dark Ages. The Swiss-born renaissance healer Paracelsus (1493–1541), also known as Philippus Aureolus Theophrastus Bombastus von Hohenheim, traveled around Europe seeking to expand his medical and healing knowledge. He earned his living as a physician and writer and, while continuing to build on Galen's theories of the four temperaments, he redirected the focus back to the four elements, which he described in his book, *Nymphs, Gnomes, Sylphs and Salamanders.*

— **Nymphs** (think mermaids) live in the water and are sensitive, beguiling, and need to be loved. They inspire those who frequent their retreats or drink of waters they guard, hence Henry Thoreau by his pond, or John Keats by his brooks, are empowered to produce prose and poetry that stirs souls and lives for ages.

— **Gnomes** live in the earth and are cranky, hard workers. They're trusted keepers of what's valuable and strive to be productive Hobbits. In addition to tending treasures, they keep cultures intact, guarding the traditions, sayings, adages, maxims, precepts, and proverbs that give a society its values.

— **Sylphs** live in the air and are thinkers, dreamers, and loners. Logical and contemplative, they're usually lost in some inquiry or calculation. Insatiably curious, they're prone to survey from the heights, staring in wide-eyed wonder, owl-like, as they try to unravel the mysteries below.

— **Salamanders** live in fires and are energetic, hot-blooded, and mischievous. Like their namesake lizard, people with these temperaments are changelings—they can take on the attributes of their environment, blending in perfectly. To the Salamander, all the world is a stage. The guiding spirit of the Salamander is the voice in the prompter's box; it whispers who and what the Salamander shall be today.

Seasons

At about the time the Pilgrims were landing their ships on the coast of North America, many Native American tribes believed that each of the four seasons had characteristics that are shared by different types of people. Here is a modern interpretation of how one of the Ojibway tribes from the Great Lakes region described these people:

— The **fall** is a time of harvest. This is when the crops are gathered in and celebrations, feasts, and festivals occur. This is a time to be sociable, to communicate and interact with others. This is the time to enjoy the bounties and share what you have with others. This is the time to marvel at the colorful leaves as you stroll hand-in-hand with a sweater-adorned loved one down a tree-lined path.

— The **winter** is a time when only the prepared survive, and winter people have prepared well. They have filled their pantries with bottled fruits and vegetables, packed their woodsheds with neatly stacked logs, filled their propane tanks with fuel, weatherproofed their windows and doors, and winterized their machinery. They have done what was expected of them in a timely fashion. They will manage just fine, thank you, in spite of what may befall them.

— The **spring** is the time of awakening, of re-birth, of newness of life. People of the spring have fertile minds and are always seeking for intellectual nutrients and supplements to help them grow and develop. They seek after light and truth, wherever it may be found. Like a spring day, these people may seem chilly when you first meet them, but as you spend more time with them, they become warmer and warmer. They like to plant new ideas and tenderly nurture them until they're strong enough to stand on their own.

— The **summer** is a time of heat, of passion, of energy. While people of the summer may be hot-blooded, they're also generous, fun loving, and entertaining to be around. Their days are long and filled with activity after activity. They love exploring the outdoors, climbing the mountains, diving in the oceans, jumping off cliffs, skiing behind boats, or just lying naked in the sun.

Life Stages

The Anishinabeg Indians, who have lived in northern Michigan for more than five hundred years, have maintained that as people progress through various stages in life, which they do on their own timetable, they take on different personality characteristics. However, since most people prefer one stage to the others, they tend to revert to that stage whenever they can.

— **Adulthood** is the stage for courting and marrying. It's a time to have children, to nurture them, to teach them. During this stage you begin to focus on the needs of others rather than your own. You're interested in what's happening in your community, how you can help improve situations, and how you can make your community a better place. As you communicate with and develop relationships with members of your community, you learn how to help other people, lift other's burdens, and strengthen those who need your help. It's a time for overcoming personal challenges and increasing spiritual growth. Young people who aspire to this stage can't wait to grow up so they can establish their families and make their mark on the word.

— **Old age** is the stage where you provide guidance and direction to others. Here your leadership abilities are put to the test, where you understand the need for maintaining traditions and respecting the time-tested ways of your people. During this time you draw on the resources you have saved over the years and rely in some measure on the younger people in the community. Therefore, you seek to make the community safe and strong, filled with dependable, responsible people. People in this stage are cautious, frugal, and systematic. They prefer things to be done in a specific way. They have a clear picture of right and wrong, good and bad, and don't hesitate to share this view with others.

— **Birth** is the stage where people learn the most, such as learning to eat, drink, sleep, walk, and talk. They learn about the world around them and their place in it. Children are naturally curious and seek to explore and understand the world around them. They ask questions, such as "Why is grass green?" or "How does the snow get up into the sky?" Those who prefer this stage as they become older are constantly trying to develop their knowledge and grow in their capacity to understand the world.

— **Youth** (puberty through early 20s) is the time for adventure and freedom. It's a time when you test your strengths and find your personal limits. It's a time when your body matures and is awakened to new passions. It's a time to leave the protecting arms of your mother and see if you can make it on your own. It's the season for change, for experimentation, for exploration, for exuberance, for energy, and for fun. Regardless of their age, people who prefer this stage are normally active and young at heart. In old age, they look upon their youth with fondness and wish to experience it again.

Parts of the Day

The Teton Sioux Indians, among others, believed there were four parts of a day that influence life on earth. People tend to receive more energy at different times of the day. Some people are more energetic in the morning, others at mid-day, others in the evening, and others in the dark, pre-dawn hours.

— The **evening** is the time to relax, to rest, to renew, to relate. People of this hour love to settle down and enjoy a good meal with friends and loved ones. They enjoy chatting about the affairs of the day, and learning what others may have done. It's at this time they're the happiest, when all the work has been done, when the family is back together, when they can snuggle with a loved one near the fire under the light of the moon.

— The **night** is the time where the body is prepared for another day's work. During this time, the unconscious body works hard to mend its muscles and convert food to energy so it can live for another day. So too do people of the night live out their days, mending what's broken and acquiring supplies for another day. They seek to be prepared for whatever the future may bring. These people are early risers—often waking before the sun rises, tending to their chores and duties while others sleep.

— The **morning** represents new beginnings as the light of the dawning sun begins a new day. People of this hour are looking for new discoveries, new advances, and new ideas. They're at their best in the morning, when their minds are rested, clear, and uncluttered with the day's events. These people seek illumination and enlightenment.

— **Noontime**, when the sun is at its peak, is the hour of warmth and energy. People on this path are powerful and full of life. They have a sunny, optimistic disposition. They're eager to get their work done so they can enjoy the rest of their day. Just like the sun sits in the middle of the sky, so these people prefer to be in the middle of the action, in the heat of the moment, at the center of attention.

Adickes

At the dawning of the twentieth century, the science of psychology was really taking off in Europe, particularly in Germany. Because of the recent industrial revolution, people were finally able to devote their entire lives to solving the mysteries behind human behavior.

One of the first individuals to publish a theory on temperament was Erich Adickes (1866–1928). He was a philosopher and educator who, in his 1907 book, *Charakter und Weltanschauung (Character and Worldview),* described four basic temperaments. Interestingly, even though he probably didn't know about the work of Plato, Galen, and the others, his temperaments describe essentially the same types of people as their theories.

— **Dogmatic** people are those who find an important social issue or cause to champion and then hang on to it with all their might. Once they find their crusade, they're eager—even zealous—to share what they have learned with others.

— **Traditional** people are careful observers of customary practices, habits, ceremonies, and rituals, regardless of where they're found. They revere and cultivate the time-honored practices of their social groups, believing this is what holds society together.

— **Agnostic** people are naturally skeptical, in spite of how much time and energy they devote to inspection and analysis. They believe there's always the potential of some new fact or figure popping up that would nullify their arguments.

— **Innovative** people are people who like to scramble things up, just to make life more interesting. They're always in the search for something new and different, something bigger and faster. If they've "been there and done that," they're determined to try something new.

Spranger

Eduard Spranger (1882–1963), another German educator and philosopher, studied personality to see how it related to political and social dimensions. As he studied the effects of culture and history on human ethics and actions, he concluded that there are four basic types of people. These were described in his 1914 work, *Lebensformen,* which translates to *Types of Life* or *Types of Men*.

— **Religious** types are those who seek out and eventually adopt a set of personal ethics they aren't willing to break—ever. They faithfully and wholeheartedly stick to their causes, philosophies, or activities, knowing they're often on the road less traveled.

— **Economic** types are those that seek to provide security when the storm comes. Like the Little Red Hen, they plant the wheat, water it, weed it, harvest it, grind it up, and bake it into loaves of bread. Then they share it, and other types of wealth or property, only with those they're duty-bound to protect and serve, or those who are worthy of such an investment.

— **Theoretic** types are logical, objective, levelheaded, and cerebral. They spend enormous amounts of time theorizing, postulating, and speculating—trying to make sense out of life as they learn a new competency.

— **Aesthetic** types know beautiful art when they see it. They know great music when they hear it. They know true love when they experience it. It must be processed with their senses, in real time, up close and personal, before it has meaningful, lasting value.

Kretschmer

Ernst Kretschmer (1888–1964) was yet another German psychiatrist who studied human personality. Like his forerunner Galen, he focused on the medical benefits that would be realized if personality characteristics could be correlated with physical and mental illness. His early writings focused on how certain body shapes were associated with specific personality traits; however, as he got older, he broadened his definitions and looked into the structure of the mind as well as the build of the body. He became convinced that many behaviors attributed to "mental illness" could actually be explained in terms of temperament rather than disease.

— When feeling unloved, unwanted, or unwelcome, the **Hyperesthetics** are oversensitive, overemotional, and over-sentimental. They wear their hearts on their sleeves and read between the lines, even when nothing is there. They act irrationally and often become frantic, self-destructive, inconsolable, even suicidal.

— When they feel they have lost control of their lives, the **Depressives** tend to sink into despair. They become unproductive, listless, disorderly, helpless, critical, and dejected.

— When they're feeling incompetent or amateurish, the **Anesthetics** can become cold, unfeeling, bitter, and cruel. They may also be anti-social, disagreeable, stubborn, arrogant, unreasonable, and perverse.

— When they're feeling caged up like a wild animal at the circus, the **Hypomanics** can be recklessly impulsive, thoughtless, irresponsible, and self-absorbed. They become overly rowdy, rude, vulgar, aggressive, even brutal at times.

Fromm

Erich Fromm (1900–1980), emigrated from Austria to the United States to escape the Nazi regime. He was a psychoanalyst and social philosopher who explored the interaction between personality and socioeconomics. He wrote several important books that helped convert many psychologists from objective behaviorism to a kindler, gentler, more subjective view of mankind.

Among other things, he believed humans are products of the cultures in which they're reared, rather than the result of unconscious, instinctive forces. Therefore, social conditioning plays a vital role in the development of an individual's personality. This was a breakthrough in thought—no longer would genetics be seen as the exclusive factor in determining human behavior.

— **Receptive** individuals are attuned, caring, idealistic, innocent, kindhearted, optimistic, pleasant, approachable, sensitive, sentimental, tolerant, and unpretentious.

— **Hoarding** individuals are careful, cautious, composed, economical, imperturbable, loyal, methodical, orderly, patient, practical, reserved, and steadfast.

— **Marketing** individuals are adaptable, clever, competent, determined, inquisitive, intelligent, open-minded, unbiased, and visionary.

— **Exploiting** individuals are active, assertive, bold, captivating, confident, fun-loving, impulsive, initiators, lively, proud, skillful, and upbeat.

Myers

In the early 1940s, two Americans, Isabel Briggs Myers (1897–1980) and her mother, Katharine Cook Briggs (1875–1968), began developing the Myers-Briggs Type Indicator (MBTI). The MBTI is a self-reporting personality inventory designed to give people information about their psychological type preferences.

The MBTI contains four separate scales (see below) that reflect how people interact with each other, gather information, and process that information. As a result of taking the test, you're given a score that plots your preferences on each continuum. The closer you are to either pole, the stronger your preferences.

The first scale deals with how you prefer to relate with others. You're either extraverted or introverted to some degree. Extroverts are naturally sociable, outgoing, and talkative. They're energized as they associate with others. Introverts tend to shrink from social contacts and are often preoccupied with their own thoughts. They are worn down by associating with others and need eventually to go off by themselves to recharge their batteries.

The second scale deals with how you prefer to gather information. If you prefer to use your five senses and are highly aware of things that are happening around you, you're a Sensory. On the other hand, if you're more introspective, imaginative, and able to see things with your mind's eye, you're an Intuitive.

The third and fourth scales deal with how you prefer to process information. These scales yield four different preferences that are identical to the four temperaments presented in the other theories in this text. Myers believed that if you prefer to use your head and are more objective and analytical, you're probably a Thinker. If you rely on your feelings and are personal and sensitive, you're probably a Feeler. If you prefer to evaluate information, put it in a category, or order it, then you're probably a Judger. If you prefer to find a good use for the information immediately or, in the alternative, throw it out and probe for other options, then you're probably a Perceiver.

The end product of the MBTI is a four-letter code that describes your personality type. E=Extraversion, I=Introversion, S=Sensory, N=Intuitive, T=Thinker, F=Feeler, J=Judger, P=Perceiver. There are 16 possible combinations of these letters, resulting in 16 personality types.

ENTJ	**ESTJ**	**ESTP**	**ENFJ**
INTJ	**ISTJ**	**ISTP**	**INFJ**
ENTP	**ESFJ**	**ESFP**	**ENFP**
INTP	**ISFJ**	**ISFP**	**INFP**

With your code in hand, you're able to spell out and describe your personality to others. For example, if you were an ENTP, you're eager to express your views to others (E), are introspective (N), are tough-minded (T), and are given to probing for options (P).

Keirsey

In the 1970s, Dr. David W. Keirsey, a clinical psychologist from California, made significant contributions to clarifying and simplifying the personality theories of Myers, Kretschmer, Adickes, and others. In his best-selling 1978 book, *Please Understand Me,* Keirsey concluded there were four basic temperaments. He named them after the Greek gods who shared the same characteristics.

— The **Apollonian** temperament is essentially a combination of Myers' ENFJ, INFJ, ENFP, and INFP personality types. The NF—the Intuitive Feeling—links these types together and forms the temperament. According to Keirsey, these people are "friendly to the core in dreaming up how to give meaning and wholeness to people's lives. Conflict in those around them is painful for NFs, something they must deal with in a very personal way, and so they care deeply about keeping morale high in their membership groups, and about nurturing the positive self-image of their loved ones." (Keirsey, David W. *Please Understand Me II.* Del Mar, CA: Prometheus Nemesis Books. 1998. pg. 18–19.)

— The **Demeterian** temperament is a combination of the ESTJ, ISTJ, ESFJ, and ISFJ personalities. They're linked by the SJ—the Sensory Judging—attribute. "For SJs, everything should be in its proper place, everybody should be doing what they're supposed to, everybody should be getting their just desserts, every action should be closely supervised, all products thoroughly inspected, all legitimate needs promptly met, all approved ventures carefully insured." (Ibid.)

— The **Promethean** temperament is the ENTJ, INTJ, ENTP, and INTP personality types. The NT—the Intuitive Thinking—links these types together. These people are "tough-minded in figuring out what sort of technology might be useful to solve a given problem. NTs require themselves to be persistently and consistently rational in their actions.... All NTs insist that they have a rationale for everything they do, that whatever they do and say makes sense." (Ibid.)

— The **Dionysian** temperament is composed of the ESTP, ISTP, ESFP, and ISFP types. They're connected by SP—the

Sensory Perceiving—characteristic. These people probe "around their immediate surroundings in order to detect and exploit any favorable options that came within reach. Having the freedom to act on the spur of the moment is very important to SPs. No chance is to be blown, no opening missed, no angle overlooked—whatever or whoever might turn out to be exciting, pleasurable, or useful is checked out for advantage." (Ibid.)

Bryce

In the 1980s, I was a typical college student studying psychology and communications. As part of my schoolwork, I began to evaluate different personality theories and how they could be used to help improve the ability of people to communicate and relate with others.

Becoming progressively intrigued with this research, I began an in-depth, multi-year analysis of hundreds of personality theories and philosophies. I began to see the need to create a simplified theory that combined many of the truths I've learned into a format that could be used in everyday situations. As a result, I developed and patented the Insight Personality Instrument™ in 1994.

Rather than simply assigning people to one of four specific groups, I propose that all of us are, in actuality, a combination of all four temperaments. And even though most of us prefer one over the others, we each have a blend that's unique so that very few people share an identical blend of preferences. Once you understand yourself, and how your preferences affect each other, you can begin to understand others.

Before ultimately deciding on using four colors to describe the four temperaments—a metaphor that had been used for years by quite a number of personality theorists—I experimented with naming the four types after rocks, gems, animals, trees, birds, historical figures, even hair styles. But nothing worked as well as the colors metaphor, especially when you try to describe someone's blend of all four types. Using the term *color spectrum* and describing someone as a Green-Orange is much better than calling someone a piece of jade surrounded by little rubies, an owl with hawkish tendencies, a Lincoln administration with a Kennedy vice president, or a crew cut with spiked sideburns.

In addition, the four colors seem to have inherent meanings that cross cultures:

— **Blue** represents tranquility and peace as found in the sky, the ocean, and a mountain lake. It is soothing, calming, and pacifying.

- — **Gold** represents wealth, royalty, standards, and excellence. Gold holds its value and is the symbol of security, status, and power.
- — **Green** things exist, grow, and thrive in the natural world, converting deadly carbon dioxide to brain-stimulating, life-giving oxygen.
- — **Orange** is seen in fire, in the brilliant sunrise and sunset, in cones that surround road hazards and designate temporary boundaries.

CHAPTER 12

Applying Colors Information

This final chapter will explain how to apply information on temperament in real-life settings. It will provide guidelines and principles that, when followed, will increase the likelihood of success.

How Do I Do?

Mixed in with my theories on personality are two bright pearls. The first is that your preferences, whether in movement, thought, or food, are an individual choice that comes from within and may be recognized early in development. And, like being left- or right-handed, most preferences are neither correct nor incorrect, but rather flow along the lines of what's usual and customary, and often easiest, for whoever holds them.

The second is that you can have a basic preference, say a strong Green, but learn to act, if only for a time, as would a person of a different temperament.

For instance, most salespeople learned long ago the importance of seeking out clues as to the temperament of their clients, and then doing what they can to "sync up to" that style whenever they're in that client's presence. For new sales staff, this is an effort, but most of the old pros do it easily and without conscious thought.

Preferences affect who we are in many ways. To have a dominant left or right eye, for instance, will determine many things, from how we shoot a gun to how we hold a pool cue. Our preferred foot is the one with which we step off, which in turn effects how we get on and off elevators, escalators, and bicycles.

Other preferences tend to be internal rather than external. One child will hate tomatoes, while another in the same family will love them. Your favorite ice cream flavor or soda pop may not be mine, even if we come from the same genetic pool.

Some preferences show themselves as personality traits. For instance, one child, predominantly Green, may be quiet, aloof, and bookish; another, likely an Orange, loud and active. Golds may tend to be obedient, helpful, and orderly, and the Blues may tend to stay in a group, or cling tightly to siblings and parents.

Whether they're manifest externally, internally, or in temperament doesn't alter the fact that these choices, whatever their emotional or physical basis, are often just that—choices. You can choose to hold your fork in either hand. However if one or the other seems more natural or comfortable, then that one is likely to be the most practiced and becomes dominant. This doesn't mean, however, that you can't practice and regain or develop the capability to use your non-dominant hand if desired.

It's my observation that one doesn't often need to change one's preferences—if that's even possible. Rather, it's usually enough to realize that everybody has them, and to respect those differences. In fact, it's always an excellent practice to at least try and operate in a different preference now and then. For instance, if you're a strong Orange, doing some Gold will never hurt you—it might even help you to get through the details and busywork of life without having to depend on some sympathetic Blue to do your paperwork for you.

Some evidence exists that the more we mature, the more we increase our ability to operate in our non-preference areas. It's unlikely that we will ever be able to move from being right-handed to left-handed, but it's likely that we can develop nearly equal facility, for some purposes, with both, as in playing a piano, or doing finger spelling in sign language. It's unlikely that we will ever change our dominant color, but it's likely that we will come to understand the strengths of each of the other colors and increase in our capacity to act like them; that is, "do" those colors, as appropriate.

Again, if you recognize each of the four colors for what they are—different temperaments—you're ahead of the game compared to so many people, who believe firmly that their way is the best and possibly the only correct way to go through life. You're especially far ahead if you recognize that temperaments are our innate, inborn tendencies that cannot easily be altered through conscious decisions or choices. This means that spending inordinate amounts of time and energy in trying to change someone to be more like you (as you see the world in your own color) is worse than waste. It's an exercise in frustration for both the person you're trying to change and the person attempting the changing.

So how can we inspire, discipline, and correct, if we are likely to fail? (The stronger one's primary color, the more unlikely a person is to change; the weaker they are, the more likely it is they can shift from one to the other. But essentially the tiger doesn't change its stripes, an owl doesn't become a woodpecker, and a young sagebrush doesn't evolve into a giant redwood—therefore a bright Orange never becomes a Gold.) The answer is in the realization that changing isn't the goal; rather, behavior is. Get an Orange to "do" some Gold, teach a Green to "act" more Blue when appropriate, and you have accomplished more than a thousand sharp-tongued, arm-twisting, pedagogues ever will! You will incline the growing tree without warping the wood.

A person's temperament comes from within, again, much as being left- or right-handed. You might as well say that people are born with their temperaments, because by the time a baby can move and function on its own, its preferences are set. The choices and attitudes that will guide it through life are selected unconsciously. They're innate preferences that feel more comfortable than the alternatives, and left to themselves, children will select them and come to depend on them to the degree that they are, for all practical purposes, innate. Your temperament is pretty much what you started out with, but you're always free to "do" other colors. It will increase your range of options as you meet situations in life, and it's one facet of personality that gets stronger and more flexible with practice.

When you reach the point that you can "do" the attributes and mannerisms of the other temperaments whenever you desire, you will inherit the rich prize of being able to cherry pick the most reliable and appropriate behaviors you see in those around you. Remember, you're only choosing to "do" a color. "You" are unchanged and unthreatened, because you know your own temperament and preferences, and can easily revert to them. Perhaps most important, you will discover an almost uncanny ability to set people at ease, gain their respect, and have them listen to your ideas and take them seriously.

The Ten Commandments of Colors

At this point in your reading, I feel compelled to be absolutely blunt with you. You see, now you have enough information about personality styles to be extremely dangerous to yourself and others.

Unfortunately, I'm not exaggerating this point. A few well-meaning novices have taken this information and have made some serious relationship faux pas. Rather than strengthening associations, they've weakened them. Rather than improving communications, they've degraded them. They've used this knowledge to manipulate rather than persuade, and have consequently done more harm than good.

I'm confident you won't consciously do these things, being the decent, upstanding citizen that you are. But to make sure you don't do it unconsciously, I've established some ground rules for using the information you now possess.

Over the years as my colleagues and I have worked with hundreds of thousands of people, we've collected a vast assortment of real-life guidelines and strategies for using this information successfully. I've boiled these down to a short list, which is called, with no offense to the ancient Israelites, the *Ten Commandments of Colors*.

1. Don't stereotype others

"Since you're a Green, you must like science." This generalization doesn't consider the fact that there are relatively few people who are only one color. Remember that everyone has a personal color spectrum composed of a unique blend of all four colors. While most people have a primary color score that's higher than the others, some people have points distributed equally among two, three, or even all four of the colors. Because of the limitless variations, a person's color spectrum is a unique thing. So while it may be true that many Greens like science, this statement won't be true of every Green. Therefore, we simply can't put individuals into neat little pigeonholes, regardless of how convenient that may be.

2. Don't try to change people

As we look at others, it's easy to notice how different they are from us. We tend to compare their characteristics to our own. Our natural response is to think, "These people must be flawed because they're different from me. Therefore, I must change this person and help him or her become more like me." Fortunately, this is impossible. Just as the alchemists haven't discovered how to turn lead into gold, psychologists haven't learned how to turn Blues into Golds.

3. Don't negate the values of others

It's vitally important to refrain from judging personality characteristics as right or wrong, or good and bad. Each personality type has its own set of values and standards that are dramatically different from the other types. It would be unfair to compare one set of values against another. For example, Oranges aren't "bad" just because they're free-spirited and fun-loving. And introverted Greens aren't "wrong" when they prefer to be reclusive and solve problems on their own.

4. Don't let strengths become liabilities

People with a positive self-image know how to put their strengths to good use. However, when they're feeling down and out, they tend to turn these same strengths into weaknesses. They consciously or unconsciously minimize or maximize their characteristics until they become liabilities. As an example, the normally orderly Gold can become obsessed over cleanliness to the point where it drives away family or friends.

5. Don't use colors as an excuse

Whether we're talking about ourselves or others, it's enormously counterproductive to blame personality type for behavior. "Because I'm Gold I can't do those creative things," or, "He's an Orange and can't be expected to sit still for the staff meeting." Remember, we're talking about preferences—not capabilities. Almost everyone is capable of doing specific behaviors, even if they don't prefer to do them.

6. Keep your observations private

Most people react negatively to being figured out so easily by others. Resist the urge to proclaim, "Oh you're a Gold, no wonder you're so worried. All you have to do is...." Instead, keep the revelation to yourself and use it to improve your own personal relationships. Eventually others may see how successful you've become, and may even come to you for advice. Then feel free to share what you know. Better yet, invite them to read this material so they can discover this information for themselves. Only then will they readily accept it.

7. Give good gifts

Do this by giving others what they value—not what you value. By now, you should have a clear understanding of what the different colors value. If you truly care about someone, you'll put your own wants and needs in the background and focus on theirs. Rather than communicating or relating in ways you prefer, you will do it in ways they prefer. They will, it is to be hoped, do the same for you.

8. Carry your colored lenses with you

If you begin to experience failure in your interpersonal relationships, try to adopt another perspective. The easiest way to do this is to look at the world through the colored lenses of another temperament. If relating in one style doesn't work, whip out a different pair of lenses—you have four to choose from. Eventually you'll find one style that's more effective than the others.

9. Validate the strengths of each color

Realize that each personality type has a set of natural strengths that the other types don't possess. The world needs the strengths of each of the colors in order to function. In fact, the success of almost every organization, relationship, business, or other endeavor relies on how well it uses the native assets of each of the different personalities. Validate these strengths in the people you know. Allow them to grow and blossom.

10. Learn from others

One of the keys in successfully adapting to what life has to offer is to learn the skills the other colors naturally possess. If you feel you're lacking in the social skills department, make friends with a Blue and emulate his or her behaviors. If you require more structure and self-discipline, look to a Gold for detailed instructions. If you need to learn some cognitive skills, seek out a Green's expert advice. If you feel you're stuck in a rut, hang around with an energetic Orange until you're ready to settle back down again. Chances are, every skill and attitude you could possibly desire to obtain has already been mastered by an acquaintance. Don't re-invent the wheel—watch them, emulate their attitudes, practice their behaviors, and soon your character debits will become credits.

Applying Colors in Different Relationship Settings

Now that you have identified your color spectrum and have been introduced to the major characteristics of the four colors, your mind is probably buzzing with possible applications. You likely sense that this tool has a lot of power to influence nearly every part of your life. Following is a sample of how knowledge of your own color, as well as having an ability to recognize the colors of others, can be a great advantage.

Romantic relationships

One of the key elements of a successful relationship is the ability to communicate—to truly understand what your partner is saying and respond to that information in a way that will make sense to your partner. Insight has the power to increase your abilities to be an effective communicator because it provides an immediate understanding of your companion's communication style.

For example, when a distressed Blue approaches a Green with a personal problem, the analytical Green calmly responds with a perfectly logical solution—after all, that's what a Green seeks when he or she approaches others with problems. However, chances are that the Blue didn't really want a solution and only came to the Green for empathy and emotional validation. Instead of getting support, the Blue simply feels demoralized and lectured to, as though the Blue couldn't have figured things out unaided. As a result, the Blue feels worse and the well-intentioned Green is mystified by the Blue's inability to accept the gift of a solution.

A proper understanding of personality styles could prevent both the Blue's anguish and the Green's bewilderment. When each person understands the viewpoint of the other and tries to respond in a way the other understands and appreciates, true communication takes place.

A different example would involve Green's outward appearance of being cold, distant, and enigmatic to a significant other, especially if they have been together for a long time. The other may feel the Green doesn't show enough affection, provide enough emotional support, or supply enough energy to the relationship. On the other hand, the Green may find the partner to be too emotional, too dependent, or spending too much time reading between the lines. The Blue may complain, "You never tell me you love me!" And the Green will respond, "I told you when we first married that I loved you. If I change my mind I'll let you know."

Imagine what a difference it would make to this relationship if each party truly understood the values and needs of the other.

What would happen if the Green tried to do a few more Blue things and the Blue tried to do a few more Green things? What if they both learned to appreciate the unique characteristics and contributions of the other? This understanding would be fundamental in building a tremendously rewarding, long-term relationship.

Parent/child relationships

The natural tendency of many parents is to try to make their children into a "chip off the old block." Trying to make children into something they are not can be a great tragedy. Persistent effort to do so sends the message that the child's values are not important. As a result, the child's self-image diminishes, misbehavior increases, individuality is lost, and relationships are permanently marred.

On the other hand, knowing the personalities of your children will draw you closer to them. It gives you much better understanding of their values, hopes, dreams, and desires, as well as greater understanding of why they do the things they do. It shows you how to build their self-esteem when they're feeling down. It explains how to communicate with them in ways that are more meaningful. It helps you anticipate problems and resolve concerns before they get out of hand.

Understanding your children's personality styles also helps you more effectively discipline your children. What works for one color won't work for another. For example, punishing Greens by sending them to their rooms is more a reward than a punishment—they would probably prefer to be alone where they could curl up with a good book. Instead, suspend their library card or escort them to a school dance.

Introducing your children to the power of colors will help you accomplish two of the most important goals of parenting: teaching children how to communicate effectively and how to build positive relationships. Even young children are able to understand the different temperaments. And when they do, the personality styles become an invaluable tool that helps them understand the world and its peculiar inhabitants.

Teacher/student relationships

Most of us are teachers at some point in our lives, regardless of whether we are employed by a school. We act as teachers when we explain to a co-worker how to work with a machine, show a child how to ride a bike, or describe to an audience the effects of spilling oil in the ocean. As educators, we each have our own particular "teaching style" and if that style doesn't accommodate the "learning style" of our audience, we will probably be unsuccessful in our efforts.

Teaching styles and learning styles can be defined in terms of color. Gold teachers instruct in a Gold way with structured environments, detailed lesson plans, traditional instructional techniques, and firm discipline. On the other hand, Blue teachers instruct in a Blue way with interactive environments, individualized lesson plans, creative and unconventional learning activities, and loose discipline.

Of course, one particular teaching style isn't inherently better or worse than another. However, if you teach in only one way, and your learners learn in a different way, true learning may not take place. For example, teaching Blue students in Gold ways will likely produce frustration—for everybody. Like Blue teachers, Blue students thrive on interaction and face-to-face dialogue. They enjoy working in small groups on artistic or significant projects. If Gold teachers don't consider these preferences and occasionally alter their presentations, the Blue students will feel alienated.

Therefore, if you're a Gold instructor who only teaches in a Gold way, and if all your students are Gold, everything is fine—you and your students are comfortable with your teaching style. But if you have students who are Green, Orange, or Blue, you need to alter your teaching style to accommodate their learning preferences.

Most professional educators are Gold, even though there are a fair number of Blues who prefer to teach in elementary schools and Greens who prefer to teach in colleges and universities. This helps explain why so many non-Gold students, especially Oranges, have trouble in school. Imagine what could happen if teachers would learn to understand, appreciate, and tolerate a variety of learning styles and if students were taught to adjust to different teaching styles.

Business relationships

Understanding personality styles plays an important role in business relationships as well. It provides valuable understanding of the strengths, wants, needs, and expectations of clients, employees, and employers. It's a crucial factor to consider as workers choose careers, as employers hire employees to perform specific jobs, as managers assemble teams to accomplish specific goals, and as salespeople try to sell to potential customers.

For example, by knowing the personality style of your customers, you're better able to approach them in ways they prefer. Golds want facts, benefits, and savings. They're more concerned with economics and quality than with other elements. Greens like all the information you can give them. Give them alternatives, details, statistics, charts, and lots of time to make decisions. Oranges will be your quickest sales—they act on impulse and intuition and respond to glitz and appeal. With Blues, you need to be personable. Appeal to their emotions and explain how the product will help them or those they love.

Apply this to selling cars. Orange buyers would be interested in sporty red convertibles. Show them how fast the car will go and how it catches the attention of other people. Green buyers would be interested in the mechanics, technology, and reliability of the cars. Show them the engine, crawl under the car with them, find them some data that support how this car is the most efficient and technologically appropriate choice. Gold buyers would be interested in practicality and safety for their families. Show them a family car, stress the safety features, stress the high resale value, and give them an economic deal. Blues would be interested in the comfort the car provides and the ability it gives to visit friends or relatives. They're likely to be easily influenced by a friendly, sincere, and gentle salesperson.

As you might imagine, certain personalities gravitate towards specific jobs. Most of the time, they take these jobs because they're able to perform the required behaviors naturally. For instance, if your organization needs a charismatic leader who can take chances, act quickly in a crisis, and maintain high-levels of enthusiasm, look for an Orange. If you need an administrative assistant who can stay on task, follow-through with assignments, and painstakingly complete paperwork, look for a Gold. If you need someone to troubleshoot complicated problems, research a new project, or suggest ways to improve efficiency, look for a Green. If you need someone to listen to customer complaints, handle personnel issues, and motivate workers to achieve their potential, look for a Blue.

Of course, you can also fill these positions with people who have learned to perform the behaviors of a color other than their own comfortably. Just remember that their long-term success requires that they're comfortable with this performance.

Managers who know the personality styles of their team members are able to increase production by rewarding them in meaningful ways. Blues need to feel they're making a difference and respond to small tokens of appreciation. Oranges need immediate rewards and recognition for their performance. Greens need to be recognized for their ideas and commended for their competence. Golds need recognition for their achievement, production, and dependability.

Suggested Reading

Adler, Alfred. (1956). *The Individual Psychology of Alfred Adler.* Ansbaucher, Heinz, & Ansbaucher, Rowena (Eds.), New York: Basic Books.

Avila, Alexander. (1999). *LoveTypes: Discover Your Romantic Style and Find Your Soul Mate.* New York: Avon.

Bennet, E. A. (1983). *What Jung Really Said*. New York: Schocken.

Bolen, Jean Shinoda, M.D. (1984). *Goddesses in Everywoman*. San Francisco: Harper & Row.

Brownsword, Alan. (1987). *It Takes All Types*. Herndon, VA: Baytree.

Calaway, Bernie L. (1984). *Forty-Four Fun Fables*. Wilton, CT: Moorehouse-Barlow.

Duniho, Terrence. (1991). *Wholeness Lies Within*. Gladwyne, PA: Type and Temperament.

Grant, W. Harold. (1983). *From Image to Likeness: A Jungian Path in the Gospel Journey*. Mahwah, NJ: Paulist.

Hirsh, Sandra Krebs. (1985). *Using the Myers-Briggs Type Indicator in Organizations*. Palo Alto, CA: Consulting Psychologists.

Hirsh, Sandra Krebs, & Kise, Jane A. G. (1998). *Soul Types*. New York: Hyperion.

Hirsh, Sandra Krebs, & Kummerow, Jean M. (1989). *Life Types*. New York: Warner Books.

———. (1987). *Introduction to Type in Organizational Settings*. Palo Alto, CA: Consulting Psychologists.

Johnson, Robert A. (1977). *He: Understanding Masculine Psychology*. New York: Harper & Row.

———. (1977). *She: Understanding Feminine Psychology*. New York: Harper & Row.

———. (1983). *We: Understanding the Psychology of Romantic Love*. New York: Harper &Row.

Jung, Carl Gustav. (1971). *Psychological Types*. Princeton, NJ: Princeton University.

Kiersey, David W. (1998). *Please Understand Me II: Temperament, Character, Intelligence*. Del Mar, CA: Prometheus Nemesis.

Kiersey, David W., & Bates, Marilyn. (1978). *Please Understand Me: Character and Temperament Types*. Del Mar, CA: Prometheus Nemesis.

Kroeger, Otto, & Thuesen, Janet M. (1994). *16 Ways to Love Your Lover*. New York: Dellacorte.

———. (1992). *Type Talk at Work*. New York: Dell.

———. (1988). *Type Talk*. New York: Dell.

LaHaye, Tim. (1982). *Why You Act the Way You Do*. Wheaton, IL: Tyndale House.

Lawrence, Gordon D. (1982). *People Types and Tiger Stripes*. 2nd ed. Gainesville, FL: Center for Application of Psychological Type.

McCaulley, Mary H. (1981). *Jung's Theory of Psychological Types and The Myers-Briggs Type Indicator*. Gainesville, FL: Center for Application of Psychological Type.

Moir, Anne, and Jessel, David. (1993). *Brain Sex: The Real Difference Between Men and Women*. New York: Dell.

Myers, Isabel Briggs. (1987). *Introduction to Type*. Rev. Ed. Palo Alto, CA: Consulting Psychologists.

Myers, Isabel Briggs, and McCaulley, Mary H. (1985). *Manual for the Myers-Briggs Type Indicator: A Guide to the Development and Use of the MBTI*. Palo Alto, CA: Consulting Psychologists.

Myers, Isabel Briggs, with Myers, Peter B. (1980). *Gifts Differing*. Palo Alto, CA: Consulting Psychologists.

Nelson, George D. (2001). *The Aristotle Effect: Breaking the Learning Barrier*. Provo, UT: CI Press.

Sanford, John A. (1982). *Between People: Communicating One to One*. Mahwah, NJ: Paulist.

Saunders, Frances W. (1991). *Katharine and Isabel*. Palo Alto, CA: Consulting Psychologists.

Stevens, Anthony. (1982). *Archetypes: A Natural History of the Self*. New York: Quill.

Tieger, Paul, & Barron-Tieger, Barbara. (1992). *Do What You Are*. Toronto: Little, Brown & Company.

Thompson, Helen B. V. M. (1982). *Journey Toward Wholeness: A Jungian Model of Adult Spiritual Growth*. Mahwah, NJ: Paulist.

Was, Mike, Combs, Allan, & Combs, Julie. (1999). *Finding Your Strong Suit*. Los Angeles: Renaissance.

Welch, John O. Carm. (1982). *Spiritual Pilgrims*. Mahwah, NJ: Paulist.